INTRODUCTION TO COMPUTING AND PROGRAMMING IN PYTHON™

A MULTIMEDIA APPROACH

Mark J. Guzdial and Barbara Ericson

College of Computing/GVU
Georgia Institute of Technology

Fourth Edition

PEARSON

Boston   Columbus   Indianapolis   New York   San Francisco   Hoboken
Amsterdam   Cape Town   Dubai   London   Madrid   Milan   Munich   Paris   Montreal   Toronto
Delhi   Mexico City   São Paulo   Sydney   Hong Kong   Seoul   Singapore   Taipei   Tokyo

Vice President and Editorial Director, ECS: *Marcia J. Horton*
Executive Editor: *Tracy Johnson*
Executive Marketing Manager: *Tim Galligan*
Marketing Assistant: *Jon Bryant*
Senior Managing Editor: *Scott Disanno*
Production Project Manager: *Greg Dulles*
Program Manager: *Carole Snyder*
Global HE Director of Vendor Sourcing and Procurement:
    Diane Hynes
Director of Operations: *Nick Sklitsis*
Operations Specialist: *Maura Zaldivar-Garcia*

Cover Designer: *Black Horse Designs*
Manager, Rights and Permissions: *Rachel Youdelman*
Associate Project Manager, Rights and Permissions:
    Timothy Nicholls
Full-Service Project Management:
    Shylaja Gattupalli, Jouve India
Composition: *Jouve India*
Printer/Binder: *RR Donnelley*
Cover Printer: *Phoenix Color/Hagerstown*
Typeface: *10.5/13 Times*

Library of Congress Cataloging-in-Publication Data
Guzdial, Mark.
    Introduction to Computing and Programming in Python : a Multimedia Approach / Mark Guzdial,
Barbara Ericson, College of Computing/GVU, Georgia Institute of Technology. – Fourth edition.
        pages cm
    Includes bibliographical references and index.
    ISBN-13: 978-0-13-402554-4
    ISBN-10: 0-13-402554-7
    1. Python (Computer program language)   2. Multimedia systems.   I. Ericson, Barbara.   II. Title.
    QA76.73.P98G99 2016
    005.13'3–dc23

                                                                                        2014045817

10 9 8 7 6 5 4 3 2 1

ISBN-10: 0-13-402554-7
ISBN-13: 978-0-13-402554-4

Dedicated to our first teachers, our parents:
Janet, Charles, Gene, and Nancy

Contents

3 TEXT, FILES, NETWORKS, DATABASES, AND UNIMEDIA 309

11 Manipulating Text with Methods and Files 311

12 Advanced Text Techniques: Web and Information 337

Preface for the Fourth Edition

We started Media Computation in the of Summer 2002, and taught it for the first time in Spring 2003. It's now over ten years later, which is a good time to summarize the changes across the second, third, and fourth editions.

Media Computation has been used successfully in an undergraduate course at Georgia Tech for the last dozen years. The course continues to have high retention rates (over 85% of students complete the class with a passing grade), and is majority female. Both students and teachers report *enjoying* the course, which is an important recommendation for it.

Researchers have found that Media Computation works in a variety of contexts. The University of Illinois-Chicago had the first Media Computation paper outside of Georgia, and they showed how switching to MediaComp improved their retention rates in classes that were much more diverse than those at Georgia Tech [41]. The University of California-San Diego adopted Media Computation as part of a big change in their introductory course, where they also started using pair-programming and peer instruction. Their paper at the 2013 SIGCSE Symposium showed how these changes led to dramatic improvements in student retention, even measured a year later in the Sophomore year. The paper also won the Best Paper award at the conference [27]. It's been particularly delightful to see Media Computation adopted and adapted for new settings, like Cynthia Bailey Lee's creation of a MATLAB Media Computation curriculum [12].

Mark wrote a paper in 2013, summarizing ten years of Media Computation research. Media Computation does often improve retention. Our detailed interview studies with female students supports the claim that they find the approach to be creative and engaging, and that's what keeps the students in the class. That paper won the Best Paper award at the 2013 International Computing Education Research (ICER) Conference [33].

HOW TO TEACH MEDIA COMPUTATION

Over the last 10 years, we have learned some of the approaches that work best for teaching Media Computation.

- *Let the students be creative.* The most successful Media Computation classes use open-ended assignments that let the students choose what media they use. For example, a collage assignment might specify the use of particular filters and compositions, but allow for the student to choose exactly what pictures are used. These assignments often lead to the students putting in a lot more time to get *just* the look that they wanted, and that extra time can lead to improved learning.

- *Let the students share what they produce.* Students can produce some beautiful pictures, sounds, and movies using Media Computation. Those products are more motivating for the students when they get to share them with others. Some schools provide online spaces where students can post and share their products. Other schools have even printed student work and held an art gallery.

- *Code live in front of the class.* The best part of the teacher actually typing in code in front of the class is that *nobody* can code for long in front of an audience and *not* make a mistake. When the teacher makes a mistake and fixes it, the students see (a) that errors are expected and (b) there is a process for fixing them. Coding live when you are producing images and sounds is fun, and can lead to unexpected results and the opportunity to explore, "How did *that* happen?"

- *Pair programming leads to better learning and retention.* The research results on pair programming are tremendous. Classes that use pair programming have better retention results, and the students learn more.

- *Peer instruction is great.* Not only does peer instruction lead to better learning and retention outcomes, but it also gives the teacher better feedback on what the students are learning and what they are struggling with. We strongly encourage the use of peer instruction in computing classes.

- *Worked examples help with creativity learning.* Most computer science classes do not provide anywhere nearly enough worked-out examples for students to learn from. Students like to learn from examples. One of the benefits of Media Computation is that we provide a lot of examples (we've never tried to count the number of `for` and `if` statements in the book!), *and* it's easy to produce more of them. In class, we do an activity where we hand out example programs, then show a particular effect. We ask pairs or groups of students to figure out which program generated that effect. The students talk about code, and study a bunch of examples.

AP CS PRINCIPLES

The Advanced Placement exam in CS Principles[1] has now been defined. We have explicitly written the fourth edition with CS Principles in mind. For example, we show how to measure the speed of a program empirically in order to contrast two algorithms (Learning Objective 4.2.4), and we explore multiple ways of analyzing CSV data from the Internet (Learning Objectives 3.1.1, 3.2.1, and 3.2.2).

Overall, we address the CS Principles learning objectives explicitly in this book as shown below:

- In *Big Idea I: Creativity*:
- LO 1.1.1: ... use computing tools and techniques to create artifacts.
- LO 1.2.1: ... use computing tools and techniques for creative expression.

---

[1]http://apcsprinciples.org

- LO 1.2.2: ... create a computational artifact using computing tools and techniques to solve a problem.
- LO 1.2.3: ... create a new computational artifact by combining or modifying existing artifacts.
- LO 1.2.5: ... analyze the correctness, usability, functionality, and suitability of computational artifacts.
- LO 1.3.1: ... use programming as a creative tool.
- In *Big Idea II: Abstraction*:
- LO 2.1.1: ... describe the variety of abstractions used to represent data.
- LO 2.1.2: ... explain how binary sequences are used to represent digital data.
- LO 2.2.2: ... use multiple levels of abstraction in computation.
- LO 2.2.3: ... identify multiple levels of abstractions being used when writing programs.
- In *Big Idea III: Data and information*:
- LO 3.1.1: ... use computers to process information, find patterns, and test hypotheses about digitally processed information to gain insight and knowledge.
- LO 3.2.1: ... extract information from data to discover and explain connections, patterns, or trends.
- LO 3.2.2: ... use large data sets to explore and discover information and knowledge.
- LO 3.3.1: ... analyze how data representation, storage, security, and transmission of data involve computational manipulation of information.
- In *Big Idea IV: Algorithms*:
- LO 4.1.1: ... develop an algorithm designed to be implemented to run on a computer.
- LO 4.1.2: ... express an algorithm in a language.
- LO 4.2.1: ... explain the difference between algorithms that run in a reasonable time and those that do not run in a reasonable time.
- LO 4.2.2: ... explain the difference between solvable and unsolvable problems in computer science.
- LO 4.2.4: ... evaluate algorithms analytically and empirically for efficiency, correctness, and clarity.
- In *Big Idea V: Programming*:
- LO 5.1.1: ... develop a program for creative expression, to satisfy personal curiosity or to create new knowledge.
- LO 5.1.2: ... develop a correct program to solve problems.
- LO 5.2.1: ... explain how programs implement algorithms.
- LO 5.3.1: ... use abstraction to manage complexity in programs.

- LO 5.5.1: ... employ appropriate mathematical and logical concepts in programming.
- In *Big Idea VI: The Internet*:
- LO 6.1.1: ... explain the abstractions in the Internet and how the Internet functions.

CHANGES IN THE FOURTH EDITION

1. We fixed lots of bugs that our crack bug-finders identified in the third edition.

2. We changed most of the pictures in the book – they were getting stale, and our kids wanted us to not use as many pictures of them.

3. We added more end-of-chapter questions.

4. We added a whole new chapter, on text as a medium and manipulating strings (to make sentences, koans, and codes). This isn't a *necessary* chapter (e.g., we introduce for and if statements, but we didn't remove the introductions later in the book). For some of our teachers, playing with text with shorter loops (iterating over all the characters in a sentence is typically smaller than the thousands of pixels in a picture) is a more comfortable way to start.

5. We gave up fighting the battle of inventing a Web scraper that could beat out the changes that Facebook made, which kept breaking the one we put in the 3rd edition and then kept updating on the teacher's website[2]. Instead, we wrote examples in this book for processing CSV (Comma-Separated Values), a common format for sharing data on the Internet. We parse the CSV from a file using string processing, then using the CSV library in Python, and then accessing the data by URL.

6. We added some new edge detection code which is shorter and simpler to understand.

7. We added more with turtles: creating dancing turtles (using sleep from the time module to pause execution) and recursive patterns.

8. We updated the book to use the latest features in JES, which include those that reduce the need to use full pathnames (a problem identified by Stephen Edwards and his students in their SIGCSE 2014 paper [43]).

ACKNOWLEDGMENTS

Our sincere thanks go out to all our reviewers and bug-finders:

- At the top of the list is Susan Schwarz of the US Military Academy at West Point. Susan runs a large course with many instructors, and pays careful attention to what's going in all of the sections of the course. She turned that attention on the third edition of this book. She caught many bugs, and gave us lots of useful feedback. Thanks, Susan!

[2]http://home.cc.gatech.edu/mediaComp and http://www.mediacomputation.org

- Our other bug finders for the book were John Rutkiewicz, U. Massachusetts–Dartmouth; Brian Dorn, U. Nebraska–Omaha; Dave Largent, Ball State University; Simon, University of Newcastle; Eva Heinrich, Massey University; Peter J. DePasquale, The College of New Jersey, and Bill Leahy, Georgia Institute of Technology.

- Matthew Frazier, North Carolina State University, worked with us in the summer of 2014 to create a new version of JES – fixing many bugs, and improving JES considerably.

- We are grateful for the feedback from our book reviewers for the 4th edition: Andrew Cencini, Bennington College; Susan Fox, Macalester College; Kristin Lamberty, University of Minnesota-Morris; Jean Smith, Technical College of the Lowcountry; and William T. Verts, University of Massachusetts-Amherst.

- We are grateful for the input from our book reviewers for the 3rd edition, too: Joseph Oldham, Centre College; Lukasz Ziarek, Purdue University;Joseph O'Rourke, Smith College; Atul Prakash, University of Michigan; Noah D. Barnette, Virginia Tech; Adelaida A. Medlock, Drexel University; Susan E. Fox, Macalester College; Daniel G. Brown, University of Waterloo; Brian A. Malloy, Clemson University; Renee Renner, California State University, Chico.

MARK GUZDIAL AND BARBARA ERICSON
Georgia Institute of Technology

Preface to the First Edition

Research in computing education makes it clear that one doesn't just "learn to program." One learns to program *something* [8, 19], and the motivation to do that something can make the difference between learning and not learning to program [5]. The challenge for any teacher is to pick a *something* that is a powerful enough motivator.

People want to communicate. We are social creatures and the desire to communicate is one of our primal motivations. Increasingly, the computer is used as a tool for communication even more than a tool for calculation. Virtually all published text, images, sounds, music, and movies today are prepared using computing technology.

This book is about teaching people to program in order to communicate with digital media. The book focuses on how to manipulate images, sounds, text, and movies as professionals might, but with programs written by students. We know that most people will use professional-grade applications to perform these type of manipulations. But, knowing *how* to write your own programs means that you *can* do more than what your current application allows you to do. Your power of expression is not limited by your application software.

It may also be true that knowing how the algorithms in a media applications work allows you to use them better or to move from one application to the next more easily. If your focus in an application is on what menu item does what, every application is different. But if your focus is on moving or coloring the pixels in the way you want, then maybe it's easier to get past the menu items and focus on what you want to say.

This book is not just about programming in media. Media-manipulation programs can be hard to write or may behave in unexpected ways. Natural questions arise, like "Why is the same image filter faster in Photoshop?" and "That was hard to debug—Are there ways of writing programs that are *easier* to debug?" Answering questions like these is what computer scientists do. There are several chapters at the end of the book that are about *computing*, not just programming. The final chapters go beyond media manipulation to more general topics.

The computer is the most amazingly creative device that humans have ever conceived. It is completely made up of mind-stuff. The notion "Don't just dream it, be it" is really possible on a computer. If you can imagine it, you can make it "real" on the computer. Playing with programming can be and *should* be enormous fun.

OBJECTIVES, APPROACH AND ORGANIZATION

The curricular content of this book meets the requirements of the "imperative-first" approach described in the ACM/IEEE *Computing Curriculum 2001* standards document [2]. The book starts with a focus on fundamental programming constructs: assignments, sequential operations, iteration, conditionals, and defining functions. Abstractions (e.g., algorithmic complexity, program efficiency, computer organization, hierarchical decomposition, recursion, and object-oriented programming) are emphasized later, after the students have a context for understanding them.

This unusual ordering is based on the findings of research in the learning sciences. Memory is associative. We remember new things based on what we associate them with. People can learn concepts and skills on the premise that they will be useful some day but the concepts and skills will be related only to the premises. The result has been described as "brittle knowledge" [25]—the kind of knowledge that gets you through the exam but is promptly forgotten because it doesn't relate to anything but being in that class.

Concepts and skills are best remembered if they can be related to many different ideas or to ideas that come up in one's everyday life. If we want students to gain *transferable* knowledge (knowledge that can be applied in new situations), we have to help them to relate new knowledge to more general problems, so that the memories get indexed in ways that associate with those kinds of problems [22]. In this book, we teach with concrete experiences that students can explore and relate to (e.g., conditionals for removing red-eye in pictures) and later lay abstractions on top of them (e.g., achieving the same goal using recursion or functional filters and maps).

We know that starting from the abstractions doesn't really work for computing students. Ann Fleury has shown that students in introductory computing courses just don't buy what we tell them about encapsulation and reuse (e.g., [7]). Students prefer simpler code that they can trace easily and they actually think that such code is *better*. It takes time and experience for students to realize that there is value in well-designed systems. Without experience, it's very difficult for students to learn the abstractions.

The **media computation** approach used in this book starts from what many people use computers for: image manipulation, exploring digital music, viewing and creating Web pages, and making videos. We then explain programming and computing in terms of these activities. We want students to visit Amazon (for example) and think, "Here's a catalog Web site—and I know that these are implemented with a database and a set of programs that format the database entries as Web pages." We want students to use Adobe Photoshop and GIMP and think about how their image filters are actually manipulating red, green, and blue components of pixels. Starting from a relevant context makes transfer of knowledge and skills more likely. It also makes the examples more interesting and motivating, which helps with keeping students in the class.

The media computation approach spends about two-thirds of the time on giving students experiences with a variety of media in contexts that they find motivating. After that two-thirds, though, they naturally start to ask questions about *computing*. "Why is it that Photoshop is faster than my program?" and "Movie code is slow—How slow do programs get?" are typical. At that point, we introduce the abstractions and the valuable insights from computer science that answer *their* questions. That's what the last part of this book is about.

A different body of research in computing education explores why withdrawal or failure rates in introductory computing are so high. One common theme is that computing courses seem "irrelevant" and unnecessarily focus on "tedious details" such as efficiency [21, 1]. A communications context is perceived as relevant by students (as they tell us in surveys and interviews [6, 18]). The relevant context is part of the explanation for the success we have had with retention in the Georgia Tech course for which this book was written.

The late entrance of abstraction isn't the only unusual ordering in this approach. We start using arrays and matrices in Chapter 3, in our first significant programs. Typically, introductory computing courses push arrays off until later, because they are obviously more complicated than variables with simple values. A relevant and concrete context is very powerful [19]. We find that students have no problem manipulating matrices of pixels in a picture.

The rate of students withdrawing from introductory computing courses or receiving a D or F grade (commonly called the *WDF rate*) is reported in the 30–50% range or even higher. A recent international survey of failure rates in introductory computing courses reported that the average failure rate among 54 U.S. institutions was 33% and among 17 international institutions was 17% [24]. At Georgia Tech, from 2000 to 2002, we had an average WDF rate of 28% in the introductory course required for all majors. We used the first edition of this text in our course *Introduction to Media Computation*. Our first pilot offering of the course had 121 students, no computing or engineering majors, and two-thirds of the students were female. Our WDF rate was 11.5%.

Over the next two years (Spring 2003 to Fall 2005), the average WDF rate at Georgia Tech (across multiple instructors, and literally thousands of students) was 15% [29]. Actually, the 28% prior WDF rate and 15% current WDF rate are incomparable, since all majors took the first course and only liberal arts, architecture, and management majors took the new course. Individual majors have much more dramatic changes. Management majors, for example, had a 51.5% WDF rate from 1999 to 2003 with the earlier course, and had a 11.2% failure rate in the first two years of the new course [29]. Since the first edition of this book was published, several other schools have adopted and adapted this approach and evaluated their result. All of them have reported similar, dramatic improvements in success rates [4, 42].

Ways to Use This Book

This book represents what we teach at Georgia Tech in pretty much the same order. Individual teachers may skip some sections (e.g., the section on additive synthesis, MIDI, and MP3), but all of the content here has been tested with our students.

However, this material has been used in many other ways.

- A short introduction to computing could be taught with just Chapters 2 (introduction to programming) and 3 (introduction to image processing), perhaps with some material from Chapters 4 and 5. We have taught even single-day workshops on media computation using just this material.
- Chapters 6 through 8 basically replicate the computer science concepts from Chapters 3 through 5 but in the context of sounds rather than images. We find the replication useful—some students seem to relate better to the concepts of iteration and conditionals when working with one medium than with the other.

Further, it gives us the opportunity to point out that the same **algorithm** can have similar effects in different media (e.g., scaling a picture up or down and shifting a sound higher or lower in pitch are the same algorithm). But it could certainly be skipped to save time.

- Chapter 12 (on movies) introduces no new programming or computing concepts. While motivational, movie processing could be skipped to save time.

- We recommend getting to at least some of the chapters in the last unit, in order to lead students into thinking about computing and programming in a more abstract manner, but clearly not *all* of the chapters have to be covered.

Python and Jython

The programming language used in this book is Python. Python has been described as "executable pseudo-code." We have found that both computer science majors and non majors can learn Python. Since Python is actually used for communications tasks (e.g., Web site development), it's a relevant language for an introductory computing course. For example, job advertisements posted to the Python Web site (`http://www.python. org`) show that companies like Google and Industrial Light & Magic hire Python programmers.

The specific dialect of Python used in this book is *Jython* (`http://www.jython. org`). Jython *is* Python. The differences between Python (normally implemented in C) and Jython (which is implemented in Java) are akin to the differences between any two language implementations (e.g., Microsoft vs. GNU C++ implementations)—the basic language is *exactly* the same, with some library and details differences that most students will never notice.

TYPOGRAPHICAL NOTATIONS

Examples of Python code look like this: x = x + 1. Longer examples look like this:

```
def helloWorld():
  print "Hello, world!"
```

When showing something that the user types in with Python's response, it will have a similar font and style, but the user's typing will appear after a Python prompt (»):

```
>>> print 3 + 4
7
```

User interface components of JES (Jython Environment for Students) will be specified using a small caps font, like SAVE menu item and the LOAD button.

There are several special kinds of sidebars that you'll find in the book.

> **Computer Science Idea: An Example Idea**
> Key computer science concepts appear like this.   ■

Common Bug: An Example Common Bug

Common things that can cause your program to fail appear like this.

Debugging Tip: An Example Debugging Tip

If there's a good way to keep a bug from creeping into your programs in the first place, it's highlighted here.

Making It Work Tip: An Example How to Make It Work

Best practices or techniques that really help are highlighted like this.

INSTRUCTOR RESOURCES

The instructor resources are available on the author's website `http://mediacomputation.org` or the Pearson Education's Instructor Resource Center at `www.pearsonhighered.com/guzdial`:

- PowerPoint® Presentation slides

ACKNOWLEDGMENTS

Our sincere thanks go out to the following:

- Jason Ergle, Claire Bailey, David Raines, and Joshua Sklare, who made the initial version of JES with surprising quality in an amazingly short amount of time. Over the years, Adam Wilson, Larry Olson, Yu Cheung (Toby) Ho, Eric Mickley, Keith McDermott, Ellie Harmon, Timmy Douglas, Alex Rudnick, Brian O'Neill, and William Fredrick (Buck) Scharfnorth III have made JES into the useful and still understandable tool that it is today.

- Adam Wilson built the MediaTools that are so useful for exploring sounds and images and processing video.

- Andrea Forte, Mark Richman, Matt Wallace, Alisa Bandlow, Derek Chambless, Larry Olson, and David Rennie helped build course materials. Derek, Mark, and Matt created many example programs.

- There were several people who really made the effort come together at Georgia Tech. Bob McMath, Vice-Provost at Georgia Tech, and Jim Foley, Associate Dean for Education in the College of Computing, invested in this effort early on. Kurt Eiselt worked hard to make this effort real, convincing others to take it seriously. Janet Kolodner and Aaron Bobick were excited and encouraging about the idea of media computation for students new to computer science. Jeff Pierce reviewed and advised us on the design of the media functions used in the book. Aaron Lanterman gave me lots of advice on how to convey the digital material content accurately. Joan Morton, Chrissy Hendricks, David White, and all the staff of the GVU Center made sure that we had what we needed and that the details were handled to make this effort come together. Amy Bruckman and Eugene Guzdial bought Mark time to get the final version completed.

- We are grateful to Colin Potts and Monica Sweat who have taught this class at Georgia Tech and given us many insights about the course.

- Charles Fowler was the first person outside of Georgia Tech willing to take the gamble and trial the course in his own institution (Gainesville College), for which we're very grateful.

- The pilot course offered in Spring 2003 at Georgia Tech was very important in helping us improve the course. Andrea Forte, Rachel Fithian, and Lauren Rich did the assessment of the pilot offering of the course, which was incredibly valuable in helping us understand what worked and what didn't. The first teaching assistants (Jim Gruen, Angela Liang, Larry Olson, Matt Wallace, Adam Wilson, and Jose Zagal) did a lot to help create this approach. Blair MacIntyre, Colin Potts, and Monica Sweat helped make the materials easier for others to adopt. Jochen Rick made the CoWeb/Swiki a great place for CS1315 students to hang out.

- Many students pointed out errors and made suggestions to improve the book. Thanks to Catherine Billiris, Jennifer Blake, Karin Bowman, Maryam Doroudi, Suzannah Gill, Baillie Homire, Jonathan Laing, Mireille Murad, Michael Shaw, Summar Shoaib, and especially Jonathan Longhitano, who has a real flair for copyediting.

- Thanks to former *Media Computation* students Constantino Kombosch, Joseph Clark, and Shannon Joiner for permission to use their snapshots from class in examples.

- The research work that led to this text was supported by grants from the National Science Foundation—from the Division of Undergraduate Education, CCLI program, and from the CISE Educational Innovations program. Thank you for the support.

- Thanks to computing students Anthony Thomas, Celines Rivera, and Carolina Gomez for allowing us to use their pictures.

- Finally but most important, thanks to our children Matthew, Katherine, and Jennifer Guzdial, who allowed themselves to be photographed and recorded for Mommy and Daddy's media project and who were supportive and excited about the class.

MARK GUZDIAL AND BARBARA ERICSON
Georgia Institute of Technology

About the Authors

Mark Guzdial is a professor in the School of Interactive Computing in the College of Computing at Georgia Institute of Technology. He is one of the founders of the ACM's International Computing Education Research workshop series. Dr. Guzdial's research focuses on learning sciences and technology, specifically, computing education research. His first books were on the programming language Squeak and its use in education. He was the original developer of "Swiki" (Squeak Wiki), the first wiki developed explicitly for use in schools. He is a Fellow and a Distinguished Educator of the ACM. He is on the editorial boards of the *Journal of the Learning Sciences* and *Communications of the ACM*. He was a recipient of the 2012 IEEE Computer Society Undergraduate Teaching Award.

Barbara Ericson is a research scientist and the director of Computing Outreach for the College of Computing at Georgia Tech. She has been working on improving introductory computing education since 2004.

She has served as the teacher education representative on the Computer Science Teachers Association board, the co-chair of the K-12 Alliance for the National Center for Women in Information Technology, and as a reader for the Advanced Placement Computer Science exams. She enjoys the diversity of the types of problems she has worked on over the years in computing including computer graphics, artificial intelligence, medicine, and object-oriented programming.

Mark and Barbara received the 2010 ACM Karl V. Karlstrom Award for Outstanding Computer Educator for their work on Media Computation including this book. They led a project called "*Georgia Computes!*" for six years, which had a significant impact in improving computing education in the US state of Georgia [31]. Together, they Mark and Barbara are leaders in the *Expanding Computing Education Pathways* (ECEP) alliance[3]

---

[3]http://www.ecepalliance.org

PART 1

INTRODUCTION

Introduction to Computer Science and Media Computation

Chapter Learning Objectives

- To explain what computer science is about and what computer scientists are concerned with.
- To explain why we digitize media.
- To explain why it's valuable to study computing.
- To explain the concept of an **encoding**.
- To explain the basic components of a computer.

1.1 WHAT IS COMPUTER SCIENCE ABOUT?

Computer science is the study of **process**: how we or computers do things, how we specify what we do, and how we specify what the stuff is that we're processing. That's a pretty dry definition. Let's try a metaphorical one.

Computer Science Idea: Computer Science Is the Study of Recipes

"Recipes" here are a special kind—one that can be executed by a computational device, but this point is only of importance to computer scientists. The important point overall is that a computer science recipe defines *exactly* what has to be done.

More formally, computer scientists study *algorithms* which are step-by-step procedures to accomplish a task. Each step in an algorithm is something that a computer already knows how to do (e.g., add two small integer numbers) or can be taught how to do (e.g., adding larger numbers including those with a decimal point). A recipe that can run on a computer is called a *program*. A program is a way to communicate an algorithm in a representation that a computer can execute.

To use our metaphor a bit more—think of an algorithm as the step-by-step way that your grandmother made her secret recipe. She always did it the same way, and had a reliably great result. Writing it down so that you can read it and do it later is like turning her algorithm into a program for you. You *execute* the recipe by *doing* it—following the recipe step-by-step in order to create something the way that your grandmother did. If you give the recipe to someone else who can read the language of the recipe (maybe English or French), then you have communicated that process to that other person, and the other person can similarly execute the recipe to make something the way that your grandmother did.

If you're a biologist who wants to describe how migration works or how DNA replicates, then being able to write a recipe that specifies *exactly* what happens, in terms that can be completely defined and understood, is *very* useful. The same is true if you're a chemist who wants to explain how equilibrium is reached in a reaction. A factory manager can define a machine-and-belt layout and even test how it works— before physically moving heavy things into position—using computer **programs**. Being able to exactly define tasks and/or simulate events is a major reason why computers have radically changed so much of how science is done and understood.

In fact, if you *can't* write a recipe for some process, maybe you don't really understand the process, or maybe the process can't actually work the way that you are thinking about it. Sometimes, trying to write the recipe is a test in itself. Now, sometimes you can't write the recipe because the process is one of the few that cannot be executed by a computer. We will talk more about those in Chapter 14.

It may sound funny to call *programs* a recipe, but the analogy goes a long way. Much of what computer scientists study can be defined in terms of recipes.

- Some computer scientists study how recipes are written: Are there better or worse ways of doing something? If you've ever had to separate egg whites from yolks, you realize that knowing the right way to do it makes a world of difference. Computer science theoreticians think about the fastest and shortest recipes, and the ones that take up the least amount of space (you can think about it as counter space—the analogy works), or even use the least amount of energy (which is important when running on low-power devices like cell phones). *How* a recipe works, completely apart from how it's written (e.g., in a program), is called the study of algorithms. Software engineers think about how large groups can put together recipes that still work. (Some programs, like the ones that keep track of credit card transactions, have literally millions of steps!) The term **software** means a collection of computer programs (recipes) that accomplish a task.

- Other computer scientists study the units used in recipes. Does it matter whether a recipe uses metric or English measurements? The recipe may work in either case, but if you don't know what a pound or a cup is, the recipe is a lot less understandable to you. There are also units that make sense for some tasks and not others, but if you can fit the units to the tasks, you can explain yourself more easily and get things done faster—and avoid errors. Ever wonder why ships at sea measure their speed in *knots*? Why not use something like meters per second? Sometimes, in certain special situations—on a ship at sea, for instance—the more common terms aren't appropriate or don't work as well. Or we may invent new kinds of units, like a unit that represents a whole other program or a computer, or a network like your friends and your friends' friends in Facebook. The study of computer science units is referred to as **data structures**. Computer scientists who study ways of keeping track of lots of data (in lots of different kinds of units) and figuring out how to access the data quickly are studying **databases**.

- Can recipes be written for anything? Are there some recipes that *can't* be written? Computer scientists know that there are recipes that can't be written. For example, you can't write a recipe that can absolutely tell whether some other recipe will actually work. How about *intelligence*? Can we write a recipe such that a computer following it would actually be *thinking* (and how would you tell if you got it right)? Computer scientists in **theory**, **intelligent systems**, **artificial intelligence**, and **systems** worry about things like this.

- There are even computer scientists who focus on whether people *like* what the recipes produce, almost like restaurant critics for a newspaper. Some of these are **human–computer interface** specialists who worry about whether people can understand and make use of the recipes ("recipes" that produce an *interface* that people use, like windows, buttons, scrollbars, and other elements of what we think about as a running program).

- Just as some chefs specialize in certain kinds of recipes, like crepes or barbecue, computer scientists also specialize in certain kinds of recipes. Computer scientists who work in *graphics* are mostly concerned with recipes that produce pictures, animations, and even movies. Computer scientists who work in *computer music* are mostly concerned with recipes that produce sounds (often melodic ones, but not always).

- Still other computer scientists study the *emergent properties* of recipes. Think about the World Wide Web. It's really a collection of *millions* of recipes (programs) talking to one another. Why would one section of the Web get slower at some point? It's a phenomenon that emerges from these millions of programs, certainly not something that was planned. That's something that **networking** computer scientists study. What's really amazing is that these emergent properties (that things just start to happen when you have many, many recipes interacting at once) can also be used to explain noncomputational things. For example, how ants forage for food or how termites make mounds can also be described as something that just happens when you have lots of little programs doing something simple and interacting. There are computer scientists today who study how the Web allows for new kinds of interactions, particularly in large groups (like Facebook or Twitter). Computer scientists who study *social computing* are interested in how these new kinds of interactions work and the characteristics of the software that are most successful for promoting useful social interactions.

The recipe metaphor also works on another level. Everyone knows that some things in a recipe can be changed without changing the result dramatically. You can always increase all the units by a multiplier (say, double) to make more. You can always add more garlic or oregano to the spaghetti sauce. But there are some things that you cannot change in a recipe. If the recipe calls for baking powder, you may not substitute baking

CHICKEN CACCIATORE

3 whole, boned chicken breasts	1 (28 oz) can chopped tomatoes
1 medium onion, chopped	1 (15 oz) can tomato sauce
1 tbsp chopped garlic	1 (6.5 oz) can mushrooms
2 tbsp and later ¼ c olive oil	1 (6 oz) can tomato paste
1 ½ c flour	½ of (26 oz) jar of spaghetti
¼ c Lawry's seasoning salt	sauce
1 bell pepper, chopped (optional)	3 tbsp Italian seasoning
any color	1 tsp garlic powder (optional)

Cut up the chicken into pieces about 1 inch square. Saute the onion and garlic until the onion is translucent. Mix the flour and Lawry's salt. You want about 1:4–1:5 ratio of seasoning salt to flour and enough of the whole mixture to coat the chicken. Put the cut up chicken and seasoned flour in a bag, and shake to coat. Add the coated chicken to the onion and garlic. Stir frequently until browned. You'll need to add oil to keep from sticking and burning; I sometimes add up to ¼ cup of olive oil. Add the tomatoes, sauce, mushrooms, and paste (and the optional peppers, too). Stir well. Add the Italian seasoning. I like garlic, so I usually add the garlic powder, too. Stir well. Because of all the flour, the sauce can get too thick. I usually cut it with the spaghetti sauce, up to ½ jar. Simmer 20–30 minutes.

FIGURE 1.1
A cooking recipe—you can always double the ingredients, but throwing in an extra cup of flour won't cut it, and don't try to brown the chicken *after* adding the tomato sauce!

soda. The order matters. If you're supposed to brown the chicken and then add tomato sauce, you won't get the same result if you add tomato sauce and then (somehow) try to brown the chicken (Figure 1.1).

The same holds for software recipes. There are usually things you can easily change: the actual names of things (though you should change names consistently), some of the **constants** (numbers that appear as plain old numbers, not as variables), and maybe even some of the data **ranges** (sections of the data) being manipulated. But the order of the commands to the computer, however, almost always has to stay exactly as stated. As we go on, you'll learn what can be safely changed, and what can't.

1.2   PROGRAMMING LANGUAGES

Computer scientists write a recipe in a **programming language** (Figure 1.2). Different programming languages are used for different purposes. Some of them are wildly popular, like Java and C++. Others are more obscure, like Squeak and Scala. Some others are designed to make computer science ideas very easy to learn, like Scheme or Python, but the fact that they're easy to learn doesn't always make them very popular or the best choice for experts building larger or more complicated recipes. It's a hard balance in teaching computer science to pick a language that is easy to learn *and* is popular and useful enough to experts that students are motivated to learn it.

Why don't computer scientists just use natural human languages, like English or Spanish? The problem is that natural languages evolved the way they did to enhance

Python/Jython

```
def hello():
  print "Hello World"
```

Java

```
class HelloWorld {
  static public void main( String args[] ) {
    System.out.println( "Hello World!" );
  }
}
```

C++

```
#include <iostream.h>

main() {
    cout << "Hello World!" << endl;
    return 0;
}
```

Scheme

```
(define helloworld
    (lambda ()
            (display "Hello World")
            (newline)))
```

FIGURE 1.2
Comparing programming languages: a common simple programming task is to print the words "Hello World!" to the screen.

communications between very smart beings—humans. As we'll explain more in the next section, computers are exceptionally dumb. They need a level of specificity that natural language isn't good at. Further, what we say to one another in natural communication is not exactly what you're saying in a computational recipe. When was the last time you told someone how a video game like *Mario Kart* or *Minecraft* or *Call of Duty* worked in such minute detail that they could actually replicate the game (say, on paper)? English isn't good for that kind of task.

There are so many different kinds of programming languages because there are so many different kinds of recipes to write and *people* use these languages. Programs written in the programming language *C* tend to be very fast and efficient, but they also tend to be hard to read, hard to write, and require units that are more about computers than about bird migrations, or DNA, or whatever else you want to write your recipe about. The programming language *Lisp* (and related languages like Scheme, Racket, and Common Lisp) is very flexible and is well suited to exploring how to write recipes that have never been written before, but Lisp *looks* so strange compared to languages like C. If you want to hire a hundred programmers to work on your project, it will be easier to find a hundred programmers who know a popular language than a less popular one—but that doesn't mean that the popular language is the best one for your task!

The programming language that we're using in this book is **Python** (visit `http://www.python.org` for more information on it). Python is a popular programming language, used very often for Web and media programming. The Web search engine *Google* uses Python. The media company *Industrial Light & Magic* also uses Python. A list of companies using Python is available at `http://css.dzone.com/articles/best-python-companies-work`. Python is easy to learn, easy to read, very flexible, but not as efficient as other programming languages. The same algorithm coded in C and in Python will probably be faster in C. Python is a good language for writing programs that work within an application, like the image manipulation language GIMP (`http://www.gimp.org`) or the 3D content creation tool Blender (`http://www.blender.org`).

The version of Python used in this book is called **Jython** (`http://www.jython.org`).[1] Jython is a form of Python that is particularly effective for programming in multimedia that will work across multiple computer platforms. You can download a version of Jython for your computer from the Jython Web site that will work for all kinds of purposes. Most programs written for Jython will work without change in Python.

In this book, we will describe how to program in Jython using a programming *environment* called **JES** (*Jython Environment for Students*) that has been developed to make it easier to program in Jython. JES has some features for working with media, like viewers for sounds and images. JES also has embedded in it some special functions for manipulating digital media that are made available to you without you doing anything special. Anything you can do in JES, you can also do in normal Jython, though you will have to explicitly include the special libraries.

Media Computation special libraries work with other environments and other forms of Python, too.

- Pythy developed by Stephen Edwards and his colleagues at Virginia Tech is a browser-based programming environment.[2] All programming occurs through a Web browser with Pythy, and programs and media are stored in the cloud. Programs that work in JES will work in Pythy.

- A team led by Paul Gries at the University of Toronto has implemented portions of the special media libraries in JES to work in other forms of Python.[3]

- The books at `http://www.interactivepython.org/` by Brad Miller at Luther College support manipulation of images in Python in all of their ebooks.

Let's revisit here two of the most important terms that we'll be using in this book:

- A **program** is a description in a programming language of a process that achieves some result that is useful to someone. A program can be small (like one that implements a calculator) or huge (like one your bank uses to track all of its accounts).

---

[1]Python is often implemented in the programming language C. Jython is Python implemented in *Java*—this means that Jython is actually a program written in Java.

[2]See `https://github.com/web-cat/pythy` for information on installing Pythy.

[3]See `https://code.google.com/p/pygraphics/` for information on the Pygraphics library.

- An **algorithm** (in contrast) is a description of a process in a step-by-step manner, not tied to any programming language. The same algorithm may be implemented in many different languages in many different ways in many different programs—but they would all be the same **process** if we're talking about the same algorithm.

Computer Science Idea: Computer Science is about People

A famous computer scientist, Edsger W. Dijkstra, once said that, "Computer Science is no more about computers than astronomy is about telescopes." Computer science is about people. People think about process in all those different ways (from a data perspective, to issues of human–computer interfaces, to artificial intelligence). People use programming languages, and they prefer different ways of communicating and thinking, so different languages result. People make the programs and the languages. Most decisions in computer science are not about computers. Most decisions in computer science are about people.

1.3   WHAT COMPUTERS UNDERSTAND

Computational recipes are written to run on computers. What does a computer know how to do? What can we tell the computer to do in the recipe? The answer is, "very, very little." Computers are exceedingly stupid. They really only know about numbers.

Actually, even to say that computers *know* numbers is not really correct. Computers use **encodings** of numbers. Computers are electronic devices that react to voltages on wires. Each wire is called a **bit**. If a wire has a voltage on it, we say that it encodes a 1. If it has no voltage on it, we say that it encodes a 0. We group these wires (bits) into sets. A set of 8 bits is called a **byte**. So, from a set of eight wires (a byte), we have a pattern of eight 0's and 1's, for example, 01001010. Using the **binary** number system, we can interpret this byte as a **number** (Figure 1.3). That's where we come up with the claim that a computer knows about numbers.[4]

A computer has a **memory** filled with bytes. Everything that a computer is working with at a given instant is stored in its memory. This means that everything a computer is working with is *encoded* in its bytes: JPEG pictures, Excel spreadsheets, Word documents, annoying Web pop-up ads, and the latest spam email.

A computer can do lots of things with numbers. It can add them, subtract them, multiply them, divide them, sort them, collect them, duplicate them, filter them (e.g., "Make a copy of these numbers, but only the even ones."), and compare them and do things based on the comparison. For example, a computer can be told in a recipe, "Compare these two numbers. If the first one is less than the second one, jump to step 5 in this recipe. Otherwise, continue on to the next step."

So far, it looks like the computer is a kind of fancy calculator, and that's certainly why it was invented. One of the first uses of a computer was to calculate projectile trajectories during World War II ("If the wind is coming from the SE at 15 mph, and you want to hit a target 0.5 miles away at an angle of 30 degrees East of North, then incline your

---

[4]We'll talk more about this level of the computer in the chapter *Speed*.

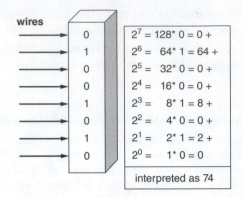

FIGURE 1.3
Eight wires with a pattern of voltages is a byte, which is interpreted as a pattern of eight 0's and 1's, which in turn is interpreted as a decimal number.

launcher to ...."). Modern computers can do billions of calculations per second. But what makes the computer useful for general recipes is the concept of *encodings*.

Computer Science Idea: Computers Can Layer Encodings

Computers can layer encodings to virtually any level of complexity. Numbers can be interpreted as characters, which can be interpreted in sets as Web pages, which can be interpreted to appear as multiple fonts and styles. But at the bottom-most level, the computer *only* "knows" voltages, which we interpret as numbers. Encodings let us forget about lower-level details. Encodings are an example of *abstraction*, which give us new concepts to use which allow us to ignore other details.

If one of these bytes is interpreted as the number 65, it could simply be the number 65. Or it could be the letter *A* using a standard encoding of numbers to letters called the *American Standard Code for Information Interchange* (**ASCII**). If the 65 appears in a collection of other numbers that we're interpreting as text, and it's in a file that ends in ".html" it might be part of something that looks like this <a href=..., which a Web browser will interpret as the definition of a link. Down at the level of the computer, that *A* is just a pattern of voltages. Many layers of recipes up, at the level of a Web browser, it defines something that you can click on to get more information.

If the computer understands only numbers (and that's a stretch already), how does it manipulate these encodings? Sure, it knows how to compare numbers, but how does that extend to being able to alphabetize a class list? Typically, each layer of encoding is implemented as a piece or layer in software. There's software that understands how to manipulate characters. The character software knows how to do things like compare names because it has encoded that *a* comes before *b* and so on, and that the numeric comparison of the order of numbers in the encoding of the letters leads to alphabetical comparisons. The character software is used by other software that manipulates text in files. That's the layer that something like Microsoft Word or Notepad or TextEdit would use. Still another piece of software knows how to interpret *HTML* (the language of the

Web), and another layer of the same software knows how to take HTML and display the right text, fonts, styles, and colors.

We can similarly create layers of encodings in the computer for our specific tasks. We can teach a computer that cells contain mitochondria and DNA, and that DNA has four kinds of nucleotides, and that factories have these kinds of presses and these kinds of stamps. Creating layers of encoding and interpretation so that the computer is working with the right units (recall back to our recipe analogy) for a given problem, is the task of **data representation** or defining the right **data structures**.

If this sounds like a lot of software, it is. When software is layered this way, it slows the computer down a bit. But the powerful thing about computers is that they're *amazingly* fast—and getting faster all the time!

Computer Science Idea: Moore's Law

Gordon Moore, one of the founders of Intel (maker of computer processing chips) claimed that the number of transistors (a key component of computers) would double at the same price every 18 months, effectively meaning that the same amount of money would buy twice as much computing power every 18 months. This means that computers keep getting smaller, faster, and cheaper. This law has held true for decades.
■

Computers today can execute literally *billions* of recipe steps per second. They can hold in memory literally encyclopedias of data! They never get tired or bored. Search a million customers for an individual cardholder? No problem! Find the right set of numbers to get the best value out of an equation? Piece of cake!

Process millions of picture elements or sound fragments or movie frames? That's **media computation**. In this book, you will write recipes that manipulate images, sounds, text, and even other recipes. This is possible because everything in the computer is represented digitally, even recipes. We would not be able to do media computation if the media were not represented digitally. By the end of the book, you will have written recipes to implement digital video special effects that create Web pages in the same way that Amazon and eBay do, and that filter images like Photoshop.

1.4   MEDIA COMPUTATION: WHY DIGITIZE MEDIA?

Let's consider an encoding that would be appropriate for pictures. Imagine that pictures are made up of little dots. That's not hard to imagine: look really closely at your monitor or at a TV screen and you will see that your images are *already* made up of little dots. Each of these dots is a distinct color. Physics tells us that colors can be described as the sum of *red*, *green*, and *blue*. Add the red and green to get yellow. Mix all three together to get white. Turn them all off and you get a black dot.

What if we encoded each dot in a picture as a collection of three bytes, one each for the amount of red, green, and blue at that dot on the screen? And we collect a bunch of these three-byte sets to determine all the dots of a given picture? That's a pretty reasonable way of representing pictures, and it's essentially how we're going to do it in Chapter 4.

Manipulating these dots (each referred to as a **pixel** or *picture element*) can take a lot of processing. There are thousands or even millions of them in a picture that you might want to work with on your computer or on the Web. But the computer doesn't get bored, and it's very fast.

The encoding that we will be using for sound involves 44,100 two-byte sets (called a *sample*) for each *second* of time. A three-minute song requires 158,760,000 bytes (twice that for stereo). Doing any processing on this takes a *lot* of operations. But at a billion operations per second, you can do lots of operations to every one of those bytes in just a few moments.

Creating encodings of this kind for media requires a change to the media. Look at the real world: it isn't made up of lots of little dots that you can see. Listen to a sound: Do you hear thousands of little bits of sound per second? The fact that you *can't* hear little bits of sound per second is what makes it possible to create these encodings. Our eyes and ears are limited: we can only perceive so much, and only things that are just so small. If you break up an image into small enough dots, your eyes can't tell that it's not a continuous flow of color. If you break up a sound into small enough pieces, your ears can't tell that the sound isn't a continuous flow of auditory energy.

The process of encoding media into little bits is called **digitization**, sometimes referred to as "*going digital*." *Digital* means (according to the *Longman Dictionaries*) "Giving information in the form of numbers; relating to the fingers and toes."[5] Making things digital is about turning things from continuous and uncountable to something that we can count, as if with our fingers.

Digital media, done well, feel the same to our limited human sensory apparatus as the original. Phonograph recordings (ever seen one?) capture sound continuously as an **analog** signal. Photographs (on film) capture light as a continuous flow. Some people say that they can hear a difference between phonograph recordings and CD recordings, but to our ears and most measurements, a CD (which *is* digitized sound) sounds just the same, or maybe clearer. Digital cameras at high enough resolutions produce photograph-quality pictures.

Why would you want to digitize media? Because then the media will be easier to manipulate, to replicate exactly, to compress, to search, to index and classify (e.g., to group similar images or sounds together), to compare, and to transmit. For example, it's hard to manipulate images that are in photographs, but it's very easy when the same images are digitized. This book is about using the increasingly digital world of media and manipulating it—and learning computation in the process.

Moore's Law has made media computation feasible as an introductory topic. Media computation relies on the computer doing lots and lots of operations on lots and lots of bytes. Modern computers can do this easily. Even with slow (but easy to understand) languages, even with inefficient (but easy to read and write) recipes, we can learn about computation by manipulating media.

---

[5]Definition of "digital" from *Longman Dictionary of Contemporary English*. Copyright © 2009 by Pearson Education. Reprinted with permission.

When we manipulate media, we need to be respectful of the author's digital rights. Modifying images and sounds for educational purposes is allowed under fair use laws (which limit or create exceptions to an owner's copyright). However, sharing or publishing manipulated images or sounds could infringe on the owner's copyright.

1.5   COMPUTER SCIENCE FOR EVERYONE

Why should you learn about computer science by writing programs that manipulate media? Why should anyone who doesn't want to be a computer scientist learn about computer science? Why should you be interested in learning about computation by manipulating media?

Most professionals today manipulate media: papers, videos, tape recordings, photographs, and drawings. Increasingly, this manipulation is done with a computer. Media are very often in a digitized form today.

We use software to manipulate these media. We use Adobe Photoshop for manipulating our images, and Audacity to manipulate our sounds, and perhaps Microsoft PowerPoint for assembling our media into slideshows. We use Microsoft Word for manipulating our text, and Google Chrome or Microsoft Internet Explorer for browsing media on the Internet.

So why should anyone who does *not* want to be a computer scientist study computer science? Why should you learn to program? Isn't it enough to learn to *use* all this great software? The following sections provide answers to these questions.

1.5.1   It's About Communication

Digital media are manipulated with software. *If you can only manipulate media with software that **someone else** made for you, you are limiting your ability to communicate.* What if you want to say something that can't be said in software from Adobe, Microsoft, Apple, and the rest? Or what if you want to say something in a way they don't support? If you know how to program, even if it would take you *longer* to do it yourself, you have the freedom to manipulate the media your way.

What about learning these tools in the first place? In our years working with computers, we have seen many types of software come and go as *the* package for drawing, painting, word processing, video editing, and so on. You can't learn just a single tool and expect to be able to use it for your entire career. If you know *how* the tools work, you have a core understanding that can transfer from tool to tool. You can think about your media work in terms of the *algorithms*, not the *tools*.

Finally, if you're going to prepare media for the Web, for marketing, for print, for broadcast, or for any use whatsoever, it's worthwhile for you to have a sense of what's possible and what can be done with media. It's even more important as a consumer of media that you know how the media can be manipulated, to know what's true and what could be just a trick. If you know the basics of media computation, you have an understanding that goes beyond what any individual tool provides.

1.5.2   It's About Process

In 1961, Alan Perlis gave a talk at MIT in which he argued that computer science, and programming explicitly, should be part of a liberal education [35]. Perlis is an important figure in the field of computer science. The highest award in computer science is the ACM Turing Award. Perlis was the first recipient of that award. He's an important figure in software engineering and he started several of the first computer science departments in the United States.

Perlis's argument can be made in comparison with calculus. Calculus is generally considered part of a liberal education: not *everyone* takes calculus, but if you want to be well educated, you will typically take at least a term of calculus. Calculus is the study of *rates*, which is important in many fields. Computer science, as stated earlier in this chapter, is the study of **process**. Process is important to nearly every field, from business to science to medicine to law. Knowing process formally is important for everyone. Using a computer to automate processes has changed every profession.

Jeannette Wing has argued that everyone should learn **computational thinking** [23]. She views the types of skills taught in computing as critical skills for all students. This is what Alan Perlis predicted: that automating computation would change the way we learn about our world.

1.5.3   You Will Probably Need It

A team of researchers at Carnegie Mellon University did a study in 2005[6] where they answered the question, "In the future, where will the programmers be, and how many will there be?" They predicted that *most* programmers would not be professional software developers. Most people who wrote programs would likely be people who needed to write little programs to do something that they needed in their daily work. They estimated that the ratio of professional software to *end-user programmers* would be as high as 1:9, i.e., for every professional programmer in the world, there are nine more people who are programming but just to help them out with their daily work. That result suggests that *many* of you now reading this book will likely need to program one day, even if you never make it your career.

The reality is that *many* people program today. Scientists and engineers write programs to create models and test them in simulations, or to analyze data. Graphics designers write programs to make program tasks in Photoshop or GIMP to save themselves time, or to move their designs onto the Web. Accountants program when they create complex spreadsheets. Many professionals need to store and manipulate process, and thus learn to program, just as Alan Perlis predicted.

PROBLEMS

1.1   *Every* profession uses computers today. Use a Web browser and a search engine like Google to find sites that relate your field of study with computer science or computing or computation. For example, search for "biology computer science" or "management computing."

1.2   The 2013 Nobel Prize in Chemistry was in some sense a Nobel Prize given for work in computer science. What was the role of computers in that Nobel Prize?

---

[6]See http://dl.acm.org/citation.cfm?id=1083231.1083232&coll=DL&dl=ACM&CFID=347064215&CFTOKEN=87606004.

1.3   Text characters are encoded in different ways. The bottom level is always binary in bytes, but a different binary pattern can be used to represent different characters. Two of these encodings are *ASCII* and *Unicode*. See if you can do Web searches on ASCII and Unicode. What's the difference between ASCII and Unicode? Why would we need Unicode if we already had ASCII?

1.4   Consider the representation for pictures described in Section 1.4, where each dot (pixel) in the picture is represented by three bytes, for the red, green, and blue components of the color at that dot. How many bytes does it take to represent a 640 by 480 picture, a common picture size on the Web? How many bytes does it take to represent a 1024 by 768 picture, a common screen size? (What do you think is meant now by a "three megapixel" camera?)

1.5   One bit can represent 0 or 1. With two bits you have four possible combinations 00, 01, 10, and 11. How many different combinations can you make with four bits or eight bits (one byte)? Each combination can be used to represent a binary number. How many numbers can you represent with 2 bytes (16 bits)? How many numbers can you represent with four bytes?

1.6   Microsoft Word *used* to use an encoding of a word-processing document called "DOC." Most recent versions of Microsoft Word use a different encoding called "DOCX." What's the difference between them?

1.7   One of the powerful ideas in computer science is that encodings can be *layered*. Most of the encodings we've talked about so far (e.g., pixels in a picture, characters, floating point numbers) are based on binary. *XML* is a way of encoding information in text, which is in turn encoded in binary. What are the advantages and disadvantages of using XML rather than binary encodings?

1.8   How can you encode a *floating-point number* in terms of bytes? Do a search on the Web for "floating point." You will find that there are different encodings of floating point numbers. Take a common one like the IEEE Floating Point Standard as an example. Assuming *single precision*, what is the largest and smallest numbers that you can represent in that encoding?

1.9   As we said in the chapter, computer science is about *people*. Start your exploration of computer science by exploring the people who are computer scientists and influence computer science. As you do, find Web sites that you believe are *credible* for your information, and include the URL in your answers—with your reasons for believing that source is credible. What general rules do you use to determine what is a credible Web site?

1.10   Look up Alan Kay, *object-oriented programming*, and the *Dynabook* on the Web. Alan is one of the inspirations for the media computation approach that we use in this book. Can you figure out what he has to do with media computation?

1.11   Look up Clarence (Skip) Ellis. Without him, Google Docs wouldn't work the way that it does to help people collaborate. What did he do?

1.12   Look up Grace Hopper on the Web. How did she contribute to programming languages?

1.13   Look up Andrea Lawrence on the Web. What computer science department did she chair?

1.14   Look up Alan Turing on the Web. What does he have to do with our notion of what a computer can do and how encodings work?

1.15   Look up Adele Goldberg on the Web. How did she contribute to programming languages?

1.16   Look up Kurt Gödel on the Web. What amazing things did he do with encodings?

1.17   Look up Ada Lovelace on the Web. What amazing things did she do before the first mechanical computer was built?

1.18   Look up Claude Shannon on the Web. What did he do for his master's thesis?

1.19   Look up Richard Tapia on the Web. What has he done to encourage diversity in computing?

1.20   Look up Marissa Mayer on the Web. What computer tool (that you probably use regularly) did she help create?

1.21   Look up Shafi Goldwasser on the Web. What major computing prize did she win in 2012 and why?

1.22   Look up Mary Lou Jepsen on the Web. What new technology is she working on?

1.23   Look up Ashley Qualls on the Web. What did she create that is worth a million dollars?

1.24   Look up Tim Berners-Lee on the Web. What did he invent?

1.25   As in every field, people in computer science build on one another's work.

- Who invented the Logo Turtle?
- Who used the Logo Turtle to have fourth graders learn about fractions in mathematics?
- Who invented a programming language that featured thousands of Logo Turtles in order to model complex behavior like ants and termites?

1.26   Now trace this series of who built on who's work.

- Who invented the laser printer?
- One of the winners of the ACM Turing Award (the closest that computer science has to a Nobel Prize) invented a computer system for typesetting books on a laser printer. Who was that?
- The winner of a recent ACM Turing Award built a computer system *on top of* the last typesetting system, to make it easier to use (but that's not what he won the Turing Award for). Who was that, and what did he win his award for?

TO DIG DEEPER

You can learn more about copyright law in the United States, including issues like fair use, at `http://www.copyright.gov/`.

James Gleick's book *Chaos* describes more on emergent properties—how small changes can lead to dramatic effects, and the unintended impacts of designs because of difficult-to-foresee interactions.

Mitchel Resnick's book *Turtles, Termites, and Traffic Jams: Explorations in Massively Parallel Microworlds* [37] describes how ants, termites, and even traffic jams and slime molds can be described pretty accurately with hundreds or thousands of very small processes (programs) running and interacting all at once.

Exploring The Digital Domain [26] is a wonderful introductory book on computation with lots of good information about digital media.

2 Introduction to Programming

Chapter Learning Objectives

The media learning goals for this chapter are:

- To make and show pictures.
- To make and play sounds.

The computer science goals for this chapter are:

- To use JES to enter and execute programs.
- To create and use variables to store values and objects, such as pictures and sounds.
- To create functions.
- To recognize different types (encodings) of data, such as integers, floating-point numbers, and media objects.
- To sequence operations in a function.

2.1 PROGRAMMING IS ABOUT NAMING

Computer Science Idea: Much of Programming Is about Naming

A computer can associate names, or *symbols*, with just about anything: with a specific byte; with a collection of bytes making up a numeric variable or a bunch of letters; with a media element like a file, sound, or picture; or even with more abstract concepts, like a named recipe (a *program*) or a named encoding (a *type*). A computer scientist sees a choice of names as being high quality in the same way that a philosopher or mathematician might: the naming scheme (the names and what they name) should be elegant, parsimonious, and usable. Naming is a form of abstraction. The name is used to refer to the thing you are naming.

Obviously, the computer itself doesn't *care* about names. Names are for humans. If the computer were just a calculator, then remembering words and their association with values would be just a waste of the computer's memory. But for humans, this is *very* powerful. It allows us to work with the computer in a natural way, even a way that extends how we think about recipes (processes) altogether.

A **programming language** is really a set of names that a computer has encodings for, such that the names make the computer do expected actions and interpret our data in expected ways. Some of the programming languages' names allow us to define *new* names that in turn allow us to create our own layers of encoding. Assigning a variable to a value is one way of defining a name for the computer. Defining a function is giving a name to a recipe.

A **program** is made from a set of names and their values, where some of these names have values of instructions to the computer ("code"). Our instructions will be in the Python programming language. Combining these two definitions means that the Python programming language gives us a set of useful names that have a meaning to the computer, and that our programs are then a selection of Python's useful names, plus names that we define, that together let us tell the computer what we want it to do.

> **Computer Science Idea: Programs Are for People, Not for Computers**
> Remember that names are only meaningful for people, not for computers. Computers just take instructions. A good program is meaningful (understandable and useful) for humans. Computers are made to serve people.

There are good names and bad names. This has nothing to do with curse words or with TLAs (three-letter acronyms). A good set of encodings and names allows us to describe recipes in a way that's natural, without having to say too much. The variety of different programming languages can be thought of as a collection of sets of namings and encodings. Some are better for some tasks than others. Some languages require you to write more to describe the same recipe than others—but sometimes that "more" leads to a much more (humanly) readable recipe that helps others to understand what you're saying.

Philosophers and mathematicians look for very similar senses of quality. They try to describe the world in a few words, seeking an elegant selection of words that cover many situations but remain understandable to their fellow philosophers and mathematicians. That's exactly what computer scientists do.

How the units and values (**data**) of a recipe can be interpreted is often also named. Remember the discussion in Section 1.3 that everything is in bytes, but bytes can be interpreted as numbers? In some programming languages, you can say explicitly that some value is a *byte*, and later tell the language to treat it as a number, an *integer* (or sometimes *int*). Similarly, you can tell the computer that this particular series of bytes is a collection of numbers (an **array of integers**), a collection of characters (a **string**), or even a more complex encoding of a single floating-point number (a **float**—any number with a decimal point in it).

In Python, we will explicitly tell the computer how to interpret our values, but we will very rarely tell it that certain names are only associated with certain encodings. Languages such as Java and C++ are *strongly typed*; that is, in these languages names are strongly associated with certain types or encodings. They require you to say that this name will only be associated with integers and that one will only be a floating-point number. Python still has *types* (encodings that you can reference by name), but they're not as explicit. Python also has **reserved words**. Reserved words are words that you can't use to name things since they already have meaning in the language.

> **Computer Science Idea: Names Are Symbols and Identifiers**
>
> We are using the word "names," but programming languages use more specific terms. Some programming languages call the name for a value or function or object a *symbol*. Python (and Java) call it an *identifier*. We can think about it as the human notion of a "name," but error messages will use the more specific terms. Probably the most common error message in Java is *Identifier expected* which typically means that there was a missing or mistyped name.

2.1.1 Files and Their Names

A programming language isn't the only place where computers associate names and values. Your computer's **operating system** takes care of the files on your disk and associates names with them. Operating systems you may be familiar with or use include Windows, MacOS, and Linux. A **file** is a collection of values (bytes) on your **hard disk** (the part of your computer that stores things after the power is turned off). If you know the name of a file and tell it to the operating system, you will be given the values associated with the name.

You may be thinking, "I've been using the computer for years, and I've *never* given a filename to the operating system." Maybe you didn't realize that you were doing it, but when you pick a file from a file-choosing dialog in Photoshop, or double-click a file in a *directory* window (or Explorer or Finder), you are asking some software somewhere to give the name you're picking or double-clicking to the operating system, and get the values back. When you write your own recipes, though, you'll be explicitly getting filenames and asking for their values.

Our hard disks today are huge. You will probably have more than one file with the same filename on them, somewhere. You probably have a couple of files named **report.doc** (maybe one for History, and another for Chemistry, and yet another for your internship) or `friends.jpg` on your disk right now. As long as they are in different directories, the same name can refer to different files entirely. The computer has a *file system* that manages the directories and files. The complete name for a file is called a *path* that describes the directories to follow to get to a specific file. We use this idea shortly.

Files are *very* important for media computation. Disks can store acres and acres of information on them. Remember our discussion of Moore's Law? Disk capacity per dollar is increasing *faster* than computer speed per dollar! Computer disks today can store whole movies, hours (days?) of sounds, and the equivalent of hundreds of film rolls of pictures.

These media are not small. Even in a *compressed* form, screen-size pictures can be over a million bytes large, and songs can be 3 million bytes or more. You need to keep them someplace where they'll last past the computer being turned off and where there's lots of space.

In contrast, your computer's **memory** is impermanent (it disappears when the power does) and relatively small. Computer memory is getting larger all the time, but it's still just a fraction of the amount of space on your disk. When you're working with media, you will load the media from the disk into memory, but you wouldn't want it to stay in memory after you're done. It's too big.

Think about your computer's memory as a dorm room. You can get to things easily in a dorm room—they're right at hand, easy to reach, and easy to use. But you wouldn't want to put everything you own (or everything you hope to own) in that one dorm room. All your belongings? Your skis? Your car? Your boat? That's silly. Instead, you store large things in places designed to store large things. You know how to get them when you need them (and maybe take them back to your dorm room if you need to or can).

When you bring things into memory, you will name the value so that you can retrieve it and use it later. In that sense, programming is something like *algebra*. To write equations and functions that were generalizable (i.e., that worked for any number or value), you wrote them with *variables*, like $PV = nRT$ or $e = Mc^2$ or $f(x) = sin(x)$. Those P's, V's, R's, T's, e's, M's, c's, and x's were names for values. When you evaluated $f(30)$ (in the equation $f(x) = sin(x)$), you knew that the x was the name for 30 when computing f, and you know that the result should be $sin(30)$. We'll be naming media (as values) in the same way when using them in programming.

2.2   PROGRAMMING IN PYTHON

The programming language that we use in this book is called **Python**. It's a language invented by Guido van Rossum. He named his language for the famous British comedy troupe *Monty Python*. Python has been used for years by people without formal computer science training—it's aimed at being easy to use. The particular form of Python that we're going to be using is **Jython** because it lends itself to cross-platform multimedia.

In this book, we program in the Jython programming language using the **JES** (**Jython Environment for Students**). JES is a simple **editor** (tool for entering program text) and interaction tool so that you can try things out in JES and create new recipes within it. The media names (functions, variables, encodings) that we'll be talking about in this book were developed to work from within JES (i.e., they're not part of a normal Jython distribution, though the basic language we'll be using is normal Python).

You can read the instructions on installing JES at `http://mediacomputation.org`. The process there will lead you to install Java, Jython, and JES, and give you a nice icon to double-click on to start JES. JES is available for Windows, Macintosh, and Linux.

Debugging Tip: Getting Java, If You Have to

For most people, dragging the JES folder onto their hard disk is all they need to do to get started. However, if you have Java installed, and it's an older version that can't run JES, you might have trouble getting JES started. If you do have problems, get a new version of Java at `http://www.java.com`.

2.3 PROGRAMMING IN JES

How you start JES depends on your platform. In Windows and Macintosh, you'll have a JES icon that you'll simply double-click. In Linux, you'll probably cd into your Jython directory and type a command like `./JES.sh`. See the instructions at the Web site for what will work for your computer.

Common Bug: JES Can Be Slow to Start

JES can take a while to load. Don't worry—you may see the splash screen for a long time, but if you see the splash screen, it will load. It will start faster after the first use. ■

Common Bug: Making JES Run Faster

As we'll talk more about later, when you're running JES, you're actually running Java. Java needs memory. If you find that JES runs slowly, give it more memory. You can do this by quitting out of other applications you're running. Your email program, your instant messenger, and your digital music player all take up memory—sometimes lots of it! Quit out of those and JES will run faster. ■

Once you start JES, it will look something like Figure 2.1. There are two main areas in JES (the bar between them moves so that you can differentially resize the two areas).

FIGURE 2.1
JES with areas labeled.

- The top part is the **Program Area**. This is where you write *your* recipes: the programs that you're creating and their names. This area is simply a text editor—think of it as Microsoft Word for your programs. The computer doesn't actually try to interpret the names that you type up in the Program Area until you press the LOAD PROGRAM button, and you can't press LOAD PROGRAM until you've saved your program (by using the SAVE menu item which is under the FILE menu).

  Don't worry if you hit LOAD PROGRAM before you remember to save. JES won't load the program until it's saved, so it will give you a chance to save the program then.

- The bottom part is the **Command Area**. This is where you literally *command* the computer to do something. You type your commands at the >>> prompt, and when you hit the RETURN (Apple) or ENTER (Windows) key, the computer will interpret your words (i.e., apply the meanings and encodings of the Python programming language) and do what you have told it to do. This interpretation will include whatever you typed and loaded from the Program Area as well.

- The area on the right is the **Help Area**. You can select something and then click the Explain button for help on that item.

Other features of JES are visible in Figure 2.1, but we won't be doing much with them yet. The watcher button opens up the **watcher (a debugger)**, a window with tools for watching how the computer executes your program. The STOP button allows you to stop a running program (e.g., if you think it's been running too long, or if you realize that it's not doing what you wanted it to do).

Making It Work Tip: Get to Know Your Help!

An *important* feature to start exploring is the HELP menu. There is a lot of great help for programming and for using JES available under this menu. Start exploring it now so that you have a sense of what's there when you start writing your own programs. ■

2.4   MEDIA COMPUTATION IN JES

We're going to start out by simply typing commands in the command area—not defining new names yet, but simply using the names that the computer already knows from within JES.

The name `print` is an important one to know. It's always used with something following it. The meaning for `print` is, "Display a readable representation of whatever follows." Whatever follows can be a name that the computer knows, or an *expression* (literally, in the algebraic sense). Try typing `print 34 + 56` by clicking in the Command Area, typing the command, and hitting ENTER—like this:

```
>>> print 34 + 56
90
```

34 + 56 is a numeric expression that Python understands. Obviously, it's composed of two numbers and an operation (in our sense, a *name*) that Python knows how to

do, + meaning "add." Python understands other kinds of expressions, not all of them numeric. We see below division (/), multiplication (*), subtraction (–), and modulo, or remainder (%)—9 divided by 2 leaves 1, and 9 divided by 3 leaves 0 (no remainder). We also see below string concatenation, which is also + but with strings of characters.

```
>>> print 34.1/46.5
0.7333333333333334
>>> print 22 * 33
726
>>> print 14 - 15
-1
>>> print 9 % 2
1
>>> print 9 % 3
0
>>> print "Hello"
Hello
>>> print "Hello" + "Mark"
HelloMark
```

Python understands quite a few standard math operations. It also knows how to recognize different kinds or **types** of numbers: integer and floating point. A floating-point number has a decimal point in it. An integer number does not have a decimal point in it. Python also knows how to recognize *strings* (sequences of characters) that are started and ended with " (quote) marks. It even knows what it means to "add" two strings together: it simply puts one right after the other. That's string concatenation.

Common Bug: Python's Types Can Produce Odd Results

Python takes types seriously. If it sees you using integers, it thinks you want an integer result from your expressions. If it sees you using floating-point numbers, it thinks you want a floating-point result. Sounds reasonable, no? But how about:

```
>>> print 1.0/2.0
0.5
>>> print 1/2
0
```

1/2 is 0? Well, sure! 1 and 2 are integers. There is no integer equal to 1/2, so the answer must be 0! Adding ".0" to an integer convinces Python that we're talking about floating-point numbers, so the result is in floating-point form. Many other programming languages work the same way. Python 3.0 does *not* interpret numbers like this, so this result may differ as Python 3.0 becomes more common.

Python supports defining numbers with exponential or scientific notation. You simply include E and the exponent for the power of 10 to apply.

```
>>> bignum = 3.0E10
>>> print bignum
3.0E10
>>> print bignum + 1
3.0000000001E10
```

```
>>> lilnum = 3.0E-5
>>> print lilnum
3.0E-5
>>> print lilnum+1
1.00003
```

Python also understands about **functions**. Remember functions from algebra? They're a "box" into which you put one value, and out comes another. One of the functions that Python knows takes a character as the *input* value (the value that goes into the box) and returns or outputs (the value that comes out of the box) the number that is the ASCII mapping for that character. The name of this function is ord (for *ordinal*), and you can use print to display the value that the function ord returns:

```
>>> print ord("A")
65
```

The function chr goes backwards. Given the number, the chr function returns the character that is encoded with that number according to the ASCII standard mapping.

```
>>> print chr(65)
A
>>> print chr(66)
B
>>> print chr(75)
K
```

Another function that's built into Python is named abs—it's the absolute value function. It returns the absolute value of the input value.

```
>>> print abs(1)
1
>>> print abs(-1)
1
```

Debugging Tip: Common Typos

If you type something that Python can't understand at all, you'll get a syntax error.

```
>>> pint "Hello"
Your code contains at least one syntax
error, meaning it is not legal Jython.
```

If you try to access a word that Python doesn't know, Python will say that it doesn't know that name.

```
>>> print a
A local or global name could not be found. You need to define
the function or variable before you try to use it in any way.
```

A *local name* is a name defined inside a function, and a *global name* is a name available to all functions (such as pickAFile which is described in the next section) in either the Command or Program Areas.

■

Another function that JES knows is one that allows you to pick a file from your disk. You may notice that we have switched from saying "Python knows" to "JES knows."

print is something that all Python implementations know. pickAFile is something that we built for JES. In general, you can ignore the difference, but if you try to use another kind of Python, it will be important to know what is common and what is not. It takes no input, as ord did, but it does return a string which is the name of the file on your disk. The name of the function is pickAFile. Python is very picky about capitalization—neither pickafile nor Pickafile will work! Try it like this: print pickAFile(). When you do, you will get something that looks like Figure 2.2.

You're probably already familiar with how to use a file picker or file dialog:

- Double-click on folders/directories to open them.
- Click to select and then click OPEN, or double-click, to select a file.

Once you select a file, what gets returned is the *full filename* as a string (a sequence of characters). (If you execute print pickAFile() then click CANCEL, you will see that None gets printed, i.e., there was nothing returned.) Try it: do print pickAFile() and OPEN a file.

```
>>> print pickAFile()
C:\ip-book\mediasources\beach.jpg
```

What you get when you finally select a file will depend on your operating system. On Windows, your filename will probably start with **C:** and will have backslashes in it (e.g., \). On Linux or MacOS, it will probably look like **/Users/guzdial/ip-book/mediasources/beach.jpg**. There are really two parts to this filename:

- The character between words (e.g., the / between "Users" and "guzdial") is called the **path delimiter** or **path separator**. Everything from the beginning of the

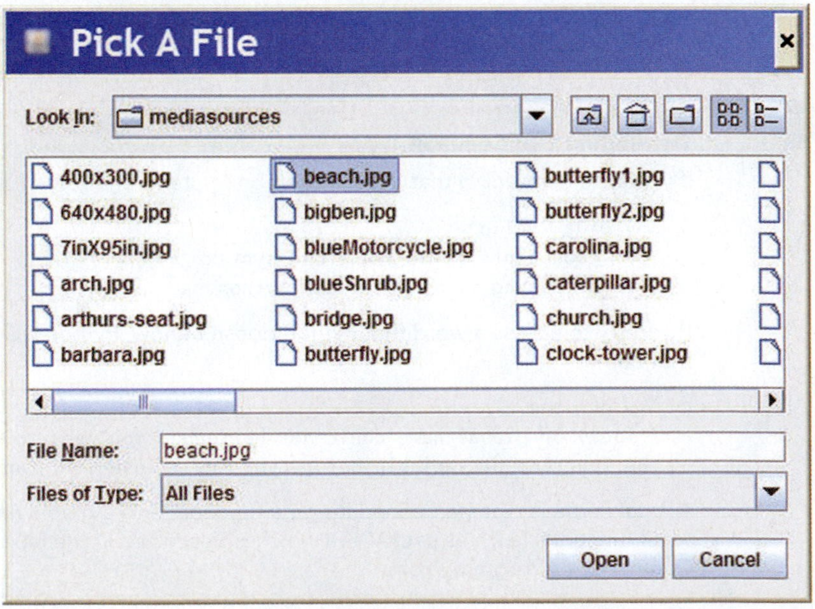

FIGURE 2.2
The file picker.

filename to the last path delimiter is the *path* to the file. That describes exactly *where* on the hard disk (in which **directory**) a file exists.

- The last part of the file (e.g., **beach.jpg**) is called the **base filename**. When you look at the file in the Finder/Explorer/Directory window (depending on your operating system), that's the part you see. The last three characters (after the period) are called the **file extension**. They identify the encoding of the file.

Files that have an extension of ".jpg" are **JPEG** files. They contain pictures. (To be more literal, they contain data that can be *interpreted* to be a *representation* of a picture—but it's close enough to say "they contain pictures.") JPEG is a standard *encoding* (representation) for any kind of image. The other media files that we'll be using frequently are ".wav" files (Figure 2.3). The ".wav" extension means that these are **WAV** files. They contain sounds. WAV is a standard encoding for sounds. There are many other kinds of extensions for files, and there are even many other kinds of media extensions. For example, there are also GIF (".gif") files for images and AIFF (".aif" or ".aiff") files for sounds. We'll stick to JPEG and WAV in this text, just to avoid too much complexity.

2.4.1   Showing a Picture

So now we know how to get a complete filename: path and base name. This *doesn't* mean that we have the file itself loaded into memory. To get the file into memory, we have to tell JES how to interpret it. *We* know that JPEG files are pictures, but we have to tell JES explicitly to read the file and make a picture from it. There is a function for that, too, named makePicture.

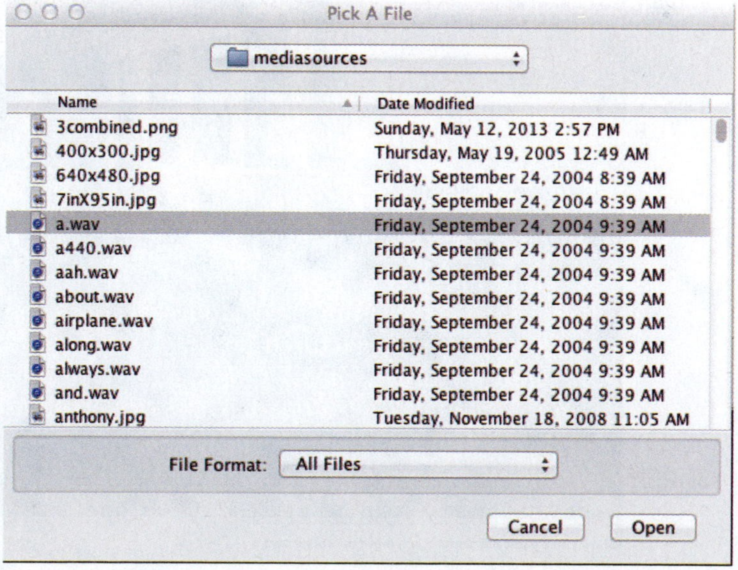

FIGURE 2.3
A MacOS X file picker with both image and sound files visible.

makePicture *does* require a **parameter**—some input to the function. Just like ord, the input is specified inside parentheses. It takes a filename. Lucky us—we know how to get one of those.

```
>>> print makePicture(pickAFile())
Picture, filename C:\ip-book\mediasources\barbara.jpg
    height 294 width 222
```

The result from print suggests that we did in fact make a picture, from a given filename and a given height and width. Success! Oh, you wanted to actually *see* the picture? We'll need another function! (Did we mention somewhere that computers are stupid?) The function to show the picture is named show. The function show *also* takes an input (or parameter)—a Picture.

But, we have a problem. We didn't name the picture that we just created and so we don't have any way to refer to it again. We can't just say show the picture that we created a second ago, but didn't name. Computers don't remember things unless we name them. Creating a name for a value is also called *declaring a variable*.

Let's start over and this time let's first name the file that we pick. We will also name the picture that we create. Then we can show the named picture as shown in Figure 2.4.

You can pick and name a file using file = pickAFile(). This means create a name file and set it to refer to the value returned from the function pickAFile(). We have seen that the function pickAFile() returns the name of the file (including

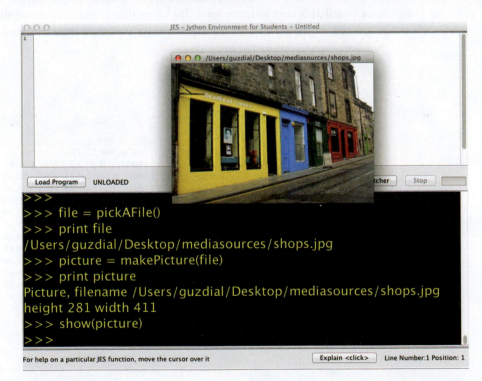

FIGURE 2.4
Picking, making, and showing a picture, and naming the pieces.

the path). We can name and create a picture using `pict = makePicture(file)`. This passes the filename into the function `makePicture` and then returns the created picture. The name `pict` refers to that created picture. We can then show the created picture by passing the name `pict` to the function `show`.

Another way to do all of this is to do it all at once because the output from one function can be used as the input for another function: `show(makePicture(pickAFile()))`. That's what we see in Figure 2.5. This will start by allowing you to pick a file and then pass the name of that file to the `makePicture` function and pass the resulting picture to the `show` function. But again, we didn't name the picture so we can't refer to it again.

Try it yourself! Congratulations—you've just worked your first media computation! To summarize, the code

```
>>> file = pickAFile()
>>> picture = makePicture(file)
>>> show(picture)
```

does the same thing as this code (assuming you pick the same file)

```
>>> picture = makePicture(pickAFile())
>>> show(picture)
```

This can even be done all in one line (without any names at all, which means that we can't show again or change the picture after this line).

```
>>> show(makePicture(pickAFile()))
```

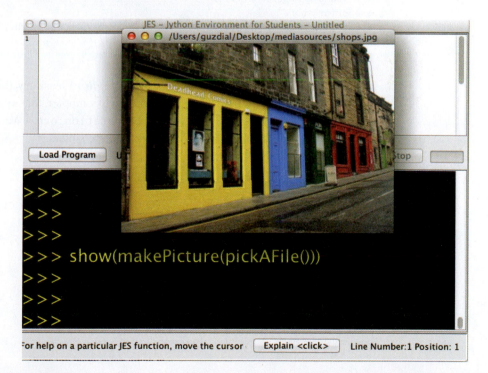

FIGURE 2.5
Picking, making, and showing a picture, using each function as input to the next.

If you try `print show(pict)`, you'll notice that the output from `show` is `None`. Functions in Python don't *have* to return a value, unlike real mathematical functions. If a function *does* something (like opening up a picture in a window), it can be useful without also needing to return a value. Computer scientists use the term **side-effect** for when a function does computation other than through its input-to-return value computation. Displaying windows and making sounds is a type of side-effect computation.

2.4.2 Playing a Sound

We can replicate this entire process with sounds.

- We still use `pickAFile` to find the file we want and get its filename. This time we pick a file that ends with .wav.
- We now use `makeSound` to make a sound. `makeSound`, as you might imagine, takes a filename as input.
- We will use `play` to play the sound. `play` takes a sound as input but returns `None`.

Here are the same steps we saw previously with pictures[1]:

```
>>> file = pickAFile()
>>> print file
/Users/guzdial/Desktop/mediasources/aah.wav
>>> sound = makeSound(file)
>>> print sound
Sound file: /Users/guzdial/Desktop/mediasources/aah.wav number of samples: 43009
>>> print play(sound)
None
```

(The number of the samples determines the *length*.) Please try this on your own, using JPEG files and WAV files that are on your own computer, that you make yourself, or that are available at `http://www.mediacomputation.org`. (We talk more about where to get the media and how to create it in future chapters.)

2.4.3 Naming Values

As we saw in the last section, we name data using =. We can check our namings using `print`, just as we have been doing.

```
>>> myVariable=12
>>> print myVariable
12
>>> anotherVariable=34.5
>>> print anotherVariable
34.5
>>> myName="Mark"
>>> print myName
Mark
```

---

[1]This example was made on a MacOS computer, so the file paths look different.

Don't read = as "equals." That's what it means in mathematics, but that's not at all what we're doing here. Read = as "becomes a name for the value." The statement `myVariable=12` thus means "`myVariable` becomes a name for the value 12." The reverse (putting the *expression* on the left and the name on the right) thus makes no sense: `12=myVariable` would then mean "12 becomes a name for the value `myVariable`." The statement 2 * 8 = x would mean "2 * 8 becomes a name for the value x" which makes even less sense. However, x = 2 * 8 means "x becomes a name for the value of 2 * 8 (or, 16)."

```
>>> x = 2 * 8
>>> print x
16
>>> 2 * 8 = x
Your code contains at least one syntax error, meaning
it is not legal Jython.
```

Common Bug: Assignment Is an Operation, Not a Statement of Truth

In mathematics, the equals sign (=) indicates truth. The physics statement $F = ma$ tells us that Force is always the product of mass times acceleration. But in computer science, the equals sign is an *assignment operation*. If we say number = 3 then the variable number takes on the value 3 *at that moment*, but if the next line is number=34.56, then number takes on the new value of 34.56. This becomes important later when we see statements like index = index + 1. Mathematically, there is no number that equals one plus itself. But in computer science, we read that as "index becomes the name for the (old) value of index plus one."

We can use names more than once.

```
>>> print myVariable
12
>>> myVariable="Hello"
>>> print myVariable
Hello
```

The *binding* (or association) between the name and the data only exists until (a) the name gets assigned to something else or (b) you quit JES. The relationship between names and data (or even names and functions) only exists during a session of JES.

Remember that data have encodings or types. How data act in expressions depends in part on their types. Note how the *integer* 12 and the *string* "12" act differently for multiplication below. Both are doing something reasonable for their type, but they are very different actions.

```
>>> myVariable=12
>>> print myVariable*4
48
>>> myOtherVariable="12"
>>> print myOtherVariable*4
12121212
```

We can assign names to the *results* of functions. If we name the result from `pickAFile`, we will get the same result each time we print the name. We don't rerun `pickAFile`. Naming code in order to re-execute it is what we're doing when we define functions, which comes up in just a few pages.

```
>>> file = pickAFile()
>>> print file
C:\ip-book\mediasources\640x480.jpg
>>> print file
C:\ip-book\mediasources\640x480.jpg
```

In the following example, we assign names to the filename and the picture.

```
>>> myFilename = pickAFile()
>>> print myFilename
C:\ip-book\mediasources\barbara.jpg
>>> myPicture = makePicture(myFilename)
>>> print myPicture
Picture, filename barbara.jpg
height 294 width 222
```

Note that the algebraic notions of *substitution* and *evaluation* work here as well. `myPicture = makePicture(myFilename)` causes the exact same picture to be created as if we had executed `makePicture(pickAFile())`,[2] because we set `myFilename` to be equal to the result of `pickAFile()`. The values are substituted for the names when the expression is evaluated. `makePicture(myFilename)` is an expression that is expanded, at evaluation time, into `makePicture("C:/ip-book/mediasources/barbara.jpg")` because **C:/ip-book/mediasources/barbara.jpg** is the name of the file that was picked when `pickAFile()` was evaluated and the returned value was named `myFilename`.

We can also replace the function *invocations* (or *calls*) with the *value* returned. `pickAFile()` returns a *string*—a bunch of characters enclosed inside quotes. We can make the last example work like this, too.

```
>>> myFilename = "C:/ip-book/mediasources/barbara.jpg"
>>> print myFilename
C:/ip-book/mediasources/barbara.jpg
>>> myPicture = makePicture(myFilename)
>>> print myPicture
Picture, filename C:/ip-book/mediasources/barbara.jpg
height 294 width 222
```

Or even substitute the actual filename for any function or variable name. (We're swapping p for `myPicture` in this example, because the actual name doesn't matter – it's up to us as the programmers what names we choose to use.)

```
>>> p = makePicture("C:/ip-book/mediasources/barbara.jpg")
>>> print p
Picture, filename C:/ip-book/mediasources/barbara.jpg
height 294 width 222
```

[2] Assuming, of course, that you picked the same file.

Common Bug: Windows Filenames and Backslashes

Windows uses backslashes as file delimiters. Python gives special meanings to certain backslash-and-character combinations, as we'll talk more about later. For example, '\n' means the same thing as the ENTER or RETURN key. These combinations can occur naturally in Windows filenames. To avoid having Python misinterpret these characters, you can use forward slashes instead as in **C:/ip-book/mediasources/barbara.jpg** or you can type your filenames with an "r" in front, like this:

```
>>> myfile=r"C:\ip-book\mediasources\barbara.jpg"
>>> print myfile
C:\ip-book\mediasources\barbara.jpg
>>> myfile
'C:\\ip-book\\mediasources\\barbara.jpg'
```

Computer Science Idea: We Can Substitute Names, Values, and Functions

We can substitute a value, a name assigned to that value, and the function returning the same value *interchangeably*. The computer cares about the value, not whether it comes from a string, a name, or a function call. The key is that the computer is *evaluating* the value, the name, and the function. As long as these *expressions* evaluate to the same thing, they can be used interchangeably.

We actually don't need to use `print` every time we ask the computer to do something. If we want to call a function that doesn't return anything (and so is pretty useless to `print`), we can just call the function by typing its name and its input (if any) and hitting return.

```
>>> show(myPicture)
```

We tend to call these statements to the computer that are telling it to do things *commands*. `print myPicture` is a command. So is `myfilename = pickAFile()`, and `show(myPicture)`. These are more than expressions: they're telling the computer to *do* something.

2.5 MAKING A PROGRAM

We have now used names to stand for values. The values are substituted for the names when the expression is evaluated. We can do the same for programs. We can name a series of commands and then just use the name whenever we want the commands to be executed. In Python, the name we define will be a *function*. A *program* in Python, then, is a collection of one or more functions that perform a useful task. We're going to use the term *recipe* to describe programs (or portions of programs) that perform a useful media operation, even if whatever is covered by the term is not enough to make a useful program in itself.

Remember when we said earlier that just about anything can be named in computers? We've seen naming values. Now we'll see naming recipes.

The name that Python understands as _defining_ the name of new recipes is `def`. `def` isn't a function—it's a command like `print`. `def` is used to _define_ new functions. There are certain things that have to come after the word `def`, though. The structure of what goes on the line with the `def` command is referred to as the **syntax** of the command— the words and characters that have to be there for Python to understand what's going on and the order of those things.

`def` needs three things to follow it on the same line:

- The name of the recipe you're defining, like `showMyPicture`.

- Whatever _inputs_ this recipe will take. The recipe can be a function that takes inputs, like `abs` or `makePicture`. The inputs are named and placed between parentheses separated by commas. If your recipe takes no inputs, you simply enter `()` to indicate no inputs.

- The line ends with a colon, `:`.

What comes after this are the commands to be executed, one after the other, whenever the recipe is told to execute. We create a collection of commands by defining a **block**. The block of commands that follow a `def` command (or _statement_) are the ones associated with the name of the function.

Most real programs that do useful things, especially those that create user interfaces, require the definition of more than one function. Imagine that you have several `def` commands in the Program Area. How do you think Python will figure out that one function has ended and a new one has begun? (Especially because it _is_ possible to define functions _inside of_ other functions.) Python needs some way of figuring out where the _function body_ ends—which statements are part of this function and which are part of the next.

The answer is **indentation**. All the statements that are part of the definition are slightly indented after the `def` statement. We recommend using exactly two spaces— it's enough to see, it's easy to remember, and it's simple. (In JES, you could also use one _tab_—a single press of the tab key.) You enter the function in the Program Area like this (where ⊔ indicates a single space, a single press of the spacebar):

```
def hello():
⊔⊔print "Hello"
```

We can now define our first program. You type this into the Program Area of JES. When you're done, save the file: Use the extension ".py" to indicate a Python file. (We saved ours as **pickAndShow.py**.)

Program 1: Pick and Show a Picture

```
def pickAndShow():
  myFile = pickAFile()
  myPict = makePicture(myFile)
  show(myPict)
```

You'll notice a thin blue box around the body of the function while you're typing. The blue box indicates the blocks in your program (Figure 2.6). All the commands in the same block as the statement containing the cursor (the vertical bar where you're typing) are enclosed in the same blue box. You know that you have the indentation right when all the commands you *expect* to be in the block *are* in the box.

Once you've typed in your recipe and saved it, you can load it. Click the LOAD PROGRAM button.

Debugging Tip: Don't Forget to Load!

The most common mistake with JES is typing in the function, saving it, and then trying the function in the Command Area before you load it. You have to click the LOAD PROGRAM button to make it available in the Command Area.

Now you can execute your program. Click in the Command Area. Since you aren't taking any input and aren't returning any value (i.e., this isn't a strict mathematical function), simply type the name of your program as a command:

```
>>> pickAndShow()
>>>
```

We can similarly define our second program to pick and play a sound.

Program 2: Pick and Play a Sound

```
def pickAndPlay():
  myFile = pickAFile()
  mySound = makeSound(myFile)
  play(mySound)
```

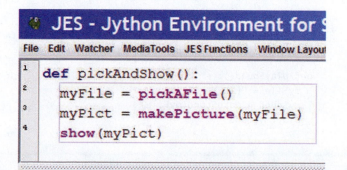

FIGURE 2.6
Visualizing the blocks in JES.

Making It Work Tip: Use the Names You Like

In the last section, we used the names `myFilename` and `myPicture`. In this program, we used `myFile` and `myPict`. Does it matter? It doesn't matter to the computer at all. We could call all our pictures `myGlyph` or even `myThing`. The computer doesn't care what names you use—they're entirely for your benefit. Pick names that are (a) meaningful to you (so that you can read and understand your program), (b) meaningful to others (so that anyone you show your program to can understand it), and (c) easy to type. Names with 25 characters, like `myPictureThatIAmGoingToOpenAfterThis` are meaningful and easy to read, but are a pain to type.

These programs probably aren't really useful. Needing to pick the file over and over again is annoying if you want the same picture to appear. Now that we have the power to define programs, we can define new ones to perform whatever tasks we want. Let's define one that will open a specific picture and another that opens a specific sound.

Use `pickAFile` to get the filename of the sound or picture you want. We're going to need the name in defining the program to play that specific sound or show that specific picture. We'll just set the value of `myFile` *directly*, instead of as a result of `pickAFile`, by putting the string between quotes directly in the recipe.

Program 3: Show a Specific Picture

Be sure to replace FILENAME below with the complete path to your own picture file; for example, **C:/ip-book/mediasources/barbara.jpg**.

```
def showPicture():
  myFile = "FILENAME"
  myPict = makePicture(myFile)
  show(myPict)
```

How It Works

The variable `myFile` takes on the value of the filename—the same one that the function `pickAFile` would return if it were to pick that file. We then make a picture from the file and name it `myPict`. Finally, we show the picture in `myPict`.

Program 4: Play a Specific Sound

Be sure to replace FILENAME below with the complete path to your own sound file; for example, **C:/ip-book/mediasources/hello.wav**.

```
def playSound():
  myFile = "FILENAME"
  mySound = makeSound(myFile)
  play(mySound)
```

Making It Work Tip: Copying and Pasting

Text can be copied and pasted between the Program and Command areas. You can use `print pickAFile()` to print a filename, then select it and COPY it (from the EDIT menu), then click in the Command Area and PASTE it. Similarly, you can copy whole commands from the Command Area up to the Program Area. That's an easy way to test the individual commands and then put them all in a recipe once you have the order right and they're working. You can also copy text within the Command Area. Instead of retyping a command, select it, COPY it, PASTE it into the bottom line (make sure the cursor is at the end of the line!), and hit ENTER to execute it. ■

2.5.1 Functions: Real Math-Like Functions That Take Input

How do we create a real function, like a function in mathematics, that takes inputs, such as ord or makePicture? Why would you *want* to?

An important reason for using a variable to specify input to the program is to make a program more *general*. Consider Program 3, showPicture. That's for a specific filename. Would it be useful to have a function that could take *any* filename, then make and show the picture? That kind of function handles the *general* case of making and showing pictures. We call that kind of generalization **abstraction**. Abstraction leads to general solutions that work in lots of situations.

Defining a program that takes input is very easy. It continues to be a matter of *substitution* and *evaluation*. We'll put a name inside those parentheses on the def line. That name is sometimes called the **parameter** or **input variable**.

When you evaluate the function by specifying its name with an **input value** (also called the **argument**) inside parentheses (like makePicture(myFilename) or show(myPicture)), the input value is *assigned* to the input variable. We say that the input variable *takes on* the input value. During the execution of the function (recipe), the input value will be *substituted* for the variable.

Here's what a program would look like that takes the filename as an input variable:

Program 5: Show the Picture File Whose Filename Is Input

```
def showNamed(myFile):
  myPict = makePicture(myFile)
  show(myPict)
```
■

Click on the LOAD PROGRAM button to tell JES to read the function or functions in the Program Area. If you have any errors in your function, you will need to fix them and click LOAD PROGRAM button again. Once you have successfully loaded your functions, you can use them in the Command Area.

When you type

```
showNamed("C:/ip-book/mediasources/barbara.jpg")
```

in the Command Area and hit ENTER, the variable myFile in the function showNamed takes on the value

```
"C:/ip-book/mediasources/barbara.jpg"
```

myPict will then refer to the picture resulting from reading and interpreting the file. Then the picture will be shown.

We can create a function to play a sound in the same way. We can type more than one function in the Program Area. Just add the function shown below after the previous one and click Load Program again.

Program 6: Play the Sound File Whose Filename Is Input

```
def playNamed(myFile):
  mySound = makeSound(myFile)
  play(mySound)
```

Try this function by typing the following in the Command Area.

```
>>> playNamed("C:/ip-book/mediasources/croak.wav")
```

You can create functions that take more than one parameter. Just separate the parameters with commas.

Program 7: Play a Sound File While Showing a Picture

```
def playAndShow(sFile, pFile):
  mySound = makeSound(sFile)
  myPict = makePicture(pFile)
  play(mySound)
  show(myPict)
```

We can also write programs that take pictures or sounds in as the input values. Here's a program that shows a picture but takes the picture object as the input value instead of the filename.

Program 8: Show the Picture Provided as Input

```
def showPicture(myPict):
  show(myPict)
```

At this point you may want to save your functions to a file so that you can use them again. Click on File and then Save Program. A file dialog window will appear that will allow you to specify where to save the file and what to call it. If you later exit JES and restart JES, you can use Open Program in the File menu to open the file again and click on Load Program to load the functions for use.

Now, what is the difference between the function showPicture and the built-in JES function show? Nothing at all. We can certainly create a function that provides a new name to another function. If that makes your code easier for you to understand, then it's a great idea.

What is the *right* input value for a function? Is it better to input a filename or a picture? And what does "better" mean here, anyway? You'll read more about all of these issues later, but here's a short answer: Write the function that is most useful to you. If defining showPicture is more readable for you than show, then that's useful. If what you really want is a function that takes care of making the picture and showing it to you, then you might find the showNamed function the most useful.

What we have done so far is to tell the computer to show and play media files, and to create functions to make it easier for us to group these commands. We have barely tapped into what makes a computer powerful. First, a computer can *repeat* operations, millions and millions of times over, without ever getting tired or bored. Second, a computer can make *choices*, that is, make comparisons and take actions dependent on the results of those comparisons. We will use repetition to process all the pixels in a picture, and choice to process only some pixels.

PROGRAMMING SUMMARY

In this chapter, we talk about several kinds of encodings of data (or objects).

Integers (e.g., 3)	Numbers without a decimal point—they can't represent fractions.
Floating-point numbers (e.g., 3.0, 3.01)	Numbers that can contain a decimal point—they can represent fractions.
Strings (e.g., "Hello!")	A sequence of characters (including spaces, punctuation, etc.) delimited on either end with a double quote.
Filename	A string whose characters represent a path and a base filename.
Pictures	Encodings of images, typically coming from a JPEG file.
Sounds	Encodings of sounds, typically coming from a WAV file.

Here are the program pieces introduced in this chapter:

print	Displays the value of an expression (variable, value, formula, etc.) in its text form.
def	Defines a function and its input variables (if any).
ord	Returns the equivalent numeric value (from the ASCII standard) for the input character.
chr	Returns the character for the input of the equivalent numeric value (from the ASCII standard).
abs	Takes a number and returns the absolute value of it.
pickAFile	Lets the user pick a file and returns the complete path name as a string. It doesn't take any input.
makePicture	Takes a path name as input, reads the file, and creates a picture from it. Returns the new picture.
show	Shows a picture provided as input. It doesn't return anything.
makeSound	Takes a path name as input, reads the file, and creates a sound from it. It returns the new sound.
play	Takes a sound and plays it. It doesn't return anything.

PROBLEMS

2.1   Computer science concept questions:

- What is an algorithm?
- What is an encoding?
- What is the difference between an *algorithm* and a `program`?

2.2   Computer science representation (encoding) questions:

- How can computers represent pictures as numbers?
- How can computers represent text as numbers?
- Remember that the computer can only represent *integer* numbers in raw binary. How can computers represent floating-point (decimal) numbers?

2.3   What does `def` mean? What does the statement `def someFunction(x,y):` do?

2.4   What does `print` mean? What does the statement `print a` do?

2.5   What is the output from `print 1 / 3`? Why do you get this output?

2.6   What is the output from `print 1.0 / 3`? Why do you get this output?

2.7   What is the output from `print 10 + 3 * 7`? Why do you get this output?

2.8   What is the output from `print (10 + 3) * 7`? Why do you get this output?

2.9   What is the output from `print "Hi" + "there"`? Why do you get this output?

2.10   What is the output from `print "Hi" + 10`? Why do you get this output?

2.11   What is the output from `print "Hi" * 10`? Why do you get this output?

2.12   What is the output from `print "Hi" + "there"`? Why do you get this output?

2.13   What is the output from `print "Hi" * "10"`? Why do you get this output?

2.14   What is the output from `print "Hi" + "10"`? Why do you get this output?

2.15   What does `show(p)` do? (Hint: There's more than one answer to this question.)

2.16   What is the output from the following?

```
>>> a = 3
>>> b = 4
>>> x = a * b
>>> print x
```

2.17   What is the output from the following?

```
>>> a = 3
>>> b = -5
>>> x = a * b
>>> print x
```

2.18   What is the output from the following?

```
>>> a = 3
>>> b = -5
>>> a = b
>>> b = 22
>>> x = a * b
>>> print x
```

2.19 What is the output from the following?
```
>>> a = 4
>>> b = 2
>>> x = a / b
>>> print x
```

2.20 What is the output from the following?
```
>>> a = 4
>>> b = 2
>>> x = b - a
>>> print x
```

2.21 What is the output from the following?
```
>>> a = -4
>>> b = 2
>>> c = abs(a)
>>> x = a * c
>>> print x
```

2.22 What is the output from the following?
```
>>> name = "Barb"
>>> name = "Mark"
>>> print name
```

2.23 What is the output from the following?
```
>>> first = "Abe"
>>> last = "Lincoln"
>>> print first + last
```

2.24 What is the output from the following?
```
>>> first = "Abe"
>>> last = "Lincoln"
>>> print first + " " + last
```

2.25 What is the output from the following?
```
>>> first = "Abe"
>>> last = "Lincoln"
>>> swap = first
>>> first = last
>>> last = swap
>>> print first + " " + last
```

2.26 What is the output from the following?
```
>>> a = ord("A")
>>> b = 2
>>> x = a * b
>>> print x
```

2.27 Type the function below into the Program Area of JES, then load the program and type into the Command Area compute(). What is being computed by the following?
```
def compute():
    distanceInMiles = 3279.8
    metersPerMile = 1609.34
    distanceInMeters = distanceInMiles * metersPerMile
    turtleSpeed = 0.5
```

```
turtleSecondsM2S = distanceInMeters / turtleSpeed
print("Time in seconds")
print("for turtle to Miami to Seattle:")
print(turtleSecondsM2S)
turtleMinutes = turtleSecondsM2S / 60
print("In minutes:")
print(turtleMinutes)
turtleHours = turtleMinutes / 60
turtleDays = turtleHours / 24
turtleWeeks = turtleDays / 7
print("In Weeks:")
print(turtleWeeks)
```

2.28   Type the function below into the Program Area of JES, then load the program and type into the Command Area compute(). What is being computed by the following?

```
def compute2():
  gravity = 6.67384E-11
  earthMass = 5.9736E24
  earthRadius = 6371000
  velocity = (2 * gravity * earthMass) / earthRadius
  result = sqrt(velocity)
  print "Escape velocity:"
  print result
```

2.29   Type the function below into the Program Area of JES, then load the program and type into the Command Area compute(). What is being computed by the following?

```
def compute3():
 heightInStories = 3
 feetPerStory = 10
 heightInFeet = heightInStories * feetPerStory
 metersPerFoot = 0.3048
 heightInMeters = heightInFeet * metersPerFoot
 gravityMeters = 9.81
 timeToFall = sqrt((2*heightInMeters)/gravityMeters)
 print("Time to fall (seconds):")
 print(timeToFall)
```

2.30   The following code gives the error message shown below. Fix the code.

```
>>> pickafile()
The error was:pickafile
Name not found globally.
A local or global name could not be found. You need
to define the function or variable before you try
to use it in any way.
```

2.31   The following code gives the error message shown below. Fix the code.

```
>>> a = 3
>>> b = 4
>>> c = d * a
The error was:d
Name not found globally.
A local or global name could not be found. You need
```

```
to define the function or variable before you try
to use it in any way.
```

2.32   Try some other operations with strings in JES. What happens if you multiply a number by a string, like `3 * "Hello"`? What happens if you try to multiply a string by a string, `"a" * "b"`?

2.33   We evaluated the expression `pickAFile()` when we wanted to execute the function named `pickAFile`. But what is the name `pickAFile` anyway? What do you get if you `print pickAFile`? How about `print makePicture`? What prints, and what do you think it means?

2.34   Try running the code below. What is the result? Why did you get that? (Hint: "becomes the name for the value of.")
```
>>> print abs(-5)
5
>>> myfunc = abs
>>> print myfunc(-5)
```

TO DIG DEEPER

The best (deepest, most material, most elegant) computer science textbook is *Structure and Interpretation of Computer Programs* by Abelson, Sussman, and Sussman [17]. It's a challenging book to get through but definitely worth the effort. A newer book more aimed at the programming novice but in the same spirit is *How to Design Programs* [36].

Neither of these books is really aimed at students who want to program because it's fun or because they have something small they want to do. They're aimed at future professional software developers. The best books for the student exploring computing are by Brian Harvey. His *Simply Scheme* uses the same programming language as the Abelson *et al.* book, but is more approachable. Our favorite of this group of books, though, is Harvey's three-volume set *Computer Science Logo Style* [9], which combines good computer science with creative and fun projects.

3

Creating and Modifying Text

Chapter Learning Objectives

The media learning goals for this chapter are:

- To create human-usable text (like stories) via programs.
- To generate text patterns, including "double dutch" language.

The computer science goals for this chapter are:

- To manipulate strings.
- To build strings with concatenation.
- To use loops to iterate over characters in a string.
- To convert strings into lists for manipulation.
- To use array notation for accessing elements of strings and lists.

3.1 STRINGS: MAKING HUMAN TEXT IN A COMPUTER

The first medium that most of us manipulate is text: words, stories, and poems. Text is typically manipulated in a program as **strings**. A string is a sequence of characters.

If we think about the computer's memory as a collection of mailboxes, like in a mailroom, then strings are a contiguous sequence of our memory mailboxes—the mailboxes right next to one another. The string "Hello" would be stored in five mailboxes right next to one another: one mailbox holding the binary code representing "H," the next one holding "e," the next one holding "l," and so on.

Strings are defined with sequences of characters inside quote marks. Python is unusual in that it allows several different kinds of quoting. We can use single quotes, double quotes, or even triple quotes. We can *nest* quotes. If we start a string with double quotes, then we can use single quotes inside the string because the string isn't ended until the next set of double quotes. If you start a string with single quotes, you can put all the double quotes you want inside the string, because Python is waiting for the single quotes to end.

```
>>> print 'This is a single-quoted string'
This is a single-quoted string
>>> print "This is a double-quoted string"
This is a double-quoted string
>>> print """This is a triple-quoted string"""
This is a triple-quoted string
```

Why triple quote? Because it allows us to embed new lines and spaces and tabs in our strings. We can't use it easily from the Command Area, but we can in the Program Area.

In the below example, we are defining a function named `sillyString` that simply prints a long, multi-line string.

```
def sillyString():
   print """This is using triple quotes.  Why?
Notice the different lines.
And we can't ignore the use of apostrophes.

Because we can do this."""
```

After we press the LOAD PROGRAM button, we can type `sillyString()` to execute (or *call*) the function.

```
>>> sillyString()
This is using triple quotes.  Why?
  Notice the different lines.
  And we can't ignore the use of apostrophes.

Because we can do this.
```

Having so many different kinds of quotes makes it easy to put quotes *inside* of strings. For example, Web pages use a code called HTML that requires double quotes inside its commands. If you want to write a Python function that creates HTML pages (a common use for Python, and something we do later in the book), then you will need strings that contain quotes. Since any of these quotes work, you can embed double quotes by simply using single quotes to start and end the string.

```
>>> print " " "
Invalid syntax
Your code contains at least one syntax error, meaning
it is not legal jython.
>>> print ' " '
 "
```

Strings are not the same as numbers. We say that they are different *types*. They can't be used interchangeably. The string "4" contains the character "4," but 4 by itself has the value of the number 4.

```
>>> print 4 + 5
9
>>> print "4"+"5"
45
>>> print 4 + "5"
The error was: 'int' and 'str'
Inappropriate argument type. An attempt was made to call a function with a
parameter of an invalid type. This means that you did something such as trying
to pass a string to a method that is expecting an integer.
```

You can *convert* a number to a string by using the function str, and you can convert a string into an integer using the function int. If you have a *floating-point number* inside the string, you can convert it with float.

```
>>> print 4 + 1
5
>>> print str(4) + str(1)
41
>>> print int("4")
4
>>> print int("abc")
The error was: abc
Inappropriate argument value (of correct type).
An error occurred attempting to pass an argument to a function.
>>> print float("124.3")
124.3
>>> print int("124.3")
The error was: 124.3
Inappropriate argument value (of correct type).
An error occurred attempting to pass an argument to a function.
```

3.1.1 Making Strings from Strings: Telling Stories

We can easily add strings together using + (also called **concatenation** of strings)

```
>>> hello = "Hello"
>>> print len(hello)
5
>>> mark = ", Mark"
>>> print hello+mark
Hello, Mark
```

We can combine the ability to define functions and to add strings together to create a Mad Lib program. A Mad Lib[1] is a word game where one player provides a list of words (like a name, and a verb, and an animal) and the second player inserts those words into a story template. Mad Libs work best when the two players don't know what the other is doing, e.g., the word picker doesn't know the template, and the story maker doesn't know what words are being selected.

We can replicate a Mad Lib by naming the words we want, then adding them into lines of a string to make up the story.

[1]Look up "mad libs" in your favorite search engine.

Program 9: Generate a Mad Lib Story

```
def madlib():
    name = "Mark"
    pet = "Baxter"
    verb = "ate"
    snack = "Krispy Kreme Doughnuts"
    line1 = "Once upon a time, "+name+" was walking"
    line2 = " with "+pet+", a trained dragon. "
    line3 = "Suddenly, "+pet+" stopped and announced,"
    line4 = "'I have a desperate need for "+snack+"'. "
    line5 = name+" complained. 'Where I am going to get that?' "
    line6 = "Then "+name+" found a wizard's wand. "
    line7 = "With a wave of the wand, "
    line8 = pet+" got "+snack+". "
    line9 = "Perhaps surprisingly, "+pet+" "+verb+" the "+snack+"."
    print line1+line2+line3+line4
    print line5+line6+line7+line8+line9
```

```
>>> madlib()
Once upon a time, Mark was walking with Baxter, a trained dragon. Suddenly,
Baxter stopped and announced,'I have a desperate need for Krispy Kreme
Doughnuts'.

Mark complained. 'Where I am going to get that?' Then Mark found a wizard's
wand. With a wave of the wand, Baxter got Krispy Kreme Doughnuts. Perhaps
surprisingly, Baxter ate the Krispy Kreme Doughnuts.
```

How It Works

The first four lines define the names that the first player would specify: a `name`, a `pet` (name), a past tense `verb`, and a `snack` name. The next nine lines create lines of the story. These could have all been one long line, but it would be harder to read. Notice that we use double quotes to begin and end each line, which lets us use apostrophes and single quotes to define what the characters are saying. You should also note that we have to insert spaces into the strings where ever we want them. Being careful with the spacing is important when adding two names together. Python doesn't really know that these are words and it knows nothing about spacing. If we want spaces, we have to put them in. At the end, we print out all the lines. We could have had nine separate lines like `print line1`, or we could have had one long line `print line1+line2+line3...+line9`. We broke it up as we did for readability.

Now, we can pretty easily run this program again with a different set of names.

Program 10: Generate a 2nd Mad Lib Story

```
def madlib2():
    name = "Ty"
    pet = "Fluffy"
    verb = "rolled on"
    snack = "a seven-layer wedding cake."
```

```
        line1 = "Once upon a time, "+name+" was walking"
        line2 = " with "+pet+", a trained dragon. "
        line3 = "Suddenly, "+pet+" stopped and announced,"
        line4 = "'I have a desperate need for "+snack+"'. "
        line5 = name+" complained. 'Where I am going to get that?' "
        line6 = "Then "+name+" found a wizard's wand. "
        line7 = "With a wave of the wand, "
        line8 = pet+" got "+snack+". "
        line9 = "Perhaps surprisingly, "+pet+" "+verb+" the "+snack+"."
        print line1+line2+line3+line4
        print line5+line6+line7+line8+line9
```

```
>>> madlib2()
Once upon a time, Ty was walking with Fluffy, a trained dragon. Suddenly, Fluffy
stopped and announced, 'I have a desperate need for a seven-layer wedding cake.'.

Ty complained. 'Where I am going to get that?' Then Ty found a wizard's wand.
With a wave of the wand, Fluffy got a seven-layer wedding cake. Perhaps
surprisingly, Fluffy rolled on the a seven-layer wedding cake.
```

Parameterizing Story

But this still doesn't really replicate the idea of a Mad Lib. We should be able to specify the names *without* seeing the rest of the story. We can do that in Python by specifying *parameters*. Here is another version of the madlib function, but this one accepts the names as *arguments* when we call the function.

Program 11: Provide a Mad Lib Story Template with Parameters

```
def madlib3(name,pet,verb,snack):
        line1 = "Once upon a time, "+name+" was walking"
        line2 = " with "+pet+", a trained dragon. "
        line3 = "Suddenly, "+pet+" stopped and announced,"
        line4 = "'I have a desperate need for "+snack+"'. "
        line5 = name+" complained. 'Where I am going to get that?' "
        line6 = "Then "+name+" found a wizard's wand. "
        line7 = "With a wave of the wand, "
        line8 = pet+" got "+snack+". "
        line9 = "Perhaps surprisingly, "+pet+" "+verb+" the "+snack+"."
        print line1+line2+line3+line4
        print line5+line6+line7+line8+line9
```

Now, we can specify the names when we call the madlib3() function—without knowing what is inside the function. The order of the strings we give

```
>>> madlib3("Lee","Spot","stomped on","Taco Bell nachos")
Once upon a time, Lee was walking with Spot, a trained dragon. Suddenly,
Spot stopped and announced,'I have a desperate need for Taco Bell nachos'.

Lee complained. 'Where I am going to get that?' Then Lee found a wizard's
wand. With a wave of the wand, Spot got Taco Bell nachos. Perhaps
surprisingly, Spot stomped on the Taco Bell nachos.
```

Multiplying Strings

An interesting feature of Python which is occasionally useful is to *multiply strings* by an integer.

```
>>> print "abc" * 3
abcabcabc
>>> print 4 * "Hey!"
Hey!Hey!Hey!Hey!
```

We can use this feature in functions, too. The below function repeats the threat of Inigo Montoya from the movie *The Princess Bride* seven times.

Program 12: Repeat the Inigo Montoya Threat

```
def mathWithStrings():
    mystring = "My name is Inigo Montoya."
    mythreat = 'You killed my father. Prepare to die.'
    print mystring + mythreat  #String concatenation
    print mystring * 6
```

A nice use for the multiplying strings is to create patterns of text. We can use the multiplication to create strings of spaces and other characters to create shapes. Here's a function that creates a "pyramid" of an input character.

Program 13: Print a Pyramid of an Input Character

```
def pyramid(char):
    space = " "
    print 4*space,char
    print 3*space,3*char
    print 2*space,5*char
    print space,7*char
    print 9*char
```

```
>>> pyramid("=")
    =
   ===
  =====
 =======
=========
```

3.2 TAKING STRINGS APART WITH FOR

A string isn't just one thing. It's easy to imagine a string like `"an apple falls"` as three words: `"an"` and `"apple"` and `"falls"`. To Python, it's really a sequence of characters.

How do we get Python to dissect the string and let us at the individual characters? The easiest way is with the `for`. Read `for` as `"for each"` and you'll get a clear idea of how it works. Let's use it first in a function, because it works a little easier there than in the Command Area.

Try this in the Program Area:

```
def parts():
  for letter in "Hello":
    print letter
```

Then try it in the Command Area:

```
>>> parts()
H
e
l
l
o
```

We can read that second line as "for each letter in 'Hello'", then `print letter`. So, each letter gets printed. We can generalize this function to work for any string.

Program 14: Print the Parts of Any String

```
def parts(string):
  for letter in string:
    print letter
```

```
>>> parts("apple")
a
p
p
l
e
```

Now, the challenge of typing this into the Command Area is that it's more than one line to use a `for` loop. Notice the pieces of a `for` loop:

- The word `"for"` which we can think of as "for each."
- The variable that will be the "each." In these examples, it's `letter`, but that will change later.
- The word `"in"` which we can think of as "in." (Who says programming is indecipherable?)
- Whatever we're taking apart in "for each." We sometimes call this the *sequence* because a string is a sequence of characters.
- A colon (":") which says to Python, "Now comes the statements I want to execute once for each 'each' in my sequence."
- And then, *indented* (I usually use two spaces) is a new line with each statement that we want to use the "each." In these examples, it's simply `print letter`. We can have more than one statement inside the `for` loop, and they would all have to be indented the same amount to be part of the same loop. We call these statements a *block*.

It turns out that JES (Jython Environment for Students) is smart enough to recognize when your statement requires a block. It changes the prompt from »> to ... to say, "I know that we are inside a loop now." To end the loop, hit return on a line by itself.

```
>>> for letter in "Hello":
...          print letter
...
H
e
l
l
o
```

The variable does not have to be "letter", and we can do something different with the letters than just printing them as-is.

```
>>> string = "Hello"
>>> for char in string:
...          print 2*char
...
HH
ee
ll
ll
oo
>>> for char in string:
...          print ord(char)
...
72
101
108
108
111
```

3.2.1   Testing the Pieces

We can use another kind of statement, called if to do something different with different characters. The statement if is followed by a *logical expression* or *test*, that if it's true, the following statements (in a *block*, all indented the same) are executed.

Here's an example that prints out *only* the vowels in the input string. The logical expression letter in "aeiou" is true only if the letter is one of "a," "e," "i," "o," or "u."

Program 15: Print Just the Vowels

```
def justvowels(string):
  for letter in string:
    if letter in "aeiou":
      print letter
```

```
>>> justvowels("hello there!")
e
o
e
e
```

We can also do the inverse of that—print out only the letters that are *not* vowels.

Program 16: Print Everything but the Vowels

```
def notvowels(string):
    for letter in string:
        if not (letter in "aeiou"):
            print letter
```

```
>>> notvowels("hello there!")
h
l
l

t
h
r
!
```

Imagine that you had *just* the vowels, or just *not* the vowels of strings in French and English.

```
>>> justvowels("bon voyage")
o
o
a
e
>>> justvowels("safe journey")
a
e
o
u
e
>>> notvowels("bon voyage")
b
n

v
y
g
>>> notvowels("safe journey")
s
f

j
r
n
y
```

If you just had the four outputs and didn't know what the input strings were, do you think you could guess which was French and which was English? Which would be easier—having the vowels, or having *not* the vowels? What is more key to our recognition of the phrases?

Dealing with Case

There is a problem with our current functions. Try this:

```
>>> justvowels("Old Brown Cow")
o
o
```

Uh, where's the "O" in "Old"? Look at our function again—we are only checking for the lowercase form of the characters. If we want both, we have to check for both.

Program 17: Print Just the Vowels, Either Case

```
def justvowels2(string):
  for letter in string:
    if letter in "aeiouAEIOU":
      print letter
```

That works fine:

```
>>> justvowels2("Old Brown Cow")
O
o
o
```

There's another way we could do it. We could force the character to be lowercase, no matter what it is. We can use a special kind of function called a *method*, which we call with a period after the variable, and then the name of the method. Here's another version of justvowels that uses the method lower (and yes, there is one called upper).

```
>>> print "HEAR ME!".lower()
hear me!
```

Program 18: Print Just the Vowels, Using lower()

```
def justvowels3(string):
  for letter in string:
    if letter.lower() in "aeiou":
      print letter
```

This one also works fine:

```
>>> justvowels3("Old Brown Cow")
O
o
o
```

Common Bug: Methods Return a Changed String, Not Change the String

Notice what got printed from `justvowels3`—a capital "O" and two lowercase "o." Now look back at our code. You might be thinking: "But we used `lower()`! The string should be lowercase!" String methods don't *change* the string. They only return a new, changed string. The original string is upper or lowercase, whatever it was before. *String methods don't change their strings.*

```
>>> string = "HEAR ME!"
>>> print string.lower()
hear me!
>>> print string
HEAR ME!
```

3.2.2   Taking String Apart, and Putting Strings Together

We *can* do more with strings than simply taking them apart with the `for` loop. We can put them back together again. We can put them back in different orders, or even double them up.

Remember that the assignment statement means to take the value of the right-hand side it and name it with the left-hand side. Read = as "becomes a name for the value." Works the same way with strings. We can make a string bigger by adding something to it on the right, and putting it in the same name on the left.

```
>>> word = "Um"
>>> print word
Um
>>> word = word + "m"
>>> print word
Umm
>>> word = word + "m"
>>> print word
Ummm
>>> word = word + "m"
>>> print word
Ummmm
```

If we combine this with a `for` loop, we can recombine letters in different ways. First, here's the most boring one: Walk the letters and stick them at the end of an empty string `pile` (one that doesn't have any characters in it to start). This just prints out the original string.

Program 19: Return a New String from Its Pieces

```
def duplicate(source):
  pile = ""
  for letter in source:
    pile = pile+letter
  print pile
```

How It Works

We start out by making the variable `pile` equal to an empty string—two quotes, one right after the other. It's a string, but with zero characters in it. We then use a `for` loop to take apart the input string `source` into characters. We add them to the end of the `pile`, and put the result back into the variable `pile`. *AFTER* the loop, we `print` the whole `pile`. How do we know that it's *after* the loop? Because the indentation of two characters goes away. We *outdent*.

```
>>> duplicate("rubber duck")
rubber duck
```

Reversing, Doubling, and Mirroring Strings

Reversing a string, then, is pretty easy. Stick each letter on the *front* of the pile.

Program 20: Reverse a String

```
def reverse(source):
  pile = ""
  for letter in source:
    pile = letter+pile
  print pile
```

```
>>> reverse("rubber duck")
kcud rebbur
```

To double the letters is to create a variation of `duplicate`. Instead of just adding the letter to the end of the string, add two of them. (We could use multiplication of a string to add as many as we want, but we'll just use concatenation right now.)

Program 21: Double the Letters in a String

```
def double(source):
  pile = ""
  for letter in source:
    pile = pile+letter+letter
  print pile
```

```
>>> double("rubber duck")
rruubbbbeerr  dduucckk
```

To mirror the string is to simply combine the duplicate, double, and the reverse code. Add each letter to both sides of the pile, and you end up with the word forward and backwards. We are "doubling" each letter in the pile, but one on either side of the growing `pile` string.

Program 22: Mirror a String

```
def reverse(source):
  pile = ""
  for letter in source:
    pile = letter+pile
  print pile
```

■

```
>>> mirror("hello")
ollehhello
```

As we'll see more in future chapters, we can use the *Watcher* in JES to see how the program is running, line-by-line. We can also watch variables (using the ADD VAR button at the top) to track what happens to the `pile` variable. You can see in the trace which line is executing when, and how the `pile` variable grows in length, by "doubling" the letter (Figure 3.1).

step	line	instruction	var: pile
1	1	def mirror(source):	–
2	2	pile = ""	
3	3	for letter in source:	
4	3	for letter in source:	
5	4	pile = letter+pile...	hh
6	3	for letter in source:	hh
7	4	pile = letter+pile...	ehhe
8	3	for letter in source:	ehhe
9	4	pile = letter+pile...	lehhel
10	3	for letter in source:	lehhel
11	4	pile = letter+pile...	llehhell
12	3	for letter in source:	llehhell
13	4	pile = letter+pile...	ollehhello
14	3	for letter in source:	ollehhello
15	5	print pile	

FIGURE 3.1
Watching the execution of string mirroring in JES.

Program 23: Double Dutch the Input Name

```
def doubledutch(name):
  pile = ""
  for letter in name:
    if letter.lower() in "aeiou":
      pile = pile + letter
    if not (letter.lower() in "aeiou"):
      pile = pile + letter + "u" + letter
  print pile
```

■

```
>>> doubledutch("mark")
mumarurkuk
>>> doubledutch("bill")
bubilullul
```

My colleague, Bill Leahy, told me that he used to play a word game when he was a kid. You would say each other's name changed such that (a) vowels would say as they were, but (b) you would double the consonants, putting a "u" between them. So, his name would be "Bubilulul."

We can write a program to generate this, but it's a little more complicated than any program we've done up until now. We still want to take the input `name` apart into letters, then add them back into a `pile`. But now, we'll have *TWO* `if` statements, so that we do something different for vowels and for *not* vowels. If it's not a vowel, we stick it back on twice, with a "u" in between.

3.2.3 Taking Strings Apart with Indices

While the `for` loop works fine, it requires us to go through *every* letter in the string. What if we want to get at *specific* letters in a string? What if we want to go through the letters *backwards* or *forwards* every *n*th letter?

There is a way of doing that in Python. We use *square bracket* notation to *index* the letters in the string. Each letter in a string has a number associated with it, which is called its *index*. Think of the index as the address of where to find the letter in the string. The index values always start at zero, and go up by one. (For bizarre historical reasons, computer scientists typically start counting indices at zero.) The characters "[" and "]" are called *square brackets*.

```
>>> phrase = "Hello world!"
>>> phrase[0]
'H'
>>> phrase[1]
'e'
>>> phrase[2]
'l'
>>> phrase[6]
'w'
```

So, `string[0]` is *always* the first character in the string. We told you that the indices always go up by one, starting from zero. That's true—but that doesn't mean that there aren't *negative indices*. An index value of −1 is considered to start from the *end* of the string and go *backwards*. Thus, `string[-1]` is always the last character in a string.

```
>>> phrase[-1]
'!'
>>> phrase[-2]
'd'
```

Another way to get the last character in the string is to compute it from the length of the string. The `len` function returns the *number* of letters in a string.

Common Bug: **The Length Is One More than the Last Index**

The most common bug in indexing is forgetting that the first index is zero. Because it's zero, the *length* of the string is *one more than* the last index in the string. The last index in a string is length minus one. If you try to get the character beyond the last index, you will get a sequence index error.

```
>>> abc = "abc"
>>> print len(abc)
3
>>> print abc[3]
The error was: 3
Sequence index out of range.
The index you're using goes beyond the size of that data (too low or high).
For instance, maybe you tried to access OurArray[10] and OurArray
only has 5 elements in it.
>>> print abc[2]
c
```

Now, what if we want to go through the whole string, but backwards or skipping every few characters? We can use the `for` loop for this, but in a different way than using it to step "for each" letter in the string. Instead, we will use the `for` loop to step "for each" index value that we want.

A `for` loop uses a variable (like `letter`) to name each value in a sequence of letters. If we can generate a sequence of indices, then we can say `for index in sequence` in a similar way. Fortunately, there is a function in Python that generates sequences of numbers. It is called `range`, and it can be used to generate indices. The range function can take one, two, or three inputs.

- The most common use of range is with two inputs, a start index and the length index. The function `range(0,3)` returns a list of indices starting at 0 with 3 elements: `[0,1,2]`. Another way to think about it is to start at 0, and count up to but *not including* the last argument, 3: 0,1,2 . . . stop!

- If you provide three inputs, it's a start index, the ending point (up to but not including), and the *increment*—how much to add between successive values. The function `range(0,11,2)` returns all the even integers up to 11 (including 0 and 10).

- Because the *most common* use of `range` is to generate indices, and the `len` function is so handy, `range(len(string))` returns the indices from 0 up to but not including the length of the string. Those are exactly all the indices in the string.

```
>>> print range(0,5)
[0, 1, 2, 3, 4]
>>> print range(0,3)
[0, 1, 2]
>>> print range(3,0)
[]
>>> print range(0,5,2)
[0, 2, 4]
```

```
>>> print range(0,7,3)
[0, 3, 6]
>>> print range(5)
[0, 1, 2, 3, 4]
```

We can now use these indices in a for loop.

```
>>> for index in range(0,3):
...          print index
...
0
1
2
>>>
```

We can print out all the elements in a string using our new index-based mechanism, rather than for letter in string. No, this isn't any *better*, but we will find that it gives us the ability to do new things.

Program 24: **Print the Parts of Any String, with Indices**

```
def parts2(string):
  for index in range(len(string)):
    print string[index]
```

```
>>> parts2("bear")
b
e
a
r
```

How It Works

Our function parts2 takes in a string as input. We use the one-input form of range to get all the indices in the input string. For the input "bear", the len is 4, and the indices are [0,1,2,3]. We use the name index to represent each of those indices, and then print the letter at each of those indices.

3.2.4   Mirroring, Reversing, and Separating Strings with Index

We can do different kinds of mirroring than we could before, because we can go part-way through a word. Here's a program for mirroring the front half of a word.

Program 25: **Mirror the Front Half of a Word**

```
def mirrorHalfString(string):
  pile=""
  for index in range(0,len(string)/2):
    pile = pile+string[index]
  for index in range(len(string)/2,0,-1):
    pile = pile+string[index]
  print pile
```

How It Works

The function `mirrorHalfString` doesn't quite work correctly. It's off by one (a common computer science problem).

```
>>> mirrorHalfString("elephant")
elephpel
>>> mirrorHalfString("something")
sometemo
```

Notice that the mirrored words don't start and end with the same letter. What's going on here?

- The program starts by creating an *accumulator* where we'll stick all the letters.
- The first loop in the program starts the index values at the beginning of the string (0) and goes up to halfway through the string (`len(string)/2`). Remember, though, that we never *get* to that value—we'll stop halfway before.
- We add all the letters referenced by those indices into our pile.
- The second loop *starts* at the halfway point (`len(string)/2`) and goes *down* to 0—but never gets there. It goes down by adding a *third* input to `range`, the step amount. We'll step by −1, thus decreasing one each step.
- Again, we add all those letters to the pile.
- At the end, we print the pile.

Do you see the problem? We ended the first loop (`len(string)/2)-1`, but started the next loop at `len(string)/2`. The first loop starts at 0, but the second loop ends at 1 (because the 0 is the ending position). If we tweak the function a little bit, we can make the two loops match up. We'll make the second loop start at (`len(string)/2)-1` and end at 0, by making −1 the end position.

Program 26: Mirror the Front Half of a Word, Exactly

```
def mirrorHalfString2(string):
  pile=""
  for index in range(0,len(string)/2):
    pile = pile+string[index]
  for index in range((len(string)/2)-1,-1,-1):
    pile = pile+string[index]
  print pile
```

This version does exactly what we want.

```
>>> mirrorHalfString2("elephant")
eleppele
>>> mirrorHalfString2("something")
someemos
```

We can now rewrite the function to reverse a string, but using indices.

Program 27: Reverse a String, Using an Index

```
def reverseString2(string):
  pile=""
  for index in range(len(string)-1,-1,-1):
    pile = pile+string[index]
  print pile
```

This one does just what you'd expect.

```
>>> reverseString2("happy holidays")
syadiloh yppah
```

We can also use the index to do something different with each letter, based on its position. Imagine that we want to collect the letters at the *even* indices, and the ones at the *odd* indices, each separate. We can do that using the index value.

Program 28: Separate Odd Letters from Even Letters

```
def separate(string):
  odds = ""
  evens = ""
  for index in range(len(string)):
    if index % 2 == 0:
      evens = evens + string[index]
    if not (index % 2 == 0):
      odds = odds +string[index]
  print "Odds: ",odds
  print "Evens: ",evens
```

```
>>> separate("rubber baby buggy bumpers")
Odds:   ubrbb ug upr
Evens:   rbe aybgybmes
```

How It Works

We create *two* string "piles" here—one for odds, and one for evens. We then generate each index from 0 to the end of the string. Remember that "%" is the *modulo* (integer division) operator, and "==" is a test for equality. The test in the if statement is index % 2 == 0 which says, "If we divide the index by 2, do we get 0 as the remainder?" If so, the index is even, so we grab that character and add it to the evens pile. If not that, we add the letter to the odds pile. At the end, we print each.

3.2.5   Encoding and Decoding Strings Using a Keyword Cipher

There is another useful string method find that returns the index where a given string occurs in a bigger string. The index is in the range 0 to the length of the bigger string minus one. If find ever returns −1, then the little string wasn't found.

```
>>> print "abcd".find("b")
1
>>> print "abcd".find("d")
3
>>> print "abcd".find("e")
-1
```

Let's say that we have a string that we want to encode. We want to replace the letters in the string with letters in an order that we and our confederates know, but nobody else knows. How do we generate the secret alphabet? You don't want to send the whole secret alphabet around. A way of *creating* a secret alphabet is a keyword cipher.[2] You input a keyword, like "earth." Now, you create a new alphabet with "earth" as the first five characters, and then the rest of the alphabet, *skipping* the letters in the key ("earth"). Here's a program that does it.

Program 29: Build a Keyword Cipher Alphabet

```
def buildCipher(key):
  alpha="abcdefghijklmnopqrstuvwxyz"
  rest = ""
  for letter in alpha:
    if not(letter in key):
      rest = rest + letter
  print key+rest
```

```
>>> buildCipher("earth")
earthbcdfgijklmnopqsuvwxyz
```

Notice that our new alphabet has each letter only once, but a bit scrambled. As long as you know the keyword, you can easily generate this new alphabet.

To encode a message, you look up letters in the original alphabet. Whatever index the letter is, you take the corresponding letter from the *keyword cipher* alphabet—which you can easily generate if you know the keyword.

Program 30: Encode a Message Using the Keyword Cipher Alphabet

```
def encode(string,keyletters):
  alpha="abcdefghijklmnopqrstuvwxyz"
  secret = ""
  for letter in string:
    index = alpha.find(letter)
    secret = secret+keyletters[index]
  print secret
```

```
>>> encode("this is a test","earthbcdfgijklmnopqsuvwxyz")
sdfqzfqzezshqs
```

[2]Please look up "keyword ciphers" in your favorite search engine.

You have to admit that "sdfqzfqzezshqs" doesn't look much like "this is a test." Now, to *decode* the message, we just do the reverse: Find the letter in the secret alphabet, and return the letter in the original alphabet.

Program 31: Decode a Message Using the Keyword Cipher Alphabet

```
def decode(secret,keyletters):
  alpha="abcdefghijklmnopqrstuvwxyz"
  clear = ""
  for letter in secret:
    index = keyletters.find(letter)
    clear = clear+alpha[index]
  print clear
```

```
>>> decode("sdfqzfqzezshqs","earthbcdfgijklmnopqsuvwxyz")
thisziszaztest
```

It works, but what's with all the z's? Spaces aren't in the alphabet, so the `find` returned -1. If we index on -1, we get the *last* letter in the string—which is "z" in our case.

3.3   TAKING STRINGS APART BY WORDS

We talked earlier about how we might take strings apart. One way of "taking strings apart" is letter by letter. But another perfectly reasonable way to do it is in terms of *words*. We can split a string into words pretty easily, too. The method for breaking a string up into words is called `split`. The method `split` returns a *list* of the words in the input.

```
>>> "this is a test".split()
['this', 'is', 'a', 'test']
>>> "abc".split()
['abc']
>>> "dog bites man".split()
['dog', 'bites', 'man']
```

We can access individual parts of that list using an index, just the same as using an index for accessing individual characters. We used square bracket notation to get at the pieces of the string, which were the characters. Here, we use square bracket notation to get at the pieces of the list, which are words.

```
>>> sentence = "Dog bites man"
>>> parts = sentence.split()
>>> print len(parts)
3
>>> print parts[0]
Dog
>>> print parts[1]
bites
>>> print parts[2]
man
```

What's cool about this is that we can now manipulate *parts* of the sentence. Let's generate a story (like with Mad Libs) where the input is a sentence, and we pull out the pieces we want. Just to do something different than Mad Lib, let's generate thoughtful puzzles, kind of like a Zen Koan[3]—a story or question that generates doubt in the listener. A famous one is, "What is the sound of one hand clapping?"

Let's take as input a simple sentence of the form noun-verb-noun, like "Dog bites man." Here's a function that chops up the pieces, and serves it back as a set of things to think about.

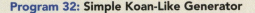

Program 32: Simple Koan-Like Generator

```
def koan(sentence):
  parts = sentence.lower().split()
  subject = parts[0]
  verb = parts[1]
  object = parts[2]
  print "Sometimes "+sentence
  print "But sometimes "+object+" "+verb+" "+subject
  print "Sometimes there is no "+subject
  print "Sometimes there is no "+verb
  print "Watch out for the stick!"
```

```
>>> koan("dog bites man")
Sometimes dog bites man
But sometimes man bites dog
Sometimes there is no dog
Sometimes there is no bites
Watch out for the stick!
```

How It Works

Our koan generator takes in a noun-verb-noun sentence as input. The first thing it does is to make the whole sentence lowercase, and to split it into parts. Turns out that we can do this all in one statement, which is pretty cool.

```
>>> "Watch OUT!".lower().split()
['watch', 'out!']
```

Next, we pull out the subject, verb, and object of the sentence. Then, we start to build the new sentences, in what's meant to be a provocative (and perhaps silly) set of statements. The end line about watching out for the stick is a reference to the *Keisaku* or "warning stick"[4] which makes an appearance in many Zen Koans.

Now, what if we want a noun-verb-noun sentence with articles in it, like "the"? We get something that might be provocative, but isn't really what we wanted.

---

[3]You can find lists of Zen Koans through your favorite search engine, including http://www. ashidakim.com/zenkoans/zenindex.html.
[4]http://ajw.asahi.com/article/behind_news/social_affairs/AJ201305300013

```
>>> koan("The woman bites the apple")
Sometimes The woman bites the apple
But sometimes bites woman the
Sometimes there is no the
Sometimes there is no woman
Watch out for the stick!
```

Can we avoid the articles? Sure, same way that we did something different with vowels than consonants. The `in` operator that we used with `if` earlier can also be used here. We can ask if a word is `in` a list of words. Note that "Sure!" doesn't get printed after the second test. There is no "banana" in that list.

```
>>> if "apple" in ["mother's", "apple", "pie"]:
...         print "Sure!"
...
Sure!
>>> if "banana" in ["mother's", "apple", "pie"]:
...         print "Sure!"
...
>>>
```

To build this more complicated program, we will keep index numbers to represent where we expect to find the subject, verb, and object of the sentence. If we find an article word ("the," or "a," or "an"), we change where expect to find the verb and the object.

Program 33: Koan Generator with Article Awareness

```
def koan2(sentence):
  parts = sentence.lower().split()
  verbindex = 1
  objindex = 2
  subject = parts[0]
  if subject in ["the","a","an"]:
    subject = parts[1]
    verbindex = 2
    objindex = 3
  verb = parts[verbindex]
  object = parts[objindex]
  if object in ["the","a","an"]:
    object = parts[4]
  print "Sometimes "+sentence
  print "But sometimes "+object+" "+verb+" "+subject
  print "Sometimes there is no "+subject
  print "Sometimes there is no "+verb
  print "Watch out for the stick!"
```

```
>>> koan2("The woman bites the apple")
Sometimes The woman bites the apple
But sometimes apple bites woman
Sometimes there is no woman
Sometimes there is no bites
Watch out for the stick!
```

How It Works

The `koan2` generator again takes a sentence, makes it all lowercase (to better fit into our story), and splits it into parts. We start out expecting the verb index (`verbindex`) to be at position 1, and the object to be at position 2. We then grab the `subject` where we expect it to be (position 0). If it's in our list of articles, we grab the subject from position 1, and update our expectation for the verb (`verbindex = 2`) and for the object (`objindex=3`). We pull out the `verb`. We pull out the `object` where we expect it to be. If it's an article, we pull it out of position 4 instead. We then generate our pseudo-Koan in the same way as before.

3.4   WHAT'S INSIDE A STRING

In memory, a string is a series of consecutive mailboxes (to continue our metaphor of memory as a mailroom), each containing the binary code for the corresponding character. The function `ord()` gives us the ASCII (American Standard Code for Information Interchange) encoding for each character. Thus, we find that the string "Hello" is five mailboxes, the first containing 72, and then 101, and then 108, and so on.

In JES, that's a slight simplification. The version of Python we're using, Jython, is built on Java, which is actually *not* using ASCII to encode its strings. It's using *Unicode*, which is an encoding for characters where two bytes are used for each character. Two bytes give us 65,536 possible combinations. All those extra possible codes allow us to go beyond a simple Latin alphabet, numbers, and punctuation. We can represent Hiragana, Katakana, and other *glyph* (graphic depictions of characters) systems.

What this should tell you is that there are many more possible characters than can be typed at the keyboard. Not only are there special symbols but there are invisible characters like tabs and pressing the return/enter key. We type these in Python strings (and in many other languages, such as Java and C) using *backslash escapes*. Backslash escapes are the backslash key \ followed by a character.

- \t is the same as typing the tab key.
- \b is the same as typing the backspace key (which is not a particularly useful character to put in a string, but you can). When you print \b, it shows up as a box on most systems—it's not actually printable (see below).
- \n is the same as typing the enter/return key.
- \uXXXX where XXXX is a code made up of 0–9 and A–F (known as a *hexadecimal* number) represents the Unicode character with that code. You can look up the codes at `http://www.unicode.org/charts`.

It is not easy to see unicode glyphs in JES,[5] but we can see how some of these special symbols effect printing.

---

[5]You can see them in CPython, with a command like `print u"\ufeed"`.

```
>>> print "hello\tthere.\nMark"
hello    there.
Mark
```

What if you want to have a string that *includes* backslash characters? If you start a string with the letter "r" then you keep all the backslash characters.

```
>>> print r"C:\ip-book\mediasources\barbara.jpg"
C:\ip-book\mediasources\barbara.jpg
```

An 'r' tells Python to read the string in *raw mode*. All the characters are treated as plain characters, i.e., backslash escapes are ignored. As we will see, that's useful for computers using the Windows operating system. File paths (descriptions of where a file exists on a computer) in Windows use backslashes as *delimiters*. Imagine that you had a file named bear.jpg. A path to that file would include the phrase \bear, and Python would view that \b as a backspace character, not as a delimiter-b. Using "r" lets you include the backlash character safely.

3.5   WHAT A COMPUTER CAN DO

At this point, we have seen six things that a computer can do:

- They can store data with names, e.g., name = "Rory".
- They can name sets of instructions, and execute those named instructions, e.g., def koan.
- They can take data apart, e.g., name[0].
- They can transform data into other forms, e.g., str(45) to make "45".
- They can do a set of commands repetitively, e.g., using a for loop.
- They can make tests (with an if) and then take actions based on whether those tests were true.

That is *all* that a computer *can* do. There are no other capabilities of a computer other than those items. No computer in the world can do more than those six things.

Before the first computer was ever created, a mathematician named Alan Turing (who, coincidentally with this chapter, was famous for code-breaking) invented the definition of a computer. He was trying to answer the question, "What is computable?" Mathematicians at the time were trying to understand the limits of mathematics—what was answerable with mathematics, and what wasn't. He defined his *Turing Machine* to be a device that could compute anything that was computable. Other definitions of a computer were also created, and they were found to all be identical—all computers can essentially do the same things mathematically. Those six statements represent one definition of a Turing Machine.

So if you understand how the computer does all six of those things, you understand what a computer can do—and that's *all* that a computer can do. Everything else is just a variation on this theme.

PROGRAMMING SUMMARY

In this chapter, we talk about several kinds of encodings of data (or objects).

Strings	A sequence of characters. When typed in directly, delimited with quotes (single, double, or triple).
Sequence	One piece of data after another. The function `range` returns a sequence of numbers. A string is a sequence of characters.
Lists	A sequence of items. We used lists of words in this chapter.
Integers	A number without a decimal point.
Floating-point numbers	A number with a decimal point.

PROGRAM PIECES

`for`	Takes a variable name and a sequence. For each value in the sequence, name the value with the variable name and execute the block.
`in`	Operator that tests if a letter is in a word, or a word in a list. Generally, tests to see if a value is in sequence.
`if`	Test a condition, and if it is true, execute the block.

STRING PROGRAM PIECES

`str`	Function to change the input number to a string.
`int`	Function to change a string into an integer.
`float`	Function to change a string into a floating-point value.
`split`	Method to separate a string into its constituent words.
`find`	Method to find a substring. Returns the index number if found, -1 if not found.

PROBLEMS

3.1 You are running a bingo game where you want to tweet the winner of each round of the game. You want to announce the name of who won, and how much they won in dollars. Make a function that takes those two words in as input, and then announces the win. For now, just `print` the statement that you will want to tweet later. (Hint: Remember that you are taking a *number* as input, which has to be converted to a string to concatenate it.)

```
>>> bingo("Mark",50)
Mark called Bingo! winning $50
```

3.2 You are a race official on an ultra marathon (100 miles), and you want to display the number and elapsed time for each runner on a big display. Write a program to generate the phrase for the display based on the runner number, the mile marker, and the elapsed time.

```
>>> runner(42,10,"1:12:09")
Runner #42 passed mile 10 at time 1:12:09
```

3.3 The `pyramid` function in this chapter doesn't quite line up with "=" character as input. Try some others, like "n" and "m" and "t". The last one seems to line up best. Why?

3.4 Create a function like the `pyramid` function that does the upside-down version. Your function `invertedPyramid` should also take an input character and print an *inverted* pyramid.

3.5 Using `for` loops and using the same techniques as the `pyramid` function, create a `textsquare` function that takes in two values as input: the character to use in making the square, and the size of the square in characters. Then print out a square of that many characters.

```
>>> textsquare("t",5)
ttttt
t   t
t   t
t   t
ttttt
```

3.6 We fixed `justvowels` so that it works with lowercase or uppercase vowels. Fix `notvowels` so that it doesn't print out uppercase vowels. (Try it as it is in the chapter, and you will see that it does print uppercase vowels, even though the function is supposed to only print *not* vowels.) Actually, do two versions of `notvowels`, using each of the two methods that we used to fix `justvowels`.

3.7 One of the below programs that when called like this (with the underscore representing a digit from 1 to 4) generates this output:

```
>>> dup_("rubber duck")
'kcud rebburrubber duck'
```

Which one?

- ```
  def dup1(source):
      target = ""
      for letter in source:
        target = target+letter
      return target
  ```

- ```
  def dup2(source):
      target = "_"
      for letter in source:
  ```

```
            target = target+source
        return target
```

- ```
  def dup3(source):
      target = ""
      for letter in source:
          target = letter+target+letter
      return target
  ```

- ```
  def dup4(source):
      target = ""
      for letter in source:
          target = letter+target
      return target
  ```

3.8   Try giving our `doubledutch` program a full name like "John Smith." What happens to the space? What if you include punctuation like periods or hyphens? How could you create more full featured `doubledutch` that gets around these problems?

3.9   Write a program that accepts a string as input, then prints out the vowels in that string and then prints the consonants in that string.

```
>>> splitem("elephant")
Vowels:  eea
Consonants:  lphnt
```

3.10   Change the `encode` function so that spaces are simply skipped.

3.11   Change the `encode` function so that punctuation is simply skipped.

3.12   The `buildCipher` function could create more complicated alphabets. As long as both the receiver and the sender generate the alphabet in the same way, the message needs to only include the keyword for encoding and decoding to work. Try building these variations:

- Put the keyword at the end of the alphabet, rather than the front.

- Reverse the alphabet before concatenating it to the keyword.

- Separate the vowels and the consonants in the rest of the alphabet so that the cipher alphabet is keyword, then the rest of the vowels, then the rest of the consonants.

3.13   One of the below programs that when called like this (with the underscore representing a digit from 1 to 4) generates this output:

```
>>> dup_("alphabet")
'_alphabetalphabetalphabetalphabetalphabetalphabetalphabetalphabet'
```

Which one?

- ```
  def dupTimes1(something):
      dup = ""
      for index in range(0,len(something)):
          dup = dup + (2*something[index])
      return dup
  ```
  ```

```
• def dupTimes2(something):
    dup = ""
    for index in range(0,len(something)):
        dup = dup + (index*something[index])
    return dup

• def dupTimes3(something):
    dup = "_"
    for index in range(0,len(something)):
        dup = dup + something[index]
    return dup

• def dupTimes4(something):
    for index in range(0,len(something)):
        dup = dup + something[index]
    dup = "_"
    return dup
```

3.14 One of the below programs that when called like this (with the underscore representing a digit from 1 to 4) generates this output:

```
>>> findem_(4)
'abcdabcdabcdabcdabcdabcda'
```

Which one?

```
• def findem1(n):
    letters = 'abcdefghijklmnopqrstuvwyz'
    pile = ''
    for index in range(0,n):
        pile = pile+letters[index]
    return pile

• def findem2(n):
    letters = 'abcdefghijklmnopqrstuvwyz'
    pile = ''
    for index in range(0,n % len(letters)):
        pile = pile+letters[index]
    return pile

• def findem3(n):
    letters = 'abcdefghijklmnopqrstuvwyz'
    pile = ''
    for index in range(1,len(letters)):
        pile = pile+letters[n % index]
    return pile

• def findem4(n):
    letters = 'abcdefghijklmnopqrstuvwyz'
    pile = ''
    for index in range(0,len(letters)):
        pile = pile+letters[index % n]
    return pile
```

3.15 One of the below programs that when called like this (with the underscore representing a digit from 1 to 4) generates this output:

```
>>> mixem_("we hold these truths")
'w.e. .h.o.l.d. .t.h.ese truths'
```

Which one?

- ```
  def mixem1(astring):
      mix = ""
      for index in range(0,len(astring),2):
          mix = mix + astring[index]
      mix = mix + "-"
      for index in range(len(astring)/2,len(astring)):
          mix = mix + astring[index]
      return mix
  ```

- ```
  def mixem2(astring):
      mix = ""
      for index in range(0,len(astring)/2):
          mix = mix + astring[index]+"."
      for index in range(len(astring)/2,len(astring)):
          mix = mix + astring[index]
      return mix
  ```

- ```
  def mixem3(astring):
      mix = ""
      for index in range(0,len(astring)/2,2):
          mix = mix + astring[index]
      mix = mix + "-"
      for index in range(1,len(astring),2):
          mix = mix + astring[index]
      return mix
  ```

- ```
  def mixem4(astring):
      mix = ""
      for index in range(len(astring)/2,0,-1):
          mix = astring[index]+mix + astring[index]
      return mix
  ```

3.16 You have written an essay for school, and it has to be at least five pages long. But your essay is only 4.5 pages long! You decide to use your new Python skills to make your essay longer by spacing out the letters. Write a function that takes a string and a number of spaces to insert between each letter, then print out the resulting string.

```
>>> spaceitout("It was a dark and stormy night",3)
```

It was a dark and stormy night

3.17 Same problem as before, but you decide to use *more* of your new Python skills. You are going to increase the spaces *between* the words. Write a function that takes a string and a number of spaces to insert between each word, then print out the resulting string.

```
>>> spaceout("It was a dark and stormy night",3)
It   was   a   dark   and   stormy   night
```

TO DIG DEEPER

Text processing is a common use for Python. There are many good books on how to use Python for manipulating and creating text. One that we can recommend is David Mertz's *Text Processing in Python* (Addison-Wesley, 2003).

Modifying Pictures Using Loops

Chapter Learning Objectives

The media learning goals for this chapter are:

- To understand how images are digitized by taking advantage of limits in human vision.

- To identify different models for color, including RGB, the most common one for computers.

- To manipulate color values in pictures, like increasing or decreasing red values.

- To convert a color picture to grayscale, using more than one method.

- To negate a picture.

The computer science goals for this chapter are:

- To use a matrix representation in finding pixels in a picture.

- To use the objects *pictures* and *pixels*.

- To use iteration (with a `for` loop) for changing the color values of pixels in a picture.

- To nest blocks of code within one another.

- To choose between having a function *return* a value and just providing a *side effect*.

- To determine the *scope* of a variable name.

4.1   HOW PICTURES ARE ENCODED

Pictures (images, graphics) are an important part of any media communication. In this chapter, we discuss how pictures are represented on a computer (mostly as *bitmap* images—each dot or *pixel* is represented separately) and how they can be manipulated. The chapters that follow this one will introduce alternative image representations, such as *vector* images.

Pictures are a two-dimensional array of *pixels*. Each of these terms will be described in this section.

For our purposes, a picture is an image stored in a JPEG file. **JPEG** is an international standard for how to store images with high quality but in little space. JPEG is a **lossy compression** format. That means that it is *compressed*, made smaller, but not with 100% of the quality of the original format. Typically, though, what you lose is quality or sharpness that you don't see or don't notice anyway. For most purposes, a JPEG image works fine. The BMP format is *lossless* but is uncompressed. A BMP file will be much larger than a JPEG file for the same image. The PNG format is lossless and compressed.

A one-dimensional array is a sequence of elements of the same type. You can assign a name to an array and then use index numbers to access elements of the array. The first element in an array is at index 0. In Figure 4.1 the value at index 0 is 15, the value at index 1 is 12, the value at index 2 is 13, and the value at index 3 is 10.

A two-dimensional array is also called a **matrix**. A matrix is a collection of elements arranged in both rows and columns. This means that both the row and column index can be specified in order to access a value in the matrix.

In Figure 4.2, you see an example matrix. We use two numbers to reference elements (the numbers) in this matrix. We will use the first number to reference which column (vertical slice) we mean, and the second number to reference which row (horizontal

0	1	2	3
15	12	13	10

FIGURE 4.1
An example array.

	0	1	2	3
0	15	12	13	10
1	9	7	2	1
2	6	3	9	10

FIGURE 4.2
An example matrix.

slice). At *coordinates* (0, 1) (horizontal, vertical), you'll find the matrix element whose value is 9. At *column* = 0 and *row* = 0 (e.g., (0, 0)) the value is 15, at *column* = 1 and *row* = 0 (e.g., (1, 0)) is value 12, and (2, 0) is value 13. We will often refer to these coordinates as (x, y) (*column, row*).

What's stored at each element in the picture is a **pixel**. The word "pixel" is short for "picture element." It's literally a dot, and the overall picture is made up of lots of these dots. Have you ever taken a magnifying glass to the pictures in a newspaper or magazine, or to a television or even your own monitor? When you look at the picture in the magazine or on the television, it doesn't look like it's broken up into millions of discrete spots, but it is.

You can get a similar view of individual pixels using the picture tool, as shown in Figure 4.3. This tool allows you to zoom in on a picture up to 500% so that each individual pixel is visible. One way to bring up the picture tool is to explore the picture as shown below.

```
>>> file = "c:/ip-book/mediasources/caterpillar.jpg"
>>> pict = makePicture(file)
>>> explore(pict)
```

Our human sensory apparatus can't distinguish (without magnification or other special equipment) the small bits in the whole. Humans have low visual *acuity*—we don't see as much detail as, say, an eagle. We actually have more than one kind of vision system in use in our brain and our eyes. Our system for processing color is different from our system for processing black and white (or **luminance**). We use luminance to detect motion and sizes of objects, for example. We actually pick up luminance detail better with the sides of our eyes than from the center of our eye. That's an evolutionary advantage, since it allows you to pick out the sabertooth tiger sneaking up on your right in those bushes over there.

The lack of resolution in human vision is what makes it possible to digitize pictures. Animals that perceive greater detail than humans (e.g., eagles or cats) may actually see the individual pixels. We break up the picture into smaller elements (pixels), but there

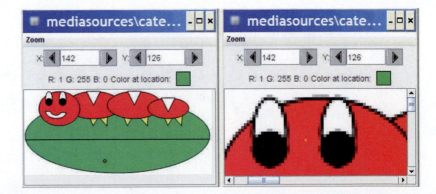

FIGURE 4.3
Image shown in the JES picture tool: 100% image (*left*) and 500% (*right*).

are enough of them and they are small enough that the picture doesn't look choppy when one looks at it overall. If you *can* see the effects of the digitization (e.g., you can see little rectangles in some spots), we call that *pixelization*—the effect when the digitization process becomes obvious.

Picture encoding is more complex in structure than sound encoding. A sound is encoded as a collection of numbers whose arrangement is inherently linear—it progresses forward in time. A picture has two dimensions, width and height. Each position in those dimensions has a color which is more complex than a single number.

Visible light is continuous—visible light is any wavelength between 370 and 730 nanometers (0.00000037 and 0.00000073 meters). But our perception of light is limited by how our color sensors work. Our eyes have sensors that trigger (peak) around 425 nanometers (blue), 550 nanometers (green), and 560 nanometers (red). Our brain determines what a particular color is based on the feedback from these three sensors in our eyes. There are some animals with only two kinds of sensors, like dogs. These animals still perceive color, but not the same colors or in the same way as humans. One of the interesting implications of our limited visual sensory apparatus is that we actually perceive two kinds of orange. There is a *spectral* orange—a particular wavelength that is natural orange. There is also a mixture of red and yellow that hits our color sensors just right so that we perceive it as the same orange.

As long as we encode what hits our three kinds of color sensors, we're recording our human perception of color. Thus, we encode each pixel as a triplet of numbers. The first number represents the amount of red in the pixel, the second is the amount of green, and the third is the amount of blue. We can make up any human-visible color by combining red, green, and blue light (Figure 4.4). Combining all three gives us pure white. Turning off all three gives us black. We call this the **RGB color model**.

There are other models for defining and encoding colors besides the RGB color model. There's the *HSV color model* which encodes Hue, Saturation, and Value (sometimes also called the *HSB* color model for Hue, Saturation, and Brightness). The advantage of the HSV model is that some changes we might want, like making a color "lighter" or "darker," involve changes to one of those three dimensions (Figure 4.5). Another color model is the *CMYK color model*, which encodes Cyan, Magenta, Yellow, and blacK (using the "K" instead of the "B" since "B" could be confused with blue). The CMYK model is what printers use. Cyan, magenta, yellow, and black are the inks that printers combine to make colors. However, four elements is more to encode on a computer than three, so the CMYK color model is less popular for digital media than RGB. RGB is the most popular color model on computers.

FIGURE 4.4
Merging red, green, and blue to make new colors.

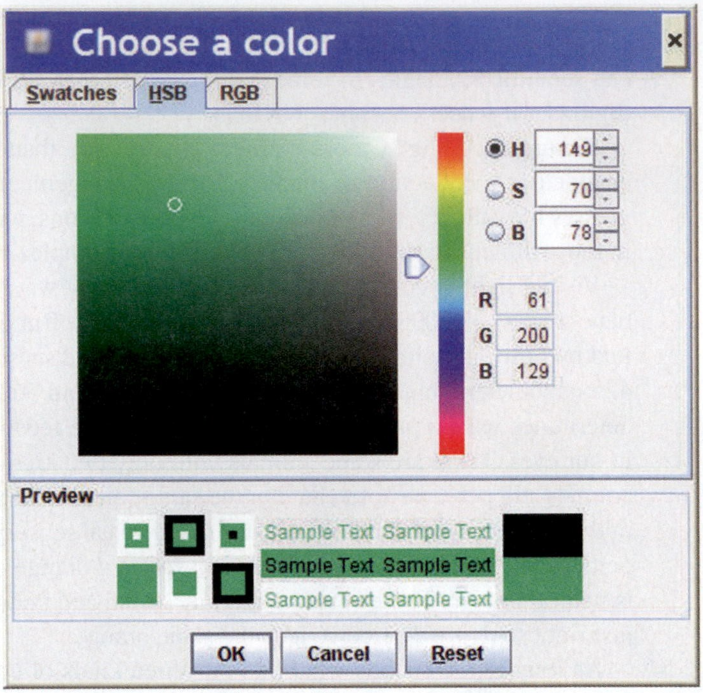

FIGURE 4.5
Picking colors using the HSB color model.

Each color component (sometimes called a **channel**) in a pixel is typically represented with a single byte, eight bits. Eight bits can represent 256 patterns (2^8): 00000000, 00000001, up through 11111111. We typically use these patterns to represent the values 0 to 255. Each pixel, then, uses 24 bits to represent colors. There are 2^{24} possible patterns of 0s and 1s in those 24 bits, which means that the standard encoding for color using the RGB model can represent 16,777,216 colors. We can actually perceive more than 16 million colors, but it turns out that it just doesn't matter. There is no technology that comes even close to being able to replicate the whole color space that we can see. We do have devices that can represent 16 million distinct colors, but those 16 million colors don't cover the entire space of color (or luminance) that we can perceive. So the 24-bit RGB model is adequate until technology advances.

There are computer models that use more bits per pixel. For example, there are 32-bit models that use the extra eight bits to represent *transparency*, that is, how much of the color "below" the given image should be blended with this color. These additional eight bits are sometimes called the **alpha channel**. There are other models that use more than eight bits for the red, green, and blue channels, but they are uncommon.

We actually perceive borders of objects, motion, and depth through a *separate* vision system. We perceive color through one system and *luminance* (how light/dark things are) through another system. Luminance is not actually the *amount* of light, but our *perception* of the amount of light. We can measure the amount of light (e.g., the number of photons reflected off the color) and show that a red spot and a blue spot are each reflecting the same amount of light, but we perceive the blue as darker. Our sense of luminance is based on comparisons with the surroundings. The optical illusion in Figure 4.6 highlights how we perceive gray levels. The two end quarters are actually the same level of gray but because the two mid-quarters end in a sharp contrast of lightness and darkness, we perceive one half as darker than the other when the difference is really only in the middle.

Most tools for allowing users to pick out colors let the users specify the color as RGB components. The color chooser in JES (which is the standard Java Swing color chooser) offers a set of sliders for controlling the amount of each color (Figure 4.7). You can pick a color by typing the following in the Command Area.

```
>>> pickAColor()
```

FIGURE 4.6
The ends of this figure are the same colors of gray but the middle two quarters contrast sharply, so the left side looks darker than the right.

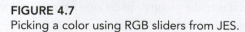

FIGURE 4.7
Picking a color using RGB sliders from JES.

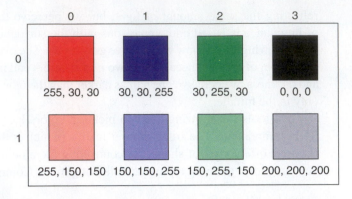

FIGURE 4.8
RGB triplets in a matrix representation.

TABLE 4.1 Number of bytes needed to store pixels at various sizes and formats

	320 × 240 image	**640 × 480 image**	**1024 × 768 image**
24-bit color	230,400 bytes	921,600 bytes	2,359,296 bytes
32-bit color	307,200 bytes	1,228,800 bytes	3,145,728 bytes

As mentioned, a triplet of (0, 0, 0) (red, green, blue components) is black, and (255, 255, 255) is white. (255, 0, 0) is pure red, but (100, 0, 0) is red too—just darker. (0, 100, 0) is a medium green, and (0, 0, 100) is medium blue. When the red component is the same as the green and as the blue, the resultant color is gray. (50, 50, 50) would be a fairly dark gray, and (100, 100, 100) is lighter.

Figure 4.8 is a representation of pixel RGB triplets in a matrix form. Thus, the pixel at (1, 0) has color (30, 30, 255), which means that it has a red value of 30, a green value of 30, and a blue value of 255—it's a mostly blue color, but not pure blue. The pixel at (2, 1) has pure green but also more red and blue (150, 255, 150), so it's a fairly light green. 150 in binary is "10010110," and 255 is "11111111" so that fairly light green color would be encoded in 24-bit color as "100101101111111110010110."

Images on disk and even in computer memory are usually stored in *compressed* form. The amount of memory needed to represent every pixel of even small images is pretty large (Table 4.1). A fairly small image of 320 pixels across by 240 pixels wide, with 24 bits per pixel, takes up 230,400 bytes—that's roughly 230 *kilobytes* (1000 bytes) or 1/4 *megabyte* (million bytes). A computer monitor with 1024 pixels across and 768 pixels vertically with 32 bits per pixel takes up three megabytes just to represent the screen.

4.2 MANIPULATING PICTURES

We manipulate pictures in JES by making a picture object out of a JPEG file, then changing the color of the pixels in the picture. To change a pixel's color, we manipulate the red, green, and blue components.

We make pictures using makePicture. We make the picture appear with show.

```
>>> file = pickAFile()
>>> print file
C:\ip-book\mediasources\beach.jpg
>>> myPict = makePicture(file)
>>> show(myPict)
>>> print myPict
Picture, filename C:\ip-book\mediasources\beach.jpg
    height 480 width 640
```

What makePicture does is to scoop up all the bytes at the input filename, bring them into memory, reformat them slightly, and place a sign on them announcing, "This is a picture!" When you execute myPict = makePicture(filename), you are saying, "The name for that picture object (note the sign on it) is now myPict."

Pictures know their width and their height. You can query them with getWidth and getHeight.

```
>>> print getWidth(myPict)
640
>>> print getHeight(myPict)
480
```

We can get any particular pixel from a picture using getPixel with the picture, and the coordinates of the pixel desired. We can also get a one-dimensional array of all the pixels with getPixels. The one-dimensional array starts with all the pixels from the first row followed by all the pixels from the second row and so on. We reference the array elements using square brackets notation. Each pixel has an index number associated with it. Think of it like an address. We can reference an individual pixel with [index].

```
>>> pixel = getPixel(myPict,0,0)
>>> print pixel
Pixel red=2 green=4 blue=3
>>> pixels = getPixels(myPict)
>>> print pixels[0]
Pixel red=2 green=4 blue=3
```

Common Bug: Don't Try Printing the Pixels Array: Way Too Big!

getPixels literally returns an array of all the pixels. If you try to print the return value from getPixels, you'll get the printout of each pixel. How many pixels are there? Well, **beach.jpg** has a width of 640 and a height of 480. How many lines would print? $640 * 480 = 307{,}200$! A printout of 307,200 lines is very big. You probably don't want to wait for it to finish. If you do this accidentally, just quit JES and restart it. ■

Pixels know where they come from. You can ask them their x and y coordinates with getX and getY.

```
>>> print getX(pixel)
0
>>> print getY(pixel)
0
```

Each pixel knows how to getRed and setRed. (Green and blue work similarly.)

```
>>> print getRed(pixel)
2
>>> setRed(pixel,255)
>>> print getRed(pixel)
255
```

You can also ask a pixel for its color with getColor, and you can also set the color with setColor. Color objects know their red, green, and blue components. You can make new colors with the function makeColor.

```
>>> color = getColor(pixel)
>>> print color
color r=255 g=4 b=3
>>> newColor = makeColor(0,100,0)
>>> print newColor
color r=0 g=100 b=0
>>> setColor(pixel,newColor)
>>> print getColor(pixel)
color r=0 g=100 b=0
```

If you change the color of a pixel, the picture to which the pixel belongs is also changed.

```
>>> print getPixel(myPict,0,0)
Pixel, color=color r=0 g=100 b=0
```

Common Bug: Seeing Changes in the Picture

If you show your picture, and then change the pixels, you may wonder why you don't see anything different. Picture displays don't automatically update. If you execute repaint with the picture, for example, repaint(picture), the picture will update.

You can also make colors from pickAColor, which gives you several ways to pick a color.

```
>>> color2=pickAColor()
>>> print color2
color r=255 g=51 b=51
```

When you have finished manipulating a picture, you can write it out with writePictureTo.

```
>>> writePictureTo(myPict,"C:/temp/changedPict.jpg")
```

Common Bug: End with .jpg

Be sure to end your filename with ".jpg" in order to get your operating system to recognize it as a JPEG file.

Common Bug: Saving a File Quickly—and How to Find It Again!

What if you don't know the whole path to a directory of your choosing? You don't have to specify anything more than the base name.

```
>>> writePictureTo(myPict,"new-picture.jpg")
```

The problem is finding the file again. In what directory was it saved? This is a pretty simple bug to resolve. The default directory (the one you get if you don't specify a path) is wherever JES is. If you have used `pickAFile()` recently, the default directory will be whatever directory you picked the file from. If you have a standard media folder (e.g., **mediasources**) where you keep your media and pick files from, that's where your files will be saved if you don't specify a complete path.

■

We don't have to write new functions to manipulate pictures. We can do it from the Command Area using the functions just described. In the below example, we use a reference to a predefined name *black*. The list of all the predefined color names appears at the end of this chapter, just before the Exercises.

```
>>> print black
color r=0 g=0 b=0
>>> file="C:/ip-book/mediasources/caterpillar.jpg"
>>> pict=makePicture(file)
>>> show(pict)
>>> pixels = getPixels(pict)
>>> setColor(pixels[0],black)
>>> setColor(pixels[1],black)
>>> setColor(pixels[2],black)
>>> setColor(pixels[3],black)
>>> setColor(pixels[4],black)
>>> setColor(pixels[5],black)
>>> setColor(pixels[6],black)
>>> setColor(pixels[7],black)
>>> setColor(pixels[8],black)
>>> setColor(pixels[9],black)
>>> repaint(pict)
```

The result, showing a small black line at the top left of the picture, appears in Figure 4.9. This black line is 10 pixels long.

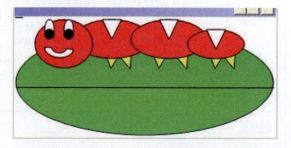

FIGURE 4.9
Directly modifying the pixel colors via commands: note the small black line in the top left corner.

Making It Work Tip: Use JES HELP!

JES has a wonderful help system. Forget what function you need? Just choose an item from the JES HELP menu (Figure 4.10—it's all hyperlinked, so hunt around for what you need). Forget what a function you're already using does? Select it and choose EXPLAIN from the HELP menu and get an explanation of what you have selected (Figure 4.11). ▪

4.2.1   Exploring Pictures

If you choose PICTURE TOOL . . . in the MEDIATOOLS menu in JES, you'll get the chance to pick a picture from picture objects that you have defined in the Command Area. First you will get to select from names for picture objects (if any) as seen in Figure 4.12. From the pop-up menu of the available picture objects (by their variable names) and the

---

| Back | Forward | Go To: | /Pictures_PictureObjects.html | Go |

Table of Contents > Understanding Pictures in JES > Picture Objects in JES

Picture Objects in JES

To understand how to work with pictures in JES, you must first understand the objects (or encodings) that represent pictures.

You can imagine that each **picture** is made up of a collection of **pixels**, which is made up of **pixel** 0, pixel 1, pixel 2, etc, and that each pixel has it's own particular **color**.

Pictures	Pictures are encodings of images, typically coming from a JPEG file.
Pixels	Pixels are a sequence of Pixel objects. They flatten the two dimensional nature of the pixels in a picture and give you instead an arraylike sequence of pixels. **pixels[0]** returns the leftmost pixel in a picture.
Pixel	A pixel is a dot in the Picture. It has a color and an (x, y) position associated with it. It remembers its own Picture so that a change to the pixel changes the real dot in the picture.
Color	It's a mixture of red, green, and blue values, each between 0 and 255.

▲jump to top

FIGURE 4.10
An example JES HELP entry.

Back   Forward   Go To: http://coweb.cc.gatech.edu/mediaCd   Go

setColor(pixel, color):
pixel: the pixel you want to set the color of
color: the Color you want to set the pixel to
Takes in a pixel and a Color, and sets the pixel to the provided color. **Example:**

```
def makeMoreBlue(pixel):
  myBlue = getBlue(pixel) + 60
  newColor = makeColor(getRed(pixel), getGreen(pixel), myBlue)
  setColor(pixel, newColor)
```

This will take in a pixel and increase its level of blue by 60.

Explain setColor   Line Number:1 Position: 1

FIGURE 4.11
An example JES EXPLAIN entry.

FIGURE 4.12
Picking a picture in the picture tool in JES.

opportunity to choose one of them by clicking OK. The JES picture tool works from picture objects that you have defined *and named* in the Command Area. If you don't have the picture named, you can't view it with the JES picture tool. `p = makePicture (pickAFile())` will allow you to define a picture and name it p. You can then explore the picture using `explore(pict)` or by using PICTURE TOOL . . . from the MEDIATOOLS menu.

The JES picture tool allows you to explore a picture. You can zoom in or out by choosing a level in the ZOOM menu. Press down with the mouse button as you move the cursor around the picture and you'll be shown the (x, y) (horizontal, vertical) coordinates and the RGB values of the pixel your mouse cursor is currently over (Figure 4.13).

- The red, green, and blue values will be displayed for the pixel you're pointing at. This is useful when you want to get a sense of how the colors in your picture map to

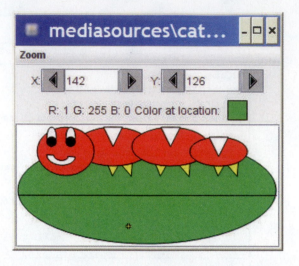

FIGURE 4.13
Selecting a pixel in the JES picture tool.

numeric red, green, and blue values. It's also helpful if you did some computation on the pixels and want to check the values.

- The *x* and *y* positions will be displayed for the pixel you're pointing at. This is useful when you want to figure out regions of the screen (e.g., if you want to process only part of the picture). If you know the range of *x* and *y* coordinates where you want to process, you can tune your for loop to reach just those sections.

4.3   CHANGING COLOR VALUES

The easiest thing to do with pictures is to change the color values of their pixels by changing the red, green, and blue components. You can get radically different effects by simply tweaking these values. Some of Adobe Photoshop's *filters* do just what we're going to be doing in this section.

The way we're going to manipulate colors is by computing a *percentage* of the original color. If we want 50% of the amount of red in the picture, we're going to set the red channel to 0.50 times whatever it is right now. If we want to increase the red by 25%, we're going to set the red to 1.25 times whatever it is right now. Recall that the asterisk (*) is the operator for multiplication in Python.

4.3.1   Using Loops in Pictures

What we could do is to get each pixel in the picture and set it to a new value of red or green or blue. Let's say that we want to decrease the red by 50%. We can always write code like this:

```
>>> file="C:/ip-book/mediasources/barbara.jpg"
>>> pict=makePicture(file)
>>> show(pict)
```

```
>>> pixels = getPixels(pict)
>>> setRed(pixels[0],getRed(pixels[0]) * 0.5)
>>> setRed(pixels[1],getRed(pixels[1]) * 0.5)
>>> setRed(pixels[2],getRed(pixels[2]) * 0.5)
>>> setRed(pixels[3],getRed(pixels[3]) * 0.5)
>>> setRed(pixels[4],getRed(pixels[4]) * 0.5)
>>> setRed(pixels[5],getRed(pixels[5]) * 0.5)
>>> repaint(pict)
```

That's pretty tedious to write, especially for all the pixels even in a small image. What we need is a way of telling the computer to do the same thing over and over again. Well, not exactly the same thing—we want to change what's going on in a well-defined way. We want to take one step each time, or process one additional pixel.

We can do this with a for loop. A for loop executes some block of commands (that you specify) for each item in an *array* (that you provide), where each time the commands are executed, a particular variable (that you name) will have the value of a different element of the array. An array is an ordered collection of data. getPixels returns an array of all the pixel objects in an input picture.

We're going to write statements that look like this:

```
for pixel in getPixels(picture):
```

Let's talk through the pieces here.

- First comes the command name for.
- Next comes the variable name that you want to use in your code for addressing (and manipulating) the elements of the sequence. We're using the word pixel here because we want to process each of the pixels in the picture.
- The word in is **required**—you must type it! Typing in makes the command more readable than leaving it out, so there's a benefit to the extra four keystrokes (space-i-n-space).
- Then you need an *array*. The variable pixel is going to be assigned to each element of the array each time through the loop: one element of the array, one iteration through the loop, the next element of the array, the next iteration through the loop. We use the function getPixels to generate the array for us.
- Finally, you need a colon (":"). The colon is important—it signifies that what comes next is a *block* (you should recall reading about blocks in Chapter 2).

What comes next are the commands that you want to execute for each pixel. Each time the commands are executed, the variable (in our example pixel) will be a different element from the array. The commands (called the *body*) are specified as a block. This means that they should follow the for statement, each on its own line, *and indented by two more spaces*! For example, here is the for loop that sets each pixel's red channel to half the original value.

```
for pixel in getPixels(picture):
  value = getRed(pixel)
  setRed(pixel,value * 0.5)
```

Let's talk through this code.

- The first statement says that we're going to have a for loop that will set the variable pixel to each of the elements of the array that is output from getPixels (picture).
- The next statement is indented, so it's part of the body of the for loop—one of the statements that will be executed each time pixel has a new value (whatever the next pixel in the picture is). It gets the current red value at the current pixel and puts that in the variable value.
- The third statement is still indented, so it's still part of the loop body. Here we set the value of the red channel (setRed) of the pixel named pixel to the value of the variable value times 0.5. This will halve the original value.

Remember that what comes after a function definition def statement is *also* a block. If you have a for loop inside a function, then the for statement is indented two spaces already, so the body of the for loop (the statements to be executed) must be indented *four* spaces. The for loop's block is inside the function's block. That's called a **nested block**—one block is nested inside the other. Here's an example of turning a loop into a function.

```
def decreaseRed(picture):
  for pixel in getPixels(picture):
    value = getRed(pixel)
    setRed(pixel,value * 0.5)
```

You don't actually have to put loops into functions to use them. You can type them into the Command Area of JES. JES is smart enough to figure out that you need to type more than one command if you're specifying a loop, so it changes the prompt from >>> to .... Of course, it can't figure out when you're done, so you'll have to just hit ENTER without typing anything else to tell JES that you're done with the body of your loop. You probably realize that we don't really need the variable value—we can simply replace the variable with the function holding the same value. Here's how to do it at the command line:

```
>>> for pixel in getPixels(picture):
...     setRed(pixel,getRed(pixel) * 0.5)
```

Now that we see how to get the computer to do thousands of commands without writing thousands of individual lines, let's try it out.

4.3.2   Increasing/Decreasing Red (Green, Blue)

A common desire when working with digital pictures is to shift a picture's *redness* (or greenness or blueness—most often the redness). You can shift it higher to "warm" the picture, or reduce it to "cool" the picture or to deal with overly red digital cameras.

The program given below reduces the amount of color 50% in an input picture. It uses the variable pix to stand for the current pixel. We used the variable pixel in the previous function. It doesn't matter—the name can be whatever we want.

Program 34: Reduce the Amount of Red in a Picture by 50%

```
def decreaseRed(picture):
  for pix in getPixels(picture):
    value=getRed(pix)
    setRed(pix,value*0.5)
```

Go ahead and type the preceding code into your JES Program Area. Click LOAD PROGRAM to get Python to process the function (be sure to save it, something like **decreaseRed.py**) and thus make the name decreaseRed stand for this function. Follow along the example below to get a better idea of how this all works.

Making It Work Tip: Program Files Can Have Any Number of Functions
We are having you save the file **decreaseRed.py** with only the single function in it, decreaseRed. We can have more than one function in a Python file. In fact, there's no actual limit to the number of functions you put in a file.

This recipe takes a picture as input—the one that we'll use to get the pixels from. To get a picture, we need a filename, and then we need to make a picture from it. We can also open a JES picture tool on a picture using the function explore(picture). This will make a copy of the current picture and show it in the JES picture tool. After we apply the function decreaseRed to the picture, we can explore it again and compare the two pictures side-by-side. Therefore, the program can be used like this:

```
>>> file="C:/ip-book/mediasources/eiffel.jpg"
>>> picture=makePicture(file)
>>> explore(picture)
>>> decreaseRed(picture)
>>> explore(picture)
```

Common Bug: Patience—For Loops Always End
The most common bug with this kind of code is to give up and hit the STOP button before it ends on its own. If you're using a for loop, the program will *always* stop. But it might take a full minute (or two!) for some of the manipulations we'll do—especially if your source image is large.

The original picture and its red-reduced version appear in Figure 4.14. 50% is obviously a *lot* of red to reduce. The picture looks like it was taken through a blue filter. Notice that the first pixel's red value was 133 and has been changed to 66.

Computer Science Idea: The Most Important Skill to Learn Is Tracing
The most important skill that you can develop in your first course in programming is the ability to *trace* your program. (This is sometimes also called *stepping* or *walking through*

FIGURE 4.14
The original picture (*left*) and red-reduced version (*right*).

your program.) To trace your program is to walk through it, line by line, and figure out what happens. Looking at a program, can you *predict* what it's going to do? You should be able to by thinking through what it does. Eventually, you want to be able to *design* new programs as well, but you have to understand well how your programs work before you can effectively make new ones.   ■

How It Works

Let's *trace* the function to decrease red and see how it worked. We want to break in at the point where we just called `decreaseRed`:

```
>>> file="C:/ip-book/mediasources/Katie-smaller.jpg"
>>> picture=makePicture(file)
>>> explore(picture)
>>> decreaseRed(picture)
>>> explore(picture)
```

What happens now? `decreaseRed` really stands for the function that we saw earlier, so it begins to execute.

```
def decreaseRed(picture):
  for p in getPixels(picture):
    value=getRed(p)
    setRed(p,value*0.5)
```

The first line we execute is `def decreaseRed(picture):`. This says that the function should expect some input and that the input will be named `picture` during the execution of the function.

Computer Science Idea: Names Inside of Functions Are Different from Names Outside of Functions

The names inside a function (like picture, p, and value in the decreaseRed example) are *completely* different from the names in the Command Area or any other function. We say that they have a different *scope*, which means the area where the name is defined. Within the function decreaseRed, the name p is in *local* scope. It cannot be accessed from the Command Area. Names created in the Command Area have a more *global* scope. Those names can be accessed from within functions defined in the Program Area. ■

Inside the computer, we can imagine what it now looks like: there is some association between the word picture and the picture object that we gave it as input.

Now we get to the line for p in getPixels(picture):. This means that all the pixels from the picture are lined up (within the computer) as a sequence (in the array), and that variable p should be assigned (associated with) the first one. We can imagine that inside the computer it now looks like this:

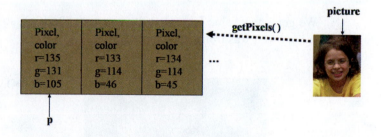

Each pixel has its own RGB values. p points at the first pixel. Note that the variable picture is still there—we may not use it anymore but it's still there.

Now we're at value=getRed(p). This simply adds another name to the ones the computer is already tracking for us and gives it a simple numeric value.

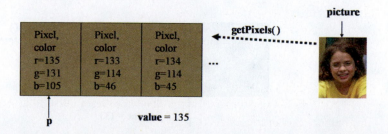

Finally, we're at the bottom of the loop. The computer executes `setRed(p,value*0.5)`, which changes the red channel of the pixel p to 50% of the `value`. The value of p is odd, so we would get 67.5 when we multiply by 0.5, but we are putting the result in an integer so that the fractional part of the number is simply thrown away. So the original red value of 135 changes to 67.

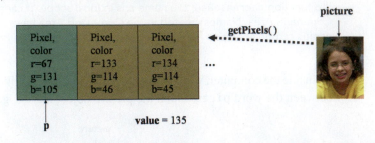

What happens next is very important: the loop starts over again! We go back to the `for` loop and take the *next* value in the array. The name p gets associated with that next value.

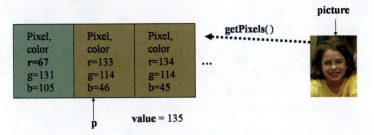

We get a new value for `value` at `value=getRed(p)`, so now `value` is 133, rather than the 135 it was from the first pixel.

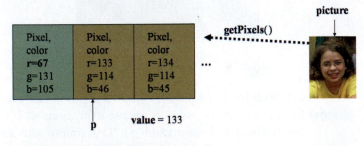

And then we change *that* pixel's red channel.

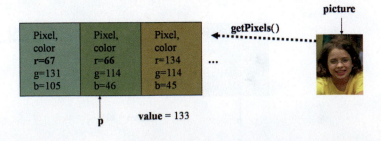

Eventually, we get Figure 4.15. We keep going through all the pixels in the sequence and changing all the red values.

4.3.3   Testing the Program: Did That Really Work?

How do we know that what we did really worked? Sure, *something* happened to the picture, but did we really decrease the red? By 50%?

Making It Work Tip: Don't Just Trust Your Own Programs!
It's easy to mislead yourself into thinking that your program worked. After all, you told the computer to do something, so you shouldn't be surprised if the computer did what you wanted. But computers are really stupid—they can't figure out what you want. They only do what you tell them. It's pretty easy to get it *almost* right. Be sure to check. ■

We can check it several ways. One way is with the JES picture tool. You can check the RGB values at the same *x* and *y* coordinates in both the before and after picture using the picture tool. Click and drag the cursor to a location to check in the before-picture and then type in the same *x* and *y* coordinates in the after-picture tool and hit ENTER. This will show you the color values at the desired *x* and *y* locations in both the before and after pictures (Figure 4.15).

We can also use the functions that we know in the Command Area to check the red values of individual pixels.

```
>>> file = pickAFile()
>>> pict = makePicture(file)
```

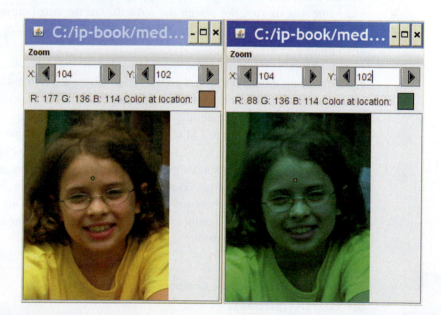

FIGURE 4.15
Using the JES picture tool to convince ourselves that the red was decreased.

```
>>> pixel = getPixel(pict,0,0)
>>> print pixel
Pixel, color=color r=168 g=131 b=105
>>> decreaseRed(pict)
>>> newPixel = getPixel(pict,0,0)
>>> print newPixel
Pixel, color=color r=84 g=131 b=105
>>> print 168 * 0.5
84.0
```

4.3.4   Changing One Color at a Time

Let's increase the red in the picture now. If multiplying the red component by 0.5 reduced it, multiplying it by something over 1.0 should increase it.

Program 35: Increase the Red Component by 20%

```
def increaseRed(picture):
  for p in getPixels(picture):
    value=getRed(p)
    setRed(p,value*1.2)
```

How It Works

We would use increaseRed using the same kind of Command Area statements as we did for decreaseRed. When we type something like increaseRed(pict), the same kind of process occurs. We get all the pixels of the input picture pict (whatever that is) then assign the variable p to the first pixel in the list. We get its red value (say, 100) and name that value. We assign the red value of the pixel currently represented by the name p to 1.2 * 100 or 120. We then repeat the process for *every* pixel p in the input picture.

What happens if you increase the red in a picture that has lots of red in it and some of the resulting red values would go over 255? There are two options in this case. The value can be clipped to a maximum of 255 or you can wrap it around using the modulo (remainder) operator. For example if the value is 200 and you try to double it to 400, it can remain at 255 or wrap to 144 (400 − 256). Try it and see what happens, then check to see how your options are set. JES provides an option to either clip color values to 255 or wrap them. To change this option, click on EDIT in the menu and then on OPTIONS. The option to change is MODULO PIXEL COLOR VALUES BY 256. To wrap is to use the *modulo* operation. To prevent from growing larger than 255 is *not* to use modulo.

We can even get rid of a color component completely. The next program erases the blue component from a picture.

Program 36: Clear the Blue Component from a Picture

```
def clearBlue(picture):
  for p in getPixels(picture):
    setBlue(p,0)
```

4.4   CREATING A SUNSET

We can certainly do more than one picture manipulation at once. Once, Mark wanted to generate a sunset out of an island scene. His first attempt was to increase the red but that doesn't work. Some of the red values in a given picture are pretty high. If you go past 255 for a channel value, the default is to *wrap-around*. If you setRed of a pixel to 256, you'll actually get *zero*. So increasing red created bright blue-green (no red) spots.

Mark's second thought was that maybe what happens in a sunset is that there is *less* blue and green, thus *emphasizing* the red, without actually increasing it. Here is the program that he wrote for that:

Program 37: Making a Sunset

```
def makeSunset(picture):
  for p in getPixels(picture):
    value=getBlue(p)
    setBlue(p,value*0.7)
    value=getGreen(p)
    setGreen(p,value*0.7)
```

How It Works

As in past examples, we take an input picture and make the variable p stand for each pixel in the input picture. We get each blue component and then set it again after multiplying its original value by 0.70. We then do the same to the green. Effectively, we're changing both the blue and green channels—reducing each by 30%. The effect works pretty well, as seen in Figure 4.16.

4.4.1   Making Sense of Functions

You probably have lots of questions about functions at this point. Why did we write these functions in this way? How is it that we're reusing variable names like picture in both

FIGURE 4.16
Original island scene (*left*) and at (fake) sunset (*right*).

the function and the Command Area? Are there other ways to write these functions? Is there such a thing as a better or worse function?

Since we're always picking a file (or typing in a filename) and *then* making a picture before calling one of our picture manipulation functions and *then* showing or exploring the picture, it's natural to ask why we don't build those in. Why doesn't *every* function have `pickAFile()` and `makePicture` in it?

We use the functions in the way that makes them more *general* and *reusable*. We want each function to do one and only one thing, so that we can use the function again in a new context where we need that one thing done. An example may make this clearer. Consider the program to make a sunset (Program 37). It works by reducing the green and blue, each by 30%. What if we rewrote this function so that it calls two *smaller* functions that just do the two pieces of the manipulation? We'd end up with something like Program 38.

Program 38: Making a Sunset as Three Functions

```
def makeSunset2(picture):
  reduceBlue(picture)
  reduceGreen(picture)

def reduceBlue(picture):
  for p in getPixels(picture):
    value=getBlue(p)
    setBlue(p,value*0.7)

def reduceGreen(picture):
  for p in getPixels(picture):
    value=getGreen(p)
    setGreen(p,value*0.7)
```

How It Works

The first thing to realize is that this actually does work. `makeSunset2` does the same thing here as in the previous recipe for `makeSunset`. The function `makeSunset` takes an input picture, then calls `reduceBlue` with the same input picture. `reduceBlue` makes p stand for each pixel in the input picture, and reduces the blue of each by 30% (by multiplying it by 0.7). `reduceBlue` then ends, and the *flow of control* (i.e., which statement executes next) returns to `makeSunset2` and then the *next* statement is executed. That is the call to the function `reduceGreen` with the same input picture. As before, `reduceGreen` touches each of the pixels and reduces the green value by 30%.

Making It Work Tip: Using Multiple Functions
It's perfectly okay to have multiple functions in one Program Area, saved in one file. It can make it easier to read and reuse functions.

It's perfectly okay to have one function (`makeSunset2` in this case) use other functions written by the programmer in the same file (`reduceBlue` and `reduceGreen`).

You use `makeSunset2` just as you did before with `makeSunset`. It's the same recipe (it tells the computer to do the same thing), but with different functions. The earlier recipe did everything in one function and this one does it in three. In fact, you can also use `reduceBlue` and `reduceGreen`—make a picture in the Command Area and pass it as input to either of them. They work just like `decreaseRed`.

What's different is that the function `makeSunset2` is somewhat simpler to read. It states pretty clearly, "To make a sunset means to reduce blue and reduce green." Being simple to read *is* important.

> **Computer Science Idea: Programs Are for People**
>
> Computers couldn't care less what a program looks like. Programs are written to communicate with *people*. Making programs easy to read and understand means that they are more easily changed and reused and they more effectively communicate process to other humans. ∎

What if we had written `reduceBlue` and `reduceGreen` with `pickAFile` and `show` and `repaint` in it? Something like this:

```
def reduceBlueNotReusable():
  picture = makePicture(pickAFile())
  show(picture)
  for p in getPixels(picture):
    value=getBlue(p)
    setBlue(p,value*0.7)
  repaint(picture)

def reduceGreenNotReusable():
  picture = makePicture(pickAFile())
  show(picture)
  for p in getPixels(picture):
    value=getGreen(p)
    setGreen(p,value*0.7)
    repaint(picture)
```

We would be asked for the picture once each time we used the function. Since these functions get their own pictures, we cannot provide a picture as an input, like we do in `makeSunset2`. Basically, these versions cannot be used for new purposes—they are not easily reused. Because we wrote the original functions `reduceBlue` and `reduceGreen` to *only* reduce the blue and reduce the green ("one and only one thing"), we can reuse them in new functions like `makeSunset2`.

Now let's say that we put `pickAFile` and `makePicture` into the `makeSunset2`, like this:

```
def makeSunset2NotReusable():
  picture = makePicture(pickAFile())
  show(picture)
  reduceBlue(picture)
  reduceGreen(picture)
  repaint(picture)
```

The functions `reduceBlue` and `reduceGreen` are completely flexible and reusable again. But `makeSunset2` is now less flexible and reusable. Is that a big deal? No, not if you only care about having the function to give a sunset look to a single frame. But what if you later want to build a movie with a few hundred frames, to each of which you want to add a sunset look? Do you really want to pick out each of those few hundred frames with `pickAFile()`? Or would you rather make a loop to go through the frames (which we'll learn how to do in a few chapters) and send each of them as input to the *more general* form of `makeSunset2`? That's why we make functions general and reusable—you never know when you're going to want to use a function again in a larger context.

Making It Work Tip: Don't Start by Trying to Write Applications

New programmers often want to write complete applications that a nontechnical user can use. You may want to write a makeSunset application that goes out and fetches a picture for a user and generates a sunset. Building good user interfaces that anyone can use is hard work. Start out more slowly. It's hard enough to make a reusable function that takes a picture as input. You can work on user interfaces later. ∎

We could also write these functions with explicit filenames by saying at the beginning of one of the recipes:

```
file="C:/ip-book/mediasources/bridge.jpg"
```

That way, we wouldn't be prompted for a file each time. But then the functions only work for the one file, and if we want them to work for some other file, we have to modify them. Do you really want to change the function each time you use it? It's easier to leave the function alone and change the picture that you hand to it.

Of course, we could change any of our functions to be handed a filename rather than a picture. For example, we could write:

```
def makeSunset3(filename):
  reduceBlue(filename)
  reduceGreen(filename)

def reduceBlue(filename):
  picture = makePicture(filename)
  for p in getPixels(picture):
    value=getBlue(p)
    setBlue(p,value*0.7)

def reduceGreen(filename):
  picture = makePicture(filename)
  for p in getPixels(picture):
    value=getGreen(p)
    setGreen(p,value*0.7)
```

Is this better or worse than the code we saw before? At some level, it doesn't matter—we can work with pictures or filenames, whichever makes more sense to us. The filename-as-input version does have several disadvantages, though. For one, it doesn't work! The picture is made in each of `reduceGreen` and `reduceBlue`, but then it isn't saved, so it gets lost at the end of the function. The earlier version of `makeSunset2` (and its *subfunctions*, the functions it calls) works by *side effects*—the function doesn't return anything, but it changes the input object directly.

We could fix the loss-of-the-picture by saving the file to disk after we're done with each function, but then the functions are doing more than "one and only one thing." There's also the inefficiency of making the picture twice, and if we were to add in the saving, saving the picture twice. Again, the best functions do "one and only one thing."

Even larger functions, like `makeSunset2`, do "one and only one thing." `makeSunset2` makes a sunset-looking picture. It does so *by* reducing green and reducing blue. It calls two other functions to do that. What we end up with is a *hierarchy* of goals—the "one and only one thing" that is being done. `makeSunset` does its one thing by asking two other functions to do their one thing. We call this **hierarchical decomposition** (breaking down a problem into smaller parts, then breaking down the smaller parts until you get something that you can easily program) and it's very powerful for creating complex programs out of pieces that you understand.

Names in functions are *completely* separate from names in the Command Area. The *only* way to get any data (pictures, sounds, filenames, numbers) from the Command Area into a function is by passing it in as input to the function. Within the function, you can use any names you want. Names that you first define within the function (like `picture` in the last example) and names that you use to stand for the input data (like `filename`) *only* exist while the function is running. When the function is done, variable names literally do not exist anymore.

This is really an advantage. Earlier, we said that naming is very important to computer scientists: we name everything, from data to functions. But if each name could mean one and only one thing *forever*, we'd run out of names. In natural language, words mean different things in different contexts (e.g., "What do you mean?" and "You are being mean!"). A function is a different context—names can mean something different than they do outside of that function.

Sometimes you will compute something inside a function that you want to return to the Command Area or to a calling function. We've already seen functions that output a value, like `pickAFile`, which outputs a filename. If you did a `makePicture` inside a function, you might want to output the picture that you created inside the function. You can do this by using `return`, which we'll talk more about later.

The name you give to a function's input can be thought of as a *placeholder*. Whenever the placeholder appears, imagine the input data appearing instead. So in a function like

```
def decreaseRed(picture):
  for p in getPixels(picture):
    value=getRed(p)
    setRed(p,value*0.5)
```

we are going to call `decreaseRed` with a statement like `decreaseRed(myPicture)`. Whatever picture is in `myPicture` *becomes known as* `picture` while `decreaseRed` is running. For those few seconds, `picture` in `decreaseRed` and `myPicture` in the

Command Area *refer to the same picture*. Changing the pixels in one changes the pixels in the other.

We've now talked about different ways of writing the same function—some better, some worse. There are other ways that are pretty much equivalent and some that are much better. Let's consider a few more ways that we can write functions.

We can pass in more than one input at a time. Consider this version of `decreaseRed`:

```
def decreaseRed(picture, amount):
  for p in getPixels(picture):
    value=getRed(p)
    setRed(p,value*amount)
```

We would use this one by saying something like `decreaseRed(mypicture, 0.25)`. This use would reduce the red by 75%. We could say `decreaseRed (mypicture, 1.25)` and *increase* red by 25%. Perhaps this function should be better named `change-Red`, because that's what it is now—a general way of changing the whole amount of red in a picture. That's a pretty useful and powerful function.

Recall seeing this code in Program 36:

```
def clearBlue(picture):
  for p in getPixels(picture):
    setBlue(p,0)
```

We could also write the same program like this:

```
def clearBlue(picture):
  for p in getPixels(picture):
    value = getBlue(p)
    setBlue(p,value*0)
```

It's important to note that this function achieves the *exact same* thing as the earlier program did. Both set the blue channel of all pixels to zero. An advantage of the latter function is that it has the same *form* as all the other color-changing functions we've seen. This may make it more understandable, which is useful. It is somewhat less efficient—it's not really necessary to *get* the blue value before setting it to zero nor is it necessary to multiply by zero when we just want the value of zero. The function is really doing more than it needs to do—it's not doing "one and only one thing."

4.5   LIGHTENING AND DARKENING

To lighten or darken a picture is pretty simple. It's the same pattern we saw previously, but instead of changing a color component, you change the overall color. Here are lightening and then darkening as programs. Figure 4.17 shows the original and darker version of a picture.

Program 39: Lighten the Picture

```
def lighten(picture):
  for px in getPixels(picture):
    color = getColor(px)
    color = makeLighter(color)
    setColor(px,color)
```

FIGURE 4.17
The original picture (*left*) and a darker version (*right*).

How It Works

The variable px is used to represent each of the pixels in the input picture. (Not p! Does it matter? Not to the computer—if p means "pixel" to you, then use it, but feel free to use px or pxl or even pixel!) color takes on the color of the pixel px. The function makeLighter returns the new lighter color. The setColor method sets the color of the pixel to the new lighter color.

Program 40: Darken the Picture

```
def darken(picture):
   for px in getPixels(picture):
     color = getColor(px)
     color = makeDarker(color)
     setColor(px,color)
```

4.6   CREATING A NEGATIVE

Creating a *negative image* of a picture is much easier than you might at first imagine. Let's think it through. What we want is the opposite of each of the current values for red, green, and blue. It's easiest to understand at the extremes. If we have a red component of 0, we want 255 instead. If we have 255, we want the negative to have a 0.

Now let's consider the middle ground. If the red component is slightly red (say, 50), we want something that is almost completely red—where the "almost" is the same amount of redness in the original picture. We want the maximum red (255), but 50 less than that. We want a red component of $255 - 50 = 205$. In general, the negative should be $255 - original$. We need to compute the negative of each of the red, green, and blue components, then create a new negative color and set the pixel to the negative color.

FIGURE 4.18
Negative of the image.

Here's the program that does it, and you can see that it really does work (Figure 4.18).

Program 41: Create the Negative of the Original Picture

```
def negative(picture):
  for px in getPixels(picture):
    red=getRed(px)
    green=getGreen(px)
    blue=getBlue(px)
    negColor=makeColor(255-red, 255-green, 255-blue)
    setColor(px,negColor)
```

How It Works

We use px to represent each of the pixels in the input picture. For each pixel px, we use the variables red, green, and blue to name the red, green, and blue components of the pixel's color. We make a *new* color with makeColor whose red component is 255-red, the green is 255-green, and the blue is 255-blue. This means that the new color is the *opposite* of the original color. Finally, we set the color of the pixel px to the new negative color (negColor) and move on to the next pixel.

4.7   CONVERTING TO GRAYSCALE

Converting to grayscale is a fun program. It's short, not hard to understand, and yet has such a striking visual effect. It's a really nice example of what one can do easily yet powerfully by manipulating pixel color values.

Recall that the resultant color is gray whenever the red component, green component, and blue component have the same value. This means that our RGB encoding supports 256 levels of gray, from ($red = 0$, $green = 0$, $blue = 0$) (black) to (1, 1, 1) through

FIGURE 4.19
Color picture converted to grayscale.

(100, 100, 100) and finally (255, 255, 255) (white). The tricky part is figuring out what the replicated value should be.

What we want is a sense of the *intensity* of the color, called the *luminance*. It turns out that there is a pretty easy way to compute it: we average the three component colors. Since there are three components, the formula we're going to use for intensity is:

$$\frac{(red + green + blue)}{3}$$

This leads us to the following simple program and Figure 4.19.

Program 42: Convert to Grayscale

```
def grayScale(picture):
  for p in getPixels(picture):
    intensity = (getRed(p)+getGreen(p)+getBlue(p))/3
    setColor(p,makeColor(intensity,intensity,intensity))
```

This is actually an overly simple notion of grayscale. Below is a program that takes into account how the human eye perceives *luminance*. Remember that we consider blue to be darker than red, even if there's the same amount of light reflected off. So we *weight* blue lower and red higher, when computing the average.

Program 43: Convert to Grayscale with Weights

```
def grayScaleNew(picture):
  for px in getPixels(picture):
    newRed = getRed(px) * 0.299
```

```
newGreen = getGreen(px) * 0.587
newBlue = getBlue(px) * 0.114
luminance = newRed+newGreen+newBlue
setColor(px,makeColor(luminance,luminance,luminance))
```

How It Works

We make px stand for each pixel in the picture. We then *weight* the redness, greenness, and blueness based on what empirical research shows about how we perceive the luminance of each of these colors. Note that $0.299 + 0.587 + 0.114$ is 1.0. We're still going to end up with a value between 0 and 255, but we're going to make *more* of the luminance value come from the green part, less from the red, and still less from blue (which, we have already established, is perceived to be darkest). We then add these three weighted values together to get our new luminance. We make the color and set the color of the pixel px to the new color we have made.

4.8   SPECIFYING PIXELS BY INDEX

In the last chapter, we used index notation for specifying positions of characters in a string and items in a list. The function getPixels is actually returning a list of pixels. We can use the square bracket ([]) indexing notation to manipulate pixels in a picture.

We will begin by rewriting the decreaseRed function to use array notation. Here's our original function again:

```
def decreaseRed(picture):
  for pixel in getPixels(picture):
    value = getRed(pixel)
    setRed(pixel,value * 0.5)
```

We need to make a few changes:

- We will use the name pixels to mean the getPixels(picture).
- The for loop will change an index variable.
- We will name the variable pixel for the pixel at position index in the list of pixels.

Here is our new version.

Program 44: Decrease Red Using Index Notation
```
def decreaseRedIndexed(picture):
  pixels = getPixels(picture)
  for index in range(0,len(pixels)):
    pixel = pixels[index]
    value = getRed(pixel)
    setRed(pixel,value * 0.5)
```

The function decreaseRedIndexed works *exactly* the same as decreaseRed. Internally, it does things just a bit different. That little bit of difference allows us to do some new things. For example, we can do something to only 1/2 of the pixels in a picture.

Program 45: Decrease Red on First Half of the Picture

```
def decreaseRedHalf(picture):
  pixels = getPixels(picture)
  for index in range(0,len(pixels)/2):
    pixel = pixels[index]
    value = getRed(pixel)
    setRed(pixel,value * 0.5)
```

Now, which half of the picture will get red decreased when we run `decrease-RedHalf`? Left half? Right half? Top half? Bottom half? It all depends on the order that `getPixels` uses to collect the pixels. Let's try it:

```
>>> file = "/Users/guzdial/Desktop/mediasources-4ed/statue-tower.jpg"
>>> pict = makePicture(file)
>>> decreaseRedHalf(pict)
>>> explore(pict)
```

As we can see (in Figure 4.20), the function `decreaseRedHalf` processes the *top* half of the pixels in the picture. This tells us that `getPixels` works from top to bottom.

FIGURE 4.20
Original picture on the left, and after half of the picture has its red reduced on the right.

Once we know how `getPixels` returns the pixels, we can do some more interesting manipulations. For example, we can copy the top half into the bottom half. We ran this program on the statue tower, and we got the result in Figure 4.21.

Program 46: Copy Top Half of Picture into Bottom Half of Picture

```
def copyHalf(picture):
 pixels = getPixels(picture)
 for index in range(0,len(pixels)/2):
   pixel1 = pixels[index]
   color1 = getColor(pixel1)
   pixel2 = pixels[index + len(pixels)/2]
   setColor(pixel2,color1)
```

How It Works

The function `copyHalf` starts out just like `decreaseRedHalf` function. We get all the `pixels`, and we construct a `for` loop so that the `index` variable will take on the values of the indices in the top half of the picture.

FIGURE 4.21
Top of the picture copied into the bottom of the picture.

- We get a pixel (named `pixel1`) from `pixels[index]`.
- We get its color, `color1 = getColor(pixel1)`. That stores a whole color (all three of the red, green, and blue components) inside the name `color1`.
- Now, we get a *second* pixel from the picture. Since we know that the index values are going from 0 to `len(pixels)/2`, we know that the second half of the pixels go from `len(pixels)/2` to `len(pixels)`. By adding `len(pixels)/2` to the `index`, we are getting a pixel in the *bottom* half of the picture.
- We set the color of this second pixel `pixel2` to the color we got from `pixel1`, stored in the variable `color1`.

In the last chapter, we learned how to mirror strings. It's a little different with pictures, but if we can *copy* half of the picture into the other half, we should also be able to mirror. Here's a function that does that.

Program 47: Mirror Top Half of Picture into Bottom Half of Picture

```
def mirrorHalf(picture):
 pixels = getPixels(picture)
 target = len(pixels) - 1
 for index in range(0,len(pixels)/2):
   pixel1 = pixels[index]
   color1 = getColor(pixel1)
   pixel2 = pixels[target]
   setColor(pixel2,color1)
   target = target - 1
```

Here's how we might use it (with the result seen in Figure 4.21):

```
>>> pict = makePicture("/Users/guzdial/Desktop/mediasources-4ed/llama.jpg")
>>> mirrorHalf(pict)
>>> explore(pict)
```

How It Works

The function `mirrorHalf` starts out just like `copyHalf` function. We get all the `pixels`, and we construct a `for` loop so that the `index` variable will take on the values of the indices in the top half of the picture. We also start a `target` index (kind of like the `pile` variables we were using before) that we will use to figure out where we copy pixels to. We want to copy the color first pixel (index 0) into the *last* pixel in the picture. We learned in the last chapter that the length of the sequence is one more than the last index, so we will start `target` at `len(pixels) - 1`.

- We get a pixel (named `pixel1`) from `pixels[index]`.
- We get its color, `color1 = getColor(pixel1)`. (So far, same as copying.)

FIGURE 4.22
Original llama picture on left, and after mirroring the top half down on the right.

- Now, we get a *second* pixel from the picture, from whatever pixel `target` is referencing.
- We set the color of this second pixel `pixel2` to the color we got from `pixel1`.
- One step further—we subtract one from the `target` value and store it back into the name `target`. Recall that assignment means to compute the value on the right, then name it on the left. This statement is reducing `target` by one. It starts out at the last pixel in the picture, then moves backwards—while `index` is moving forwards. The result is mirroring (Figure 4.22).

PROGRAMMING SUMMARY

In this chapter, we talk about several kinds of encodings of data (or objects).

Pictures	Encodings of images, typically created from a JPEG file.
Pixels	A one-dimensional array (sequence) of pixel objects. The code `pixels[0]` returns the top leftmost pixel in a picture.
Pixel	A dot in the picture. It has a color and an (x, y) position associated with it. It remembers its own picture so that a change to the pixel changes the real dot in the picture.
Color	A mixture of red, green, and blue values, each between 0 and 255.

PICTURE PROGRAM PIECES

getPixels	Takes a picture as input and returns a one-dimensional array of pixel objects in the picture with the pixels from the first row first and then the pixels from the second row and so on.
getPixel	Takes a picture, an *x* position and a *y* position (two numbers), and returns the pixel object at that point in the picture.
getWidth	Takes a picture as input and returns its width in the number of pixels across the picture.
getHeight	Takes a picture as input and returns its length in the number of pixels top-to-bottom in the picture.
writePictureTo	Takes a picture and a filename (string) as input, then writes the picture to the file as a JPEG. (Be sure to end the filename in ".jpg" for the operating system to understand it properly.)

PIXEL PROGRAM PIECES

getRed, getGreen, getBlue	Each of these functions takes a pixel object and returns the value (between 0 and 255) of the amount of redness, greenness, and blueness (respectively) in that pixel.
setRed, setGreen, setBlue	Each of these functions takes a pixel object and a value (between 0 and 255) and sets the redness, greenness, or blueness (respectively) of that pixel to the given value.
getColor	Takes a pixel and returns the color object at that pixel.
setColor	Takes a pixel object and a color object and sets the color for that pixel.
getX, getY	Takes a pixel object and returns the *x* or *y* position (respectively) of where that pixel is at in the picture.

COLOR PROGRAM PIECES

makeColor	Takes three inputs for the red, green, and blue components (in order), and returns a color object.
pickAColor	Takes no input but puts up a color picker. Find the color you want and the function will return the color that you picked.
makeDarker, makeLighter	Each takes a color and returns a slightly darker or lighter version (respectively) of the color.

There are a bunch of **constants** that are useful in this chapter. These are variables with predefined values. These values are colors: `black`, `white`, `blue`, `red`, `green`, `gray`, `darkGray`, `lightGray`, `yellow`, `orange`, `pink`, `magenta`, and `cyan`. These are defined inside of JES, actually using Python code that looks like this:

```
#Constants
black = Color(0,0,0)
white = Color(255,255,255)
blue = Color(0,0,255)
red = Color(255,0,0)
green = Color(0,255,0)
gray = Color(128,128,128)
darkGray = Color(64,64,64)
lightGray = Color(192,192,192)
yellow = Color(255,255,0)
orange = Color(255,200,0)
pink = Color(255,175,175)
magenta = Color(255,0,255)
cyan = Color(0,255,255)
```

PROBLEMS

4.1   Picture concept questions:

  - Why don't we see red, green, and blue spots at each position in our picture?
  - What is hierarchical decomposition? What is it good for?
  - What is luminance?
  - Why is the maximum value of any color component (red, green, or blue) 255?
  - The color encoding we're using is RGB. What does this mean, in terms of the amount of memory required to represent color? Is there a limit to the number of colors that we can represent? Are there *enough* colors representable in RGB?

4.2   Program 34 (page 89) obviously reduces the red by too much. Write a version that only reduces the red by 10%, then one by 20%. Can you find pictures where each is most useful? Note that you can always repeatedly reduce the red in a picture but you don't want to have to do it *too* many times.

4.3   Write the blue and green versions of the reduce red function—Program 34 (page 89).

4.4   Each of the following is equivalent to the increase red function—Program 35 (page 94). Test them and convince yourself that they work. Which do you prefer and why?

```
def increaseRed2(picture):
    for p in getPixels(picture):
        setRed(p,getRed(p)*1.2)

def increaseRed3(picture):
    for p in getPixels(picture):
        redC = getRed(p)
```

```
        greenC = getGreen(p)
        blueC = getBlue(p)
        newRed=int(redC*1.2)
        newColor = makeColor(newRed,greenC,blueC)
        setColor(p,newColor)
```

4.5   If you keep increasing the red value and wrapping is on, eventually some pixels become *bright* green and blue. If you check those pixels with the picture tool, you'll find that the values of red are very *low*. What do you think is going on? How did they get so small? How does wrapping work?

4.6   Write a function to swap the values of two colors, for example, swap the red value with the blue value.

4.7   Write a function to set the red, green, and blue values to zero. What is the result?

4.8   Write a function to set the red, green, and blue values to 255. What is the result?

4.9   What does the following function do?
```
def test1 (picture):
    for p in getPixels(picture):
        setRed(p,getRed(p) * 0.3)
```

4.10   What does the following function do?
```
def test2 (picture):
    for p in getPixels(picture):
        setBlue(p,getBlue(p) * 1.5)
```

4.11   What does the following function do?
```
def test3 (picture):
    for p in getPixels(picture):
        setGreen(p,0)
```

4.12   What does the following function do?
```
def test4 (picture):
    for p in getPixels(picture):
        red = getRed(p) + 10
        green = getGreen(p) + 10
        blue = getBlue(p) + 10
        color = makeColor(red, green, blue)
        setColor(p,color)
```

4.13   What does the following function do?
```
def test5 (picture):
    for p in getPixels(picture):
        red = getRed(p) - 20
        green = getGreen(p) - 20
        blue = getBlue(p) - 20
        color = makeColor(red,green,blue)
        setColor(p,color)
```

4.14   What does the following function do?
```
def test6 (picture):
    for p in getPixels(picture):
        red = getRed(p)
        green = getGreen(p)
        blue = getBlue(p)
```

```
        color = makeColor(blue, red, green)
        setColor(p,color)
```

4.15   What does the following function do?
```
def test7 (picture):
    for p in getPixels(picture):
        red = getRed(p)/2
        green = getGreen(p)/2
        blue = getBlue(p)/2
        color = makeColor(red,green,blue)
        setColor(p,color)
```

4.16   What does the following function do? By reading the program without running it, do you think that the result of test8 will be lighter or darker than the result of test7?
```
def test8 (picture):
    for p in getPixels(picture):
        red = getRed(p) /3
        green = getGreen(p) /3
        blue = getBlue(p) /3
        color = makeColor(red,green,blue)
        setColor(p,color)
```

4.17   What does the following function do? By reading the program without running it, do you think that the result of test9 will be lighter or darker than the result of test7?
```
def test9 (picture):
    for p in getPixels(picture):
        red = getRed(p) * 2
        green = getGreen(p) * 2
        blue = getBlue(p) * 2
        color = makeColor(red,green,blue)
        setColor(p,color)
```

4.18   Write a function to "blue-ify" a face. Write a function that accepts a picture as input. If any pixel has a blue value less than 150, then set that pixel's color to white. Try it on a picture of a face and see what you get.

4.19   Write a general "blue-ify" function. Write a function that accepts a picture as input, then doubles the blue value of every pixel and cut the red and green values in half.

4.20   Write a general "red-ify" function. Write a function that accepts a picture as input, then doubles the red value of every pixel and cut the blue and green values in half.

4.21   Write a function to change a picture to grayscale and *then* negate it.

4.22   Write a function to create a lightened grayscale image. First, lighten the image by adding 75 to the red, green, and blue components of every pixel. Since higher numbers are closer to white, this should make the pixel lighter. Now, grayscale the new image.

4.23   Write a function to create a lightened grayscale image, by use makeLighter. First, lighten the image by using the makeLighter function on each color.

Now, grayscale the new image. Compare the result to the picture created by the previous problem. How does makeLighter compare to adding 75 to each of the red, green, and blue components of every pixel?

4.24 Write three functions, one to clear blue (Program 36 (page 94)) and one to clear red, and one to clear green. For each of these, which would be the most useful in actual practice? How about combinations of them?

4.25 Rewrite the clear blue program (Program 36 (page 94)) to *maximize* blue (i.e., set it to 255) instead of clearing it. Is this useful? Would the red or green versions of the maximize function be useful? Under what conditions?

4.26 Write a function that takes a picture as input, and make the top half of the picture black.

4.27 The function copyHalf copied the top half of the picture into the bottom half. Write a new function copyUpHalf that copies the bottom half of the picture into the top.

4.28 The function mirrorHalf mirrors the top half of the picture onto the bottom half. Write a new function mirrorUpHalf that mirrors the top half of the picture into the top.

TO DIG DEEPER

A wonderful book on how vision works, and how artists have learned to manipulate it, is *Vision and Art: The Biology of Seeing* by Margaret Livingstone [28].

5

Picture Techniques with Selection

Chapter Learning Objectives

The media learning goals for this chapter are:

- To implement controlled color changes, like red-eye removal, sepia tones, and posterizing.
- To use background subtraction to separate foreground from background images and to understand when and how it will work.
- To use chromakey to separate foreground from background images.
- To draw lines and borders based on position.

The computer science goals for this chapter are:

- To use conditionals to select certain pixels.
- To use `if`, `else`, and `elif`.

5.1 REPLACING COLORS: RED-EYE, SEPIA TONES, AND POSTERIZING

Replacing colors with another color is pretty easy. We can do it broadly (across the entire picture) or just within a range (of *x* and *y* values). More useful perhaps is to change colors that are *close* to the color we want. This technique allows us to create some interesting effects across the entire picture, or tune the effect to do something specific to the picture, like turn the white of someone's teeth into purple.

Here's how we do the more interesting technique—we have the computer make a *decision*. In our program, we tell it what to *test*, and if the test proves true, we tell it what to do. We have the computer *select* certain pixels using an `if` statement.

An `if` statement uses a *test* and a block. If the test is true, the block of code is executed. The general form looks like this:

```
if (some test):
    print "The test was true."
print "This will print whether or not the test is true"
```

The "some test" can be any kind of *logical expression.* 1 < 2 is a logical expression that is always true. a < 2 is a logical expression that depends on the value of a. We can test on <, <= (less than or equal), == (for equality), >, >=, or <> (for not equal).

For the color replacement technique, we need a way to figure out if one color is *close* to another. We have a function in JES to do that called `distance`. The `distance` function returns a number that represents how close two colors are to one another. It does not figure out how similar colors are to a human's eye, which would be the best way of doing it. Instead, it computes a Euclidean distance between two colors in Cartesian coordinate space. That probably sounds complicated, but you probably learned the formula for telling the distance between (x_1, y_1) and (x_2, y_2) when you were in school.

$$\sqrt{((x_1 - x_2)^2 + (y_1 - y_2)^2)}$$

Think about what that would mean for the distance between two colors (red_1, $green_1$, $blue_1$) and (red_2, $green_2$, $blue_2$).

$$\sqrt{(red_1 - red_2)^2 + (green_1 - green_2)^2 + (blue_1 - blue_2)^2}$$

Here's how the distances work out in JES:

```
>>> print red
color r=255 g=0 b=0
>>> print magenta
color r=255 g=0 b=255
>>> print pink
color r=255 g=175 b=175
>>> print black
color r=0 g=0 b=0
>>> print white
color r=255 g=255 b=255
>>> print distance(white,black)
441.6729559300637
>>> print distance(white,pink)
113.13708498984761
>>> print distance(black,pink)
355.3519382246282
>>> print distance(magenta,pink)
192.41881404893857
>>> print distance(red,magenta)
255.0
>>> print distance(red,pink)
247.48737341529164
```

FIGURE 5.1
Changing brown to red.

We can use the `distance` function as part of a test for `if` to select just those pixels whose colors are close to the ones that we want to change. If the distance from a given pixel's color to a color that we want to change is less than a certain value, we go ahead and change the color. We consider the color "close enough."

Here's a program that replaces the brown color in Katie's hair with red. We used the JES picture tool to figure out roughly what the RGB values were for Katie's brown hair, then wrote a program to look for colors close to that and increase the redness of those pixels. We played a lot with the value that we used for distance (here, 50.0) and the amount to multiply the red value by (here, 2). The result is that the couch behind her gets increased too (Figure 5.1).

Program 48: Turn Katie into a Redhead

```
def turnRed():
  brown = makeColor(42,25,15)
  file="/Users/guzdial/Desktop/mediasources/katieFancy.jpg"
  picture=makePicture(file)
  for px in getPixels(picture):
    color = getColor(px)
    if distance(color,brown)<50.0:
      r=getRed(px)*2
      b=getBlue(px)
      g=getGreen(px)
```

```
        setColor(px,makeColor(r,g,b))
  show(picture)
  return picture
```

■

How It Works

This is actually quite similar to our increase-red program but uses an alternative method of setting the color.

- We create a `brown` color, which is what we found in Katie's hair using the picture tool in JES.

- We create the picture of Katie.

- For each of the pixels `px` in the picture, we get the color and then compare the color to the `brown` color we identified earlier. We want to know if the color at pixel `px` is *close enough* to `brown`. How do we define "close enough?" We say that it's within 50.0. Where did we get that number? We tried 10.0, but very little changed. We tried 100.0, and way too much matched (like the stripes in the couch behind Katie's head). We tried different numbers until we got the effect we wanted.

- If the color is "close enough," we get the red, green, and blue components of the color at `px`. We double the red by multiplying it by 2.

- We then set the color at `px` to a new color with the adjusted red and the same blue and green components. Then move on to the next pixel.

With the JES picture tool we can also figure out the coordinates just around Katie's face in order to do *just* the browns near her face. The upper left-hand corner of where Katie's face is at row 6 ($y = 6$) and column 63 ($x = 63$). The lower right-hand corner is $x = 125$ and $y = 76$. Each pixel actually knows where it is positioned in a picture. The function `getX(pixel)` returns the x-coordinate of the pixel. The function `getY(pixel)` returns the y-coordinate of the pixel. We can use the `if` statement to ask, "Is this pixel within the range of where we want to treat the pixels? Is the x between 63 and 125, and the y is between 6 and 76?" The effect isn't too good, though it's clear that it worked. The line of redness is too sharp and rectangular, e.g., you can see that it reaches the couch behind her for just a little bit (Figure 5.2).

Program 49: Color Replacement in a Range

```
def turnRedInRange():
  brown = makeColor(42,25,15)
  file="/Users/guzdial/Desktop/mediasources/katieFancy.jpg"
  picture=makePicture(file)
  for px in getPixels(picture):
    x = getX(px)
    y = getY(px)
    if 63 <= x <= 125:
      if 6 <= y <= 76:
        color = getColor(px)
        if distance(color,brown)<50.0:
          r=getRed(px)*2
```

FIGURE 5.2
Double red in rectangular area range.

```
        b=getBlue(px)
        g=getGreen(px)
        setColor(px,makeColor(r,g,b))
   show(picture)
   return picture
```

How It Works

We get the same brown color as before. We get the filename for KATIEFANCY.JPG, and make a picture from it. We address each pixel in the picture using the variable px. We get the *x*-coordinate and the *y*-coordinate from px. If x is in the right range (63 <= x <= 125), then we test the y. If the y is in the right range (6 <= y <= 76), then we get the color and check it against our brown. If it matches, we double the red.

5.1.1 Reducing Red-Eye

"Red-eye" is the effect where the flash from the camera bounces off the back of the subject's eyes. Reducing red-eye is a really simple matter. We find the pixels that are "pretty close" (a distance from red of 165 works well) to red, then insert a replacement color.

We probably don't want to change the whole picture. In Figure 5.3, Jenny is wearing a red dress. We don't want to wipe out that red. We'll fix that by only changing the *range* where Jenny's eyes are. Using the JES picture tool, we find the upper left and lower right corners of her eyes. Those points were (109, 91) and (202, 107).

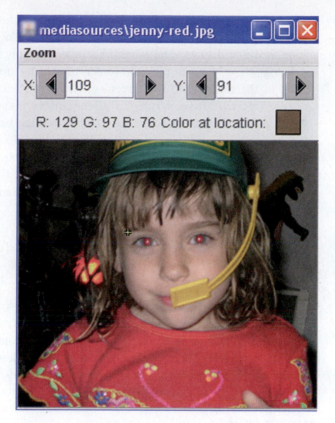

FIGURE 5.3
Finding the range of where Jenny's eyes are red.

Rather than the two `if` statements that we had in the last example, we can have a *single* `if` statement that specifies the whole test. We want to process the pixel if the *x*-coordinate is in the right range (`(startX <= x <= endX)`) *and* the *y*-coordinate is in the right range (`(startY <= y <= endY)`). Python understands the word and to join two logical expressions. The whole expression is *only* true if *both* of the side expressions are true.

Program 50: Reduce Red-Eye

```
def removeRedEye(pic,startX,startY,endX,endY,endColor):
  for px in getPixels(pic):
    x = getX(px)
    y = getY(px)
    if (startX <= x <= endX) and (startY <= y <= endY):
      if (distance(red,getColor(px)) < 165):
        setColor(px,endColor)
```

Let's try out this program using something new. Typing in long paths to a file-name is challenging. One character wrong, and it won't work. Using `pickAFile()`

isn't the right thing to do if we always want to use the same file–it's requiring extra work from the user. JES understands having a *media folder* or media path where your media will always be stored. Use the function setMediaPath() to open up a dialog where you can pick the folder where you store your media, or provide an input of the full path to the directory where you will be storing your media, e.g., setMediaPath("/Users/guzdial/Desktop/mediasources-4ed"). After you set your media path, you can reference files by just their base names, e.g., barbara.jpg. JES will know to check in the media folder for that file. If you need to get the full path to the file, you can execute getMediaPath("barbara.jpg"), and that will give you the full path to that file in the media path.

Once we setMediaPath, we can use our red-eye removal program like this:

```
>>> jenny=makePicture("jenny-red.jpg")
>>> # Same thing to say:
>>> # jenny = makePicture(getMediaPath("jenny-red.jpg"))
>>> removeRedEye(jenny, 109, 91, 202, 107, black)
>>> explore(jenny)
```

In this example, we replace the red with black—certainly other colors could be used for the replacement color. The result was good, and we can check that the eye really does now have all-black pixels (Figure 5.4). Note that this program is using the color name black. You may remember that JES predefines a bunch of colors for you: black, white, blue, red, green, gray, lightGray, darkGray, yellow, orange, pink, magenta, and cyan.

How It Works

This algorithm is really very similar to the one that we used for changing Katie's hair to red. In that program, we looked for a specific shade of brown, then doubled red when there was a match. Here, we're looking for pixels near to red, then replace it with an input endcolor.

- For each pixel px, we get the x and y for that pixel.
- We check to see if the pixel is within the range we need for the eyes: if (startX <= x <= endX) and (startY <= y <= endY):.
- If we're in the right range, we check to see if the color of this pixel px is close to red (the predefined color red). We determine "close enough" by looking for a distance within a *threshold value*. We tried different distances and settled on 165 as the distance that caught most of the eye redness that we cared about. If the match is good, we replace the pixel color with the endcolor.

5.1.2   Sepia-Toned and Posterized Pictures: Using Conditionals to Choose the Color

So far, we've done color subtraction by simply replacing one color with another. We can be more sophisticated in our color swapping. We can look for a range of colors by using if and choosing to replace some function of the original color or by changing to a specific color. The results are quite interesting.

FIGURE 5.4
Checking that the red has been changed to black.

For example, we might want to generate sepia-toned prints. Older prints sometimes have a yellowish tint. We could just do an overall color change but the end result isn't aesthetically pleasing. By looking for different kinds of colors—highlights, shadows—and treating them differently, we can get a better effect (Figure 5.5).

The way we do this is to first convert everything to grayscale, both because older prints were in a grayscale and because it makes it a little easier to work with. We then look for high, middle, and low ranges of color (really, luminance) and change them separately. (Why these particular values? Trial and error—tweaking them until we liked the effect.)

Program 51: Convert a Picture to Sepia Tones

```
def sepiaTint(picture):
  #Convert image to grayscale
  grayScaleNew(picture)

  #loop through picture to tint pixels
  for p in getPixels(picture):
    red = getRed(p)
```

FIGURE 5.5
Original scene (*left*) and using our sepia-tone program (*right*).

```
blue = getBlue(p)

#tint shadows
if (red < 63):
  red = red*1.1
  blue = blue*0.9

#tint midtones
 if (red > 62 and red < 192):
  red = red*1.15
  blue = blue*0.85

#tint highlights
if (red > 191):
  red = red*1.08
  if (red > 255):
    red = 255
  blue = blue*0.93

#set the new color values
setBlue(p, blue)
setRed(p, red)
```

How It Works

The function starts by taking in a picture as input, then uses our grayScaleNew function to convert it to grayscale. (We recommend that you copy the grayScaleNew function into the Program Area along with sepiaTint—we just don't show it here.) For each of the pixels, we grab the redness and blueness of the pixel. We know that the red and blue will be the *same* values, since the picture is now all gray, but we'll want the redness and blueness for *changing*. We look for specific ranges of colors and treat them differently. Note that with tinting the highlights (where the light is brightest), we have an if inside an if block. The idea here is that we don't want the values to wrap around—if red gets too high, we want to cap it at 255. Finally, we set the blue and red values to the new red and blue values, and move on to the next pixel.

Posterizing is a very similar process that results in converting a picture to a smaller number of colors. We're going to do that by looking for a specific range of values, then setting all values in that range to *one* value. The result is that we reduce the number of colors in the picture (Figure 5.6). For example, in the program below, if red is 1, 2, 3, ... , or 64, we make it 31. We thus wipe a whole range of red variance and make it one specific red value. We tried this on a picture of a computing student, Anthony. The file we are processing has a path like "c:/ip-book/mediasources/anthony.jpg", but if we have used setMediaPath(), we can just say "anthony.jpg".

```
>>> student = makePicture("anthony.jpg")
>>> explore(student)
>>> posterize(student)
>>> explore(student)
```

FIGURE 5.6
Reducing the colors (*right*) from the original (*left*).

Program 52: Posterizing a Picture

```
def posterize(picture):

    #loop through the pixels
    for p in getPixels(picture):
        #get the RGB values
        red = getRed(p)
        green = getGreen(p)
        blue = getBlue(p)

        #check and set red values
        if(red < 64):
            setRed(p, 31)
        if(red > 63 and red < 128):
            setRed(p, 95)
        if(red > 127 and red < 192):
            setRed(p, 159)
        if(red > 191 and red < 256):
            setRed(p, 223)

        #check and set green values
        if(green < 64):
            setGreen(p, 31)
        if(green > 63 and green < 128):
            setGreen(p, 95)
        if(green > 127 and green < 192):
            setGreen(p, 159)
        if(green > 191 and green < 256):
            setGreen(p, 223)

        #check and set blue values
        if(blue < 64):
            setBlue(p, 31)
        if(blue > 63 and blue < 128):
            setBlue(p, 95)
        if(blue > 127 and blue < 192):
            setBlue(p, 159)
        if(blue > 191 and blue < 256):
            setBlue(p, 223)
```

An interesting effect comes from using both grayscale and posterize together. We do this by computing a luminance but then only set the pixel's color to either black or white—only two levels. The result is a picture that looks a bit like a stamped image or like a charcoal drawing (Figure 5.7). We found that 64 is a good value for choosing when to make something black or white, but try other ones, too.

Program 53: Posterize to Two Gray Levels

```
def grayPosterize(pic):
    for p in getPixels(pic):
```

FIGURE 5.7
Picture posterized to two gray levels.

```
r = getRed(p)
g = getGreen(p)
b = getBlue(p)
luminance = (r+g+b)/3
if luminance < 64:
  setColor(p,black)
if luminance >= 64:
  setColor(p,white)
```

Debugging Tip: Parentheses Are Not Necessary, but Can Be Useful

Notice that we wrote if luminance < 64 above, not if (luminance < 64). You do not *have* to have parentheses around the logical test. However, if you start creating more complicated logical tests with and and or, you may want the parentheses to help make sense of what you are testing.

5.2   COMPARING PIXELS: EDGE DETECTION

Edge detection is a process where we compare pixels to decide whether to set the pixel to black or white. We want to use the idea of luminance, which we saw earlier can be estimated by summing or averaging the red, green, and blue components of the pixel. The goal is to try to draw lines the way an artist might see lines and sketch a drawing.

It's really an amazing feature of our visual systems that we can look at a line drawing of someone and pick out a face or other features. Look at the world around you. There really aren't sharp lines defining features of the world. There are no clear lines around your nose or eyes, but any child can draw a face with a checkmark for a nose and two circles for eyes—and we will all recognize it as a face! Typically, we *see* a line where there is a difference in luminance.

Here's a couple of different ways to do edge detection. In each one, we're going to compare a given pixel to the one below and to the right. Comparing to more pixels (say, top and left, too) might make for a better edge detection. These two examples give a sense for how it all works.

In our first attempt, we will do something simpler than computing luminance. We sum the red, green, and blue from our current pixel px, and the red, green, and blue from the pixel to the bottom and right of the current pixel. We then compute the *difference* of the two sums, and set the color to that difference in the red, green, and blue components. The effect is a white sketch over a black background (Figure 5.8).

You might be wondering how we get that *other* pixel, the one at the bottom and right of our current pixel. We will use getPixel which takes a picture, an *x*-coordinate, and a *y*-coordinate as inputs. It returns the pixel at that *x* and *y*. Given the *x* and *y* from our current pixel px, it's pretty easy to use getPixel to get the pixel at $x + 1$ and $y + 1$. We just have to make sure that we don't try to end up getting a pixel beyond the edge of the picture.

Program 54: Create a Simple Line Drawing Using Simple Edge Detection

```
def edge(source):
  for px in getPixels(source):
    x = getX(px)
    y = getY(px)
    if y < getHeight(source)-1 and x < getWidth(source)-1:
      sum = getRed(px)+getGreen(px)+getBlue(px)
      botrt = getPixel(source,x+1,y+1)
      sum2 = getRed(botrt)+getGreen(botrt)+getBlue(botrt)
      diff = abs(sum2-sum)
      newcolor = makeColor(diff,diff,diff)
      setColor(px,newcolor)
```

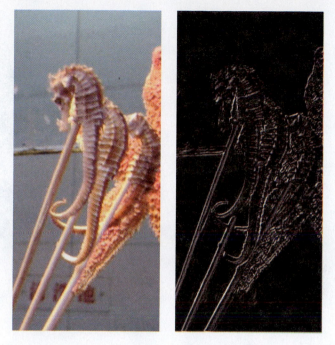

FIGURE 5.8
Sea horses on a stick (*left*) converted to a "line drawing" (*right*).

How It Works

We walk through all the pixels, where each pixel is px. We get the x and y from the pixel. Since we are going to look to the bottom and right of each pixel, i.e., getPixel(source,x+1,y+1), we only want to process those pixels *before* the right and bottom edge. So we test if y < getHeight(source)-1 and x < getWidth (source)-1.

We then do a bit of a trick. Since the luminance is the average of the three pixels, and we're going to compare two pixels, we simply sum the red, green, and blue components of each, the pixel at px and the bottom right pixel (botrt = getPixel(source,x+1, y+1)). We get the difference of the two color sums, using the *absolute* value (abs) because we only care about the *difference* between the two color sums. We don't really care which one is larger. We use the difference for the red, green, and blue components of the color that we put into px. Since most of the differences are small, the colors are mostly very dark. When there's a larger difference, the colors look more white (Figure 5.8).

While this code works, it's not *obvious* how it works. We can compute the luminance explicitly and compare the luminance between the current pixel and the one at the bottom right (Figure 5.9). To make it easier to write this code, we introduce a *helper function* named luminance that takes a pixel in as input and *returns* the luminance for that pixel. Think of returning a value as being what the functions abs or pickAFile or makePicture do. It turns out that we can write functions that return values, too.

FIGURE 5.9
Sea horses on a stick converted to a "line drawing" with our new process.

Program 55: Create a Simple Line Drawing Using Clearer Edge Detection

```
def luminance(pixel):
  r = getRed(pixel)
  g = getGreen(pixel)
  b = getBlue(pixel)
  return (r+g+b)/3

def edgedetect(source):
  for px in getPixels(source):
    x = getX(px)
    y = getY(px)
    if y < getHeight(source)-1 and x < getWidth(source)-1:
      botrt = getPixel(source,x+1,y+1)
      thislum = luminance(px)
      brlum = luminance(botrt)
      if abs(brlum-thislum) > 10:
        setColor(px,black)
      if abs(brlum-thislum) <= 10:
        setColor(px,white)
```

How It Works

Like the gray-levels posterizing, the goal here is to set each pixel to either black or white, depending on whether there is a luminance difference or not.

The first five lines define our `luminance` function. It accepts a `pixel` as input. The function then pulls out the red, green, and blue components, and returns the average of the three of them. Once we define the `luminance` function, we can simply call `luminance` with a pixel, and trust that the number it returns is the luminance value.

We can then define our `edgedetect` function. Like the `edge` function, we process all pixels `px`, get each pixel's `x` and `y`. We test to make sure that we are still within bounds, and we get the pixel at the bottom right `botright`. Here comes the difference.

Now, we compute a luminance value for the pixel `px`, and another luminance value for the pixel at `botrt`. We call this first one `thislum` (*this* luminance value) and the second one `brlum` (bottom right luminance). We check if the absolute value of the difference is greater than 10, and if so, we make `px` black. If the difference is less than or equal to 10, we make it white. (Why 10? Just because it worked. Do try different values!) The effect (Figure 5.9) is kind of the inverse of the `edge` function (Figure 5.8), with maybe a bit more detail.

There are algorithms to do much better edge detection and line drawing. For example, here we're simply setting each pixel to black or white. We're not really considering the notion of a "line." We could use techniques like blurring to smooth the image and make the dots seem more like lines. We could also make pixels black only if we are going to make nearby pixels black; that is, create a line rather than simply make dots.

5.3   BACKGROUND SUBTRACTION

Let's imagine that you have a picture of someone and a picture of where they stood without them there (Figure 5.10). Could you *subtract* the background of the person (i.e., figure out where the colors are exactly the same), and then replace another background? Say, of the moon (Figure 5.11)?

Program 56: Subtract the Background and Replace It with a New One

```
def swapBack(pict,bg,newBg):
  for px in getPixels(pict):
    x = getX(px)
    y = getY(px)
```

FIGURE 5.10
A picture of a child (Katie) and the background without her.

FIGURE 5.11
A new background: the moon.

```
bgPx = getPixel(bg,x,y)
pxcol = getColor(px)
bgcol = getColor(bgPx)
if (distance(pxcol,bgcol)<15.0):
  newcol=getColor(getPixel(newBg,x,y))
  setColor(px,newcol)
```

We run it like this:

```
>>> kid = makePicture("kid-in-frame.jpg")
>>> bg = makePicture("bgframe.jpg")
>>> moon = makePicture("moon-surface.jpg")
>>> swapBack(kid,bg,moon)
>>> explore(kid)
```

How It Works

The function `swapBack` (swap background) takes a picture (with both foreground and background in it), a picture of the background, and a new background. For all the pixels in the input picture:

- We walk through all the pixels `px` in the picture `pict`. We get the `x` and `y` from that pixel.
- We get the matching pixel (same *x* and same *y*) from the `bg` picture.
- We get the colors from `px` and from `bgPx`.
- Compare the distances between the colors. We use a threshold value here of 15.0, but do try it with others.
- If the distance is small (less than the threshold value), then assume that the pixel is part of the background. Take the color from the pixel at the same coordinates in the *new* background (`newBg`) and set the pixel in the input picture to the new color from the new background.

You can do this, but the effect isn't as good as you'd like (Figure 5.12). Our daughter's shirt color was too close to the color of the wall, so the moon bled into her shirt. Though the light was dim, a shadow is definitely having an effect here. The shadow wasn't in the background picture, so the algorithm treats the shadow as part of the foreground. This result suggests that the difference in color between the background and the foreground is important for making background subtraction work—and so is having good lighting!

Mark tried the same thing with a picture of our dog on a chair. Mark really tried to get the pixels to line up (camera on a table, not moving), but there were subtle differences between them (Figure 5.13). The leaves in the background moved, and the camera moved just enough so that the grain in the wood and siding behind the dog didn't line up. The background swap (with the moon) worked, but didn't work as well as with Katie. We tried twice, with a threshold of 20 and with 50. The threshold value

FIGURE 5.12
Katie on the moon.

FIGURE 5.13
A dog sitting on a chair (*left*) and a chair without the dog (*right*).

FIGURE 5.14
Putting the dog on the moon, with a threshold of 20 (*left*) and 50 (*right*).

of 50 is closer, but we then we get bleed-through around the dog's eyes and we still can't make up for the leaves moving in the background (Figure 5.14).

```
>>> dog = makePicture("dog-bg.jpg")
>>> bg = makePicture("nodog-bg.jpg")
>>> swapBack(dog,bg,moon)
>>> explore(dog)
```

Simply changing the threshold doesn't always improve things. It certainly makes more of the foreground get classified as background. But for problems like bleed-through because of matching colors between the clothes and the background, the threshold value doesn't help much.

5.4   CHROMAKEY

Television weather forecasters wave to show a storm front coming in across a map. The reality is that they are being filmed standing before a background of a fixed color (usually blue or green) and then that background color is replaced digitally with pixels from the desired map. This is called **chromakey**. It's easier to replace a known color and isn't as sensitive to lighting problems. Mark took our son's blue sheet, attached it to the family entertainment center, then took a picture of himself in front of it using a timer on a camera (Figure 5.15).

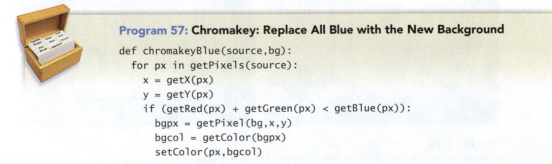

Program 57: Chromakey: Replace All Blue with the New Background

```
def chromakeyBlue(source,bg):
  for px in getPixels(source):
    x = getX(px)
    y = getY(px)
    if (getRed(px) + getGreen(px) < getBlue(px)):
      bgpx = getPixel(bg,x,y)
      bgcol = getColor(bgpx)
      setColor(px,bgcol)
```

FIGURE 5.15
Mark in front of a blue sheet.

How It Works

Here we take in just a source (with both foreground and background in it) and a new background bg. *These must be the same size!* Mark used the JES picture tool to come up with a rule for what would be "blue" for this program. He didn't want to look for equality or even a distance to the color (0, 0, 255) because he knew that very little of the blue would be *exactly* full-intensity blue. He found that pixels he thought of as blue tended to have smaller red and green values, and in fact, the blue values were greater than the sum of the red and the green. So that's what he looked for in this program. Wherever the blue was greater than the red and green, he swapped in the new background pixel's color instead.

The function walks through all of the pixels using the variable px. For each one, the x and y positions are computed. If the blue of that pixel px is greater than the red plus the green, then we get the background pixel at the same *x* and *y*. We get the color from that pixel, and set it as the color in the source picture at the pixel px.

The effect is really quite striking (Figure 5.16). Do note the "folds" in the lunar surface, though.

You don't really want to do chromakey with a common color like red—something that there's a lot of in your face. Mark tried it with the two pictures in Figure 5.17—one with the flash on and the other with the flash off. He changed the test to if getRed(p) > (getGreen(p) + getBlue(p)):. The one without the flash was terrible—the student's face was "jungle-ified." The one with the flash was better but the flash is still visible after the swap (Figure 5.18). It's clear why moviemakers and weather people use blue or green backgrounds for chromakey—there's less overlap with common colors, like face colors.

Getting chromakey to work just right takes some careful photography, e.g. good lighting and good choice of background color. But in an animation program, it is really easy to get all those aspects just right. Barbara generated the image in Figure 5.19

FIGURE 5.16
Mark on the moon.

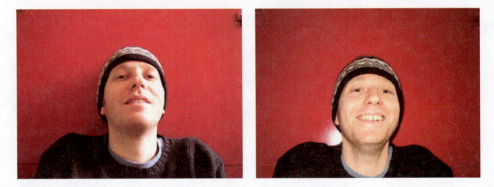

FIGURE 5.17
Student in front of a red background without the flash (*left*) and with flash on (*right*).

using the programming language Alice.[1] It's the character Alice in front of a completely green background. (Alice has blue eyes and a blue dress, so green is a better choice for chromakey for her.)

We wrote a slightly different chromakey function. This one replaces green pixels with a background color.

Program 58: ChromakeyGreen: Replace All Green with the New Background

```
def chromakeyGreen(source,bg):
  for px in getPixels(source):
    x = getX(px)
    y = getY(px)
    if (getRed(px) + getBlue(px) < getGreen(px)):
```

[1]http://www.alice.org

FIGURE 5.18
Using chromakey program with red background, flash off (*left*) and flash on (*right*).

FIGURE 5.19
The character Alice on a completely green background.

```
bgpx = getPixel(bg,x,y)
bgcol = getColor(bgpx)
setColor(px,bgcol)
```

We ran this one twice. Once, with the image saved from Alice as JPEG and once as PNG. Consider the results in Figure 5.20. Both clearly show Alice in the jungle, but look at the feet. Why does the PNG Alice have shoes on, while the JPEG Alice does not? JPEG is a *lossy* format. Some detail is lost in terms of color values when saving a picture as JPEG. PNG is a *lossless* format. PNG maintains color detail. Our suspicion is that the JPEG version of Alice blended the shoe color with the background color

FIGURE 5.20
Alice JPEG in the jungle (*top*) and PNG (*bottom*).

enough that the chromakey function got confused. The PNG version kept the black of
the shoes distinct, so they were retained after the chromakey function.

```
>>> alice = makePicture("Alice.jpg")
>>> chromakeyGreen(alice,jungle)
>>> explore(alice)
>>> alice = makePicture("Alice.png")
>>> chromakeyGreen(alice,jungle)
>>> explore(alice)
```

The devices and software that implement chromakey professionally use a somewhat
different process than this. Our algorithm looks for the color to be replaced, then does
the replacement. In professional chromakey, a *mask* is produced. A mask is of the same
size as the original image, where pixels to be changed are white in the mask, and those

that should not be changed are black. The mask is then used to decide which pixels are to be changed. An advantage to using a mask is that we separate the processes of (a) detecting which pixels are to be changed and (b) making the changes to the pixels. By separating them, we can improve on each, and thus improve the whole effect.

5.5   COLORING IN RANGES

In this chapter, we have used a general technique of iterating across all pixels, computing the x- and y-coordinates, then using an if statement to decide if the pixel needed to be manipulated based on its position. We can use this general approach to do a wide variety of changes to a picture. We can put borders on a picture, or apply image techniques to only part of the picture.

5.5.1   Adding a Border

For example, let's say that we wanted to put a blue and white border on the picture of Greek ruins. Blue and white are the colors on the Greek flag. We want to create the effect seen in Figure 5.21.

Program 59: Add Blue and White Borders

```
def greekBorder(pic):
  bottom = getHeight(pic)-10
  for px in getPixels(pic):
    y = getY(px)
    if y < 10:
      setColor(px,blue)
    if y > bottom:
      setColor(px,white)
```

FIGURE 5.21
An image of Greek ruins (*left*) with a blue and white border added at top and bottom (*right*).

How It Works

This function adds a blue border 10 pixels high to the top of the input picture, and a white border 10 pixels high to the bottom of the input picture. The coordinates of the top border are easy. We want to color blue all pixels whose *y* value is less than 10. The bottom is a little trickier. We compute a `bottom` value which is the height of the picture minus 10. We want to color white all pixels whose *y* value is greater than the `bottom`.

At the top of the function, we compute `bottom`. We iterate over all pixels `px`, but we only need to get the y value. If y is less than 10, we set the pixel to blue. If the x is greater than the bottom, we make the pixel white.

5.5.2   Lightening the Right Half of a Picture

We learned earlier how to process the vertical halves of a picture differently. We can index the pixels and use a `range` of 0 to `len(pixels)/2` to process the top half of a picture. But how do we process horizontal slices of the picture?

We can use our technique of iterating across all pixels, getting the coordinates of the pixel, and then using an `if` statement to process the pixels we care about. The function `rightHalfBright` below makes the right half of a picture brighter (Figure 5.22).

Program 60: Lighten the Right Half of a Picture

```
def rightHalfBright(pic):
  halfway = getWidth(pic) / 2
  for px in getPixels(pic):
    x = getX(px)
    if x > halfway:
      color = getColor(px)
      setColor(px,makeLighter(color))
```

FIGURE 5.22
An image of a garden (*left*) and with the right side lightened (*right*).

How It Works

The function `rightHalfBright` takes a picture in as input. We compute the `halfway` point, the middle of the picture horizontally. For each pixel `px` in the pixels of the picture, we get the *x*-coordinate, then check to see if the `x` is greater than (right of) the halfway point. If it's on the right-hand side, we get the color, make it lighter, and set it back to the pixel.

5.6   SELECTING WITHOUT RETESTING

Consider the `grayPosterize` function from earlier in the chapter:

```
def grayPosterize(pic):
  for p in getPixels(pic):
    r = getRed(p)
    g = getGreen(p)
    b = getBlue(p)
    luminance = (r+g+b)/3
    if luminance < 64:
      setColor(p,black)
    if luminance >= 64:
      setColor(p,white)
```

If the `luminance` is not less than 64, it *must* be greater than or equal to 64. To test `luminance` again does seem somewhat inefficient. We just *did* that. We basically want to take a fork here: Either set the pixel to white, or to black—and there is no other option.

Because that decision fork happens so often, Python (and many other languages) gives you a way of making just this kind of choice, with an `else`. An `else` comes after an `if` and precedes a block. The *else block* only occurs if the `if` test is *false*.

We can rewrite that program like this:

Program 61: Gray Posterize to Two Levels, with `else`

```
def grayPosterize(pic):
  for p in getPixels(pic):
    r = getRed(p)
    g = getGreen(p)
    b = getBlue(p)
    luminance = (r+g+b)/3
    if luminance < 64:
      setColor(p,black)
    else:
      setColor(p,white)
```

Now sometimes you want to take a fork with three options. If something is true, you want to do one thing, then you want to make a choice of two other paths. You want to say `if` this, then do one thing, `else if` this other thing is true, take path two, `else` take path three. That `else if` combination is so common, it can be abbreviated `elif`.

Here is an example where we posterize to black, white, and red. If the luminance is low, we make the pixel red. If the luminance is very high, we make it white. If between, we make it red. The result can be seen in Figure 5.23. We test it using the same picture of Anthony that we used earlier (Figure 5.7) for comparison.

Program 62: Gray Posterize to Three Levels, with `elif`

```
def posterizeBWR(pic):
  for p in getPixels(pic):
    r = getRed(p)
    g = getGreen(p)
    b = getBlue(p)
    luminance = (r+g+b)/3
    if luminance < 64:
      setColor(p,black)
    elif luminance > 120:
      setColor(p,white)
    else:
      setColor(p,red)
```

Did that paragraph describing `else` and `elif` get confusing? That's the problem of `else` and `elif`. Compare the two versions of posterizing to black and white. They both

FIGURE 5.23
Anthony posterized to black, white, and red.

do the exact same thing. The second one *implies* the test of `luminance >= 64` in the `else`—but it isn't explicit. Is that a bad thing? Turns out that it's bad for computers but great for humans.

An `else` keeps the computer from making a second test, which is a bit more efficient. But making it *explicit* actually improves readability. In at least one study,[2] having that explicit second test can improve the ability of new programmers to understand their programs by *ten times*!

To repeat: Programs are for people, not for computers. Write your programs to be understandable first. Worry about efficiency second.

PROGRAMMING SUMMARY

Here are the functions introduced in this chapter:

`setMediaPath()`	Lets you pick the media directory using a file chooser.
`setMediaPath(directory)`	Lets you specify the media directory.
`getMediaPath(baseName)`	Takes a base filename, then returns the complete path to that file (assuming it's in the media directory).

PROBLEMS

5.1 Write a function called `changeColor` that takes as input a picture *and* an amount to increase or decrease a color by *and* a number 1 (for red), 2 (for green), or 3 (for blue). The amount will be a number between −.99 and .99.

- `changeColor(pict,-.10,1)` should decrease the amount of red in the picture by 10%.

- `changeColor(pict,.30,2)` should increase the amount of green in the picture by 30%.

- `changeRed(pict,0,3)` should do nothing at all to the amount of blue (or red or green) in the picture.

5.2 Imagine that you have a picture, and you are painting a copy of it. But you have only eight colors. Write a function that inputs a picture, and makes these changes to each pixel. For each of red, green, and blue, if the component is less than 100, make it zero. Otherwise, make it 255.

5.3 Write a function that inputs a picture, a color, and a number. The number is the width of a border that you are to draw *on all four sides* of the picture, with the given color. You can assume that the number will always be an integer less than 50.

[2]Sime, M., Green, T., & Guest, D. (1976). Scope marking in computer conditionals: A psychological evaluation. *International Journal of Man-Machine Studies*, 9, 107–118.

5.4   The process we used to draw borders could actually be used to draw lines as well. For example, if you have a square picture, every pixel whose x value equals its y value lies on the diagonal from upper-left to lower-right corners. Write a function that inputs a square picture (you can assume square) and an input color, and draws a diagonal line from upper-left to lower-right using the input color for the line color.

5.5   Write a function that uses the same process to draw a vertical line down the middle of the picture, and a horizontal line across the middle of the picture, neatly separating the picture into four quadrants. This function can work for any square or rectangular picture.

5.6   It's a little more trickier to write a function that draws a diagonal from lower-left to upper-right for a square picture. Note that the sum of the x and the y should be equal to the number of pixels in the line.

5.7   Write a function to put 10 pixel wide "prison cell bars" on the left border, center, and right border of an input picture.

5.8   Write a function that posterizes an input picture along a very specific process. If the red value is greater than 180, then set the pixel to red. If not, then check if the blue value is greater than 180, and if so, set the pixel to blue. If not, then check if the green value is greater than 180, and if so, set the pixel to green. If none of the three channels is greater than 180, set the pixel to black.

5.9   Write a function that pinkifies white in a picture. Input a picture, then check each pixel to see if the red, green, and blue are all over 100. If so, set that pixel to pink.

5.10   Write a function that decreases red by 50% on the left side of the picture, and increases it by 200% on the right side.

5.11   Write a function to make lighter the left side of a picture, and turn the right side into a grayscale.

5.12   Write a function that treats horizontal thirds of the picture differently. Make the top third of an input picture brighter, then the middle third decrease blue and green by 30%, then the bottom third should be made negative.

5.13   Rewrite Program 52 (page 124) using this helper function to make it much shorter.
```
def pickPosterizeValue(current):
  if (current < 64):
    return 31
  if (current > 63 and current < 128):
    return 95
  if (current > 127 and current < 192):
    return 159
  if (current > 191 and current < 256):
    return 223
```

5.14   What will be printed for this function if you executed each of these:

    (a) testMe (1, 2, 3)

(b) `testMe (3, 2, 1)`

(c) `testMe (5, 75, 20)`

```
def testMe(p,q,r):
  if q > 50:
    print r
  value = 10
  for i in range(0,p):
    print "Hello"
    value = value - 1
  print value
  print r
```

5.15 Start with a picture of someone you know and make some specific color changes to it:

- Turn the teeth purple.

- Turn the eyes red.

- Turn the hair orange.

Of course, if your friend's teeth are already purple, or eyes red, or hair orange, choose a different target color.

5.16 Write a program `checkLuminance` that will input red, green, and blue values, and compute the luminance using the weighted average (as below). But then print out a warning to the user based on the computed luminance:

- If the luminance is less than 10, "That's going to be awfully dark."

- If the luminance is between 50 and 200, "Looks like a good range."

- Over 250, "That's going to be nearly white!"

5.17 Try doing chromakey in a range. The picture "statue-tower.jpg" has a blue, but not blue enough background to work with `chromakeyBlue`. However, if you change the rule to `getRed(px) + getGreen(px) < getBlue(px)+100`, it works great for the sky—but messes up near the ground.

- Change `chromakeyBlue` to use the modified rule, and apply it to "statue-tower.jpg."

- Now, write `chromakeyBlueAbove` to take in an input picture, a new background, and a number. The number is a *y* value, and you should only do chromakey to pixels above that input *y*. Apply it to "statue-tower.jpg" so that the blue of the sky gets changed to the moon or the jungle, but the area near the ground is not touched.

5.18 Try doing background subtraction in a range. Take the "dog-bg.jpg" and "nodog-bg.jpg" pictures as input, with an upper left-hand corner *x* and *y*, and lower right-hand corner *x* and *y*. Do background subtraction *just* around the dog in the chair, leaving the leaves and the house alone.

5.19 Write a function to blend two pictures, starting with the top third of the first picture and then blend the two together in the middle third and then show the last third of the second picture. This works best if the two pictures are the same size.

5.20 Write a function to interleave two pictures taken as input. Take the first 20 pixels from the first picture and then 20 pixels from the second picture and then the next 20 pixels from the first picture and then the next 20 pixels from the second picture and so on till all the pixels have been used.

5.21 Write a function to blend two pictures: 25% of one picture blended with 75% of another.

5.22 Rewrite Program 52 (page 124) to use an `if` with an `else`.

5.23 Why do moviemakers use a green or blue screen for special effects instead of a red screen?

5.24 Get some green posterboard and take a picture of a friend in front of it. Now use chromakey to put her or him in the jungle. Or better yet, in Paris.

TO DIG DEEPER

John Maeda designed a processing environment (`http://www.processing.org`) for the development of interactive art, live video processing, and data visualization. Processing allows you to do some of the same effects as in this chapter.

CHAPTER

6

Modifying Pixels by Position

Chapter Learning Objectives

The media learning goals for this chapter are:

- To mirror pictures horizontally or vertically.
- To compose pictures into one another and create collages.
- To rotate pictures.
- To scale pictures smaller and larger.
- To use blending to combine images.
- To be able to add text and shapes to existing pictures.
- To use blurring to smooth degradation.

The computer science goals for this chapter are:

- To use nested loops for addressing elements of a matrix.
- To loop through only part of an array.
- To develop some debugging strategies—specifically, to use print statements to explore executing code.
- To be able to choose between using vector and bitmapped image formats.
- To be able to choose when one should write a program for a task versus using existing applications software.

6.1   PROCESSING PIXELS FASTER

In the last chapter, we manipulated only part of a picture, by looping through all of the pixels and picking out the ones we wanted to manipulate based on their x and y position. This worked well. But it worked slowly.

The loop `for pixel in getPixels(picture):` processes *every* pixel. The `if` statement pulls out the ones that we care about. But processing *every* pixel can take a long time, especially in a big picture. If we only want to do something to a small number of pixels, it is a waste of our time to process all the pixels, when we only want to process a few of them.

So far, we have used a `for` loop to process all pixels. A `for` loop is actually a general statement for looping. We can use it to loop over *only* the pixels that we actually care about. To do that, we need to use a `range` function.

Here's a way to think about the `range` function. Ask someone to clap her hands 10 times. How do you know if she did it right? You probably counted each clap. So the first time she clapped you thought 1, the second time 2, and so on till she stopped. If the count was 10 when she stopped, then she clapped 10 times. What value did the count start at? If you thought 1 after she clapped one time then the count was actually zero before the first clap.

A `for` loop that is used to compute an *index* is similar to this. It makes an index variable take on each value in turn from a sequence. We've used sequences of pixels generated from `getPixels` but it turns out that we can easily generate sequences of numbers using the Python function `range`. The function `range` takes two inputs: an integer starting point and an integer ending point. The second number *is not included in the sequence*. While it may seem strange, we will see that it is actually handy for the things that we want to index. Here are some examples of the `range` function. The range function starts at the first number, and keeps adding numbers until it gets up to the second number. In the last example, the first number is larger than the first, so no numbers get generated at all.

```
>>> print range(0,3)
[0, 1, 2]
>>> print range(0,10)
[0, 1, 2, 3, 4, 5, 6, 7, 8, 9]
>>> print range(3,1)
[]
```

The square bracket stuff is (e.g., `[0,1,2]` in the first example above) indicating a sequence, or for our purposes, an *array*. It's how Python prints out a series of numbers to show that this is an array.[1] If we use `range` to generate the array for the `for` loop, our variable will walk through each of the sequential numbers we generate.

Optionally, `range` can take a third input: how much to increment between elements of the sequence.

```
>>> print range(0,10,3)
[0, 3, 6, 9]
>>> print range(0,10,2)
[0, 2, 4, 6, 8]
```

Since most loops do start with zero (e.g., when indexing some data), providing only a *single* input to `range` *presumes* a zero starting point.

---

[1]Technically, `range` returns a *sequence*, which is a somewhat different collection of data than an array.

```
>>> print range(10)
[0, 1, 2, 3, 4, 5, 6, 7, 8, 9]
```

6.1.1   Looping across the Pixels with Range

If we want to know both the *x* and *y* values for a pixel we will have to use *two* `for` loops—one to move horizontally (*x*) across the pixels and the other to move vertically (*y*) to get every pixel. The function `getPixels` did this inside itself, to make it easier to write simple picture manipulations. The inner loop will be *nested* inside the outer loop, literally inside its block. At this point, you're going to have to be careful in how you indent your code to make sure that your blocks line up right.

You will need to understand how coordinates for pixels in a picture work. Let's get a picture (Figure 6.1) and look at its coordinates.

```
>>> h = makePicture("horse.jpg")
>>> print h
Picture, filename /Users/guzdial/Desktop/mediasources-4ed/horse.jpg height 640 width 480
>>> print getHeight(h)
640
>>> print getWidth(h)
480
>>> print getPixel(h,0,0)
Pixel red=62 green=78 blue=49
>>> print getPixel(h,479,639)
Pixel red=113 green=89 blue=77
>>> print getPixel(h,480,640)
getPixel(picture,x,y): x (= 480) is less than 0 or bigger than the width (= 479)
```

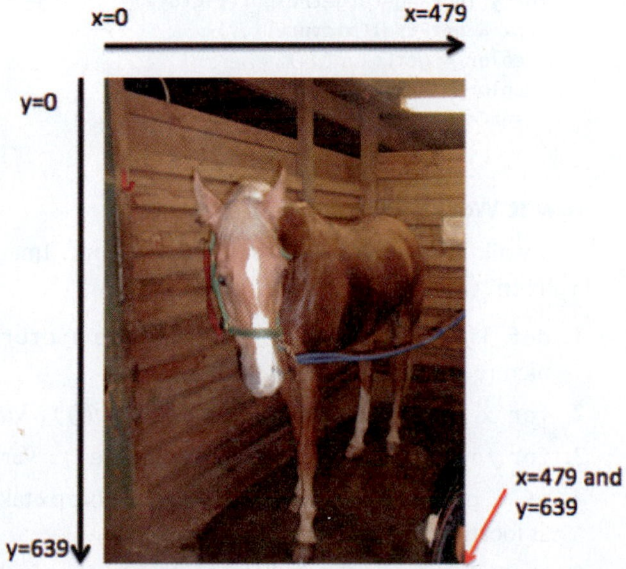

FIGURE 6.1
The picture coordinates.

```
The error was:
Inappropriate argument value (of correct type).
An error occurred attempting to pass an argument to a function.
```

The picture in (Figure 6.1) is 480 pixels across, and 640 pixels top to bottom. We say that the width is 480, and the height is 640. That means that the upper leftmost pixel is at (0, 0), where $x=0$ and $y=0$. The bottom rightmost pixel is *not* at (480, 640)—that's beyond the edge of the picture and accessing it generates an error. The bottom rightmost pixel is (479, 630).

To process all those pixels, our loops will look something like this:

```
for x in range(0,getWidth(picture)):
  for y in range(0,getHeight(picture)):
    pixel=getPixel(picture,x,y)
```

We call these *nested loops* because the *y* loop is inside the *x* loop. For each value of *x*, we generate all the values of *y*. For each value of *x* and *y*, the body of the loop (e.g., `pixel=getPixel(picture,x,y)` in the example) is executed once. Here is where the fact that the `range` function goes up to *but does not include* the last second input works. The *x* coordinate goes up to *but does not include* the `getWidth` of the picture, and the *y* coordinate goes up to *but does not include* the `getHeight` of the picture.

Here's an example of rewriting an early function, Program 39 (page 100), using explicit x and y indices to access the pixel.

Program 63: Lighten the Picture Using Nested Loops

```
def lighten2(picture):
  for x in range(0,getWidth(picture)):
    for y in range(0,getHeight(picture)):
      px = getPixel(picture,x,y)
      color = getColor(px)
      color = makeLighter(color)
      setColor(px,color)
```

How It Works

Let's walk through (trace) how it would work. Imagine that we have just executed `lighten2(myPicture)`.

1. `def lighten2(picture):` The variable `picture` becomes the new name for the picture in `myPicture`.

2. `for x in range(0,getWidth(picture)):` Variable x takes on the value 0.

3. `for y in range(0,getHeight(picture)):` Variable y takes on the value 0.

4. `px = getPixel(picture,x,y):` Variable px takes on the value of the pixel object at location (0, 0).

5. `setColor(px,color):` We set the pixel at (0, 0) to be the new lighter color.

6. `for y in range(0,getHeight(picture)):` Variable y now becomes 1. We had just modified the color at pixel (0, 0), and now we're going to process the pixel at

(0, 1). In other words, we're slowly moving down the first column of pixels, the column where x is 0.

7. `px = getPixel(picture,x,y)`: px becomes the pixel at position (0, 1).

8. We lighten that color.

9. `for y in range(0,getHeight(picture))`: Variable y now becomes 2. We will then process pixel at (0, 2), then (in the next loop) (0, 3), (0, 4), and so on, until y becomes the height of the picture *minus 1* (e.g., up to *but not including* the last value).

10. `for x in range(0,getWidth(picture))`: Variable x takes on the value 1.

11. Now y becomes 0 again, and we start down the next column where x is 1. We process pixel at (1, 0), then (iterating on the y variable) (1, 1), (1, 2), and so on until y equals the height of the picture *minus 1* (e.g., up to *but not including* the last value). Then we increase x and start down column $x = 2$, and process each y so that we address pixels (2, 0), (2, 1), (2, 2), and so on.

12. This continues until all the colors of all the pixels are lightened.
The function `lighten2` uses nested loops, but is essentially doing the same thing as the original function, i.e., every pixel is manipulated. A better example is `removeRedEye2` which removes red eye by *only* processing the pixels in the area we care about. We saw the original version in the prior chapter.

Program 64: Reduce Red-Eye Using Nested Loops

```
def removeRedEye2(pic,sX,sY,eX,eY,endColor):
  for x in range(sX,eX):
    for y in range(sY,eY):
      px = getPixel(pic,x,y)
      if (distance(red,getColor(px)) < 165):
        setColor(px,endColor)
```

We use this version just like the previous one:

```
>>> jenny=makePicture("jenny-red.jpg")
>>> removeRedEye2(jenny, 109, 91, 202, 107, black)
>>> explore(jenny)
```

This new version does *exactly* the same thing in terms of replacing the red in Jenny's eyes with an end color (black in this example). But this version only takes 1/10 the time. We can actually *time* the difference, and we do that in the next section.

6.1.2   Writing Faster Pixel Loops

We can show that using a `for` loop to generate indexes for pixel positions is *way* faster than using `for pixel in getPixels(picture)`. Imagine that you have a picture in which you want to draw a small yellow box, say, 10×10 pixels, with an upper left hand corner at (10, 10) and a lower right hand corner at (19, 19). We can draw the code in two different ways: by processing all pixels and selecting only the ones in the range, or by using nested loops to only process those pixels.

Python provides a special library function called `clock` which returns a time in seconds. By taking the time at the beginning and at the end of the function, the difference tells us how long the code was running. To use this function, we have to pull it out of the library by using the command `from time import clock` at the top of our program.

Here are two functions for making a yellow box.

Program 65: Make a Yellow Box, Both in Two Ways

```
from time import clock

def yellowbox1(pict):
  start = clock()
  for px in getPixels(pict):
    x = getX(px)
    y = getY(px)
    if 10 <= x < 20 and 10 <= y < 20:
      setColor(px,yellow)
  print "Time:",clock()-start

def yellowbox2(pict):
  start = clock()
  for x in range(10,20):
    for y in range(10,20):
      setColor(getPixel(pict,x,y),yellow)
  print "Time:",clock()-start
```

Here's what it looks like when we run it.

```
>>> b = makePicture("bridge.jpg")
>>> b
Picture, filename /Users/guzdial/Desktop/mediasources-4ed/bridge.jpg
    height 640 width 480
>>> yellowbox1(b)
Time: 1.317775
>>> yellowbox2(b)
Time: 0.00316000000001
```

The function `yellowbox1` which processes all pixels ran in 1.3 seconds. The function `yellowbox2` which uses nested loops ran in 0.003 seconds. That's essentially 1/1000th of the time. That's for a small picture of 640x480. That's 1/3 of a megapixel. For a 12 megapixel picture, `yellowbox1` would probably take about 47 seconds. The function `yellowbox2` would take 0.1 seconds. Now imagine if you were processing frames of a movie, with 30 photographs (frames) per second. That is a pretty big difference.

Nested loops let us focus on which pixels we care about, which leads to much faster code. Using nested loops buys us more than that. Because it allows us to focus on particular pixels at particular x and y values, we can do some cool things that are harder to do with our all-pixels method.

6.2   MIRRORING A PICTURE

Let's mirror a picture along its vertical axis. It's an interesting effect that is occasionally useful and is fun to do. In other words, imagine that you have a mirror and you place it on a picture so that the left side of the picture shows up in the mirror. That's the effect we're going to implement. We'll do it in a couple of different ways.

First, let's think through what we're going to do. And let's simplify things a bit. Let's think about mirroring a two-dimensional array of numbers. We'll pick a horizontal `mirrorPoint`—halfway across the picture, `getWidth(picture)/2`.

When the width of the picture is even, we will copy half the picture from the left to the right, as shown in Figure 6.2. The width of this array is 2 so the mirrorPoint is 2 / 2 = 1. We need to copy from x=0,y=0 to x=1,y=0 and from x=0,y=1 to x=1,y=1. Notice that the `mirrorPoint` is not actually the *middle* of the picture, because the width of the picture is an even number. Think through what would happen if the width of the picture was 4. What pixels would get copied where?

When the width of the picture is odd, we will not copy the middle column of pixels, as shown in Figure 6.2. We need to copy from x=0,y=0 to x=2,y=0 and from x=0,y=1 to x=2,y=1.

Whenever we mirror, we start x at 0 and y at 0. We iterate across all values x ranging from 0 to the `mirrorPoint-1` and y ranging from 0 to the height minus one. To mirror a picture from left to right, the color at the first column should be copied to the last

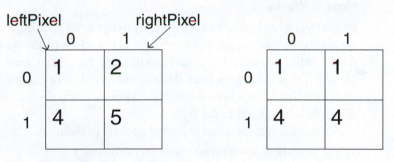

mirrorPoint = 2 / 2 = 1

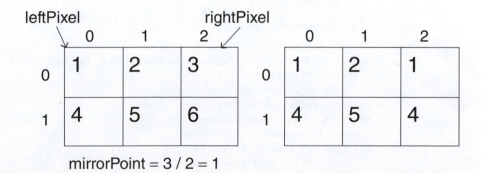

mirrorPoint = 3 / 2 = 1

FIGURE 6.2
Copying pixels from left to right around a mirror point.

column in the same row. The color at the second column should be copied to the second to last column in the same row and so on. So when x equals 0, we will copy the color from the pixel at x=0 and y=0 to x = width-1 and y = 0. When x equals 1, we will copy the color from the pixel at x=1 and y=0 to x=width-2 and y = 0. When x equals 2, we will copy the color from the pixel at x=2 and y=0 to x=width-3 and y = 0. Each time we are copying the color from the pixel on the left at the current x and y values to a pixel on the right at the width of the picture minus the current x value minus 1.

Take a look at Figure 6.2 to convince yourself that we'll actually reach every pixel using this scheme. Here's the actual program.

Program 66: Mirror Pixels in a Picture along a Vertical Line

```
def mirrorVertical(source):
  mirrorPoint = getWidth(source) / 2
  width = getWidth(source)
  for y in range(0,getHeight(source)):
    for x in range(0,mirrorPoint):
      leftPixel = getPixel(source,x,y)
      rightPixel = getPixel(source,width - x - 1,y)
      color = getColor(leftPixel)
      setColor(rightPixel,color)
```

How It Works

mirrorVertical takes a source picture as input. We're using a vertical mirror halfway across the picture, so the mirrorPoint is the width of the picture divided by 2. We do the entire height of the picture, so the loop for y goes from 0 to the height of the picture. The x value goes from 0 to mirrorPoint-1 (e.g., up to but not including the mirrorPoint). Each time through the loop, we copy the color from another column of pixels from the left to the right.

We'd use it like this (and the result appears in Figure 6.3).

```
>>> picture=makePicture("blueMotorcycle.jpg")
>>> explore(picture)
>>> mirrorVertical(picture)
>>> explore(picture)
```

Can we mirror horizontally? Sure!

Program 67: Mirror Pixels Across a Horizontal Line, Top to Bottom

```
def mirrorHorizontal(source):
  mirrorPoint = getHeight(source) / 2
  height = getHeight(source)
  for x in range(0,getWidth(source)):
    for y in range(0,mirrorPoint):
      topPixel = getPixel(source,x,y)
      bottomPixel = getPixel(source,x,height - y - 1)
      color = getColor(topPixel)
      setColor(bottomPixel,color)
```

FIGURE 6.3
Original picture (*left*) and mirrored along the vertical axis (*right*).

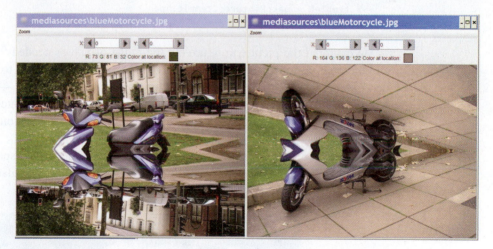

FIGURE 6.4
Mirroring horizontally, top to bottom (*left*) and bottom to top (*right*).

Now this last program copies from the top of the picture onto the bottom (see Figure 6.4). You can see that we're getting the color from `topPixel`, which is from the current x and y, which will always be *above* the `mirrorPoint` because smaller values of y are nearer the top of the picture. To copy from the bottom up, simply swap `topPixel` and `bottomPixel` (Figure 6.4).

Program 68: Mirror Pixels Horizontally, Bottom to Top

```
def mirrorBotTop(source):
  mirrorPoint = getHeight(source) / 2
  height = getHeight(source)
```

```
for x in range(0,getWidth(source)):
  for y in range(0,mirrorPoint):
    topPixel = getPixel(source,x,y)
    bottomPixel = getPixel(source,x,height - y - 1)
    color = getColor(bottomPixel)
    setColor(topPixel,color)
```

Mirroring Usefully

While mirroring is mostly used for interesting effects, occasionally it has some more serious (but still fun) purposes. Mark took a picture of the Temple of Hephaestus in the ancient agora in Athens, Greece, when traveling to a conference (Figure 6.5). By sheer luck, he got the pediment dead horizontal. The pediment of the Temple of Hephaestus is damaged. He wondered if he could "fix" it by mirroring the good part onto the broken part.

To find the coordinates where we need to mirror, use the picture tool in JES to explore the picture.

```
>>> templeP = makePicture("temple.jpg)
>>> explore(templeP)
```

He explored the picture to figure out the range of values needed for the mirroring and the point to mirror around (Figure 6.6). The function he wrote to do the repair is described in this section, and the final picture is shown in Figure 6.7—it worked pretty well! It is still possible to tell that the result was digitally manipulated. For example, if you check the shadows, you can see that the sun must have been on the left and the right at the same time.

Since the function we are building in this section will be written specifically for the temple picture, we will be using our notion of a *media path*. It's particularly helpful when

FIGURE 6.5
Temple of Hephaestus from the ancient agora in Athens.

FIGURE 6.6
Coordinates where we need to do the mirroring.

you want to deal with several pieces of media in the same directory but don't want to spell out the whole directory name. You just have to remember to use `setMediaPath()` first. The function `setMediaPath()` puts up a file picker dialog box that lets you choose a folder (or directory—different terms meaning the same thing in the file system), then prints out the *path* to the new folder that you have selected.

```
>>> setMediaPath()
New media folder: 'C:\\ip-book\\mediasources\\'
```

In the above example when we executed `setMediaPath()`, we set the media folder to **mediasources** which is inside the directory **ip-book** which sits on the root (main directory) of the hard disk C: (which tells you that this example was on a Windows computer). If we were to execute `setMediaPath()` on a Mac OS X computer, we might see something like this:

```
>>> setMediaPath()
'/Users/guzdial/Desktop/MediaComp/mediasources/'
```

The same thing is happening in this example. A file picker dialog box is displayed, a directory is selected, and then it is printed. On a Mac OS X, the main hard disk root is simply called "/" and the path above suggests that the folder **Users** sits on the main disk directory, and there's a directory within that called **guzdial**, and then **Desktop**, and then **MediaComp**, and finally media are stored in the folder **mediasources** within that.

FIGURE 6.7
The manipulated temple.

All that `getMediaPath` does is to prepend the path found in `setMediaPath` to the input filename.

```
>>> getMediaPath("barbara.jpg")
'C:\\ip-book\\mediasources\\barbara.jpg'
>>> barb=makePicture(getMediaPath("barbara.jpg"))
```

But JES is also smart enough that if you tell `makePicture` to open a base filename, it will look in the media path first. So this works, too:

```
>>> barb=makePicture("barbara.jpg")
```

Program 69: Mirror the Temple of Hephaestus

```
def mirrorTemple():
 source = makePicture("temple.jpg")
 mirrorPoint = 276
 for x in range(13,mirrorPoint):
  for y in range(27,97):
   pleft = getPixel(source,x,y)
   pright = getPixel(source,mirrorPoint + mirrorPoint - 1 - x,y)
   setColor(pright,getColor(pleft))
 show(source)
 return source
```

Common Bug: Set the Media Folder First!

If you're to use code that uses getMediaPath(baseName), you'll need to execute setMediaPath() first.

How It Works

We found the mirrorPoint (276) by exploring the picture in JES. We don't really have to copy from 0 to 276, because the edge of the temple is at an x index of 13.

This program is also one of the first ones we've written where we explicitly return a value. The keyword return sets the value that the function provides as output. In mirrorTemple(), the return value is the picture object source where the repaired temple is stored. If we invoked this function with fixedTemple = mirrorTemple(), the name fixedTemple would represent the picture returned from mirrorTemple().

Common Bug: The Keyword return Is Always Last

The keyword return specifies what the return value is from the function but it also has the effect of *ending* the function. A common bug is to try to print or show *after* a return statement but that won't work. Once return is executed, no more statements in the function are executed.

Why do we return the fixed temple picture object? Why *haven't* we ever returned before? The functions we've written before this directly manipulate the input picture—this is called computation by *side effect*. There are no inputs to mirrorTemple(). We create the picture we're manipulating inside the function. The rule of thumb on when to return is this: If you *create* the object of interest inside the function, you need to return it or else the object will just disappear when the function ends. Because the picture object source is created (using makePicture) inside the function mirrorTemple(), the object only exists within the function.

Why return anything at all? We do it for future use. Can you imagine *possibly* wanting to do something with the mirrored temple? Maybe composing it into a collage, or changing its color? You should return the object so that you will have that option later.

The temple example is a good one to ask ourselves about. If you really understand it, you can answer questions like, "What is the *first* pixel to be mirrored in this function?" and "How many pixels get copied anyway?" You should be able to figure out the answers by thinking through the program—pretend you're the computer and execute the program in your mind.

If that's too hard, you can insert `print` statements, like this:

```
def mirrorTemplePrinting():
 source = makePicture("temple.jpg")
 mirrorPoint = 276
 for x in range(13,mirrorPoint):
  for y in range(27,97):
   print"Copying color from",x,y,"to",mirrorPoint+mirrorPoint-1-x,y
   pleft = getPixel(source,x,y)
   pright = getPixel(source,mirrorPoint+mirrorPoint-1-x,y)
   setColor(pright,getColor(pleft))
 show(source)
 return source
```

When we run this version (`mirrorTemplePrinting()`), it takes a *long* time to finish. Hit STOP after a little bit, since we only really care about the first few pixels. Here's what we got:

```
>>> p2=mirrorTemple()
Copying color from 13 27  to  538 27
Copying color from 13 28  to  538 28
Copying color from 13 29  to  538 29
```

It copies from (13, 27) to (538, 27) where the 538 is calculated from the `mirror` `Point` (276) plus the `mirrorPoint` (552) minus 1 (551) then minus x (551−13 = 538).

How many pixels did we process? We can have the computer figure that one out too. Before the loops, we say that our count is 0. Each time we copy a pixel, we add 1 to our count.

```
def mirrorTempleCounting():
  source = makePicture("temple.jpg")
  mirrorPoint = 276
  count = 0
  for x in range(13,mirrorPoint):
   for y in range(27,97):
    pleft = getPixel(source,x,y)
    pright = getPixel(source,mirrorPoint + mirrorPoint - 1 - x,y)
    setColor(pright,getColor(pleft))
    count = count + 1
  show(source)
  print "We copied",count,"pixels"
  return source
```

This comes back with `We copied 18410 pixels`. Where did this number come from? We copy 70 rows of pixels (y goes from 27 to 96). We copy 263 columns of pixels (x goes from 13 to 275). 70×263 is 18,410.

6.3 COPYING AND TRANSFORMING PICTURES

We can create wholly new pictures when we copy pixels *across* pictures. We're going to end up keeping track of a *source* picture that we take pixels from and a *target* picture that we're going to set pixels in. Actually, we don't copy the pixels—we simply make the pixels in the target the same color as the pixels in the source. Copying pixels requires us to keep track of multiple index variables: the (x, y) position in the source and the (x, y) in the target.

What's exciting about copying pixels is that making some small changes in how we deal with the index variables leads not only to *copying* the image but to *transforming* it. In this section, we're going to talk about copying, cropping, rotating, and scaling pictures.

Our target picture will be a blank picture that we create with makeEmptyPicture. The function makeEmptyPicture needs at least two inputs: a number representing the width of a new picture, and a number representing the height of the new picture.

```
>>> pic = makeEmptyPicture(1000,1000)
>>> print pic
Picture, filename None height 1000 width 1000
```

We could show or explore the picture pic, but it's kind of boring. It's a big white sheet. Optionally, the function makeEmptyPicture can take a third argument: a color to fill the new picture. The default is white. If we were to execute blank = makeEmptyPicture(1000,1000,red), the name blank would represent a big *red* blank picture.

6.3.1 Copying

To copy a picture from one object to another, we simply make sure that we increment sourceX and targetX variables (the source and target index variables for the *x*-axis) together, and the sourceY and targetY variables together. We could use a for loop, but that only increments *one* variable. We have to make sure that we increment the *other* variable (whichever one is *not* in the for loop) using an expression at the same time (as close as we can) as when the for loop increments things. We'll do this using two steps:

1. by setting initial values *just before* the loop starts,
2. then adding to the index variable at the *bottom* of the loop.

Here's a program for copying the picture of the horse to the canvas.

Program 70: Copying a Picture to a Canvas

```
def copyHorse():
  # Set up the source and target pictures
  src = makePicture("horse.jpg")
  canvas = makeEmptyPicture(1000,1000)
  # Now, do the actual copying
  targetX = 0
  for sourceX in range(0,getWidth(src)):
    targetY = 0
    for sourceY in range(0,getHeight(src)):
      color = getColor(getPixel(src,sourceX,sourceY))
      setColor(getPixel(canvas,targetX,targetY), color)
```

```
        targetY = targetY + 1
      targetX = targetX + 1
  show(src)
  show(canvas)
  return canvas
```

■

Computer Science Idea: Comments Are Good!

You see in Program 70 the use of lines with "#" at the start of them. This symbol says to Python, "Ignore the rest of this line." What good is that? It allows you to put messages in the program to be read by humans and not the computer—messages that explain how things work, what sections of the program do, and why you did what you did. Remember that programs are for humans, not computers. Comments make the programs better suited to humans.

■

How It Works

This program copies the picture of the horse to the canvas (Figure 6.8).

- The first few lines just set up the source (src) and target (canvas) pictures.
- Next comes the loop for managing the *X* index variables, sourceX for the source picture and targetX for the target picture. Here are the key parts of the loop:

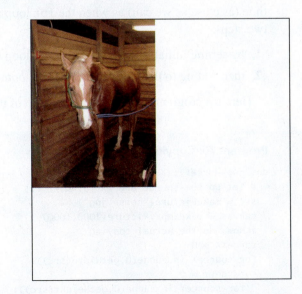

FIGURE 6.8
Copying a picture to a canvas.

```
targetX = 0
for sourceX in range(0,getWidth(src)):
  # Y LOOP GOES HERE
  targetX = targetX + 1
```

Because of the way these statements are arranged, from the point of view of the *Y* loop, `targetX` and `sourceX` are always incremented together. `targetX` becomes 0 just before `sourceX` becomes 0 in the `for` loop. At the end of the `for` loop, `targetX` is incremented by 1, and then the loop starts over again and `sourceX` is also incremented by 1 through the `for` statement.

The statement to increment `targetX` may look a little strange. `targetX = targetX + 1` isn't making a mathematical statement (which couldn't possibly be true). Instead it's giving directions to the computer. It says "Make the value of `targetX` to be (right side of =) whatever the *current* value of `targetX` is *plus* 1."

- Inside the loop for the *X* variables is the loop for the *Y* variables. It has a very similar structure, since its goal is to keep `targetY` and `sourceY` in sync in exactly the same way.

```
targetY = 0
for sourceY in range(0,getHeight(src)):
  color = getColor(getPixel(src,sourceX,sourceY))
  setColor(getPixel(canvas,targetX,targetY), color)
  targetY = targetY + 1
```

It's inside the *Y* loop that we actually get the color from the source and set the corresponding pixel in the target to the same color.

It turns out that we can just as easily put the target variables in the `for` loops and set the source variables. The program that follows does the same as Program 70.

Program 71: Copying a Picture to a Canvas Another Way

```
def copyHorse2():
  # Set up the source and target pictures
  src = makePicture("horse.jpg")
  canvas = makeEmptyPicture(1000,1000)
  # Now, do the actual copying
  sourceX = 0
  for targetX in range(0,getWidth(src)):
    sourceY = 0
    for targetY in range(0,getHeight(src)):
      color = getColor(getPixel(src,sourceX,sourceY))
      setColor(getPixel(canvas,targetX,targetY), color)
      sourceY = sourceY + 1
    sourceX = sourceX + 1
  show(src)
  show(canvas)
  return canvas
```

Of course, we don't have to copy from (0, 0) in the source to (0, 0) in the target. We can easily copy somewhere else in the canvas. All we have to do is to change where the target *X* and *Y* coordinates *start*. The rest stays exactly the same (Figure 6.9).

Program 72: Copy Elsewhere into the Canvas

```
def copyHorseMidway():
  # Set up the source and target pictures
  src = makePicture("horse.jpg")
  canvas = makeEmptyPicture(1000,1000)
  # Now, do the actual copying
  targetX = 100
  for sourceX in range(0,getWidth(src)):
    targetY = 200
    for sourceY in range(0,getHeight(src)):
      color = getColor(getPixel(src,sourceX,sourceY))
      setColor(getPixel(canvas,targetX,targetY), color)
      targetY = targetY + 1
    targetX = targetX + 1
  show(src)
  show(canvas)
  return canvas
```

Similarly, we don't have to copy a *whole* picture. *Cropping* is taking only part of a picture out of the whole picture. Digitally, that's just a matter of changing your start and end coordinates. To grab just the horse's face out of the picture, we only have to figure out what the coordinates are where the face is located, then use those coordinates in the range function for sourceX and sourceY (Figure 6.10). We can do this by exploring the picture. The face is at (104, 114) (upper left) to (266, 421) (lower right).

FIGURE 6.9
Copying a picture midway into a canvas.

FIGURE 6.10
Copying part of a picture onto a canvas.

Program 73: Cropping a Picture onto a Canvas

```
def copyHorseFace():
  # Set up the source and target pictures
  src = makePicture("horse.jpg")
  canvas = makeEmptyPicture(1000,1000)
  # Now, do the actual copying
  targetX = 100
  for sourceX in range(104,267):
    targetY = 200
    for sourceY in range(114,422):
      color = getColor(getPixel(src,sourceX,sourceY))
      setColor(getPixel(canvas,targetX,targetY), color)
      targetY = targetY + 1
    targetX = targetX + 1
  #show(src)
  show(canvas)
  return canvas
```

How It Works

The only difference between this program and the previous ones is the ranges on the source indices. We only want the x pixels between 104 and 266, so the inputs are 104, 267 for the range for sourceX. We only want the y pixels between 114 and 421, so the inputs to range are 114, 422 that we use for sourceY. We have commented out the show(src) line, because we are sure you know what that does now.

We can still swap which variables are in the for loop and which are incremented. Computing the range for the target is a little complicated, though. If we want to start copying to (100, 200), then the width of the picture is $267 - 204 = 163$ and the height is $422 - 114 = 308$. Here's the program.

Program 74: Cropping the Face into the Canvas Differently

```
def copyHorseFace2():
  # Set up the source and target pictures
  src=makePicture("horse.jpg")
  canvas = makeEmptyPicture(1000,1000)
  # Now, do the actual copying
  sourceX = 104
  for targetX in range(100,100+163):
    sourceY = 114
    for targetY in range(200,200+308):
      color = getColor(getPixel(src,sourceX,sourceY))
      setColor(getPixel(canvas,targetX,targetY), color)
      sourceY = sourceY + 1
    sourceX = sourceX + 1
  show(canvas)
  return canvas
```

How It Works

Let's look at a small example to see what's going on in the copying program. We start out with a source and a target, and copy from the source to the target, pixel by pixel. Imagine that we're copying from (0, 0) in the source to (3, 1) in the target.

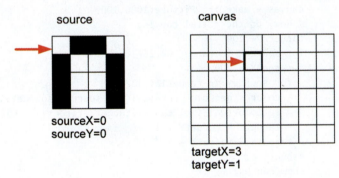

We then increment both `sourceY` and `targetY`, and copy again.

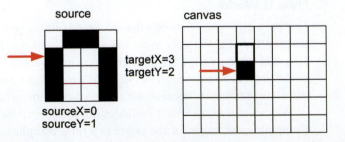

We continue down the column, incrementing both *Y* index variables.

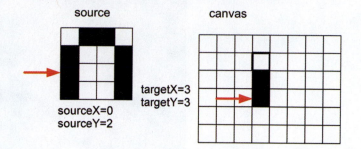

When done with that column, we increment the *X* index variables and move on to the next column, until we have copied every pixel.

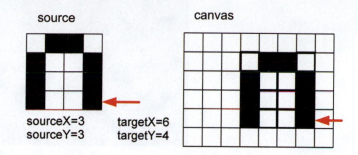

6.3.2 Copying Smaller and Modifying

Once we know what the width and height of *just* the horse's face is, we don't really need to copy it into a 1000 × 1000 pixel canvas. We can copy *just* the face. This function works very similarly to the copyHorseFace function, except that we make a smaller target and we copy into (0, 0) in the target (Figure 6.11).

Program 75: Cropping the Face into a Smaller Canvas

```
def copyHorseFaceSmall():
  # Set up the source and target pictures
  src = makePicture("horse.jpg")
  canvas = makeEmptyPicture(163,308)
  # Now, do the actual copying
  targetX = 0
  for sourceX in range(104,267):
    targetY = 0
    for sourceY in range(114,422):
      color = getColor(getPixel(src,sourceX,sourceY))
      setColor(getPixel(canvas,targetX,targetY), color)
      targetY = targetY + 1
    targetX = targetX + 1
  show(canvas)
  return canvas
```

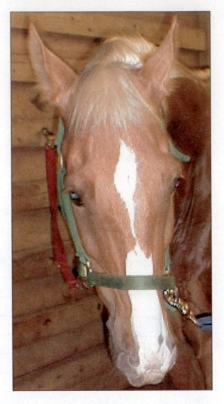

FIGURE 6.11
Copying part of a picture onto a canvas just that size.

While we are copying the colors of the pixels, we can also *do* something with them. If you check the color of brown on the horse, it's *red* = 216, *green* = 169, *blue* = 143. Just like we did in the last chapter, we can look for colors close to that, and then change them. Here, we give the horse black highlights (Figure 6.12).

Program 76: Changing the Face while Copying

```
def copyHorseFaceSmallBlack():
  hcol = makeColor(216,169,143)
  # Set up the source and target pictures
  src = makePicture("horse.jpg")
  canvas = makeEmptyPicture(163,308)
  # Now, do the actual copying
  targetX = 0
  for sourceX in range(104,267):
    targetY = 0
    for sourceY in range(114,422):
      color = getColor(getPixel(src,sourceX,sourceY))
      if distance(color,hcol) < 40:
        setColor(getPixel(canvas,targetX,targetY), black)
      else:
        setColor(getPixel(canvas,targetX,targetY), color)
```

FIGURE 6.12
Copying part of a picture and changing the colors while copying.

```
    targetY = targetY + 1
  targetX = targetX + 1
show(canvas)
return canvas
```

6.3.3   Copying and Referencing

When we input a number into a function, we are doing something different than when we copy a picture into a function. It's worth pausing to see the difference.

Computer Science Idea: Copy Versus Reference

 When we copy colors from the source picture to the target picture, the target picture contains just the color information. It does not know anything about the source picture. If we change the source picture, the target would not change. In computer science we can also make *references*. A reference is a pointer to another object. If the target picture contained a reference to the source picture, and we change the source picture, the target would also change.

This is a deep idea in computer science, so let's do a little experimentation to explain it better. When we use simple variables (e.g., ones that just contain numbers), assignment *copies* values from one place to another.

```
>>> a = 100
>>> b = a
>>> print a,b
100 100
>>> b = 200
>>> print a,b
100 200
>>> a = 300
>>> print a,b
300 200
```

In this example, we copy the value 100 to the variable a when we say a = 100. When we assign b = a, we are copying the value from a (which is 100) into b. They now both have the value 100. When we change b by copying the value 200 into it, we don't change a. How could we? The variables a and b just hold values copied into them. So a is still 100, and b is now 200. When we copy 300 into a, we don't change b.

Things are a little different when we assign to complex *objects* like pictures and pixels. Assigning a pixel to another object is creating a *reference*. Changing one changes the other.

```
>>> pictureBarb = makePicture("barbara.jpg")
>>> pixel1 = getPixelAt(pictureBarb,0,0)
>>> print pixel1
Pixel red=168 green=131 blue=105
>>> anotherpixel = pixel1
>>> print anotherpixel
Pixel red=168 green=131 blue=105
>>> setColor(pixel1,black)
>>> print pixel1
Pixel red=0 green=0 blue=0
>>> print anotherpixel
Pixel red=0 green=0 blue=0
```

In this example, we make a picture, and assign pixel1 to represent the first pixel in the picture, the one at (0, 0). It has the color red = 168, green = 131, blue = 105. When we assign anotherpixel to pixel1, these become two different names for the *same* object. When we print anotherpixel, it has the same color as pixel1. We then set the color of pixel1's pixel to black. When we print it, it's all 0's. But when we print anotherpixel, it's *also* all 0's. There was only one pixel involved, and changing the pixel through either name would result in the same change in both names. That's the difference between a reference and a copy.

When we think about it from what the computer is doing, both examples are using copies. In the first example, values are being copied. In the second example, what is being copied is a *reference* to the pixel object. Think of getPixelAt(pictureBarb, 0,0) as returning the address of where to find the first pixel in the picture pictureBarb. First, pixel1 gets a copy of that address. When we assign anotherpixel = pixel1, we *copy* the address into `anotherpixel`. The function call `setColor(pixel1,black)` is saying "Change the pixel *at this address (pixel1)* to black." That's the same address as `anotherpixel`, so they both reference the same pixel, which has just been given the color black.

6.3.4   Creating a Collage

Here are a couple images of flowers (Figure 6.13), each 100 pixels wide and high. Let's make a *collage* of them by combining several of our effects to create different flowers. We'll copy them all into the blank image **640x480.jpg**. All we really have to do is to copy the pixel colors to the right places.

Here's how we create the collage (Figure 6.14):

```
>>> flowers=createCollage()
```

FIGURE 6.13
Flowers to use in the collage.

FIGURE 6.14
Collage of flowers.

Common Bug: **Referenced Functions Must Be in the File!**

This program uses functions that we wrote previously. These functions must be copied to the same file as the `createCollage` function in order for this to work. (Later we will see how to do this with an `import` instead.)

Program 77: **Creating a Collage**

```
def createCollage():
  flower1=makePicture("flower1.jpg")
  print flower1
  flower2=makePicture("flower2.jpg")
  print flower2
  canvas=makeEmptyPicture(640,480)
  print canvas
  #First picture, at left edge
  targetX=0
  for sourceX in range(0,getWidth(flower1)):
    targetY=getHeight(canvas)-getHeight(flower1)-5
    for sourceY in range(0,getHeight(flower1)):
      px=getPixel(flower1,sourceX,sourceY)
      cx=getPixel(canvas,targetX,targetY)
      setColor(cx,getColor(px))
      targetY=targetY + 1
    targetX=targetX + 1
  #Second picture, 100 pixels over
  targetX=100
  for sourceX in range(0,getWidth(flower2)):
    targetY=getHeight(canvas)-getHeight(flower2)-5
    for sourceY in range(0,getHeight(flower2)):
      px=getPixel(flower2,sourceX,sourceY)
      cx=getPixel(canvas,targetX,targetY)
      setColor(cx,getColor(px))
      targetY=targetY + 1
    targetX=targetX + 1
  #Third picture, flower1 negated
  negative(flower1)
  targetX=200
  for sourceX in range(0,getWidth(flower1)):
    targetY=getHeight(canvas)-getHeight(flower1)-5
    for sourceY in range(0,getHeight(flower1)):
      px=getPixel(flower1,sourceX,sourceY)
      cx=getPixel(canvas,targetX,targetY)
      setColor(cx,getColor(px))
      targetY=targetY + 1
    targetX=targetX + 1
  #Fourth picture, flower2 with no blue
  clearBlue(flower2)
  targetX=300
  for sourceX in range(0,getWidth(flower2)):
```

```
    targetY=getHeight(canvas)-getHeight(flower2)-5
    for sourceY in range(0,getHeight(flower2)):
      px=getPixel(flower2,sourceX,sourceY)
      cx=getPixel(canvas,targetX,targetY)
      setColor(cx,getColor(px))
      targetY=targetY + 1
    targetX=targetX + 1
  #Fifth picture, flower1, negated with decreased red
  decreaseRed(flower1)
  targetX=400
  for sourceX in range(0,getWidth(flower1)):
    targetY=getHeight(canvas)-getHeight(flower1)-5
    for sourceY in range(0,getHeight(flower1)):
      px=getPixel(flower1,sourceX,sourceY)
      cx=getPixel(canvas,targetX,targetY)
      setColor(cx,getColor(px))
      targetY=targetY + 1
    targetX=targetX + 1
  show(canvas)
  return canvas
```

■

How It Works

While this program looks long, it's really just the same copying loop we've seen repeatedly now, but one loop after the other.

- First we create the `flower1`, `flower2`, and canvas picture objects. We will copy `flower1` and `flower2` to the `canvas`.

- The first flower is just a plain copy of `picture1` at the leftmost edge of the canvas. We want the bottom of the flower to be five pixels from the edge, so `targetY` starts at the height of the canvas minus the flower's height, minus 5. As `targetY` gets incremented (added to), it will grow *down* toward the bottom. It will get incremented for the number of pixels in the height of the flower (see the `sourceY` loop), so the maximum value `targetY` will take is the canvas height minus 5.

- We next copy the second picture in, starting `targetX` 100 pixels to the right, but using the same loops really.

- Now we negate `flower1`, then copy it in, moving farther to the right (`targetX` is now starting at 300).

- Then we clear the blue from `flower2` and copy it into the canvas even farther to the right.

- The fifth flower decreases the red of `flower1`, *which is already negated* (from the third set of loops).

- We then `show` the canvas and `return` it. We need to return the canvas because we made it inside the collage function. If we don't return it, it simply disappears when the function ends.

6.3.5   General Copying

The code to create the collage is very long and repetitive. Each time we copy a picture to the target, we calculate the `targetY` and set the `targetX`. We then loop through all the pixels in the source picture and copy them all to the target. Is there any way to make this shorter? What if we create a general copy function that takes in a picture to copy, the target, and specifies where to start the copy in the target?

Program 78: A General Copy Function

```
def copy(source, target, targX, targY):
  targetX = targX
  for sourceX in range(0,getWidth(source)):
    targetY = targY
    for sourceY in range(0,getHeight(source)):
      px=getPixel(source,sourceX,sourceY)
      tx=getPixel(target,targetX,targetY)
      setColor(tx,getColor(px))
      targetY=targetY + 1
    targetX=targetX + 1
```

Now we can rewrite the collage function to use this new general copy function.

Program 79: Improved Collage with the General Copy Function

```
def createCollage2():
  flower1=makePicture("flower1.jpg")
  flower2=makePicture("flower2.jpg")
  canvas=makeEmptyPicture(640,480)
  #First picture, at left edge
  copy(flower1,canvas,0,getHeight(canvas)-getHeight(flower1)-5)
  #Second picture, 100 pixels over
  copy(flower2,canvas,100,getHeight(canvas)-getHeight(flower2)-5)
  #Third picture, flower1 negated
  negative(flower1)
  copy(flower1,canvas,200,getHeight(canvas)-getHeight(flower1)-5)
  #Fourth picture, flower2 with no blue
  clearBlue(flower2)
  copy(flower2,canvas,300,getHeight(canvas)-getHeight(flower2)-5)
  #Fifth picture, flower1, negated with decreased red
  decreaseRed(flower1)
  copy(flower1,canvas,400,getHeight(canvas)-getHeight(flower2)-5)
  return canvas
```

Now the code to create the collage is much easier to read, change, and understand. (Notice that we removed the `show()` at the end, so you will need to `show` or `explore` what `createCollage2` returns.) Writing functions so that they take parameters makes them easier to reuse. Repeating code several times in a function also can be a problem if the repeated code contains an error. You have to fix the error in several places instead of just one place.

Making It Work Tip: Reuse Functions Rather than Copy

Try to write functions that can be reused by specifying parameters. Try to resist copying code to several places because it makes code longer and can make errors harder to fix. ■

6.3.6   Rotation

The image can be transformed by using the index variables differently or incrementing them differently but otherwise keeping the same copying algorithm. Let's rotate Barb to the left 90 degrees—at least that's the way it will seem. What we'll really do is to flip the image across the diagonal. We'll do that by simply swapping the *X* and *Y* variables in the target—we increment them the exact same way but we'll *use X* for *Y* and *Y* for *X* (Figure 6.15).

Program 80: Rotating (Flipping) a Picture

```
def flipHorseSideways():
  # Set up the source and target pictures
  src = makePicture("horse.jpg")
  canvas = makeEmptyPicture(1000,1000)
  # Now, do the actual copying
  targetX = 0
  for sourceX in range(0,getWidth(src)):
    targetY = 0
```

FIGURE 6.15
Flipping a picture to a canvas.

```
    for sourceY in range(0,getHeight(src)):
      color = getColor(getPixel(src,sourceX,sourceY))
      # Change is here
      setColor(getPixel(canvas,targetY,targetX), color)
      targetY = targetY + 1
    targetX = targetX + 1
  show(canvas)
  return canvas
```

How It Works

Rotating (flipping across the diagonal) starts with the same source and target, and even the same variable values, but since we *use* the target *X* and *Y* differently, we get a different effect. To make this problem easier to understand, let's use a small matrix of color values.

Now, as we increment the *X* variables, we're moving *across* the source array, but *down* the target array. Here's what it looks like after the second iteration of the sourceX loop, with the src table on the top and the canvas on the bottom. The variable sourceX has taken on the values 0 and 1, and we've pasted those colors into y-axis in the canvas 0 and 1.

	X=0	X=1	X=2
Y=0	Red	Green	Purple
Y=1	Blue	Yellow	White
Y=2			

	X=0	X=1	X=2
Y=0	Red		
Y=1	Green		
Y=2			

When we're done, we will have copied every color, but the *x* and *y* are swapped from the source (top) to the target (bottom).

	X=0	X=1	X=2
Y=0	Red	Green	Purple
Y=1	Blue	Yellow	White
Y=2			

	X=0	X=1	X=2
Y=0	Red	Blue	
Y=1	Green	Yellow	
Y=2	Purple	White	

How would we *really* rotate 90 degrees? We need to think about where we want each pixel. The program below actually *does* a 90 degree rotation of the picture. The key difference is in the `setColor` function call. We still need to swap the x and y indices, as we did when we flipped. But rather than use `targetX` for the y coordinate, we *compute* a value for the *y*: `width - targetX - 1`. Compare Figure 6.15 with Figure 6.16 to convince yourself that there is a difference between flipping across the diagonal and rotating the picture.

Program 81: Rotating a Picture

```
def rotateHorseSideways():
 # Set up the source and target pictures
 src = makePicture("horse.jpg")
 canvas = makeEmptyPicture(1000,1000)
 # Now, do the actual copying
 targetX = 0
 width = getWidth(src)
 for sourceX in range(0,getWidth(src)):
  targetY = 0
  for sourceY in range(0,getHeight(src)):
   color = getColor(getPixel(src,sourceX,sourceY))
   # Change is here
   setColor(getPixel(canvas,targetY,width - targetX - 1), color)
   targetY = targetY + 1
  targetX = targetX + 1
 show(canvas)
 return canvas
```

FIGURE 6.16
Rotating a picture to a canvas.

How would we do a different rotation? Maybe 45 degrees? Or 33.3 degrees? Now it gets really hard, because pixels are only at discrete, integer positions. There are pixels at (0, 0) and (1, 2), but not (0.33, 2.5). There are no pixel coordinates with decimal components, so you compute the rotation with decimal values, then figure out how to translate those to integer coordinates. We won't get into those computations here.

6.3.7   Scaling

A very common transformation for pictures is to scale them. Scaling up means to make them larger and scaling down makes them smaller. It's common to scale a 1-megapixel or 3-megapixel picture down to a smaller size to make it easier to place on the Web. Smaller pictures require less disk space, and less network bandwidth, and thus are easier and faster to download.

Scaling a picture requires the use of *sampling*, which we'll also use with sounds later. To scale a picture *smaller*, we are going to take *every other* pixel when copying from the source to the target. To scale a picture *larger*, we are going to take *every pixel twice*.

Scaling the picture down is the easier function. We are going to start from the program on page 161. We are only going to copy the face, which we calculated before is 163 pixels across and 308 pixels top to bottom. So, we only need a picture that is 82 pixels across and 155 pixels high. Instead of incrementing the source X and Y variables by 1, we increment by 2. We reduce the amount of space by 2, since we'll fill half as much room—our length will be 82/2 (converted to integer using `int` because `range` can't handle non-integer values) and the height will be 308/2. The result is a small copy of the horse face.

Program 82: Scaling a Picture Down (Smaller)

```
def copyHorseFaceSmaller():
  # Set up the source and target pictures
  src=makePicture("horse.jpg")
  canvas = makeEmptyPicture(82,155)
  # Now, do the actual copying
  sourceX = 104
  for targetX in range(0,int(163/2)):
    sourceY = 114
    for targetY in range(0,int(308/2)):
      color = getColor(getPixel(src,sourceX,sourceY))
      setColor(getPixel(canvas,targetX,targetY), color)
      sourceY = sourceY + 2
    sourceX = sourceX + 2
  show(canvas)
  return canvas
```

How It Works

- We start out creating the picture objects: `src` as our source, and a `canvas` into which we'll compose the horse face, which is just the right size to hold a half-size horse face.

- The horse's face is in the rectangle (104, 114) to (266, 405). That means that the sourceX starts at 104 and the sourceY starts at 114. We don't specify the end of the range for the source indices because they're controlled by the for loops for the target indices.

- We're going to start targetX and targetY at 0 each, since we are copying. What are the end points for the ranges? We want to get *all* of the horse's face. The width of the face is 163 pixels (the maximum x index minus the minimum x index, plus one since we want those pixels inclusive, $266 - 104 + 1$). Since we want to shrink the horse's face by half (in each direction), we'll be skipping every other row and column of pixels. That means that we'll have only half the width in the final composition: (163)/2 across. The *y*-axis and the variable targetY work the same way: from 0 to half of our width of 308.

- Because we want to skip every other row and column in the source, we increment sourceX and sourceY by 2 each time through the loop.

Scaling down a picture is literally *throwing away* every other pixel. It is inherently a *lossy* process. We get rid of some information, eliminating some of the pixel information that was in the original picture. This is *lossy* in the same sense of JPEG, which throws away some information to make it easier to compress the picture to a smaller file.

Scaling up the picture (making it larger) is a little trickier. We want to take every row and column of pixels twice. We will do this twice. The first time, we are just to literally take every pixel twice.

Program 83: Scaling a Picture Larger by Taking Every Pixel Twice

```
def copyHorseLarger():
  # Set up the source and target pictures
  src = makePicture("horse.jpg")
  w = getWidth(src)
  h = getHeight(src)
  canvas = makeEmptyPicture(w*2,h*2)
  srcPixels = getPixels(src)
  trgPixels = getPixels(canvas)
  trgIndex = 0
  # Now, do the actual copying
  for pixel in srcPixels:
    color = getColor(pixel)
    # Once
    trgPixel = trgPixels[trgIndex]
    setColor(trgPixel,color)
    trgIndex = trgIndex + 1
    # Twice
    trgPixel = trgPixels[trgIndex]
    setColor(trgPixel,color)
    trgIndex = trgIndex + 1
  show(canvas)
  return canvas
```

How It Works

- We get the `src` picture (our horse), and make a canvas that is twice its size in each dimension. What's different is that we will also `getPixels` from each.
- We set a name `trgIndex` to be our index in the target pixels (`trgPixels`).
- For each source pixel `pixel`, we get the `color` of that pixel.
- We get a target pixel at `trgIndex`. We copy the color there. We increment the target index `trgIndex`.
- We then *do it again*. We literally copy each pixel twice.

The result isn't quite what we want it to be (Figure 6.17). The horse is stretched horizontally. Why? Because when we copy each row and column twice, we're actually taking each pixel *four* times. It is hard to get this exactly right using simple index notation. It's also hard to crop, like if you wanted to scale up just *part* of the picture.

A better way to do scaling-up is to use the same function `copyHorseFaceSmaller`, but increment the source index variables by 0.5. Think about incrementing an index to values like 1.5. We can't index pixels at 1.5. But if we use the index *int*(1.5) (integer function) we'll get 1 again, and that will work. The sequence of 1, 1.5, 2, 2.5 … will become 1, 1, 2, 2 … The result is a larger form of the picture (Figure 6.18), and we can grab just the part we want (e.g., the horse's face).

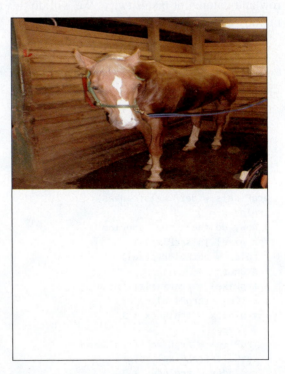

FIGURE 6.17
Doubling every pixel.

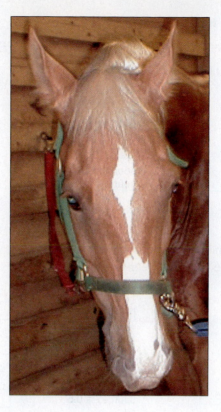

FIGURE 6.18
Scaling up a picture.

Program 84: Scaling the Picture Up (Larger)

```
def copyHorseFaceLarger():
  # Set up the source and target pictures
  src=makePicture("horse.jpg")
  canvas = makeEmptyPicture(163*2,308*2)
  # Now, do the actual copying
  sourceX = 104
  for targetX in range(0,163*2):
    sourceY = 114
    for targetY in range(0,308*2):
      srcpx = getPixel(src,int(sourceX),int(sourceY))
      color = getColor(srcpx)
      setColor(getPixel(canvas,targetX,targetY), color)
      sourceY = sourceY + 0.5
    sourceX = sourceX + 0.5
  show(canvas)
  return canvas
```

How It Works

We start from the same place as the original copy.

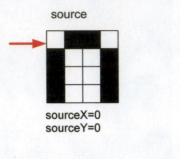

source

sourceX=0
sourceY=0

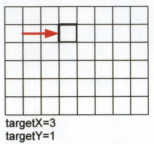

canvas

targetX=3
targetY=1

When we increment `sourceY` by 0.5, we end up referring to the same pixel in the source but the target has moved on to the next pixel.

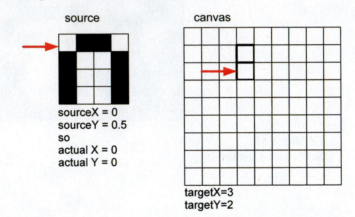

source

sourceX = 0
sourceY = 0.5
so
actual X = 0
actual Y = 0

canvas

targetX=3
targetY=2

When we increment `sourceY` a second time by 0.5, we now move on to the next pixel, which we'll end up copying twice vertically. Thus, each row of the pixel gets copied twice.

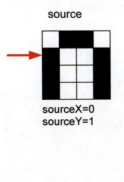

source

sourceX=0
sourceY=1

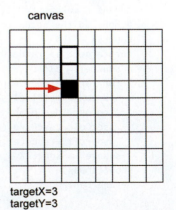

canvas

targetX=3
targetY=3

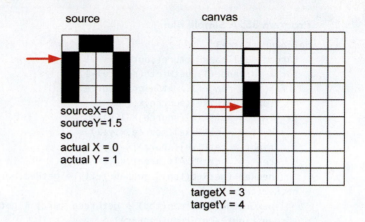

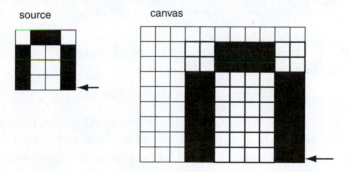

When we move to a new column in the target, we stay in the *same* column in the source. Notice that each column also appears twice. Thus, we end up duplicating every pixel in both the horizontal and vertical dimensions.

Eventually we end up doubling the picture in both directions, effectively quadrupling the area of the figure. Note that the end result is degraded a bit: it's choppier than the original. This is a degradation of quality, but isn't *lossy* in the same sense as scaling down—we *lost* no information that wasn't in the original picture. Could we make it less choppy? What if you didn't just copy a second time, but instead *blended* two pixel color values (say to the left and right)? There are lots of ways to estimate what color the duplicated value should be to avoid the choppiness (called *pixelation*).

6.4 COMBINING PIXELS: BLURRING

When we make pictures larger (scaling them up), we usually get rough edges: sharp steps in lines that we call **pixelation**. Look at the green around the horse's face in Figure 6.18. We can reduce pixelation by *blurring* the image—purposefully making some of the hard edges "soft" (i.e., smoother and more curved). This is a loss of information, but it makes the picture more pleasing to the eye.

There are *many* ways (algorithms) for blurring. We're going to use a simple one here. What we do is set each pixel to a color that is an *average* of its color and the colors of the pixels around it.

Program 85: A Simple Blur

```
def blur(source):
  target=duplicatePicture(source)
  for x in range(1, getWidth(source)-1):
    for y in range(1, getHeight(source)-1):
      top = getPixel(source,x,y-1)
      left = getPixel(source,x-1,y)
      bottom = getPixel(source,x,y+1)
      right = getPixel(source,x+1,y)
      center = getPixel(target,x,y)
      newRed=(getRed(top)+ getRed(left) + getRed(bottom) + getRed(right)¬
+ getRed(center))/5
      newGreen=(getGreen(top) + getGreen(left) + getGreen(bottom)+¬
getGreen(right)+getGreen(center))/5
      newBlue=(getBlue(top) + getBlue(left) + getBlue(bottom) + getBlue¬
(right)+ getBlue(center))/5
      setColor(center, makeColor(newRed, newGreen, newBlue))
  return target
```

¬These lines of the program should continue with the next lines. A single command in Python may not break across multiple lines.   ■

Making It Work Tip: **Don't Break Lines Midway in Python**

In examples like these, you may see lines "wrap." Lines that you would expect to be all on one line actually appear on two. That's a necessity to fit the code onto the page but we can't really break lines that way in Python. We can't break lines by hitting ENTER until the statement or expression is completed.

■

Here is a good example of the advantages of using `return`. Figure 6.19 using this one line:

```
>>> explore(blur(copyHorseFaceLarger()))
```

Figure 6.19 shows the same face as in Figure 6.18. You can see the pixelation in the original face, particularly around the curve of the halter—the sharp, blocky edges. With the blur, some of the pixelation goes away. More careful blurs take regions of colors into account (so that edges between colors are kept sharp) and thus are able to reduce pixelation without removing sharpness.

How It Works

We call `blur` with the picture that we want to blur. We use the JES function `duplicatePicture` to make a copy that is (obviously) the same size as the original. We modify only the `target` so that we always average *original* colors from the `source`. We walk through the *x* index values from 1 to the width minus 1—here we're explicitly taking advantage of the fact that `range` won't include the end values. We do the same with the *y* indices. The reason we are not starting with zero and not going to the width/height is that we're going to add 1 and subtract 1 from each *x* and *y* to get the pixels for the averages. We won't be blurring the pixels at the very edge of the picture,

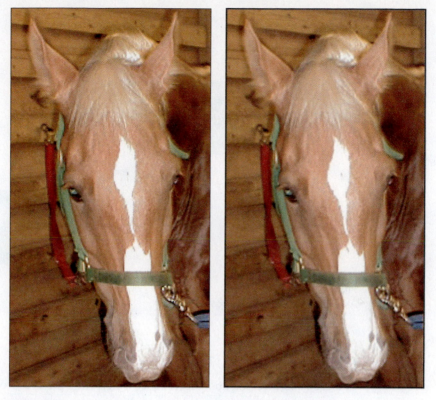

FIGURE 6.19
Original scaled picture (*left*), and blurred horse face picture (*right*).

but it'll be pretty hard to tell. For each (x, y), we get the pixel to the left $(x - 1, y)$, to the right $(x + 1, y)$, above $(x, y - 1)$, and below $(x, y + 1)$, as well as the pixel itself at the center (x, y) (from `target` because we can be sure that we haven't changed (x, y) yet). We compute the average of the reds of all five pixels, the greens, and the blues, then set color at (x, y) to the average color.

Let's imagine that we're looking at the pixel in the center of Figure 6.20, whose $(red, green, blue)$ (RGB) values are $(10, 200, 40)$. We are going to average its RGB values with the pixels above (top), left, right, and below (bottom). To compute the new red value, we get the average of 100 (top), 10 (left), 10 (center), 20 (right), and 5 (below), for a value of 29. We repeat the averaging to get the green (168) and the blue (30). Notice that we *set* the pixel in the `target`, while we read the pixels from the `source`. If we used just one picture for reading and setting, we would not get the blur we want, because we would be setting pixels whose values we would be reading later.

While this works surprisingly well (Figure 6.19), it's not quite as good as we might get. Some detail is lost when you simply blur like this. What if we blurred to get rid of pixelation but kept detail? How might we do that? What if we checked luminance values before we computed the average—perhaps we shouldn't blur across large luminance boundaries because that would reduce detail? That's just one idea—there are lots of good algorithms for blurring.

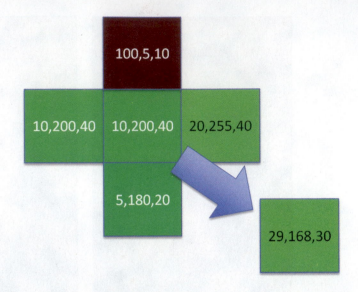

FIGURE 6.20
An example of a blurring calculation.

6.5   BLENDING PICTURES

In this chapter, we talk about techniques for creating pictures from other pieces. We'll compose pictures in new ways (e.g., pulling someone out from one background and putting them in a new setting) and create pictures from scratch without explicitly setting every pixel.

One of the ways that we can combine pictures to create new pictures is by mixing the colors of the pixels to reflect both pictures. When we create collages by copying, any overlap typically means that one picture shows *over* another. The last picture painted on is the one that appears on top of the other. But it doesn't have to be that way. We can *blend* pictures by multiplying their colors and adding them. This gives us the effect of *transparency*.

We know that 100% of something is the whole thing; 50% of one and 50% of another also is a whole. In the program below, we blend a picture of the mother and the daughter with an overlap of 70 (the width of Barbara minus 150) columns of pixels (Figure 6.21).

Program 86: Blending Two Pictures

```
def blendPictures():
  barb = makePicture("barbara.jpg")
  katie = makePicture("Katie-smaller.jpg")
  canvas = makeEmptyPicture(640,480)
  #Copy first 150 columns of Barb
  sourceX=0
  for targetX in range(0,150):
    sourceY=0
```

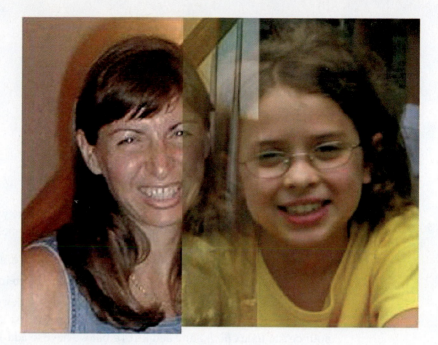

FIGURE 6.21
Blending the picture of mom and daughter.

```
    for targetY in range(0,getHeight(barb)):
        color = getColor(getPixel(barb,sourceX,sourceY))
        setColor(getPixel(canvas,targetX,targetY),color)
        sourceY = sourceY + 1
      sourceX = sourceX + 1
#Now, grab the rest of Barb
# at 50% Barb and 50% Katie
overlap = getWidth(barb)-150
sourceX=0
for targetX in range(150,getWidth(barb)):
  sourceY=0
  for targetY in range(0,getHeight(katie)):
    bPixel = getPixel(barb,sourceX+150,sourceY)
    kPixel = getPixel(katie,sourceX,sourceY)
    newRed= 0.50*getRed(bPixel)+0.50*getRed(kPixel)
    newGreen=0.50*getGreen(bPixel)+0.50*getGreen(kPixel)
    newBlue = 0.50*getBlue(bPixel)+0.50*getBlue(kPixel)
    color = makeColor(newRed,newGreen,newBlue)
    setColor(getPixel(canvas,targetX,targetY),color)
    sourceY = sourceY + 1
  sourceX = sourceX + 1
# Last columns of Katie
sourceX=overlap
for targetX in range(150+overlap,150+getWidth(katie)):
  sourceY=0
```

```
      for targetY in range(0,getHeight(katie)):
        color = getColor(getPixel(katie,sourceX,sourceY))
        setColor(getPixel(canvas,targetX,targetY),color)
        sourceY = sourceY + 1
      sourceX = sourceX + 1
  show(canvas)
  return canvas
```

How It Works

This function has three parts to it—the part where Barb is there without Katie, the part where there's some of each, and the part where there's just Katie.

- We start out by creating the picture objects for barb, katie, and the target canvas.
- For 150 pixel columns, we simply copy pixels from barb into the canvas.
- The next section is the actual blending. Our targetX index starts at 150, because we already have 150 columns from barb in the canvas. We're using sourceX and sourceY to index *both* barb and katie but we have to add 150 to sourceX when indexing barb because we've already copied 150 pixels of barb. Our *y* index will only go up to the height of the katie picture because it's shorter than the barb picture.
- The body of the loop is where the blending occurs. We get a pixel from barb and call it bPixel. We get one from katie and call it kPixel. We then compute the red, green, and blue for the target pixel (the one at targetX and targetY) by taking 50% of the red, green, and blue of each of the source pictures.
- Finally, we end up copying in the rest of the katie pixels.

6.6   DRAWING ON IMAGES

Sometimes you want to create your *own* images from scratch. We know that this is just a matter of setting pixel values to whatever color we want. As we saw in the last chapter, it's not too hard to draw vertical or horizontal lines, or to draw borders. Setting individual pixel values to draw a line or a circle or some letters is hard in the general case.

As we saw in the last chapter, one way of drawing on images is to simply set the pixels appropriately. By using nested loops, we can draw more sophisticated images than we could with just a getPixels loop. Here's an example that creates horizontal and vertical lines over Carolina, a former computing student at Georgia Tech (Figure 6.22). The program works by asking you to pick a file and then creates a picture from the file. Then it calls a function verticalLines that draws vertical lines on the picture 5 pixels apart. Then it calls a function horizontalLines that draws horizontal lines on the picture 5 pixels apart. It shows and returns the resulting picture.

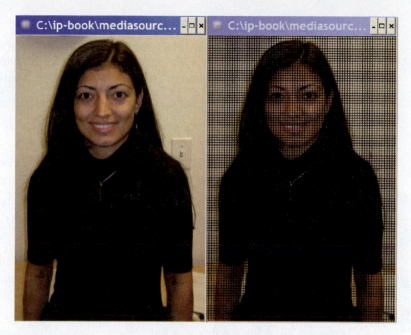

FIGURE 6.22
Carolina normal (*left*) and with lines added (*right*).

Program 87: Draw Lines by Setting Pixels

```
def lineExample():
  img = makePicture(pickAFile())
  verticalLines(img)
  horizontalLines(img)
  show(img)
  return img

def horizontalLines(src):
  for x in range(0,getHeight(src),5):
    for y in range(0,getWidth(src)):
      setColor(getPixel(src,y,x),black)

def verticalLines(src):
  for x in range(0,getWidth(src),5):
    for y in range(0,getHeight(src)):
      setColor(getPixel(src,x,y),black)
```

We can imagine drawing anything we want like this by simply setting individual pixels to whatever colors we want. We could draw rectangles or circles simply by figuring out what pixels need to be what color. We could even draw letters—by setting the appropriate pixels to the appropriate colors, we could make any letter we want. While we could do it, it would involve a lot of work to do all the math for all the different shapes and letters. That's work that lots of people need, so basic drawing tools have been built into libraries for you.

6.6.1   Drawing with Drawing Commands

Most modern programming languages with graphics libraries provide functions that enable us to draw directly a variety of different kinds of shapes onto pictures and to draw text directly onto a picture. Here are some of those functions:

- addText(pict,x,y,string) puts the string starting at position (x, y) in the picture.
- addLine(pict,x1,y1,x2,y2) draws a line from position $(x1, y1)$ to $(x2, y2)$.
- addRect(pict,x1,y1,w,h) draws a rectangle with black lines with the upper-left-hand corner at $(x1, y1)$, a width of w, and a height of h.
- addRectFilled(pict,x1,y1,w,h,color) draws a rectangle filled with the color that you specify with the upper-left-hand corner at $(x1, y1)$, a width of w, and a height of h.

We can use these commands to add things to existing pictures. What would it look like if a mysterious red box washed up on the beach? We can make that scene appear with these kinds of commands (Figure 6.23).

Program 88: Adding a Box to a Beach

```
def addABox():
  beach = makePicture("beach.jpg")
  addRectFilled(beach,190,320,50,50,red)
  show(beach)
  return beach
```

Below is another example of using these drawing commands (Figure 6.24).

Program 89: An Example of Using Drawing Commands

```
def littlepicture():
  canvas=makePicture(getMediaPath("640x480.jpg"))
  addText(canvas,10,50,"This is not a picture")
```

FIGURE 6.23
A box washed up on the shore of the beach.

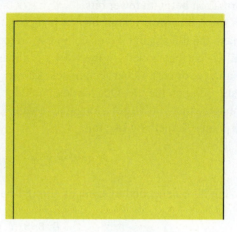

FIGURE 6.24
A very small, drawn picture.

```
addLine(canvas,10,20,300,50)
addRectFilled(canvas,0,200,300,500,yellow)
addRect(canvas,10,210,290,490)
return canvas
```

6.6.2 Vector and Bitmap Representations

Here's a thought: Which of these is smaller, the picture (Figure 6.24) or the program? The picture, on the disk, is about 15 kilobytes (a *kilobyte* is 1000 bytes). The `littlepicture` function is less than 100 bytes. But for many uses, they are *equivalent*. What if you just saved the program and not the pixels? That's what a **vector representation** for graphics is about.

Vector-based graphical representations are executable programs that generate the picture when desired. Vector-based representations are used in PostScript, Flash, and AutoCAD. When you make a change to an image in Flash or AutoCAD, you are actually making a change to the underlying representation—essentially, you're changing the program, like the one in Program `littlepicture`. The program is then executed again to make the image appear. But thanks to Moore's Law, the execution and new display occur so fast that it feels like you're changing the picture.

Font-definition languages like PostScript and TrueType actually define miniature programs (or equations) for each and every letter or symbol. When you want the letter or symbol at a particular size, the program is run to figure out which pixels should be set to what values. (Some specify more than one color to create the effect of smoother curves.) Because the programs are written to handle desired font size as an input, the letters and symbols can be generated at any size.

Bitmap graphical representations, on the other hand, store every individual pixel or a compressed representation of the pixels. Formats like BMP, GIF, and JPEG are essentially bitmap representations. GIF and JPEG are compressed representations—they don't represent each and every pixel with 24 bits. Instead, they represent the same information but with fewer bits.

What does **compression** mean? It means that various techniques have been used to make the file smaller. Some compression techniques are **lossy compression**—some detail is lost but hopefully the least significant detail (perhaps even invisible to the human eye, or ear). Other techniques, known as **lossless compression**, lose no detail but still scrunch the file. One lossless technique is **run length encoding** (RLE).

Imagine that you've got a long line of yellow pixels in a picture, surrounded by some blue pixels. Something like this:

B B Y Y Y Y Y Y Y Y Y B B

What if you encoded this, not as a long line of pixels, but as something like

B B 9 Y B B

In words, you encode "blue, blue, then nine yellows, then blue and blue." Since each of the yellow pixels takes 24 bits (3 bytes for red, green, and blue), but recording "nine" takes just a single byte, there's a huge savings. We say that we're encoding the *length* of the *run* of yellows—thus, encoding the run length. That's just one of the compression methods that is used to make pictures smaller.

There are several benefits to vector-based representations over bitmap representations. If you can represent the picture you want to send (say, over the Internet) using a vector-based representation, it's much smaller than sending all the pixels—in a sense, vector notation is already compressed. Essentially, you're sending the *instructions* for how to make the picture, rather than sending the picture itself. For very complex images, however, the instructions can be as long as the image (imagine sending all the directions on how to paint the *Mona Lisa*), so there is no benefit. But when the images are simple enough, representations like those used in Flash make for faster upload and download times than sending the same JPEG images.

The real benefit of vector-based notations comes when you want to change the image. Let's say that you're working on an architectural drawing, and you extend a line in your drawing tool. If your drawing tool is only working with bitmapped images (sometimes called a **painting tool**), then all you have are more pixels on the screen that are adjacent to the other pixels on the screen representing the line. There's nothing in the computer that says that all those pixels represent a line of any kind—they're just pixels. But if your drawing tool is working with vector-based representations (sometimes called a **drawing tool**), then extending a line means that you're changing an underlying representation of a line.

Why is that important? The underlying representation is actually a *specification* of the drawing, and it can be used anywhere that a specification is needed. Imagine taking the drawing of a part, then actually running the cutting and stamping machines based on that drawing. This happens regularly in many shops and it's possible because the drawing isn't just pixels—it's a specification of the lines and their relationships, which can then be scaled and used to determine the behavior of machines.

You might be wondering, "But how could we *change* the program? Can we write a program that would essentially retype the program or parts of the program?" Yes, we can, and we do it in a later chapter.

6.7   PROGRAMS AS SPECIFYING DRAWING PROCESS

Drawing functions like these can be used to create pictures that are exactly specified—things that might be too hard to do by hand. Take, for example, Figure 6.25.

This is a rendering of a famous optical illusion and it's not as effective as the famous ones—but it's simple to understand how this version works. Our eyes tell us that the left half of the picture is lighter than the right half, even though the end quarters are exactly the same shade of gray. Only the middle quarters are really changed. The effect is caused by the sharp boundary between the middle quarters, where left-of-center quarter moves (left to right) from gray to white, and the right-of-center moves from black to gray (left to right).

The image in Figure 6.25 is a carefully defined and created picture. It would be very hard to do with pencil and paper. It would be possible with something like Photoshop, but it wouldn't be easy. By using the graphics functions in this chapter, however, we can easily specify exactly what that picture should be.

Program 90: Draw the Gray Effect

```
def grayEffect():
  pic = makeEmptyPicture(640,480)
  # First, 100 columns of 100-gray
  gray = makeColor(100,100,100)
  for x in range(0,100):
    for y in range(0,100):
      setColor(getPixel(pic,x,y),gray)
  # Second, 100 columns of increasing grayness
  grayLevel = 100
  for x in range(100,200):
    gray = makeColor(grayLevel, grayLevel, grayLevel)
    for y in range(0,100):
```

FIGURE 6.25
A programmed grayscale effect.

```
      setColor(getPixel(pic,x,y),gray)
    grayLevel = grayLevel + 1
  # Third, 100 columns of increasing grayness, from 0
  grayLevel = 0
  for x in range(200,300):
    gray = makeColor(grayLevel, grayLevel, grayLevel)
    for y in range(0,100):
      setColor(getPixel(pic,x,y),gray)
    grayLevel = grayLevel + 1
  # Finally, 100 columns of 100-gray
  gray = makeColor(100,100,100)
  for x in range(300,400):
    for y in range(0,100):
      setColor(getPixel(pic,x,y),gray)
  return pic
```

Graphics functions are very good at drawings that are repeated where the positions of lines and shapes and the selection of colors can be made by mathematical relationships. Notice something interesting in the next program. We use a negative *step* on the range function. The expression `range(25,0,-1)` counts from 25 down to 1, by −1.

6.7.1　Why Do We Write Programs?

Why do we write programs, especially programs that draw pictures? Could we draw pictures (Figures 6.26 and 6.27) like these in Photoshop or Visio? Certainly we can, but we'd have to know *how*, and that's not easy knowledge to come by. Could we *teach* you how to do this in Photoshop? Probably, but that may take a lot of effort—Photoshop isn't simple.

Program 91: **Draw the Picture in Figure 6.26**
```
def coolPic():
  canvas=makeEmptyPicture(640,480)
  for index in range(25,0,-1):
    color = makeColor(index*10,index*5,index)
    addRectFilled(canvas,0,0,index*10,index*10,color)
  show(canvas)
  return canvas
```

Program 92: **Draw the Picture in Figure 6.27**
```
def coolPic2():
  canvas=makeEmptyPicture(640,480)
  for index in range(25,0,-1):
    addRect(canvas,index,index,index*3,index*4)
    addRect(canvas,100+index*4,100+index*3,index*8,index*10)
  show(canvas)
  return canvas
```

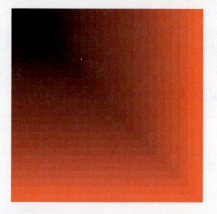

FIGURE 6.26
Nested colored-rectangles image.

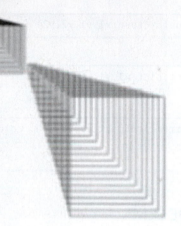

FIGURE 6.27
Nested blank-rectangles image.

But if we *give* you these programs, you can create the picture anytime you want. What's more, by giving you the program, I'm giving you the *exact* definition that you can go and change for yourself.

Computer Science Idea: We Write Programs to Encapsulate and Communicate Process
The reason why we write programs is to exactly specify a process and communicate it to others.

Imagine that you have some process to communicate. It doesn't have to be drawing—imagine that it's a financial process (such that you could do it in a spreadsheet or in a program like Quicken) or something that you do with text (such as laying out text for a book or a brochure). If you can do something by hand, you should just do it. If you need to *teach* someone else to do it, consider writing a program to do it. If you need to explain how to do it to *lots* of people, definitely use a program. If you want lots of people to be able to do the process themselves, without someone having to teach them something first, definitely write a program and give the people the program.

PROGRAMMING SUMMARY

`range`	Function that creates a sequence of numbers. Useful for creating indices for an array or matrix.
`makeEmptyPicture(width,height)`	Takes a height and width and returns an empty (all white) picture of the desired size. Optionally, makeEmptyPicture can take a third input which will fill the new empty picture.
`addText(pict,x,y,string)`	Puts the string starting at position (x, y) in the picture.
`addLine(picture,x1,y1,x2,y2)`	Draws a line from position $(x1, y1)$ to $(x2, y2)$.
`addRect(pict,x1,y1,w,h)`	Draws a rectangle with black lines with the upper-left-hand corner at $(x1, y1)$, a width of w, and a height of h.
`addRectFilled(pict,x1,y1,w,h, color)`	Draws a rectangle filled with the `color` that you pick with the upper-left-hand corner at $(x1, y1)$, a width of w, and a height of h.

PROBLEMS

6.1 Write a function to pull out just Jenny's eyes, rather than remove the red in them, and paste them into a canvas.

6.2 Rewrite the Jenny's eyes function to double Jenny's eyes, making them appear twice.

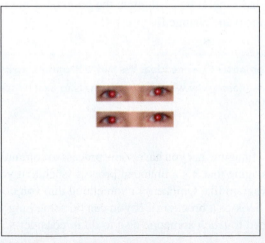

6.3   The black in the function `copyHorseFaceSmallBlack` doesn't look great on that horse. Would `red` look better? Try it.

6.4   Create a movie poster by drawing text on a picture.

6.5   Create a comic strip by putting three to four pictures next to each other horizontally and adding text.

6.6   Using the drawing functions, draw a bull's eye.

6.7   Using the drawing tools presented here, draw a house—just go for the simple child's house with one door, two windows, walls, and a roof.

6.8   Draw horizontal and vertical lines on a picture with 10 pixels between the lines.

6.9   Draw horizontal and vertical lines on a picture where the gap between the lines increases linearly. Start at 10, then 12, then 14.

6.10 Draw diagonal lines on a picture from top left to bottom right using `addLine`.

6.11 Draw diagonal lines on a picture from top right to bottom left using `addLine`.

6.12 What is a vector-based image? How does it differ from a bitmapped image? When is it better to use a vector-based image?

6.13 Draw a house on the beach where we put the mysterious box previously.

6.14 Now use your house function to draw a town with dozens of houses at different sizes. You'll probably want to modify your house function to draw at an input coordinate, then change the coordinate where each house is drawn.

6.15 Write a function to draw a simple face with eyes and a mouth. on a picture

6.16 Now use your simple face function in a loop to draw a whole crowd of people.

6.17 Draw a rainbow—use what you know about colors, pixels, and drawing operations to draw a rainbow. Is this easier to do with our drawing functions or by manipulating individual pixels? Why?

6.18 Which of the programs below takes a picture and removes all the blue from every pixel that already has a blue value of more than 100?

1. A only

2. D only

3. B and C

4. C and D

5. None

6. All

What do the other ones do?

```
A.   def blueOneHundred(picture):
        for x in range(0,100):
            for y in range(0,100):
                pixel = getPixel(picture,x,y)
                setBlue(pixel,100)
```

B.
```
def removeBlue(picture):
    for p in getPixels(picture):
        if getBlue(p) > 0:
            setBlue(p,100)
```

C.
```
def noBlue(picture):
    blue = makeColor(0,0,100)
    for p in getPixels(picture):
        color = getColor(p)
        if distance(color,blue) > 100:
            setBlue(p,0)
```

D.
```
def byeByeBlue(picture):
    for p in getPixels(picture):
        if getBlue(p) > 100:
            setBlue(p,0)
```

6.19
```
def newFunction(a, b, c):
    print a
    list1 = range(0,4)
    value = 0
    for x in list1:
        print b
        value = value +1
    print c
    print value
```
If you call the function above by typing: newFunction("I", "you", "walrus"), what will print?

6.20   We've seen that if you increment the source picture index by 2 while incrementing the target picture index by 1 for each copied pixel, you end up with the source being scaled down onto the target. What happens if you increment the target picture index by 2 as well? What happens if you increment both by 0.5 and use int to get just the integer part?

6.21   Write a function to mirror along the diagonal from (0, 0) to (*width, height*).

6.22   Write a function to mirror along the diagonal from (0, *height*) to (*width*, 0).

6.23   The function copyHorseLarger didn't really work when we copied the pixel twice. What if we copied it four times? Does that look better?

6.24   What do you get from copyHorseLarger you skipped a pixel between every other pixel?

6.25   Write a function that will scale up just part of the picture. Try making someone's nose longer.

6.26   Write a function that will scale down just a part of the picture. Make someone's head look smaller.

6.27   Write a function to flip a picture over so that if someone was looking right, they end up looking left.

6.28   Write a general crop function that takes a source picture, the start *X* value, the start *Y* value, the end *X* value, and the end *Y* value. Create and return the new picture and copy just the specified area into the new picture.

6.29   Write a general `scaleUp` function that takes in any picture and creates and returns a new picture twice as big using `makeEmptyPicture(width,height)`.

6.30   Write a general `scaleDown` function that takes in any picture and creates and returns a new picture half as big using `makeEmptyPicture(width,height)`.

6.31   Modify any of the functions from the last chapter to use a nested loop. Check the result to make sure it still does the same thing.

6.32   Write a general function to copy a triangular area from one picture to another.

6.33   Write a function to mirror the input picture's leftmost 20 pixels to pixels 20 to 40.

6.34   Using nested loops, write a function that reduces red in the top third of a picture and clears blue in the bottom third.

6.35   Write a function named `makeCollage` to create a collage of the same image at least four times fit onto the **7in.x95in.jpg** blank JPEG. (You are welcome to add additional images.) One of those four copies can be the original picture. The other three should be modified forms. You can scale, crop, or rotate the image, create a negative of the image, shift or alter colors on the image, and make it darker or lighter.

    After composing your image, *mirror it*. You can do this vertically or horizontally (or otherwise), in any direction—just make sure that your four base images are still visible after mirroring.

    Your single function should make all of this happen—all of the effects and compositing must occur from the single function `makeCollage`. Of course, it is perfectly okay to *use* other functions, but make it so that a tester of your program need only call `setMediaPath()`, put all your input pictures in a **mediasources** directory, and then execute `makeCollage()` in order to see a collage generated, shown, and returned.

*6.36   Think about how the grayscale algorithm works. Basically, if you know the *luminance* of anything visual (e.g., a small image, a letter), you can replace a pixel with that visual element in a similar way to create a collage image. Try implementing this. You'll need 256 visual elements of increasing lightness, all of the same size. You can create a collage by replacing each pixel in the original image with one of these visual elements.

6.37   One of the four functions below generated this picture.

*More challenging problem

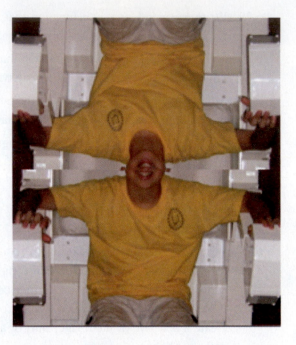

Which one is it?

A.
```
def flip1(picture):
    allpixels = getPixels(picture)
    ln = len(allpixels)-1
    address = ln
    for index in range(0,ln/2):
      mypixel = allpixels[index]
      color = getColor(mypixel)
      newpixel = allpixels[address]
      setColor(newpixel,color)
      address = address - 1
    show(picture)
```

B.
```
def flip2(picture):
    allpixels = getPixels(picture)
    ln = len(allpixels)-1
    address = ln/2
    for index in range(ln/4,(3*ln)/4):
      mypixel = allpixels[index]
      color = getColor(mypixel)
      newpixel = allpixels[address]
      setColor(newpixel,color)
      address = address - 1
    show(picture)
```

C.
```
def flip3(picture):
    allpixels = getPixels(picture)
    ln = len(allpixels)-1
    address = 0
    for index in range(ln,ln/2,-1):
      mypixel = allpixels[index]
```

```
      color = getColor(mypixel)
      newpixel = allpixels[address]
      setColor(newpixel,color)
      address = address + 1
    show(picture)
```

D.
```
def flip4(picture):
  allpixels = getPixels(picture)
  ln = len(allpixels)-1
  address = ln
  for index in range(0,ln/2,2):
    mypixel = allpixels[index]
    color = getColor(mypixel)
    newpixel = allpixels[address]
    setColor(newpixel,color)
    address = address - 1
  show(picture)
```

6.38   One of the four functions below generated this picture.

Which one is it?

A.
```
def newpic1(inpic):
  w = getWidth(inpic)
  h = getHeight(inpic)
  outpic = makeEmptyPicture(w,h)
  outX = w-1
  for inX in range(0,w/2):
    outY = h-1
    for inY in range(0,h/2):
      inpixel = getPixelAt(inpic,inX,inY)
      color = getColor(inpixel)
      newpixel = getPixelAt(outpic,outX,outY)
      setColor(newpixel,color)
      outY = outY - 1
    outX = outX - 1
  show(outpic)
  return(outpic)
```

B.
```
def newpic2(inpic):
  w = getWidth(inpic)
  h = getHeight(inpic)
  outpic = makeEmptyPicture(w,h)
  outX = 0
  for inX in range(0,w/2):
    outY = 0
    for inY in range(0,h/2):
      inpixel = getPixelAt(inpic,inX,inY)
      color = getColor(inpixel)
```

```
              newpixel = getPixelAt(outpic,outX,outY)
              setColor(newpixel,color)
              outY = outY + 1
          outX = outX + 1
      show(outpic)
      return(outpic)
```

C.
```
def newpic3(inpic):
    w = getWidth(inpic)
    h = getHeight(inpic)
    outpic = makeEmptyPicture(w,h)
    outX = w/2
    for inX in range(w/2,w):
        outY = 0
        for inY in range(0,h/2):
            inpixel = getPixelAt(inpic,inX,inY)
            color = getColor(inpixel)
            newpixel = getPixelAt(outpic,outX,outY)
            setColor(newpixel,color)
            outY = outY + 1
        outX = outX - 1
    show(outpic)
    return(outpic)
```

D.
```
def newpic4(inpic):
    w = getWidth(inpic)
    h = getHeight(inpic)
    outpic = makeEmptyPicture(w,h)
    outX = w-1
    for inX in range(0,w/2):
        outY = 0
        for inY in range(0,h/2):
            inpixel = getPixelAt(inpic,inX,inY)
            color = getColor(inpixel)
            newpixel = getPixelAt(outpic,outX,outY)
            setColor(newpixel,color)
            outY = outY + 1
        outX = outX - 2
    show(outpic)
    return(outpic)
```

TO DIG DEEPER

The "bible" of computer graphics is *Introduction to Computer Graphics* [20]. It's highly recommended.

PART 2 SOUND

Chapter Learning Objectives

The media learning goals for this chapter are:

- To understand how we digitize sounds, and the limitations of human hearing that allow us to digitize sounds.
- To use the Nyquist theorem to determine the sampling rate necessary for digitizing a desired sound.
- To manipulate volume.
- To create (and avoid) clipping.

The computer science goals for this chapter are:

- To understand and use arrays as a data structure.
- To use the formula that n bits result in 2^n possible patterns in order to figure out the number of bits needed to save values.
- To use the sound object.
- To debug sound programs.
- To use iteration (in `for` loops) for manipulating sounds.
- To use scope to understand when a variable is available for use.

7.1   HOW SOUND IS ENCODED

There are two parts to understand how sound is encoded and manipulated.

- First, what are the physics of sound? How is it that we hear a variety of sounds?
- Next, how can we then map sounds into numbers on a computer?

7.1.1   The Physics of Sound

Physically, sounds are waves of air pressure. When something makes a sound, it makes ripples in the air just like stones or raindrops dropped into a pond cause ripples on the surface of the water (Figure 7.1). Each drop causes a wave of pressure to pass over the surface of the water, which causes visible rises in the water, and also less visible but just as large depressions in the water. Where the water rises, the pressure there is increased. Where the water dips, the pressure is decreased. Some of the ripples we see actually arise from *combinations* of ripples—some waves are the sums and interactions of other waves.

In the air, we call these increases in pressure *compressions* and decreases in pressure *rarefactions*. It's these compressions and rarefactions that allow us to hear sounds. The shape of the waves, their *frequency*, and their *amplitude* all impact what we perceive in the sound.

The simplest sound in the world is a **sine wave** (Figure 7.2). In a sine wave, the compressions and rarefactions arrive with equal size and regularity. In a sine wave, one compression plus one rarefaction is called a **cycle**. At some point in the cycle, there has to be a point where there is zero pressure, just between the compression and the rarefaction. The distance from the zero point to the greatest pressure (or least pressure) is called the **amplitude**.

In general, amplitude is the most important factor in our perception of *volume*: if the amplitude rises, we typically perceive the sound as being louder. When we perceive an increase in volume, we say that we're perceiving an increase in the *intensity* of sound.

Human perception of sound is not a direct mapping from the physical reality. The study of the human perception of sound is called *psychoacoustics*. One of the odd facts about psychoacoustics is that most of our perceptions of sound are *logarithmically* related to the actual phenomena.

We measure the change in intensity in **decibels** (dB). That's probably the unit that you most often associate with volume. A decibel is a logarithmic measure, so it matches the way we perceive volume. It's always a ratio, a comparison of two values. $10 * \log_{10}(I_1/I_2)$ is the change in intensity in decibels between two intensities, I_1 and I_2. If two amplitudes are measured under the same conditions, we can express the same definition as amplitudes: $20 * \log_{10}(A_1/A_2)$. If $A_2 = 2 * A_1$ (i.e., the amplitude doubles), the difference is roughly 6 dB.

FIGURE 7.1
Raindrops causing ripples on the surface of the water just as sound causes ripples in the air.

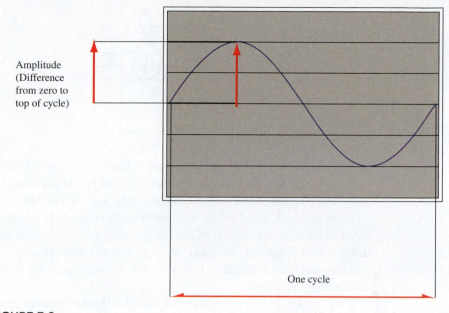

Amplitude
(Difference
from zero to
top of cycle)

One cycle

FIGURE 7.2
One cycle of the simplest sound: a sine wave.

When decibel is used as an absolute measurement, it's in reference to the threshold of audibility at *sound pressure level* (SPL): 0 dB SPL. Normal speech has an intensity of about 60 dB SPL. Shouted speech is about 80 dB SPL.

How often a cycle occurs is called the **frequency**. If a cycle is short, then there can be lots of them per second. If a cycle is long, then there are fewer of them. As the frequency increases, we perceive the **pitch** to increase. We measure frequency in *cycles per second* (cps) or *Hertz* (Hz).

All sounds are periodic—there is always some pattern of rarefaction and compression that leads to cycles. In a sine wave, the notion of a cycle is easy. In natural waves, it's not so clear where a pattern repeats. Even in the ripples in a pond, the waves aren't as regular as you might think. The time between peaks in waves isn't always the same—it varies. This means that a cycle may involve several peaks and valleys until it repeats.

Humans hear between 2 and 20,000 Hz (or 20 kilohertz, abbreviated 20 kHz). Again, as with amplitudes, that's an enormous range. To give you a sense of where music fits into that spectrum, the note A above middle C is 440 Hz in traditional *equal temperament* tuning (Figure 7.3).

Like intensity, our perception of pitch is almost exactly proportional to the log of the frequency. We don't perceive absolute differences in pitch but the *ratio* of the frequencies. If you heard a 100 Hz sound followed by a 200 Hz sound, you'd perceive the same pitch change (or *pitch interval*) as a shift from 1000 Hz to 2000 Hz. Obviously, a difference of 100 Hz is a lot smaller than a change of 1000 Hz, but we perceive it to be the same.

FIGURE 7.3
The note A above middle C is 440 Hz.

In standard tuning, the ratio in frequency between the same notes in adjacent octaves is 2 : 1. Frequency doubles each octave. We told you earlier that A above middle C is 440 Hz. You know, then, that the next A up the scale is 880 Hz.

How we think about music is dependent upon our cultural standards but there are some universals. Among them are the use of pitch intervals (e.g., the ratio between notes C and D remains the same in every octave), the constant relationship between octaves, and the existence of four to seven main pitches (not considering sharps and flats here) in an octave.

What makes the experience of one sound different from another? Why does a flute playing a note sound *so* different from a trumpet or a clarinet playing the same note? We still don't understand everything about psychoacoustics and what physical properties influence our perception of sound, but here are some of the factors that lead us to perceive different sounds (especially musical instruments) as distinct:

- Real sounds are almost never single-frequency sound waves. Most natural sounds have *several* frequencies in them, often at different amplitudes. These additional frequencies are sometimes called *overtones*. When a piano plays the note C, for example, part of the richness of the tone is that the notes E and G are *also* in the sound, but at lower amplitudes. Different instruments have different overtones in their notes. The central tone, the one we're trying to play, is called the *fundamental*.

- Instrument sounds are not continuous with respect to amplitude and frequency. Some come slowly up to the target frequency and amplitude (like wind instruments), while others hit the frequency and amplitude very quickly, and then the volume fades while the frequency remains pretty constant (like a piano).

- Not all sound waves are well represented by sine waves. Real sounds have funny bumps and sharp edges. Our ears can pick these up, at least in the first few waves. We can do a reasonable job of synthesizing with sine waves, but synthesizers sometimes also use other kinds of waveforms to get different kinds of sounds (Figure 7.4).

7.1.2 Investigating Different Sounds

There is a variety of tools that will let you display visualizations of sound in real-time. Using these, you can get insight about the characteristics of sound which you might manipulate in software. You can actually observe sounds as they come into your computer's microphone to get a sense of what louder and softer sounds look like, and what higher- and lower-pitched sounds look like.

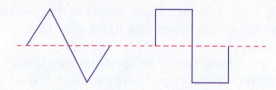

FIGURE 7.4
Some synthesizers use triangular (or *sawtooth*) or square waves.

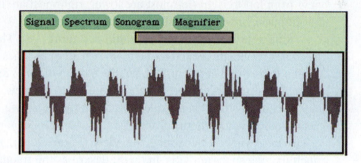

FIGURE 7.5
Sound editor main tool.

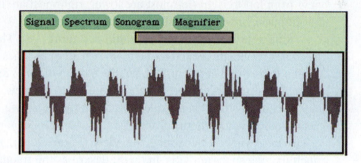

FIGURE 7.6
Viewing the sound signal as it comes in.

We have used the tool *Sonogram*[1] successfully, and it works on Mac OS X, Windows, and Linux. At `http://www.mediacomputation.org`, you can find the MediaTools application which also lets you look at sounds in different ways. The MediaTools application contains tools for sound, graphics, and video. You will also find a MediaTools menu in JES. The tools in that menu also allow you to inspect sounds and pictures, but you can't look at sounds in real time, as you can with the Sonogram, MediaTools, and similar applications.

The MediaTools application sound editor looks like that in Figure 7.5. You can record sounds, open WAV files on your disk, and view the sounds in a variety of ways. (Of course, assuming that you have a microphone on your computer!)

To view sounds, click the RECORD VIEWER button, then the RECORD button. (Hit the STOP button to stop recording.) There are three kinds of views that you can make of the sound.

The first is the **signal view** (Figure 7.6). In the signal view, you're looking at raw sound—each increase in air pressure results in a rise in the graph and each decrease in sound pressure results in a drop in the graph. Note how rapidly the wave changes.

[1]`http://www.christoph-lauer.de/Homepage/Sonogram.html`

Try some softer and louder sounds so that you can see how their look changes. You can always get back to the signal view from another view by clicking the SIGNAL button.

The second view is the **spectrum view** (Figure 7.7). The spectrum view is a completely different perspective on the sound. You read earlier that natural sounds are often actually composed of several different frequencies at once. The spectrum view shows these individual frequencies. This view is also called the *frequency domain*.

Frequencies increase in the spectrum view from left to right. The height of a column indicates the amount of energy (roughly, the volume) of that frequency in the sound. Natural sounds look like Figure 7.7 with more than one *spike* (rise in the graph). (The smaller rises around a spike are often seen as *noise*.)

The technical term for how a spectrum view is generated is called a **Fourier transform**. A Fourier transform takes the sound from the *time domain* (rises and falls in the sound over time) into the frequency domain (identifying which frequencies are in a sound, and the energy of those frequencies, over time). Frequencies increase in this view from left to right (leftmost are lower, rightmost are higher), and more energy at that frequency results in a taller spike.

A sung note has fewer spikes within it (Figure 7.8). There is a dominant *tone* and *overtones* which are related to the tone. A pattern of tones and overtones are common in sounds we think of as musical, but the pattern of tones and overtones is different for different instruments. Figure 7.9 shows the spectrum view of playing a harmonica note and plucking a string on a ukulele. Later in the book, we sum sine waves together to create sounds with patterns of frequencies at different energies.

The third view is the **sonogram view** (Figure 7.10). The sonogram view is very much like the spectrum view in that it describes the frequency domain but it presents these frequencies over time. Each column in the sonogram view, sometimes called a *slice* or *window (of time)*, represents all the frequencies at a given moment in time. The frequencies increase in the slice from lower (bottom) to higher (top). Figure 7.10 represents normal speech, then a whistle (which is almost a perfect single sine wave) that rises and falls. The *darkness* of the spot in the column indicates the amount of energy of that frequency in the input sound at the given moment.

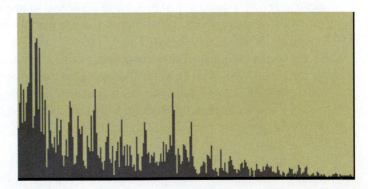

FIGURE 7.7
Viewing normal speech in spectrum view with multiple spikes.

FIGURE 7.8
A sung note in a spectrum view.

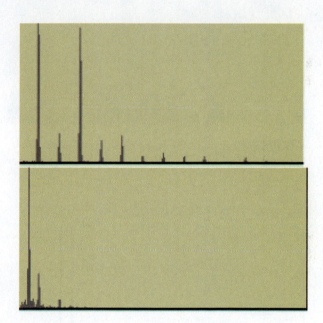

FIGURE 7.9
Harmonica and Ukulele notes in a spectrum view.

The sonogram view is great for studying how sounds change over time, for example how the sound of a piano key being struck changes as the note fades, how different instruments differ in their sounds, or how different vocal sounds differ. For example, we can see in Figure 7.10 how the whistle changes in pitch in the sonogram view. In Figure 7.11 we can see several harmonica notes and ukulele notes. Each has a unique pattern of tones and overtones. Notice that the harmonica tones stay pretty consistent for their entire duration. That is common with wind instruments. Notice that the ukulele notes fade after initially being plucked, with some overtones disappearing earlier than others. That is common with plucked string instruments. The pattern of how a note rises and fades (called *decay*) is called its *envelope*. We can write functions that shape a sound to have a particular envelope.

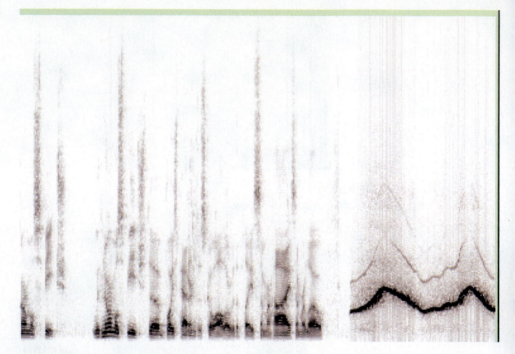

FIGURE 7.10
Viewing normal speech and a whistle in a sonogram view.

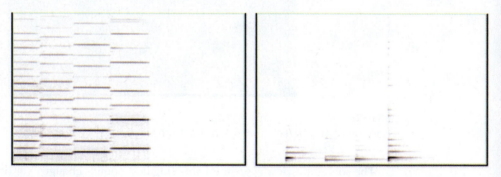

FIGURE 7.11
Viewing harmonica (*left*) and ukulele (*right*) notes in a sonogram view.

Making It Work Tip: Explore Sounds!
You really should try different views on real sounds, in whatever tool you choose. You'll get a much better understanding of sound and of what the manipulations we're doing in this chapter are doing to the sounds.

7.1.3 Encoding the Sound

You just read about how sounds work physically and how we perceive them. To manipulate sounds on a computer and play them back on a computer, we have to digitize them. To digitize sound means to take this flow of waves and turn it into numbers. We want to be able to capture a sound, perhaps manipulate it, and then play it back (through the computer's speakers) and hear what we captured as exactly as possible.

The first part of the process of digitizing sound is handled by the computer's hardware, the physical machinery of the computer. If a computer has a microphone and appropriate sound equipment (like a SoundBlaster sound card on Windows computers), then it's possible, at any moment, to measure the amount of air pressure against the microphone as a single number. Positive numbers correspond to rises in pressure, and negative numbers correspond to rarefactions. We call this an *analog-to-digital conversion (ADC)*—we've moved from an analog signal (a continuously changing sound wave) to a digital value. This means that we can get an instantaneous measure of the sound pressure, but it's only one step along the way. Sound is a continuously changing pressure wave. How do we store that in our computer?

By the way, playback systems on computers work essentially the same in reverse. Sound hardware does *digital-to-analog conversion (DAC)*, and the analog signal is then sent to the speakers. The DAC process also requires numbers representing pressure.

If you know calculus, you have some idea of how we might do this. You know that we can get close to measuring the area under a curve with more and more rectangles whose height matches the curve (Figure 7.12). With this idea, it's pretty clear that if we capture enough of those microphone pressure readings, we capture the wave. We call each pressure reading a *sample*—we are literally "sampling" the sound at that moment. But how many samples do we need? In integral calculus, you compute the area under the curve by (conceptually) having an infinite number of rectangles. While computer memories are growing larger and larger all the time, we can't capture an infinite number of samples per sound.

Mathematicians and physicists wondered about these kinds of questions long before there were computers and the answer to how many samples we need was actually computed long ago. The answer depends on the highest *frequency* you want to capture.

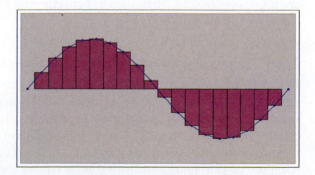

FIGURE 7.12
Area under a curve estimated with rectangles.

Let's say that you don't care about any sounds higher than 8000 Hz. The **Nyquist theorem** says that we would need to capture 16,000 samples per second to completely capture and define a wave whose frequency is less than 8000 cycles per second.

> **Computer Science Idea: Nyquist Theorem**
> To capture a sound of at most *n* cycles per second, you need to capture 2*n* samples per second. ∎

You can get the basic reasoning of the Nyquist theorem with just a little thought. It seems pretty clear that sampling at anything less than the frequency of the highest pitch in the sound would result in missing a lot of cycles. Imagine that you sampled the sound at the same frequency as the sound itself. You might accidentally capture every cycle at its peak, or at its trough. When you looked at all the values, they would just be a straight line. When you get to twice the frequency, you have a reasonable chance of catching each cycle at its peak and its trough.

The Nyquist theorem isn't just a theoretical result. It influences applications in our daily life. It turns out that human voices don't typically get over 4000 Hz. That's why our telephone system is designed around capturing 8000 samples per second. That's why playing music through the telephone doesn't really work very well. The limit of (most) human hearing is around 22,000 Hz. If we were to capture 44,000 samples per second, we would be able to capture any sound that we could actually hear. CD's are created by capturing sound at 44,100 samples per second—just a little bit more than 44 kHz for technical reasons and for a fudge factor.

We call the rate at which samples are collected the *sampling rate*. Most sounds that we hear in daily life are at frequencies far below the highest limits of our hearing. You can capture and manipulate sounds in this class at a sampling rate of 22 kHz (22,000 samples per second) and they will sound quite reasonable. If you use too low a sampling rate to capture a high-pitched sound, you'll still hear something when you play the sound back, but the pitch will sound strange.

Typically, each of these samples are encoded in 2 bytes, or 16 bits. Though there are larger *sample sizes*, 16 bits works perfectly well for most applications. CD-quality sound uses 16-bit samples.

7.1.4   Binary Numbers and Two's Complement

In 16 bits, the numbers that can be encoded range from $-32,768$ to $32,767$. These aren't magic numbers—they make perfect sense when you understand the encoding. These numbers are encoded in 16 bits using a technique called **two's complement notation** but we can understand it without knowing the details of that technique. We've got 16 bits to represent positive and negative numbers. Let's set aside one of these bits (remember, it's just 0 or 1) to represent whether we're talking about a positive (0) or negative (1) number. We call this the *sign bit*. That leaves 15 bits to represent the actual value. How many different patterns of 15 bits are there? We could start counting:

```
000000000000000
000000000000001
000000000000010
000000000000011
...
111111111111110
111111111111111
```

This looks foreboding. Let's see if we can figure out a pattern. If we've got two bits, there are four patterns: 00, 01, 10, 11. If we've got three bits, there are eight patterns: 000, 001, 010, 011, 100, 101, 110, 111. It turns out that 2^2 is four, and 2^3 is eight. Play with four bits. How many patterns are there? $2^4 = 16$. It turns out that we can state this as a general principle.

Computer Science Idea: 2^n Patterns in n Bits

If you have n bits, there are 2^n possible patterns in those n bits. ∎

$2^{15} = 32,768$. Why is there one more value in the negative range than the positive? Zero is neither negative nor positive, but if we want to represent it as bits, we need to define some pattern as zero. We use one of the positive range values (where the sign bit is zero) to represent zero, so that it takes up one of the 32,768 patterns.

The way that computers often represent positive and negative integers is called *two's complement*. In two's complement, positive numbers are shown as usual in binary. The number 9 is 00001001 in binary. The two's complement of a negative number can be calculated by starting with the positive number in binary and inverting it so that all the 1's become 0's and all the 0's become 1's. Finally, add 1 to the result. So −9 starts as 00001001 which after inversion is 11110110 and then adding 1 results in 11110111. One advantage to representing numbers in two's complement is that if you add a negative number (−3) to the positive number of the same value (3), the result is zero, since 1 plus 1 is 0, carry the 1 (Figure 7.13).

7.1.5 Storing Digitized Sounds

The sample size is a limitation on the amplitude of the sound that can be captured. If you have a sound that generates a pressure greater than 32,767 (or a rarefaction greater than −32,768), you'll only capture up to the limits of the 16 bits. If you were to look

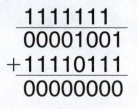

FIGURE 7.13
Adding 9 and −9 in two's complement.

at the wave in the signal view, it would look like somebody had taken some scissors and *clipped* off the peaks of the waves. We call this effect *clipping* for that very reason. If you play (or generate) a sound that's clipped, it sounds bad—it sounds like your speakers are breaking.

There are other ways of digitizing sound but this is by far the most common. The technical term for this way of encoding sound is *pulse coded modulation (PCM)*. You may encounter this term if you read further in audio or play with audio software.

What this means is that a sound in a computer is a long list of numbers, each of which is a sample in time. There is an ordering in these samples: if you played the samples out of order, you wouldn't get the same sound at all. The most efficient way to store an ordered list of data items on a computer is with an **array**. An array is literally a sequence of bytes right next to one another in memory. We call each value in an array an **element**.

We can easily store the samples that make up a sound in an array. Think of each two bytes as storing a single sample. The array will be large—for CD-quality sounds, there will be 44,100 elements for every second of recording. A minute-long recording will result in an array with 26,460,000 elements.

Each array element has a number associated with it called its **index**. The index numbers increase sequentially. The first element of the array is at index 0, the second

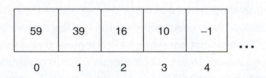

FIGURE 7.14
A depiction of the first five elements in a real sound array.

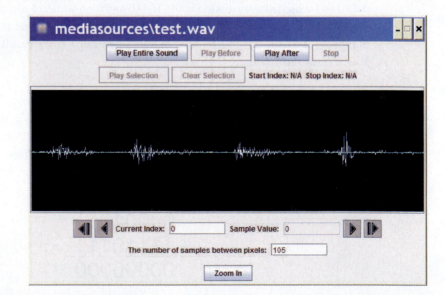

FIGURE 7.15
A sound recording graphed in MediaTools.

one is at index 1, and so on. The last element in the array is at an index equal to the number of elements in the array minus 1. You can think about an array as a long line of boxes, each one holding a value and each box having an index number (Figure 7.14).

Using the MediaTools, you can explore a sound (Figure 7.15) and get a sense of where the sound is quiet (small amplitudes) and loud (large amplitudes). This is important if you want to manipulate the sound. For example, the gaps between recorded words tend to be quiet—at least quieter than the words themselves. You can pick out where words end by looking for the gaps, as in Figure 7.15.

You will soon read about how to read a file containing a recording of a sound into a *sound object*, view the samples in the sound, and change the values of the sound array elements. By changing the values in the array, you change the sound. Manipulating a sound is simply a matter of manipulating the elements in an array.

7.2   MANIPULATING SOUNDS

Now that we know how sounds are encoded, we can manipulate sounds using our Python programs. Here's what we'll need to do.

1. We'll need to get the filename of a WAV file and make a sound from it.

2. You will often get the samples of the sound. Sample objects are easy to manipulate, and they know that when you change them, they should automatically change the original sound. You'll read first about manipulating the samples to start with, then about how to manipulate the sound samples from within the sound itself.

3. Whether you get the sample objects out of a sound or just deal with the samples in the sound object, you will then want to do something to the samples.

4. You may want to explore both the original sound and the modified sound to check that the results match what you expected to happen.

5. You may want to write the sound back out to a new file for use elsewhere.

7.2.1   Open Sounds and Manipulating Samples

You can get the full pathname for a file by picking it with `pickAFile` and then make a sound object with `makeSound`. Here's an example of doing that in JES (on Windows).

```
>>> filename=pickAFile()
>>> print filename
C:/ip-book/mediasources/preamble.wav
>>> aSound=makeSound(filename)
>>> print aSound
Sound file: C:\ip-book\mediasources\preamble.wav
    number of samples: 421110
```

If we store our sounds in the same media folder, and execute `setMediaPath()` in the Command Area, we can reduce the above example to something that looks like this (on Mac OS X):

```
>>> aSound = makeSound("preamble.wav")
>>> print aSound
```

```
Sound file: /Users/guzdial/Desktop/mediasources-4ed/preamble.wav
     number of samples: 421110
```

What makeSound does is to scoop up all the bytes from the filename provided as input, dump them into memory, and place a big sign on them saying, "This is a sound!" When you execute aSound = makeSound(filename), you are saying, "Call that sound object over there aSound!" When you use the sound as input to functions, you are saying, "Use that sound object over there (yeah, the one I named aSound) as input to this function."

You can get the samples from a sound using getSamples. The function getSamples takes a sound as input and returns an array of all the samples as sample objects. When you execute this function, it may take quite a while before it finishes—longer for longer sounds, shorter for shorter sounds.

The function getSamples makes an array of sample *objects* out of the basic sample array. An *object* is more than just a simple value like you read about earlier—for one difference, a sample object also knows what sound it came from and what its index is. You will read more about objects later but take it at face value now that getSamples provides you with a bunch of sample objects that you can manipulate—and in fact makes manipulation pretty easy. You can get the value of a sample object by using getSampleValue (with a sample object as input) and you set the sample value with setSampleValue (with a sample object and a new value as input).

But before we get to the manipulations, let's look at some other ways to get and set sample values. We can use the function getSampleValueAt to ask the sound to give us the values of specific samples at specific indices. The input values to getSampleValueAt are a sound and an index number.

```
>>> print getSampleValueAt(aSound,0)
36
>>> print getSampleValueAt(aSound,1)
29
```

Valid index values are any integer (0.1289 is not a good index value) between 0 and 1 less than the length of the sound in samples. We get the length with getLength(). Note the error that we get below if we try to get a sample using the length of the array.

```
>>> print getLength(aSound)
421110
>>> print getSampleValueAt(aSound,421110)
You are trying to access the sample at index: 421110,
but the last valid index is at 421109
The error was:
Inappropriate argument value (of correct type).
An error occurred attempting to pass an argument
to a function.
```

Debugging Tip: Getting More Information on Errors

If you're getting an error and want more information on it, go to the OPTIONS item in the EDIT menu of JES and choose EXPERT instead of NORMAL (Figure 7.16).[2] Expert mode can sometimes give you more details—maybe more than you wanted, but it can be helpful sometimes. Expert mode shows you errors as they would appear in Jython outside of JES.

We can similarly change sample values by using setSampleValueAt. It takes a sound, an index, but also a new value for the sample at that index. We can check it again with getSampleValueAt.

```
>>> print getSampleValueAt(aSound,0)
36
>>> setSampleValueAt(aSound,0,12)
>>> print getSampleValueAt(aSound,0)
12
```

Common Bug: Mistyping a Name

You just saw a whole bunch of function names and some of them are pretty long. What happens if you type one of them wrong? JES will complain that it doesn't know what you mean, like this:

```
>>> writeSndTo(aSound,"mysound.wav")
Name not found globally.
A local or global name could not be found. You need to
define the function or variable before you try to use
it in any way.
```

JES Options		
Mode:	Normal	▼
	Normal	
Font:	Expert	
Line Numbers:	☑	
Show Indentation Help:	☑	
Show Turning Menu:	☐	
Logging:	☑	
Auto save on load:	☐	
Save a backup copy on save:	☑	
Modulo pixel color values by 256 (356 mod 256 = 100)	☐	
Skin:	Metal	▼
Cancel		Done

FIGURE 7.16
Turning on Expert errors mode.

[2]Depending on what version of JES you are using, you may see more options in the Preferences pane.

It's no big deal. Use the up arrow key on the keyboard to bring up the last thing you typed and use the left arrow to go to the spot to fix. Fix the error. Be sure to go back to the last character on the line using the right arrow key before you press ENTER.

What do you think would happen if we played this sound? Would it really sound different than it did before, now that we've turned the first sample from the number 36 to the number 12? Not really. To explain why not, let's find out what the sampling rate is for this sound, using the function `getSamplingRate`, which takes a sound as its input.

```
>>> print getSamplingRate(aSound)
22050.0
```

The sound that we're manipulating in this example (a recording of Mark reading part of the U.S. Constitution's preamble) has a sampling rate of 22,050 samples per second. Changing one sample changes 1/22,050 of the first second of the sound. If you can hear that, you have amazingly good hearing—and we will have doubts about your truthfulness!

Obviously, to make a significant manipulation to the sound, we have to manipulate hundreds if not thousands of samples. We're certainly not going to do that by typing thousands of lines of

```
setSampleValueAt(aSound,0,12)
setSampleValueAt(aSound,1,24)
setSampleValueAt(aSound,2,100)
setSampleValueAt(aSound,3,99)
setSampleValueAt(aSound,4,-1)
```

We need to take advantage of the computer executing our recipe, by telling it to go do something hundreds or thousands of times. That's the topic for the next section.

But we will end this section by talking about how to write your results back out to a file. Once you've manipulated your sound and want to save it out to use elsewhere, you use `writeSoundTo`, which takes a sound and a new filename as input. Be sure that your file ends with the extension ".wav" if you're saving a sound so that your operating system knows what to do with it.

```
>>> print filename
C:/ip-book/mediasources/preamble.wav
>>> writeSoundTo(aSound,"C:/ip-book/mediasources/new-preamble.wav")
```

You'll probably figure out, when playing sounds a lot, that if you use `play` a couple of times in quick succession, you'll mix the sounds. The second `play` starts before the first one ends. How do you make sure that the computer plays only a single sound and then waits for it to end? You use `blockingPlay`. This works the same as `play` but it waits for the sound to end so that no other sound can interfere while it's playing.

7.2.2   Using the JES MediaTools

The JES MediaTools are available from the MEDIATOOLS menu in JES. When you choose the picture or sound tool, you will be offered a pop-up menu of *variable* names of pictures or sounds, appropriate to whichever tool you chose. Click OK and you'll enter the JES sound tool. You can also bring up the sound tool by exploring the sound, just like you did with pictures.

```
>>> explore(aSound)
```

The sound tool lets you explore a sound.

- You can play the sound, then click anywhere in it to set a cursor point, then play it before or after the cursor.
- You can select a region (by clicking and dragging) and then play only that region (Figure 7.17).
- As you set a cursor, you're shown the sample index and sample value at that point.
- You can also zoom in to see every sound value (Figure 7.18); you will have to scroll to see all the values.

Common Bug: Windows and WAV Files

The world of WAV files isn't as compatible and smooth as one might like. WAV files created with other applications (e.g., Windows Recorder) *may* not play in JES and JES WAV files may not play in all other applications (e.g., WinAmp 2). Apple QuickTime Player Pro (http://www.apple.com/quicktime) is good at reading *any* WAV file and exporting a new one that almost any other application can read.

7.2.3   Looping

The problem we're facing is a common one in computing: How do we get the computer to do something over and over again? We need to get the computer to **loop or iterate**.

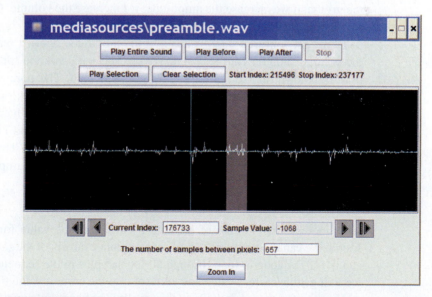

FIGURE 7.17
Exploring a sound in JES.

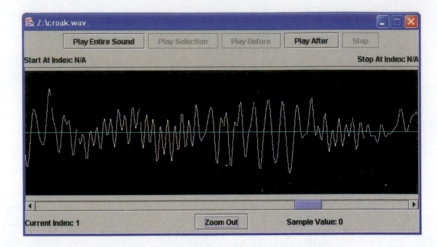

FIGURE 7.18
Zooming in to see every sound value.

Python has commands especially for looping (or iterating). We're mostly going to use the command `for`. A `for` loop executes commands (that you specify) for a sequence (that you provide), where each time the commands are executed, a particular variable (that you name) will have the value of a different element of the sequence.

7.3   CHANGING THE VOLUME OF SOUNDS

Earlier, we said that the amplitude of a sound is the main factor in the volume. This means that if we increase the amplitude, we increase the volume. Or if we decrease the amplitude, we decrease the volume.

Don't get confused here—changing the amplitude doesn't reach out and twist up the volume knob on your speakers. If your speaker's volume (or computer's volume) is turned down, the sound will never get very loud. The point is getting the sound itself louder. Have you ever watched a movie on TV where, without changing the volume on the TV, the sound becomes so low that you can hardly hear it? (Marlon Brando's dialogue in the movie *The Godfather* comes to mind.) Or have you noticed how commercials are always louder than normal TV programs? That's what we're doing here. We can make sounds *shout* or *whisper* by tweaking the amplitude.

7.3.1   Increasing Volume

Let's increase the volume of a sound by doubling the value for each sample in the sound. We can use `getSamples` to get a sequence (array) of the samples in a sound. We can use a `for` loop to loop through all the samples in the sequence. For each sample, we will get the current value and then set it to the current value times 2.

Here's a function that doubles the amplitude of an input sound.

Program 93: Increase an Input Sound's Volume by Doubling the Amplitude

```
def increaseVolume(sound):
  for sample in getSamples(sound):
    value = getSampleValue(sample)
    setSampleValue(sample,value * 2)
```

Go ahead and type the above into your JES Program Area. Click LOAD PROGRAM to get Python to process the function and to allow us to use the name `increaseVolume`. Follow along the example below to get a better idea of how this all works.

To use this recipe, you have to create a sound first, then pass the sound to the function `increaseVolume` as input. In the example below, we assume that you have used `setMediaPath()` to tell JES where your media folder is. You can then make a sound using the base filename, rather than the whole path.

```
>>> s=makeSound("test.wav")
>>> explore(s)
>>> increaseVolume(s)
>>> explore(s)
```

We create a sound that we name `s`. We then explore the sound which will bring up the JES sound tool on a copy of the sound. Next we evaluate `increaseVolume(s)`, the sound that is named `s` is *also* named `sound` but just within that function. This is a *very* important point. Both names refer to the same sound! The changes that take place in `increaseVolume` are really changing the *same* sound. You can think of each name as an *alias* for the other: they refer to the same *thing*.

There's a point to mention here just in passing, but it becomes more important later: when the function `increaseVolume` ends, the name `sound` *has no value*. It only exists during the duration of that function's execution. We say that it only exists within the *scope* of the function `increaseVolume`. The scope of a variable is the area in which it is known. For instance, variables that are defined in the Command Area have Command Area scope. They are only known in the Command Area. Variables that are defined in a function have function scope. They are only known in that function.

We can now play the file to hear that it's louder and write it to a new file.

```
>>> play(s)
>>> writeSoundTo(s,"c:/ip-book/mediasources/test-louder.wav")
```

Common Bug: Keep Sounds Short
Longer sounds take up more memory and will process more slowly.

7.3.2   Did That Really Work?

Now, is it really louder, or does it just seem that way? We can check this in several ways. You could always make the sound even louder by evaluating `increaseVolume` on our sound a few more times—eventually, you'll be totally convinced that the sound is louder. But there are ways to test even more subtle effects.

If we compared graphs of the two sounds using the JES MediaTools sound tool, you'd find that the graph of the sound does have greater amplitude after increasing it using our function. Check it out in Figure 7.19.

Maybe you're unsure that you're really seeing a larger wave in the second picture. You can use the JES sound tool to check the individual sample values. Click on a part of the wave that has a value other than 0 in one sound tool and then enter the index in the other sound tool and press ENTER. Compare the sample values. Notice in Figure 7.19 that the value at index 18,375 was −1290 originally and after the volume was increased it is −2580, so the function did double the value.

Finally, you can always check for yourself from within JES. If you've been following along with the example,[3] then the variable s is now the louder sound. Go ahead and make a new sound object which is the *original* sound—named below as sOriginal (for *sound original*). Check any sample value that you want. It's always true that the louder sound has twice the sample values of the original sound.

```
>>> print s
Sound file: C:/ip-book/mediasources/test.wav number of samples: 67585
>>> sOriginal=makeSound("test.wav")
>>> print getSampleValueAt(s,0)
0
>>> print getSampleValueAt(sOriginal,0)
0
>>> print getSampleValueAt(s,18375)
-2580
>>> print getSampleValueAt(sOriginal,18375)
-1290
>>> print getSampleValueAt(s,1000)
4
>>> print getSampleValueAt(sOriginal,1000)
2
```

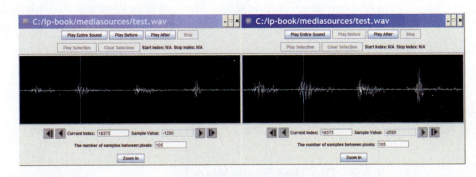

FIGURE 7.19
Comparing the graphs of the original sound (*left*) and the louder one (*right*).

[3]What? You haven't? You *should!* It'll make much more sense if you try it yourself.

You can see that negative values become *more* negative. That's what's meant by "increasing the amplitude." The amplitude of the wave goes in *both* directions. We have to make the wave larger in both the positive and negative dimensions.

It's important to do what you just read in this chapter: *doubt* your programs. Did that *really* do what I wanted it to do? The way you check is by *testing*. That's what this section is about. You just saw several ways to test:

- By checking pieces of the results (using the JES sound tool).

- By writing additional code statements that check the results of the original program.

How It Works

Let's walk through the code, slowly, and consider how this program works.

```
def increaseVolume(sound):
  for sample in getSamples(sound):
    value = getSampleValue(sample)
    setSampleValue(sample,value * 2)
```

Recall our picture of how the samples in a sound array might look. This shows the first values in the sound created from the file **gettysburg.wav**.

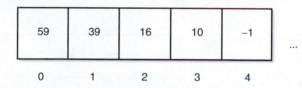

This is what getSamples(sound) would return: an array of sample values, each numbered. The for loop allows us to walk through each sample, one at a time. The name sample will be assigned to each sample in turn.

When the for loop begins, sample will be the name for the first sample.

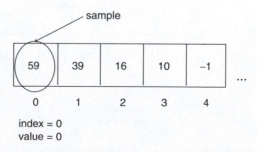

The variable value will take on the value of 59 when value=getSampleValue-(sample) is executed. The sample that the name sample references will then be doubled with setSampleValue(sample,value*2).

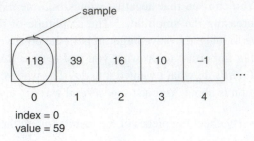

index = 0
value = 59

That's the end of the first pass through the body of the for loop. Python will then start the loop again and move `sample` on to point at the *next* element in the array.

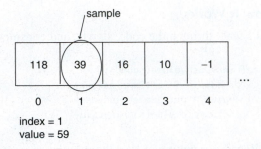

index = 1
value = 59

The `value` is again set to the value of the sample, then the sample will be doubled.

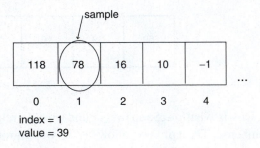

index = 1
value = 39

This is what it will look like after five times through the loop.

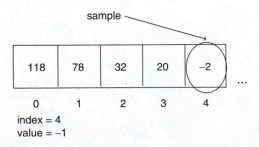

index = 4
value = −1

The for loop *keeps* going through all the samples—tens of thousands of them! Thank goodness it's the *computer* executing this program!

One way to think about what's happening here is that the for loop doesn't really *do* anything, in the sense of changing anything in the sound. Only the *body* of the loop does work. The `for` loop tells the computer *what* to do. It's a manager. What the computer actually does is something like this:

```
sample = sample #0
value = value of the sample, 59
change sample to 118
sample = sample #1
value = 39
change sample to 78
sample = sample #2
...
sample = sample #4
value = -1
change sample to -2
...
```

The `for` loop is only saying, "Do all of this for every element in the array." It's the *body* of the loop that contains the Python commands that are executed.

What you have just read in this section is called **tracing** the program. We slowly went through how each step in the program was executed. We drew pictures to describe the data in the program. We used numbers, arrows, equations, and even plain English to explain what was going on in the program. This is the single most important technique in programming. It's part of *debugging*. Your program will *not* always work. Absolutely, guaranteed, without a shadow of a doubt—you will write code that does not do what you want. But the computer *will* do *something*. How do you figure out what it *is* doing? You debug, and the most powerful way to do that is by tracing the program.

7.3.3   Decreasing Volume

To decrease volume, we need to make the amplitude of the sound wave *smaller*. By *dividing* each sound by two (i.e., multiplying by 1/2), we make the wave smaller while keeping its shape and the frequency the same.

Program 94: Decrease an Input Sound's Volume by Halving the Amplitude

```
def decreaseVolume(sound):
  for sample in getSamples(sound):
    value = getSampleValue(sample)
    setSampleValue(sample,value * 0.5)
```

How It Works

- Our function takes a sound object as input. Within the function `decreaseVolume`, the input sound will be called `sound`—no matter what name it has in the Command Area.

- The variable `sample` will stand for each and every sample in the input sound.

- Each time `sample` is assigned a new sample, we will get the *value* of the sample. We put it in the variable `value`.

- We then set the sample value to 50% of its current value by multiplying `value` by 0.5, and setting the sample value to that.

We can use it like this.

```
>>> f=pickAFile()
>>> print f
C:/ip-book/mediasources/louder-test.wav
>>> sound=makeSound(f)
>>> explore(sound)
>>> play(sound)
>>> decreaseVolume(sound)
>>> explore(sound)
>>> play(sound)
```

We can even do it again, and lower the volume even further.

```
>>> decreaseVolume(sound)
>>> explore(sound)
>>> play(sound)
```

7.3.4   Using Array Index Notation

The function `getSamples` returns an array of samples which can be indexed using the index notation that we have used previously with strings, lists, and arrays of pixels. Square brackets ("[" and "]") can allow us to index the samples from `getSamples`. When we are processing *all* the samples, the array notation is not much help. It can be more valuable in the next chapter when we are trying to figure out specific places in the sound to manipulate.

Program 95: Increase a Sound's Volume Using Index Notation

```
def increaseVolume2(sound):
  samples = getSamples(sound)
  for index in range(len(samples)):
    sample = samples[index]
    value = getSampleValue(sample)
    setSampleValue(sample, value * 2)
```

How It Works

Just like in `increaseVolume`, the function `increaseVolume2` takes in a sound as input. All the samples in the sound get named `samples`. We use the one input version of `range` to specify all the indices from 0 to `len(samples)-1`.[4] We pull the `sample` we want out of `samples[index]`. The rest of the function works exactly like `increaseVolume`.

---

[4]Recall that `range` goes up to but does not include the end value.

7.3.5   Making Sense of Functions in Sounds

The lessons about how functions work in pictures (from Section 4.4.1) apply here in sounds as well. For example, we could put all the pickAFile and makeSound calls directly into our functions like increaseVolume and decreaseVolume but that would mean that the functions are doing more than *one and only one thing*. If we had to increase or decrease the volume to a bunch of sounds, we'd find it annoying to have to keep picking files.

We can write functions that take multiple inputs. For example, here's a program to changeVolume. It accepts a factor that is multiplied by each sample value. This function can be used to increase or decrease the amplitude (and thus, the volume).

Program 96: Change a Sound's Volume by a Given Factor

```
def changeVolume(sound, factor):
  for sample in getSamples(sound):
    value = getSampleValue(sample)
    setSampleValue(sample,value * factor)
```

This program is clearly more flexible than increaseVolume or decreaseVolume. Does that make it better? Certainly it is for some purposes (e.g., if you were writing software to do general audio processing), but for other purposes, having separate and clearly named functions for increasing and decreasing volume is better. Remember that software is written for humans—write software that is understandable for the people who will be reading and using your software.

We are reusing the name sound a lot. We use it to name sounds that we read from disk in the Command Area and we're using it to serve as a placeholder for inputs to functions. *That's okay.* Names can have different meanings depending on the context. Inside a function is a different context than the Command Area. If you create a variable in a function context (like value in Program 96), then that variable won't exist when you get back out to the Command Area. We can return values from a function context back out to the Command Area (or other calling function) by using return, which we'll talk more about later.

7.4   NORMALIZING SOUNDS

If you think about it, you may find it strange that the last two programs work. We can multiply the numbers representing a sound—and the sound will seem (essentially) the same to our ears but louder. The way we experience a sound depends less on the specific numbers than on the *relationship* between them. Remember that the overall shape of the sound waveform is dependent on *many* samples. In general, if we multiply all the samples by the same multiplier, we only affect our sense of volume (intensity), not the sound itself. (We'll work to change the sound itself in future sections.)

A common operation that people want to do with sounds is to make them as **loud as possible**. This is called **normalizing**. It's not really hard to do but it takes a few more variables. Here's the recipe, in English, that we need to tell the computer to do.

- We have to figure out what the largest sample in the sound is. If it's already at the maximum value (32,767), then we can't really increase the volume and still get what seems like the same sound. Remember that we have to multiply all the samples by the same multiplier.

  It's an easy recipe (*algorithm*) to find the largest value—sort of a *subrecipe* within the overall normalizing recipe. Define a name (say, `largest`) and assign it a small value (0 works). Now check all the samples. If you find a sample larger than `largest`, change `largest` to have that larger value. Keep checking the samples, now comparing to the *new* largest. Eventually, the very largest value in the array will be in the variable `largest`.

  To do this, we'll need a way of figuring out the maximum value of two values. Python provides a built-in function called `max` that can do this.

```
>>> print max(8,9)
9
>>> print max(3,4,5)
5
```

- Next we need to figure out what value to multiply all the samples by. We want the largest value to become 32,767. Thus we want to figure out a *multiplier* such that (*multiplier*)(*largest*) = 32,767.

  Solve for the multiplier:

  multiplier = 32,767/*largest*. The multiplier will need to be a floating-point number (have a decimal component), so we need to convince Python that not everything here is an integer. Turns out that that's easy—use 32,767.0. Simply stick on ".0."

- Now loop through all the samples, as we did for `increaseVolume`, and multiply the sample by the multiplier.

  Here's a program to normalize sounds.

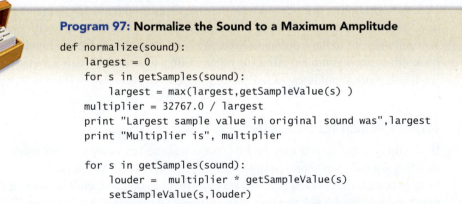

Program 97: Normalize the Sound to a Maximum Amplitude

```
def normalize(sound):
    largest = 0
    for s in getSamples(sound):
        largest = max(largest,getSampleValue(s) )
    multiplier = 32767.0 / largest
    print "Largest sample value in original sound was",largest
    print "Multiplier is", multiplier

    for s in getSamples(sound):
        louder =  multiplier * getSampleValue(s)
        setSampleValue(s,louder)
```

There are several things to note about this program.

- There are blank lines in there! Python doesn't care about them. Adding blank lines can be useful to break up and improve the understandability of longer programs.

- There are `print` statements in there! `print` statements can be *really* useful. First, they give you some feedback that the program is running—a useful thing in long-running programs. Second, they show you what it's finding, which can be interesting. Third, it's a terrific testing method and a way to debug your programs. Let's imagine that the printout showed that the multiplier was less than 1.0. We know that this kind of multiplier *decreases* volume. You should probably suspect that something went wrong.

- Some of the statements in this program are pretty long, so they wrap around in the text. *Type them as a single line!* Python doesn't let you hit ENTER until the end of the statement—make sure that your print statements are all on one line.

Here's what the program looks like running.

```
>>> s = makeSound("test.wav")
>>> explore(s)
>>> normalize(sound)
Largest sample value in original sound was 11702
Multiplier is 2.8001196376687747
>>> explore(s)
>>> play(sound)
```

Exciting, huh? Obviously, the interesting part is hearing the much louder volume, which is awfully hard to demonstrate in a book.

7.4.1 Generating Clipping

Earlier, we talked about *clipping*, the effect when the normal curves of the sound are broken by the limitations of the sample size. One way of generating clipping is to keep increasing the volume. Another way is to explicitly force clipping.

What if you *only* had the largest and smallest possible sample values? What if all the positive values were the *maximum* values and all the negative values were the *minimum* values? Try this program, particularly on sounds with words in them.

Program 98: Set All Samples to Maximum Values

```
def onlyMaximize(sound):
  for sample in getSamples(sound):
    value = getSampleValue(sample)
    if value >= 0:
      setSampleValue(sample,32767)
    if value < 0:
      setSampleValue(sample,-32768)
```

The end result looks really strange (Figure 7.20). When you play the sound back, you'll hear some awful noises. Some of that awful sound is clipping. Other parts of how bad it sounds is that every small background noise has now been made *AS LOUD AS IT POSSIBLY CAN BE!* The really amazing thing is that you can *still* make out the words in the sounds that you manipulate with this function. Why is that? Notice that the *frequency* information is exactly the same in both the original and the maximized sounds. Our ability to decipher words from noise is based mostly on frequency information and is incredibly powerful.

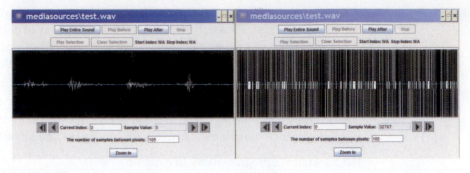

FIGURE 7.20
Original sound and the one with only maximum values.

Computer Science Idea: We Only Need One Bit per Sample for Legible Speech

How many bits are there in each sample in our maximized sound? We know that the computer is storing 16 bits of value for each sample, but the term *bit* really refers to an amount of information. Each sample in the maximized sound only has two possible *states* or values. A piece of information with only two values is one bit. Therefore, we are only using one bit of information to record the maximized sound—and it is legible speech. We now know that, if our sampling rate is high enough, we can record legible speech with only one bit per sample.

PROGRAMMING SUMMARY

In this chapter, we talk about several kinds of encodings of data (or objects).

Sounds	Encodings of sounds, typically coming from a WAV file.
Samples	Collections of sample objects, each indexed by a number (e.g., sample #0, sample #1). `samples[0]` is the first sample object. You can manipulate each sample in the samples like this: `for s in samples:`.
Sample	A value between −32,000 and 32,000 (roughly) representing the voltage that a microphone would generate at a given instant when recording a sound. The length of the instant is typically either 1/44,100 of a second (for CD-quality sound) or 1/22,050 of a second (for good-enough sound on most computers). A sample object remembers what sound it came from, so if you change its value, it knows to go back and change the right sample in the sound.

Here are the functions used or introduced in this chapter:

`int`	Returns the integer part of the input value.
`max`	Takes as many numbers as you want and returns the largest value.

SOUND FILE FUNCTIONS AND PIECES

pickAFile	Lets the user pick a file and returns the complete pathname as a string. No input.
makeSound	Takes a filename as input, reads the file, and creates a sound from it. Returns the sound.

SOUND OBJECT FUNCTIONS AND PIECES

play	Plays a sound provided as input. No return value.
getLength	Takes a sound as input and returns the number of samples in the sound.
getSamples	Takes a sound as input and returns the samples in the sound in a one-dimensional array.
blockingPlay	Plays the sound provided as input and makes sure that no other sound plays at the exact same time. (Try two play's right after each other.)
playAtRate	Takes a sound and a rate (1.0 means normal speed, 2.0 is twice as fast, and 0.5 is half as fast) and plays the sound at that rate. The duration is always *the same* (e.g., if you play it twice as fast, the sound plays *twice* to fill the given time).
playAtRateDur	Takes a sound, a rate, and a duration as the number of samples to play.
writeSoundTo	Takes a sound and a filename (a string) and writes the sound to the file as a WAV file. (Make sure that the filename ends in ".wav" if you want the operating system to treat it right.)
getSamplingRate	Takes a sound as input and returns the number representing the number of samples in each second for the sound.
getLength	Returns the length of the sound as a number of samples.

SAMPLE-ORIENTED FUNCTIONS AND PIECES

getSampleValueAt	Takes a sound and an index (an integer value) and returns the value of the sample (between −32,000 and 32,000) for that object.
setSampleValueAt	Takes a sound, an index, and a value (should be between −32,000 and 32,000) and sets the value of the sample at the given index in the given sound to the given value.

getSampleObjectAt	Takes a sound and an index (an integer value) and returns the sample object at that index.
getSampleValue	Takes a sample object and returns its value (between −32,000 and 32,000). getValue will also work.
setSampleValue	Takes a sample object and a value and sets the sample to the value. setValue will also work.
getSound	Takes a sample object and returns the sound that it is part of.

PROBLEMS

7.1   Define the following terms.

1. Clipping

2. Normalize

3. Amplitude

4. Frequency

5. Rarefactions

7.2   Write the number −9 in two's complement. Write the number 4 in two's complement. Write the number −27 in two's complement.

7.3   Open up a SONOGRAM view in the MediaTools application or a similar sound visualization tool say some vowel sounds. Is there a distinctive pattern? Do "oh's" always sound the same? Do "ah's"? Does it matter whether you switch people: Are the patterns the same?

7.4   Get a couple of different instruments and play the same note on them in the MediaTools application's sound editor with the sonogram view open. Are all "C's" made equal? Do they have the same tones and overtones? Using the MediaTools visualization, can you *see* the differences between the sounds?

7.5   Try out a variety of WAV files as instruments, using the piano keyboard in the MediaTools application sound editor. What kinds of recordings work best as instruments?

7.6   The increase volume recipe (Program 93 (page 221)) takes a sound as input. Write a function increaseVolumeNamed that takes a filename as input, then plays the louder sound.

7.7   Write a function to increase the volume for all the positive values and decrease the volume for all the negative values. Can you still understand any words in the sound?

7.8   Write a function to set all the negative values of a sound to zero. Can you still understand any words in the sound?

7.9   Write a function to find the smallest value in a sound and print it out.

7.10 Write a function to count the number of times the value of a sample is 0 and print out the total.

7.11 Write a function to set values that are greater than 0 to the maximum positive value (32,767) in a sound, but leave all the negative values the same. Can you still understand any words in the sound?

7.12 Sometimes people think that the way to increase volume is to *add* a value (like 1000) to every sample. Write the function `fauxIncreaseVolume(sound, increment)` to add an input value `increment` to every sample in an input sound. Try your function with an increment of 1000. Can you hear a difference in the sound? Why or why not?

7.13 Get a sound. Run `increaseVolume` on the sound, and then `onlyMaximize` on the same sound. Get an original copy of the sound. Now, run `fauxIncrease-Volume` on the new copy, and then `onlyMaximize` on the output of `faux-IncreaseVolume`. The sounds will sound different. If the sound had words in it, the words will be much clearer after running `fauxIncreaseVolume`. Why is that?

7.14 Rewrite increase volume (Program 93) so that it takes two inputs: the sound to increase in volume and a filename where the newly louder sound should be stored. Then increase the volume and write the sound out to the name file. You might also try rewriting it so that it takes an input filename instead of the sound, so that inputs are both filenames.

7.15 Rewrite increase volume (Program 93) so that it takes two inputs: a sound to increase in volume and a *multiplier*. Use the multiplier as *how much* to increase the amplitude of the sound samples. Can we use the same function to both increase and decrease the volume? Demonstrate commands that you would execute to do each.

7.16 In Section 7.3.2, we walked through how Program 93 worked. Draw the pictures to show how Program 94 (page 225) works in the same way.

7.17 What happens if you increase a volume too far? Explore this by creating a sound object, then increasing the volume once, and again, and again. Does it always keep getting louder? Or does something else happen? Can you explain why?

7.18 Try sprinkling in some specific values into your sounds. What happens if you set the value of a few thousand samples in the middle of a sound to 32,767? Or a few thousand to −32,768? Or set the few thousand sample to a bunch of zeroes? What happens to the sound in each of these cases?

TO DIG DEEPER

Mark gave a lecture for TEDxGeorgia Tech that included some of the material in this chapter, especially analyzing sound. You can see that at `http://bit.ly/guzdial-tedxgt`.

There are many wonderful books on psychoacoustics and computer music. One of Mark's favorites for understandability is *Computer Music: Synthesis, Composition, and Performance* by Dodge and Jerse [10]. The *bible* of computer music is Curtis Roads' massive *The Computer Music Tutorial* [11].

When you are using the MediaTools application, you are actually using a programming language called *Squeak*, developed initially and primarily by Alan Kay, Dan Ingalls, Ted Kaehler, John Maloney, and Scott Wallace [13]. Squeak is open-source[5] and is an excellent cross-platform multimedia tool. There is a book that introduces Squeak including its sound capabilities [32] and another book on Squeak [30] that includes a chapter on *Siren*, a variation of Squeak by Stephen Pope especially designed for computer music exploration and composition.

---

[5]http://www.squeak.org

8

Modifying Samples in a Range

Chapter Learning Objectives

The media learning goals for this chapter are:

- To splice sounds together to make sound compositions.
- To reverse sounds.
- To mirror sounds.

The computer science goals for this chapter are:

- To iterate an index variable for an array across a range.
- To use comments in programs and understand why.
- To identify some algorithms that cross media boundaries.
- To describe and use scope more carefully.

8.1   MANIPULATING DIFFERENT SECTIONS OF THE SOUND DIFFERENTLY

In the last chapter, we described some useful things to do to sounds overall but really interesting effects come from chopping up sounds and manipulating each piece differently: some words this way, other sounds that way. How would you do that? We need to be able to loop through *portions* of the sample, without walking through the whole thing. Turns out to be an easy thing to do, but we need to manipulate samples somewhat differently (e.g., we have to use index numbers), and we have to use our `for` loop in a slightly different way.

Recall that each sample has an associated number (an *index*), which we can think of as an address, a description of where that sample is in the overall sound. We can get each individual sample with getSampleValueAt (with a sound and an index number as input). We can set any sample with `setSampleValueAt` (with inputs of a sound, an index number, and a new value). That's how we can manipulate samples without using `getSamples` and sample objects. But we still don't want to have to write code like:

```
setSampleValueAt(sound,1,12)
setSampleValueAt(sound,2,28) ...
```

Not for tens of thousands of samples!

Using `range`, we can do everything that we were doing with `getSamples`, but now directly referencing the index numbers. Here's Program 93 (page 221) rewritten using `range`.

Program 99: Increase an Input Sound's Volume Using range

```
def increaseVolumeByRange(sound):
  for sampleIndex in range(0,getLength(sound)):
    value = getSampleValueAt(sound,sampleIndex)
    setSampleValueAt(sound,sampleIndex,value * 2)
```

Try it—you'll find that it performs just like the previous one.

But now we can do some really fun things with sounds because we can control which samples we're talking to. The next program *increases* the sound for the first half of the sound, then *decreases* it in the second half. See if you can trace how it's working.

Program 100: Increase the Volume, Then Decrease It

```
def increaseAndDecrease(sound):
  for sampleIndex in range(0,getLength(sound)/2):
    value = getSampleValueAt(sound,sampleIndex)
    setSampleValueAt(sound,sampleIndex,value * 2)
  for sampleIndex in range(getLength(sound)/2,getLength(sound)):
    value = getSampleValueAt(sound,sampleIndex)
    setSampleValueAt(sound,sampleIndex,value * 0.2)
```

How It Works

There are two loops in `increaseAndDecrease`, each of which deals with one half of the sound.

- The first loop deals with the samples from 0 to halfway through the sound. These samples all get multiplied by 2 to double their amplitude.

- The second loop goes from halfway through to the end of the sound. Here, we multiply each sample by 0.2, thus decreasing the volume by 80%.

8.1.1   Revisiting Index Array Notation

We have already touched on the use of square bracket notation to index sequences. Many languages use square brackets ([ ]) as a standard notation for accessing elements of arrays. Let's revisit the notation in this section, because sometimes it makes sound code easier to work with.

For any sequence, `sequence[index]` returns the index-th element in the array. The number inside the square brackets is always an index variable, but it's sometimes referred to as a *subscript* because of the way that mathematicians refer to the *i*-th element of *a*, for example, a_i.

Let's do it here with samples to demonstrate.

```
>>> sound = makeSound("a.wav")
>>> samples = getSamples(sound)
>>> print samples[0]
Sample at 0 with value -90
>>> print samples[1]
Sample at 1 with value -113
>>> print getLength(sound)
9508
>>> samples[9507]
Sample at 9507 with value -147
>>> samples[9508]
The error was: 9508
Sequence index out of range.
The index you're using goes beyond the size of that data
    (too low or high). For instance, maybe you tried to
    access OurArray[10] and OurArray only has 5 elements
    in it.
```

The first element in an array is at index 0. The last element in an array is at the length of the array minus 1. Notice what happens when we reference an index *beyond* the end of the array. We get an error indicating that the "Sequence index out of range."

Let's use `range` to make an array,[1] then reference it the same way.

```
>>> myArray = range(0,100)
>>> print myArray[0]
0
>>> print myArray[1]
1
>>> print myArray[99]
99
>>> mySecondArray = range(0,100,2)
>>> print mySecondArray[35]
70
```

The code `range(0,100)` creates an array with 100 elements in it. The first element is at index 0 and the last is at index 99. The array holds all the values from 0 to 99. Remember that when you specify a range using `range(begin,end)`, the `begin` number is in the returned array but the `end` number is not.

If we use an index number *below* the end of the array (i.e., a negative number), Python will compute the index as an offset from the end of the array. Notice that reference to

---

[1]Technically, a *sequence*, which can be indexed like an array but does not have all the characteristics of an array. For our purposes, the way a sequence works is pretty much the same as an array.

myArray[-1] below is the same as myArray[99] above. Any reference *above* the end of the array generates the same error we saw previously.

```
>>> myArray[-1]
99
>>> myArray[100]
The error was: 100
Sequence index out of range.
The index you're using goes beyond the size of that data
    (too low or high). For instance, maybe you tried to
    access OurArray[10] and OurArray only has 5 elements
    in it.
>>> myArray[101]
The error was: 101
Sequence index out of range.
The index you're using goes beyond the size of that data
    (too low or high). For instance, maybe you tried to
    access OurArray[10] and OurArray only has 5 elements
    in it.
```

We can rewrite function increaseAndDecrease using array notation. This version, increaseAndDecrease2 does *exactly* the same thing. Notice that we are using getSampleValue and setSampleValue instead of getSampleValueAt and setSampleValueAt. Instead, we use square bracket indexing to specify the sample we want. There is an advantage that we can continue to use the same getSampleValue/setSampleValue that we did in the last chapter.

Does this kind of notation make the function easier or harder to read for you?

Program 101: Increase the Volume, Then Decrease, Using Index Notation

```
def increaseAndDecrease2(sound):
  samples = getSamples(sound)
  for index in range(len(samples)/2):
    value = getSampleValue(samples[index])
    setSampleValue(samples[index],value * 2)
  for index in range(len(samples)/2,len(samples)):
    value = getSampleValue(samples[index])
    setSampleValue(samples[index],value * 0.2)
```

8.2   SPLICING SOUNDS

Splicing sounds is a term that dates back to when sounds were recorded on tape—juggling the order of things on the tape involved literally cutting the tape into segments and then gluing it back together in the right order. That's "splicing." When everything is digital, it's *much* easier.

To splice sounds, we simply have to copy elements around in the array. It's easiest to do this with two (or more) arrays, rather than copy within the same array. If you copy all the samples that represent someone saying the word "the" to the beginning of a sound (starting at index number 0), then you make the sound start with the word "the." Splicing lets you create all kinds of sounds, speeches, nonsense, and art.

The easiest kind of splice is when the sounds are in separate files. All that you need to do is to copy each sound, in order, into a target sound. Here's a program that creates the start of a sentence "Guzdial is . . .". (Readers are welcome to complete the sentence.)

Program 102: Merging Words into a Single Sentence

```
def merge():
  guzdialSound = makeSound("guzdial.wav")
  isSound = makeSound("is.wav")
  target = makeEmptySoundBySeconds(5)
  index = 0
  # Copy in "Guzdial"
  for source in range(0,getLength(guzdialSound)):
    value = getSampleValueAt(guzdialSound,source)
    setSampleValueAt(target,index,value)
    index = index + 1
  # Copy in 0.1 second pause (silence) (0)
  for source in range(0,int(0.1*getSamplingRate(target))):
    setSampleValueAt(target,index,0)
    index = index + 1
  # Copy in "is"
  for source in range(0,getLength(isSound)):
    value = getSampleValueAt(isSound,source)
    setSampleValueAt(target,index,value)
    index = index + 1
  play(target)
  return target
```

How It Works

There are three loops in the function merge, each of which copies one segment into the target sound—a segment being either a word or a silence between words.

- The function starts by creating sound objects for the word "Guzdial" (guzdial-Sound) and the word "is" (isSound).

- We use makeEmptySoundBySeconds to create the target sound named (target). There is a matching function called makeEmptySound that takes a *number of samples* as input. The second one allows us finer grained control over the length. Instead of using a 3-second silent sound as the target in this function, we could make an empty sound of a particular length using makeEmptySound(lengthInSamples). We can create a sound that is just long enough to fit what we want to copy into it (with 0.1 seconds of silence between words):

```
guzLen = getLength(guzdialSound)
silenceLen = int(0.1 * 22050)
isLen = getLength(isSound)
target = makeEmptySound(guzLen + silenceLen + isLen)
```

The default sampling rate for a new sound is 22,050 samples per second. So if we want a tenth of a second of silence between the words, the length of that in samples is (0.1 * 22,050). We must convert that back to an integer using `int(0.1 * 22050)`. We can also create a new silent sound using `makeEmptySound(length, samplingRate)`.

- Note that we set `index` (for the target) equal to 0 before the first loop. We then increment it in every loop, but we never again set it to a specific value. That's because `index` is always the index for the *next empty sample* in the target sound. Because each loop follows the previous one, we just keep tacking samples onto the end of the target.

- In the first loop, we copy each and every sample from `guzdialSound` into the `target`. We have the index `source` go from 0 to the length of `guzdialSound`. We get the sample value at `source` from `guzdialSound`, then set the sample value at `index` in the `target` sound to the value that we got from `guzdialSound`. We then increment `index` so that it points at the next empty sample index.

- In the second loop, we create 0.1 seconds of silence. Since `getSamplingRate(target)` gives us the number of samples in 1 second of `target`, 0.1 times tells us the number of samples in 0.1 seconds. We don't get any source value here—we simply set the `index`-th sample to 0 (for silence), then increment the `index`.

- Finally, we copy in all the samples from `isSound`, just like the first loop where we copied in `guzdialSound`.

- We `normalize` the sound to make it louder. This means that the function `normalize` *must* be in the Program Area with `merge`, even though we're not showing it here. We then `play` and `return` the sound.

    We return the target sound using `return target` because we created the sound in the function. The target sound wasn't handed in as input to the function. If we didn't return the sound we created in `merge`, it would disappear with the end of the `merge` function context (*scope*). By returning it, we allow another function to use the resulting sound.

Compare the function `merge` to the below function `merge2` that uses index notation.

Program 103: Merging Words Using Index Notation

```
def merge2():
  guzdialSound = makeSound("guzdial.wav")
  isSound = makeSound("is.wav")
  target = makeEmptySoundBySeconds(5)
  index = 0
  src1 = getSamples(guzdialSound)
  src2 = getSamples(isSound)
  trg = getSamples(target)
  # Copy in "Guzdial"
  for index1 in range(len(src1)):
    value = getSampleValue(src1[index1])
    setSampleValue(trg[index],value)
    index = index + 1
  # Copy in 0.1 second pause (silence) (0)
  for index0 in range(0,int(0.1*getSamplingRate(target))):
```

```
    setSampleValue(trg[index],0)
    index = index + 1
# Copy in "is"
for index2 in range(len(src2)):
  value = getSampleValue(src2[index2])
  setSampleValue(trg[index],value)
  index = index + 1
play(target)
return target
```

■

The more common kind of splicing is when the words are in the middle of an existing sound and you need to pull them out from there. The first thing to do in splicing like that is to figure out the index numbers that delimit the pieces you're interested in. Using the JES sound tool, that's pretty easy to do.

- Open your WAV file in the JES sound tool. You can do this by creating the sound and exploring it.
- Scroll and move the cursor (by dragging in the graph) until you think that the cursor is before or after a sound of interest.
- Check your positioning by playing the sound before and after the cursor, using the buttons in the sound tool.

Using exactly this process, Mark found the ending points of the first few words in **preamble10.wav** (Figure 8.1). He assumed that the first word started at index 0.

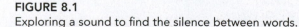

FIGURE 8.1
Exploring a sound to find the silence between words.

Word	Ending Index
We	15730
the	17407
People	26726
of	32131
the	33413
United	40052
States	55510

Writing a loop that copies things from one array to another requires a little bit of juggling. You need to think about keeping track of two indices: where you are in the array that you're copying *from* and where you are in the array that you're copying *to*. These are two different variables, tracking two different indexes. But they both increment in the same way.

The way that we're going to do it (a *subrecipe* or *subprogram*) is to use one index variable to point at the right entry in the *target* array (the one we're copying *to*), use a for loop to have the second index variable move across the right entries in the *source* array (the one we're copying *from*), and (*very important!*) move the target index variable each time we do a copy. This is what keeps the two index variables synchronized.

We make the target index move by adding 1 to it. Very simply, we'll tell Python to do `targetIndex = targetIndex + 1`. Remember that this changes the value of `targetIndex` to be whatever it currently is *plus* 1, which moves (increases) the target index. If we put this in the body of the loop where we're changing the source index, we'll get them moving in synchrony.

The general form of the subprogram is:

```
targetIndex = Where-the-incoming-sound-should-start
for sourceIndex in range(startingPoint,endingPoint)
  setSampleValueAt(target, targetIndex,
    getSampleValueAt(source, sourceIndex))
  targetIndex = targetIndex + 1
```

Below is the program that changes the preamble from "We the people of the United States" to "We the *united* people of the United States."

Program 104: Splice the Preamble to Have United People

Be sure to change the `file` variable before trying this on your computer.

```
# Splicing
# Using the preamble sound,
#  make "We the united people"
def splicePreamble():
    source = makeSound("preamble10.wav")
    # This will be the newly spliced sound
    target = makeEmptySoundBySeconds(10)
```

```
# targetIndex starts at just after
# "We the" in the new sound
targetIndex=17408
# Where the word "United" is in the sound
for sourceIndex in range(33414, 40052):
    value = getSampleValueAt(source, sourceIndex)
    setSampleValueAt(target, targetIndex, value)
    targetIndex = targetIndex + 1

# Where the word "People" is in the sound
for sourceIndex in range(17408, 26726):
    value = getSampleValueAt(source, sourceIndex)
    setSampleValueAt(target, targetIndex, value)
    targetIndex = targetIndex + 1

#Stick some quiet space after that
for index in range(0,1000):
    setSampleValueAt(target, targetIndex,0)
    targetIndex = targetIndex + 1

#Let's hear and return the result
play(target)
return target
```

We'd use this function like this:

```
>>> newSound=splicePreamble()
```

How It Works

There's a lot going on in this program. Let's walk through it, slowly.

Note that there are lots of lines with "#" in them. The hash character signifies that what comes after that character on the line is a note to the programmer *and should be ignored by Python.* It's called a *comment*.

Making It Work Tip: Comments Are Good!

Comments are great ways to explain what you're doing to others—and to yourself! The reality is that it's hard to remember all the details of a program, so it's often *very* useful to leave notes about what you did in case you ever play with the program again, or if someone else is trying to understand it.

The function `splicePreamble` takes no parameters. Sure, it would be great to write a single function that can do any kind of splicing we want, in the same way as we've done generalized increasing volume and normalization. But how would you do this? How do you generalize all the start and end points? It's easier, at least to start, to create single programs that handle specific splicing tasks.

We see here three of the copying loops like we set up earlier. Actually, there are only two. The first one copies the word "united" into place. The second one copies the word "people" into place. "But wait," you might be thinking. "The word 'people' was *already* in the sound!" That's true, but when we copy "united" in, we overwrite some of the word "people," so we copy it in again.

At the very end of the program, we return the `target` sound. The `target` sound was created in the function and not passed into it. If we didn't return it we wouldn't have any way to refer to it again. By returning it, it's possible to give it a name and play it (and even further manipulate it) after the function stops executing.

Here's the simpler form. Try it and listen to the result:

```
def spliceSimpler():
    source = makeSound("preamble10.wav")
    # This will be the newly spliced sound
    target = makeSound("preamble10.wav")
    # targetIndex starts at just after "We the" in the new sound
    targetIndex=17408
    # Where the word "United" is in the sound
    for sourceIndex in range(33414, 40052):
        value = getSampleValueAt(source, sourceIndex)
        setSampleValueAt(target, targetIndex, value)
        targetIndex = targetIndex + 1
    #Let's hear and return the result
    play(target)
    return target
```

Let's see if we can figure out what's going on mathematically. Recall the table back on page 242. We're going to start inserting samples at sample index 17,408. The word "united" has $(40,052 - 33,414)$ 6638 samples. (Exercise for the reader: How long is that in seconds?) This means that we'll be writing into the target from 17,408 to $(17,408 + 6638)$ sample index 24,046. We know from the table that the word "people" ends at index 26,726. If the word "people" is more than $(26,726 - 24,046)$ 2680 samples, then it will start earlier than 24,046, and our insertion of "united" is going to trample on part of it. If the word "united" is over 6000 samples, we doubt that the word "people" is less than 2000. That's why it sounds crunched. Why does it work with where the "of" is? The speaker must have paused in there. If you check the table again, you'll see that the word "of" ends at sample index 32,131 and the word before it ends at 26,726. The word "of" takes fewer than $(32,131 - 26,726)$ 5405 samples, which is why the original program works.

The third loop in the original Program 104 (page 242) looks like the same kind of copy loop but it's really only putting in a few 0's. Samples with a value of 0 represent silence. Putting a few in creates a pause that sounds better. (There's an exercise which suggests pulling them out and seeing what you hear.)

Figure 8.2 shows the original **preamble10.wav** file in the top sound editor and the new spliced one (saved with `writeSoundTo`) on the bottom. The lines are drawn so that the spliced section lies between them, while the rest of the sounds are identical.

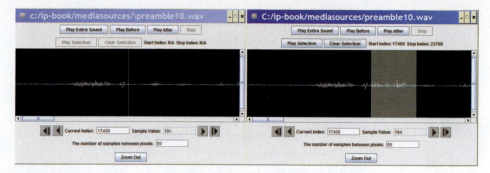

FIGURE 8.2
Comparing the original sound (*left*) to the spliced sound (*right*).

8.3   GENERAL CLIP AND COPY

The previous functions were a bit complicated. What would make them easier? It would be nice to have a general clip method that took a sound and a start and end index and returned a new sound clip with just that part of the original sound in it. Then it would be easy to create a clip with just "united" in it.

Program 105: Create a Sound Clip

```
def clip(source,start,end):
  target = makeEmptySound(end - start)
  targetIndex = 0
  for sourceIndex in range(start,end):
    sourceValue = getSampleValueAt(source,sourceIndex)

    setSampleValueAt(target,targetIndex,sourceValue)
    targetIndex = targetIndex + 1
  return target
```

Now we can create a sound clip with just the word "united" in it by doing the following:

```
>>> preamble = makeSound(getMediaPath("preamble10.wav"))
>>> explore(preamble)
>>> united = clip(preamble,33414,40052)
>>> explore(united)
```

It would also be nice to have a general copy method that would take a source sound and a target sound and copy all of the source into the target at a passed starting location in the target.

Program 106: General Copy

```
def copy(source,target,start):
  targetIndex = start
  for sourceIndex in range(0,getLength(source)):
```

```
      sourceValue = getSampleValueAt(source,sourceIndex)
      setSampleValueAt(target,targetIndex,sourceValue)
      targetIndex = targetIndex + 1
```

Now we can insert "united" into the preamble again using the new functions.

Program 107: Using the General Clip and Copy

```
def createNewPreamble():
  preamble = makeSound("preamble10.wav")
  united = clip(preamble,33414,40052)
  start = clip(preamble,0,17407)
  end = clip(preamble,17408,55510)
  len = getLength(start) + getLength(united) + getLength(end)
  newPre = makeEmptySound(len)
  copy(start,newPre,0)
  copy(united,newPre,17407)
  copy(end,newPre,getLength(start) + getLength(united))
  return newPre
```

Notice how this function calls the new general clip and copy. You can put all three of these in the same file. It would be nice if you could have a file of general sound functions that other functions can use, without having to have all the functions in the same file.

You can do this by *importing* functions from other files. You will need to add from media import * as the first line in the file with the general sound functions, in order to use the multimedia functions that JES provides like getMediaPath or getRed. JES imports the media functions for you automatically, but now we won't be loading this general file through JES, so we must explicitly import the media functions. Let's call the general sound functions file **mySound.py** so that it doesn't conflict with other things in JES that use the name **Sound**.

```
from media import *

def clip(source,start,end):
  target = makeEmptySound(end - start)
  targetIndex = 0
  for sourceIndex in range(start,end):
    sourceValue = getSampleValueAt(source,sourceIndex)
    setSampleValueAt(target,targetIndex,sourceValue)
    targetIndex = targetIndex + 1
  return target

def copy(source,target,start):
  targetIndex = start
  for sourceIndex in range(0,getLength(source)):
    sourceValue = getSampleValueAt(source,sourceIndex)
    setSampleValueAt(target,targetIndex,sourceValue)
    targetIndex = targetIndex + 1
```

To use the new general sound functions, you must first use `addLibPath(path)`. This function tells Python where to look for the files that you are importing. The path is the full pathname to the directory with the file that contains the general functions.

```
>>> addLibPath("c:/ip-book/programs/")
```

To use the general sound functions `copy` and `clip` in another file, we add `from mySound import *` as the first line in the file. The `from mySound import *` is like copying the general functions into the same file as `createNewPreamble` but it is actually better than copying the functions. If we copy the general functions to lots of files, and *then* change the general functions, we have to change them everyplace that we copied them. But, if we import general functions and then change the general function file, the improved functions are the ones that are used everywhere.

```
from mySound import *

def createNewPreamble():
 preamble = makeSound("preamble10.wav")
 united = clip(preamble,33414,40052)
 start = clip(preamble,0,17407)
 end = clip(preamble,17408,55510)
 len = getLength(start) + getLength(united) + getLength(end)
 newPre = makeEmptySound(len)
 copy(start,newPre,0)
 copy(united,newPre,17407)
 copy(end,newPre,getLength(start) + getLength(united))
 return newPre
```

General functions are also a form of *abstraction* like the general `copy` function that we used with pictures. By creating a file of general functions that we import, we are allowing others (including ourselves if we forget) to use the abstraction without understanding the details of how these functions are implemented. This is like how we have been using `getRed` and `getMediaPath` without knowing the details of how they work.

Making It Work Tip: A General Function Directory

If you put all the files that contain general functions in the same directory, you can use `setLibPath` once to allow you to access all of the general function files using `import`. You can have general function files for sounds, pictures, movies, and so on. ■

8.4 REVERSING SOUNDS

In the splicing example, we copied the samples from the words just as they were in the original sound. We don't have to always go in the same order. We can reverse the words—or make them faster, slower, louder, or softer. As an example, here's a program that reverses a sound (Figure 8.3).

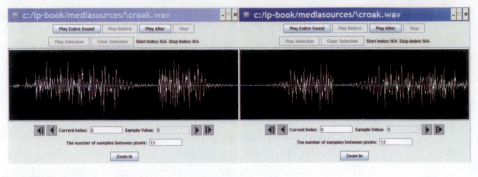

FIGURE 8.3
Comparing the original sound (*left*) to the reversed sound (*right*).

Program 108: Play the Given Sound Backwards (Reverse It)

```
def reverse(source):
  target = makeEmptySound(getLength(source))
  sourceIndex = getLength(source)-1
  for targetIndex in range(0,getLength(target)):
    sourceValue = getSampleValueAt(source,sourceIndex)
    setSampleValueAt(target,targetIndex,sourceValue)
    sourceIndex = sourceIndex - 1
  return target
```

You can try this out by typing the following in the Command Area:

```
>>> croak = makeSound(getMediaPath("croak.wav"))
>>> explore(croak)
>>> revCroak = reverse(croak)
>>> explore(revCroak)
```

How It Works

This program uses another variant of the array element copying subprogram that we've already seen.

- It first creates the `target` sound as an empty sound the same length as the `source` sound.
- It starts the `sourceIndex` at the *end* of the array rather than the front (the length minus 1).
- The `targetIndex` moves from 0 to the length minus 1, during which time the program
  - gets the sample value in the source at the `sourceIndex`:
  - copies that value into the target at the `targetIndex`: and
  - *reduces* the `sourceIndex` by 1, meaning that the `sourceIndex` moves from the end of the array back to the beginning.

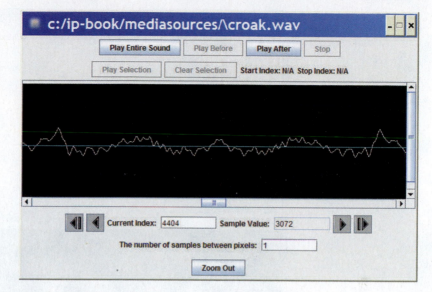

FIGURE 8.4
Mirroring a sound from front (*left*) to back (*right*).

8.5   MIRRORING

Once we know how to play sounds forwards and backwards, *mirroring* a sound is the exact same process as mirroring a picture (Figure 8.4). Compare this to Program 66 (page 152). Do you agree that this is the same *algorithm* even though we're dealing with a different medium?

Program 109: Mirror a Sound Front to Back

```
def mirrorSound(sound):
  len = getLength(sound)
  mirrorpoint=len/2
  for index in range(0,mirrorpoint):
    left = getSampleObjectAt(sound,index)
    right = getSampleObjectAt(sound,len-index-1)
    value = getSampleValue(left)
    setSampleValue(right,value)
```

8.6   ON FUNCTIONS AND SCOPE

Function parameters and scope can be confusing. The same *name* can have different meanings (i.e., different values) depending on whether the name is created inside the function or outside the function. Imagine that you were using this (stupid, meaningless) set of functions in JES (Figure 8.5):

```
def fun1(a):
  print a
```

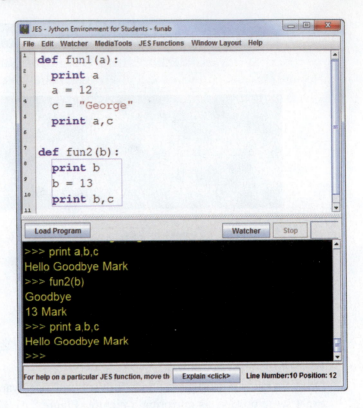

FIGURE 8.5
Two sample functions to explore parameters and scope.

```
a = 12
c = "George"
print a,c

def fun2(b):
  print b
  b = 13
  print b,c
```

Now, in the Command Area, let's define three variables, a, b, and c.

```
>>> a = "Hello"
>>> b = "Goodbye"
>>> c = "Mark"
>>> print a,b,c
Hello Goodbye Mark
```

Let's call fun1 with an input of b.

```
>>> fun1(b)
Goodbye
12 George
>>> print a,b,c
Hello Goodbye Mark
```

When we call the function fun1, the value of b from the Command Area becomes known as a. The name a *inside* fun1 will get a copy of the value of b, that is, "Goodbye." **The parameter variable a in fun1 has nothing to do with the variable a in the Command Area.** The Command Area has its own *scope*.

When we change a inside of fun1, we only change the parameter, which is a *local* variable. So, fun1 will print out "Goodbye." We then assign the variable c, which is *local* to the function fun1. A local variable only exists within the *scope* of the function. Assigning a value to c changes **nothing** about the variables in the Command Area. From within fun1, we print out a and c, and we see "12 George." But back in the Command Area, when we print a, b, and c, we see (again), "Hello Goodbye Mark."

Now, what happens if we call fun1 with a, the same name as the parameter? Pretty much the same thing, except that we print "Hello" instead of "Goodbye." The variable a inside fun1 is a completely different variable than the one with the same name in the Command Area.

```
>>> print a,b,c
Hello Goodbye Mark
>>> fun1(a)
Hello
12 George
>>> print a,b,c
Hello Goodbye Mark
```

How about fun2? It takes an input of b. If we give it the b from the Command Area, we still cannot change the b in the Command Area. The parameter is *local* to the function.

```
>>> print a,b,c
Hello Goodbye Mark
>>> fun2(b)
Goodbye
13 Mark
>>> print a,b,c
Hello Goodbye Mark
```

Notice that fun2 *references* the variable c. It does not assign c, and it does not have c as a parameter. What happens when we print b, c? The variable c will be the variable from the Command Area, because there is no local copy inside fun2. We print the parameter b and the variable c from the Command Area, so we print "13 Mark." We say that the scope of fun2 is *within* the scope of the Command Area. If we do not define a local variable with the same name, we can access the external scope's variables. We can think about the Command Area's scope as being *global*, across all functions. If within a function we define a local variable with the same name, the local variable overrides the global variable, effectively blocking access.

Here are the three ideas that you should take away from this:

- When a function is called, the input values are copied into the parameter variables.[2] Changing the parameter variables does not change the input variable, nor does it change the variables in other scopes.
- All variables that are local (which include parameter variables) disappear at the end of the function. Changing the local variables does not change variables in other scopes.
- We can reference variables in the external scope of a function, but only if we do not have a local variable with the same name.

PROGRAMMING SUMMARY

In this chapter, we talk about several kinds of encodings of data (or objects).

Sounds	Encodings of sounds, typically coming from a WAV file.
Samples	Collections of sample objects, each indexed by a number (e.g., sample #0, sample #1). `samples[0]` is the first sample object. You can manipulate each sample in the samples like this: `for s in samples:`.
Sample	A value between −32,000 and 32,000 (roughly) representing the voltage that a microphone would generate at a given instant when recording a sound. The length of the instant is typically either $1/44,100$ of a second (for CD-quality sound) or $1/22,050$ of a second (for good-enough sound on most computers). A sample object remembers what sound it came from, so if you change its value, it knows to go back and change the right sample in the sound.

Here are the functions used or introduced in this chapter:

range	Takes two numbers and returns an array of all integers starting at the first number and stopping before the last number.
range	Can also take three numbers, and then returns an array of all the integers from the first up to, but not including, the second, incrementing each time by the third.
addLibPath	Tells JES to look in a specified directory for libraries that might be imported.

PROBLEMS

8.1   Rewrite Program 100 (page 236) so that two input values are provided to the function: the sound and a *percentage* of how far into the sound to go before changing from increasing to decreasing the volume.

---

[2]If the input value is an object, the parameter variable becomes an alias, another name for that object.

8.2　Rewrite Program 100 so that you normalize the first second of a sound, then slowly decrease the sound in steps of 1/5 for each following second. (How many samples are in a second? getSamplingRate is the number of samples per second for the given sound.)

8.3　Try rewriting Program 100 so that you have a linear increase in volume to halfway through the sound, then linearly decrease the volume down to zero in the second half.

8.4　What happens if you take out the bit of silence added in to the target sound in the splicing example (Program 104 (page 242))? Try it? Can you hear any difference?

8.5　Write a new version of Program 104 to copy "We the" into a new sound and then copy in "united" and finally copy in "people." Be sure to add 2250 samples with a value of 0 in between the words. Return the new sound.

8.6　Write a new version of Program 104 to use index array notation (with square brackets).

8.7　The general functions like Program 108 (page 248) are the kind where the index array notation is really useful. Write reverse, copy, and clip using index array notation.

8.8　We think that if we're going to say "We the united people" in the splice (Program 104), "united" should be really emphasized—really loud. Change the program so that the word "united" is maximally loud (normalized) in the phrase "united people."

8.9　Try using a stopwatch to time the execution of the programs in this chapter. Time from hitting return on the command until the next prompt appears. What is the relationship between execution time and the length of the sound? Is it a linear relationship (i.e., longer sounds take longer to process and shorter sounds take less time to process)? Or is it something else? Compare the individual programs. Does normalizing a sound take longer than raising (or lowering) the amplitude a constant amount? How much longer? Does it matter whether the sound is longer or shorter?

8.10　Make an audio collage. Make it at least 5 seconds long, and include at least two different sounds (i.e., they come from different files). Make a copy of one of those different sounds and modify it using any of the techniques described in this chapter (i.e., mirroring, splicing, volume manipulations). Splice together the original two sounds and the modified sound to make the complete collage.

8.11　Compose a sentence that no one ever said by combining words from other sounds into a grammatically correct new sound. Write a function named audio-Sentence to generate a sentence out of individual words. Use at least three words in your sentence. You can use the words in the mediasource folder from the Web site or record your own words. Be sure to include a tenth (1/10) of a second pause between the words. (*Hint 1:* Remember that zeroes for the sample values generate silence. *Hint 2:* Remember that the sampling rate is the number of samples per second. From there, you should be able to figure out how many samples need to be made zero to generate a tenth of a second of silence.) Be sure to access your sounds in your Media Folder using `getMediaPath` so that it will work for users of your program as long as they first execute `setMediaPath`.

8.12   Write a function to add 1 second of silence to the beginning of a sound. It should take the sound as input, create the new empty target sound, then copy the original sound starting after the first second in the target.

8.13   Search the Web for songs that have hidden messages that you can hear when you reverse the sound.

8.14   Write a function that splices together words and music.

8.15   Write a function that interleaves two sounds. It starts with 2 seconds of the first sound and then 2 seconds of the second sound. Then it continues with the next 2 seconds of the first sound and the next 2 seconds of the second sound and so on until both sounds have been fully copied to the target sound.

8.16   Write a function called `erasePart` to set all the samples in the 2nd second of **thisisatest.wav** to 0's—essentially, making the 2nd second go silent. (*Hint:* Remember that `getSamplingRate(sound)` tells you the number of samples in a single second in a sound.) Play and return the partially erased sound.

8.17   Can you write a function that finds the silence between words? What should it return?

8.18   Write a function to increase the volume on the passed sound just between the passed start and end index.

8.19   Write a function to reverse part of the passed sound just between the passed start and end index.

8.20   Write a function `mirrorBackToFront` that mirrors the second half of a sound onto the first half.

8.21   Write a function `mirrorFrontToBack` that mirrors the first half of a sound onto the second half.

8.22   Write a function called `reverseSecondHalf` that takes a sound as input, then reverses just the second half of the sound and returns the result. For example, if the sound said "MarkBark," the returned sound should say "MarkkraB."

8.23   There is a Python keyword called `global`. Learn what it does, then change `fun1` from the last section to access *and change* a variable c in the Command Area. (You can change how you define the variable in the Command Area, too.)

TO DIG DEEPER

Gareth Loy's books "MusiMathics: The Mathematical Foundations of Music" (Volumes 1 and 2, MIT Press, 2011) go much deeper into how sound arises from vibration and how the qualities of music can be understood in terms of pressure waves.

CHAPTER 9

Making Sounds by Combining Pieces

Chapter Learning Objectives

The media learning goals for this chapter are:

- To blend sounds so that one fades into another.
- To create echoes.
- To change the frequency (pitch) of a sound.
- To create sounds that don't exist in nature by composing more basic sounds (sine waves).
- To choose between sound formats such as MIDI and MP3 for different purposes.

The computer science goals for this chapter are:

- To use file paths to reference files at different places on the disk.
- To explain blending as an algorithm that crosses media boundaries.
- To build programs from multiple functions.

9.1 COMPOSING SOUNDS THROUGH ADDITION

Creating sounds digitally that didn't exist previously is lots of fun. Rather than simply copying sample values around or multiplying them, we actually change their values and add waves together. The result are sounds that never existed until you made them.

In physics, adding sounds involves issues of canceling waves out and enforcing other factors. In math, it's about matrices. In computer science, it's one of the easiest processes that one can imagine. Let's say that you've got a sound, `source`, that you want to add in to the `target`. *Simply add the values at the same index numbers* (as in Figure 9.1). That's it!

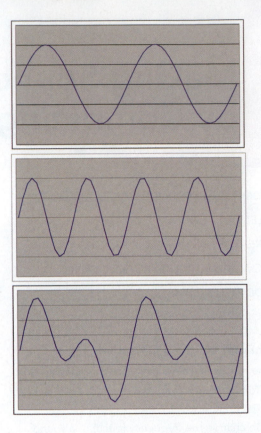

FIGURE 9.1
The top and middle waves are added together to create the bottom wave.

```
for sourceIndex in range(0,getLength(source)):
  targetValue=getSampleValueAt(target,sourceIndex)
  sourceValue=getSampleValueAt(source,sourceIndex)
  setSampleValueAt(target,targetIndex,sourceValue+targetValue)
```

The function `setSampleValueAt` takes three inputs: a sound, the index of the sample (within the sound) to change, and the new value for that sample. It is similar to `setSampleValue` except that you don't have to first pull out the sample from the sound.

9.2   BLENDING SOUNDS

In this example, we take two sounds—someone saying "Aah!" and a bassoon instrument sound of C in the fourth octave—and *blend* them. To do this we copy part of the "Aah!," then add 50% of each, and then copy the C. This is very much like mixing 50% of each at a sound mixing board. It's also very much like the way we blended pictures in Program 86 (page 184).

This function assumes that you have already executed `setMediaPath()` in the Command Area. Where we write `bass = makeSound("bassoon-c4.wav")` below, we could instead write `bass = makeSound(getMediaPath("bassoon-c4.wav"))`. The latter form (with `getMediaPath`) is explicitly specifying that `"bassoon-c4.wav"` is to be found in the media folder. Without specifying `getMediaPath`, we are relying on the fact that JES will search the media for files without a complete path.

Program 110: Blending Two Sounds

```
def blendSounds():
 bass = makeSound("bassoon-c4.wav")
 aah = makeSound("aah.wav")
 canvas = makeEmptySoundBySeconds(3)
 for index in range(0,20000):
  aahSample = getSampleValueAt(aah,index)
  setSampleValueAt(canvas,index,aahSample)
 for index in range(0,20000):
  aahSample = getSampleValueAt(aah,index+20000)
  bassSample=getSampleValueAt(bass,index)
  newSample = 0.5*aahSample + 0.5*bassSample
  setSampleValueAt(canvas,index+20000,newSample)
 for index in range(20000,40000):
  bassSample = getSampleValueAt(bass,index)
  setSampleValueAt(canvas,index+20000,bassSample)
 play(canvas)
 return canvas
```

How It Works

Like blending the pictures (Program 86 (page 184)), there are loops in this function for each segment of the blended sound.

- We start by creating the `bass` and `aah` sounds for blending and a silent sound `canvas` that we're blending into. The length of these sounds is over 40,000 samples but we're just going to use the first 40,000 as an example.

- In the first loop, we simply get 20,000 samples from `aah` and copy them into `canvas`. Note that we're not using a separate index variable for the `canvas`—instead, we're using the same index variable, `index`, for both sounds.

- In the next loop, we copy 20,000 samples from both `aah` and `bass` blended into `canvas`. We use the index variable, `index`, to index all three sounds—we use the basic `index` for accessing `bass` and add 20,000 to `index` to access `aah` and `canvas` (since we have already copied 20,000 samples from `aah` into `canvas`). We get a sample from each of `aah` and `bass`, then multiply each by 0.5 and add the results together. The result is a sample that represents 50% of each.

- Finally, we copy another 20,000 samples from `bass`. The resultant sound is returned (since it would disappear otherwise), which sounds like "Aah," a little of each, then just a bassoon note.

9.3   CREATING AN ECHO

Creating an echo effect is similar to the splicing recipe (Program 104 (page 242)) that we saw in the last chapter but involves creating sounds that didn't exist before. We do this by *adding* wave forms. What we're doing here is adding samples from a delay number of samples away into the sound but multiplied by 0.6 so that they're fainter.

Program 111: Make a Sound and a Single Echo of It

```
def echo(delay,s1):
    s2 = duplicateSound(s1)
    for index in range(delay, getLength(s1)):
        # set delay value to original value + delayed value * .6
        echoSample = 0.6*getSampleValueAt(s2, index-delay)
        comboSample = getSampleValueAt(s1,index) + echoSample
        setSampleValueAt(s1, index,comboSample)
    play(s1)
    return s1
```

How It Works

The echo function takes as input a sound and the amount of delay between echoes. The function echo returns the echoed sound. Try this with different amounts of delay. With low values of delay, the echo will sound more like *vibrato*. Higher values (try 10,000 or 20,000) will give you a real echo.

- This function creates a copy of the input sound, s1. The function also uses s1 as the canvas where we'll create the echoed sound. The variable s2 is a copy of s1, and is where we'll get the original, unadulterated samples for creating the echo.
- Our index loop skips over the delay samples, then loops to the end of the sound.
- The echoed sound is delay samples back, so index-delay is the sample we need. We multiply it by 0.6 to make it softer in volume.
- We then add the echoed sample to the current sample in comboSample, then store it at index.
- At the end, we play the sound and return it.

Figure 9.2 provides an example how this program works. Think of the first row ("100,200,1000,−150,−350,200,500,10...") as the original sound. Imagine a delay of 3 (which is way too small to hear, but works for an example). We make a copy of the sound and multiply it by 0.6 to give us the new row "60, 120, 600, −90, −210.0, 120, 300, 6...". We add these two rows together, but offset by the delay. So we keep 100, 200, 1000, then add −150 + 60 to get 90, then −350 + 120 to get −230, and so on. The result is that we've added the sound into itself, but delayed and less loud (multiplied by 0.6).

What would happen if we only used a single sound? You can do it if you move from the back of the sound to the front. That way you avoid *feedback*. This function will do it. Try it with a delay of 5000.

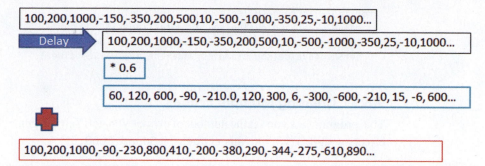

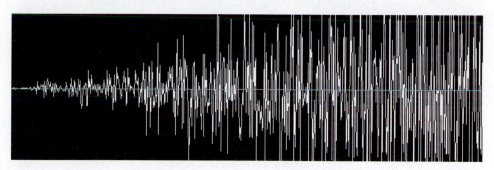

FIGURE 9.2
An example of how echo works.

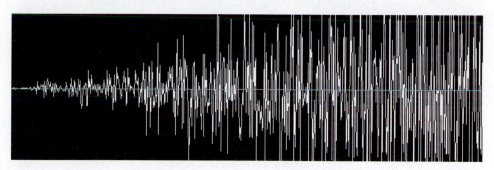

FIGURE 9.3
Creating a feedback loop with echo.

Program 112: Create Echo with a Single Sound

```
def echoOne(delay, sound):
  soundSamples = getSamples(sound)
  for index in range(len(soundSamples)-delay,0,-1):
    value = getSampleValue(soundSamples[index])
    value2 = getSampleValue(soundSamples[index-delay])
    setSampleValue(soundSamples[index],value+value2)
```

You might actually *want* to create feedback, because it's an interesting effect. If your index goes forward and you add samples together, you are fetching from indices where you have *already* added samples. The result is a feedback loop, just as when a microphone is too close to a speaker. Here is a program for creating exactly that, and Figure 9.3 shows you what the sound looks like (starting from the sound "test.wav").

Program 113: Creating Feedback by Echoing into a Single Sound

```
def echoFeedback(sound):
  delay = 5000
  soundSamples = getSamples(sound)
```

```
for index in range(0,len(soundSamples)-delay):
  value = getSampleValue(soundSamples[index])
  value2 = getSampleValue(soundSamples[index+delay])
  setSampleValue(soundSamples[index+delay],value+value2)
```

9.3.1 Creating Multiple Echoes

This program lets you set the number of echoes you get. You can generate some amazing effects with it. Try it like this echoes(mySound,5000,5).

Program 114: Creating Multiple Echoes

```
def echoes(s1, delay,num):
  # Create a new snd, that echoes the input soundfile
  # num number of echoes, each delay apart
  ends1 = getLength(s1)
  ends2 = ends1 + (delay * num)
  s2 = makeEmptySound(ends2)

  echoAmplitude = 1.0
  for echoCount in range(1,num):
    # 60% smaller each time
    echoAmplitude = echoAmplitude * 0.6
    for posns1 in range(0,ends1):
      posns2 = posns1+(delay*echoCount)
      values1 = getSampleValueAt(s1,posns1)*echoAmplitude
      values2 = getSampleValueAt(s2,posns2)
      setSampleValueAt(s2,posns2,values1+values2)
  play(s2)
  return s2
```

9.3.2 Creating Chords

A musical chord is three or more notes that create a harmonious sound when played together. The C major chord is a combination of the notes C, E, and G. To create the chord, we can just add the values together at the same index. The provided media folder contains sound files for the notes C, E, and G each played on a bassoon. All three are exactly the same length.

Program 115: Creating a Chord

```
def createChord():
  c = makeSound("bassoon-c4.wav")
  e = makeSound("bassoon-e4.wav")
  g = makeSound("bassoon-g4.wav")
  chord = makeEmptySound(getLength(c))
  for index in range(0,getLength(c)):
    cValue = getSampleValueAt(c,index)
    eValue = getSampleValueAt(e,index)
```

```
    gValue = getSampleValueAt(g,index)
    total = cValue + eValue + gValue
    setSampleValueAt(chord,index,total)
  return chord
```

9.4   HOW SAMPLING KEYBOARDS WORK

Sampling keyboards are keyboards that use recordings of sounds (e.g., pianos, harps, trumpets) to create music by playing them in the desired pitch. Modern music and sound keyboards (and synthesizers) allow musicians to record sounds in their daily lives and turn them into "instruments" by shifting their original frequencies. How do the synthesizers do this? It's not really complicated. The interesting part is that it allows you to use any sound you want as an instrument.

Sampling keyboards use huge amounts of memory to record lots of different instruments at different pitches. When you press a key on the keyboard, the recording *closest* (in pitch) to the note you pressed is selected and then is shifted to exactly the pitch you requested.

This first program works by creating a sound that *skips* every other sample. You read that right—after being so careful to treat all the samples the same, we're now going to skip half of them! In the **mediasources** directory, you'll find a sound named **c4.wav**. This is the note C, in the fourth octave of a piano, played for one second. It makes a good sound to experiment with, but any sound will work.

Program 116: Double the Frequency of a Sound

```
def double(source):
  len = getLength(source) / 2 + 1
  target = makeEmptySound(len)
  targetIndex = 0
  for sourceIndex in range(0, getLength(source), 2):
    sourceValue = getSampleValueAt(source,sourceIndex)
    setSampleValueAt(target, targetIndex, sourceValue)
    targetIndex = targetIndex + 1
  play(target)
  return target
```

Here's how to use it:

```
>>> c4 = makeSound("c4.wav")
>>> play(c4)
>>> c4doubled=double(c4)
```

This program looks like it's the array-copying algorithm we saw earlier. Note that the range uses the third parameter—we're incrementing by 2. If we increment by 2, we end up skipping every other sample.

Try it![1] You can easily hear that the sound really does double in frequency. If you explore the first sound, and the new doubled sound (using **c4.wav**), it will look like

---

[1]You are now trying this out as you read, aren't you?

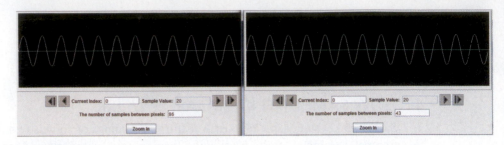

FIGURE 9.4
A sound wave doubled.

Figure 9.4. Both sounds *look* the same, but notice "the number of pixels between samples." It's 43 in one and 86 in the other. The sound did double—the wave form looks the same, and that is exactly as it should be.

How did that happen? It's not really all that complicated. Think of it this way: the frequency of the basic file is really the number of cycles that pass by in a certain amount of time. If you skip every other sample, the new sound has just as many cycles, but has them in *half* the amount of time.

Now let's try the other way. Let's take every sample twice. What happens then?

We will use the same `int` trick that we used with scaling up a picture, in order to return the integer portion of an index.

```
>>> print int(0.5)
0
>>> print int(1.5)
1
```

Here's the program that *halves* the frequency. We're using the array-copying subrecipe again but we're sort of reversing it. The `for` loop moves the `targetIndex` along the length of the sound. The `sourceIndex` is now being incremented—but only by 0.5. The effect is that we'll take every sample in the source twice. The `sourceIndex` will be 1, 1.5, 2, 2.5, and so on, but because we're using the `int` of that value, we'll take samples 1, 1, 2, 2, and so on.

Program 117: Halve the Frequency

```
def halve(source):
  target = makeEmptySound(getLength(source) * 2)
  sourceIndex = 0
  for targetIndex in range(0, getLength(target)):
    value = getSampleValueAt(source, int(sourceIndex))
    setSampleValueAt(target, targetIndex, value)
    sourceIndex = sourceIndex + 0.5
  play(target)
  return target
```

How It Works

The function `halve` takes the source sound as input. It creates a target sound that is twice as long as the source sound. The `sourceIndex` is set to 0 (that's where in the source we're copying from) and we have a loop for `targetIndex` from 0 to the end of the `target` sound. We get a sample value from `source` at the *integer* value (`int`) of the `sourceIndex`. We set the sample value at `targetIndex` to the value that we got from the `source` sample. We then add 0.5 to the `sourceIndex`. This means that the `sourceIndex`, each time through the loop, will take on the values 0, 0.5, 1, 1.5, 2, 2.5, and so on. But the integer part of this sequence is 0, 0, 1, 1, 2, 2, and so on. The result is that we take each sample from the `source` sound *twice*.

Think about what we're doing here. Imagine that the number 0.5 above was actually 0.75, or 2, or 3. Would this work? The `for` loop would have to change but essentially the idea is the same in all these cases. We are *sampling* the source data to create the target data. Using a *sample index* of 0.5 slows down the sound and halves the frequency. A sample index larger than 1 speeds up the sound and increases the frequency.

Let's try to generalize this sampling with the program that follows. (Note that this one *won't* work right.)

Program 118: Shifting the Frequency of a Sound: BROKEN!

```
def shift(source,factor):
  target = makeEmptySound(getLength(source))
  sourceIndex = 0

  for targetIndex in range(0, getLength(target)):
    sourceValue = getSampleValueAt(source,int(sourceIndex))
    setSampleValueAt(target, targetIndex, sourceValue)
    sourceIndex = sourceIndex + factor

  play(target)
  return target
```

Here's how we could use this:

```
>>> cF=getMediaPath("c4.wav")
>>> print cF
c:/ip-book/mediasources/c4.wav
>>> c4 = makeSound(testF)
>>> lowerC4=shift(c4,0.75)
```

That seems to work. But, what if the `factor` for sampling is *more* than 1.0?

```
>>> higherTest=shift(c4,1.5)
You are trying to access the sample at index: 67585,
but the last valid index is at 67584
The error was:
Inappropriate argument value (of correct type).
An error occurred attempting to pass an argument to a
function. Please check line 218 of C:\ip-book\
programs\mySound.py
```

Why? What's happening? Here's how you could see it: print out the `sourceIndex` just before the `setSampleValueAt`. You'd see that the `sourceIndex` becomes *larger* than the length of the source sound. Of course, that makes sense. If each time through the loop, we increment the `targetIndex` by 1, but increment the `sourceIndex` by *more than* 1, we'll get past the end of the source sound before we reach the end of the target sound. But how do we avoid this?

Here's what we want to happen: if the `sourceIndex` ever gets larger than the length of the source, we want to reset the `sourceIndex` back to zero. In Python we use an `if` statement to only execute the code in the following block if the test is true. Try it with commands like `shift(t,0.33)` and `shift(t,2.5)`.

Program 119: Shifting the Frequency of a Sound

```
def shift(source,factor):
  target = makeEmptySound(getLength(source))
  sourceIndex = 0

  for targetIndex in range(0, getLength(target)):
    sourceValue = getSampleValueAt(source,int(sourceIndex))
    setSampleValueAt(target, targetIndex, sourceValue)
    sourceIndex = sourceIndex + factor
    if (sourceIndex >= getLength(source)):
      sourceIndex = 0

  play(target)
  return target
```

We can actually set the factor so that we get whatever frequency we want. We call this factor the *sampling interval*. For a desired frequency f_0, the sampling interval should be:

$$samplingInterval = (sizeOfSourceSound)\frac{f_0}{samplingRate}$$

This is how a keyboard synthesizer works. It has recordings of pianos, voices, bells, drums, whatever. By *sampling* those sounds at different sampling intervals, it can shift the sound to the desired frequency.

The last program in this section plays a single sound at its original frequency, then at two times, three times, four times, and five times.

Program 120: Playing a Sound in a Range of Frequencies

```
def playASequence(inSound):
  # Play the sound five times, increasing the frequency
  for factor in range(1,6):
    sound = duplicateSound(inSound)
    target = shift(sound,factor)
    blockingPlay(target)
```

9.4.1 Sampling as an Algorithm

You should recognize a similarity between the halving recipe, Program 117 (page 262), and the recipe for scaling a picture up (making it larger), Program 84 (page 179). To halve the frequency, we take each sample twice by incrementing by 0.5 and using the `int()` function to get the integer part of that. To make the picture larger, we take each pixel twice, adding 0.5 to our index variables and using the `int()` function on them. These are using the same *algorithm*—the same basic process is being used in each. The details of pictures vs. sounds aren't critical. The point is that the same basic process is being used in each.

We have seen other algorithms that cross media boundaries. Obviously, our increasing-red and increasing-volume functions (and the decreasing versions) are essentially doing the same thing. The way we blend pictures or sounds is the same. We take the component color channels (pixels) or samples (sounds) and add them using percentages to determine the amount from each that we want in the final product. As long as the percentages total 100%, we'll get a reasonable output that reflects the input sounds or pictures at the correct percentages.

Identifying algorithms like these is useful for several reasons. If we understand the algorithm in general (e.g., when it's slow and when it's fast, what it works for and what it doesn't, what the limitations are), then the lessons learned apply in the specific picture or sound instances. Knowing the algorithms is also useful for designers. When you are designing a new program, keep the algorithms in mind so that you can use them when they apply.

When we double or halve the sound frequency, we are also shrinking or doubling the length of the sound. You might want a target sound whose length is *exactly* the length of the sound rather than have to clear out extra stuff from a longer sound. You can do that with `makeEmptySound`. The function `makeEmptySound(22050 * 10)` returns a new empty sound of 10 seconds in length with a sampling rate of 22,050.

9.5 ADDITIVE SYNTHESIS

Additive synthesis creates sounds by adding sine waves together. We saw earlier that it's really pretty easy to add sounds together. With additive synthesis, you can shape the waves yourself, set their frequencies, and create "instruments" that have never existed.

9.5.1 Making Sine Waves

Let's figure out how to produce a set of samples to generate a sound at a given frequency and amplitude. An easy way to do this is to create a sine wave. A whistle, for example, is almost a perfect sine wave. The trick is to create a sine wave with the desired frequency.

If you took values from 0 to 2π, computed the sine of each value, and graphed the computed values, you'd get a sine wave. From your really early math courses, you know that there's an infinity of numbers between 0 and 1. Computers don't handle infinity very well, so we'll actually only take *some* values between 0 and 2π.

To create the graph shown below, Mark filled 20 rows (a totally arbitrary number) of a spreadsheet with values from 0 to 2π (about 6.28). Mark added about 0.314 (6.28/20) to each preceding row. In the next column, he took the sine of each value in the first column, then graphed it.

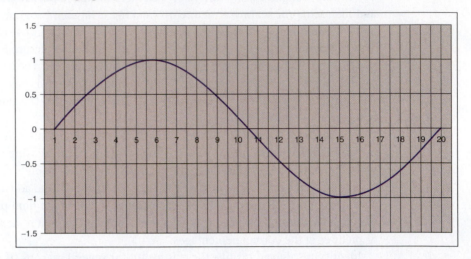

If we want to create a sound at a given frequency, say 440 Hz, we have to fit an entire cycle like the one in the graph into 1/440 of a second (440 cycles per second, meaning that each cycle fits into 1/440 second, or 0.00227 seconds). Mark made the graph using 20 values. Call it 20 *samples*. How many samples do we have to chop up the 440 Hz cycle into? That's the same as asking how many samples must go by in 0.00227 seconds. We know the sampling rate—that's the number of samples in one second. Let's say that it's 22,050 samples per second (our default sampling rate). Each sample is then 1/22,050 which equals 0.0000453 seconds. How many samples fit into 0.00227? That's 0.00227/0.0000453, or about 50. What we just did here mathematically is:

$$interval = 1/frequency$$

$$samplesPerCycle = \frac{interval}{1/samplingRate} = (samplingRate)(interval)$$

Now let's spell this out as Python. To get a wave form at a given frequency, say 440 Hz, we need 440 of these waves in a single second. Each one must fit into the interval of 1/*frequency*. The number of samples that needs to be produced during the interval is the sampling rate divided by the frequency, or interval $(1/f) * (sampling\ rate)$. Call that the *samplesPerCycle*.

At each entry of the sound *sampleIndex*, we want to:

- Get the fraction of *sampleIndex/samplesPerCycle*.
- Multiply that fraction by 2π. That's the number of radians we need. Take the *sine* of $(sampleIndex/samplesPerCycle) * 2\pi$.
- Multiply the result by the desired amplitude and put it in the `sampleIndex`.

Our sine wave generator will input a frequency, a desired amplitude, and the length of the desired sound in seconds. We'll provide an amplitude as input that will be the *maximum* amplitude of the sound. (Since sine generates between -1 and 1, the range of amplitudes will be between −*amplitude* and *amplitude*.) We can use it like this explore(sineWave(440,2000,3)) to generate a sine wave at 440 Hz, with a maximum amplitude of 2000, for 3 seconds.

Program 121: Generate a Sine Wave at a Given Frequency and Amplitude

```
def sineWave(freq,amplitude,secs):

    # Get a blank sound
    buildSin = makeEmptySoundBySeconds(secs)

    # Set sound constant
    sr = getSamplingRate(buildSin)          # sampling rate

    interval = 1.0/freq       # Make sure it's floating point
    samplesPerCycle =  interval * sr    # samples per cycle
    maxCycle = 2 * pi

    for pos in range (0,getLength(buildSin)):
        rawSample = sin((pos / samplesPerCycle) * maxCycle)
        sampleVal = int(amplitude*rawSample)
        setSampleValueAt(buildSin,pos,sampleVal)

    return buildSin
```

Note that we used 1.0 divided by freq to calculate the interval. We used 1.0 instead of 1 to make sure that the result is a floating point and not an integer. If Python sees us only using integers it will give us an integer result by throwing away anything after the decimal. By using at least one floating-point number (1.0), it will give us the result as a floating point.

9.5.2   Adding Sine Waves Together

Now let's add sine waves together. As we said at the beginning of the chapter, that's pretty easy: just add the samples at the same indices together. Here's a function that adds one sound into a second sound.

Program 122: Add Two Sounds Together

```
def addSounds(sound1,sound2):
  for index in range(0,getLength(sound1)):
    s1Sample = getSampleValueAt(sound1,index)
    s2Sample = getSampleValueAt(sound2,index)
    setSampleValueAt(sound2,index,s1Sample+s2Sample)
```

Let's add together 440 Hz, 880 Hz (twice 440), and 1320 Hz (880 + 440) but we'll have the amplitudes increase. We'll double the amplitude each time: 2000, then 4000, then 8000. We'll add them all up into the name f440 and explore the result. At the end, we will generate a 440 Hz sound so that we can listen to them both and compare.

```
>>> f440 = sineWave(440,2000,3)
>>> f880 = sineWave(880,4000,3)
>>> f1320 = sineWave(1320,8000,3)
>>> addSounds(f880,f440)
>>> addSounds(f1320,f440)
>>> play(f440)
>>> explore(f440)
>>> just440=sineWave(440,2000,3)
>>> play(just440)
>>> explore(f440)
```

Common Bug: Beware of Adding Amplitudes Past 32,767

When you add sounds, you add their amplitudes also. A maximum of 2000 + 4000 + 8000 will never be greater than 32,767 but don't worry about that. Remember what happened when the amplitude got too high in the last chapter...

9.5.3   Checking Our Result

How do we know if we really got what we wanted? If we explore the original f440 sound and the modified f440 sound, which is really the combination of the three sounds, you will notice that the wave forms look very different (Figure 9.5). That tells you that we did *something* to the sound...but what?

We can test our code by using the sound tools in MediaTools or other sound visualizer. First, we save out a sample wave (just 400 Hz) and the combined wave.

```
>>> writeSoundTo(just440,"C:/ip-book/mediasources/just440.wav")
>>> writeSoundTo(f440,"C:/ip-book/mediasources/combined440.wav")
```

The way you can really check your additive synthesis is with an FFT (fast fourier transform). Generate the FFT for each signal by using the MediaTools application. You'll see that the 440 Hz signal has a single spike (Figure 9.6). That's what you'd expect—it's supposed to be a single sine wave. Now look at the combined wave form's FFT. It's what it's supposed to be. You see three spikes there and each succeeding one is double the height of the last one.

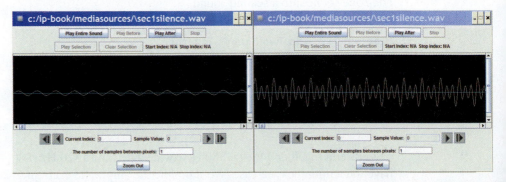

FIGURE 9.5
The raw 440 Hz signal (*left*) and the 440 + 880 + 1320 Hz signal (*right*).

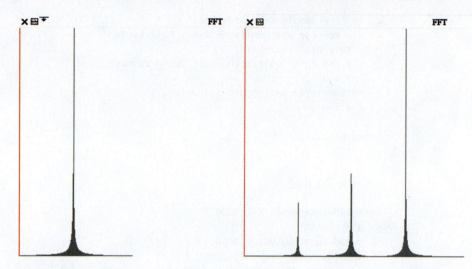

FIGURE 9.6
FFT of the 440 Hz sound (*left*) and the combined sound (*right*).

9.5.4 Square Waves

We don't have to just add sine waves. We can also add *square waves*. These are literally square-shaped waves, moving between +1 and −1. The FFT will look very different, and the *sound* will be very different. It can actually be a much richer sound.

Try swapping this program in for the sine wave generator and see what you think. Note the use of an `if` statement to swap between the positive and negative sides of the wave halfway through a cycle.

Program 123: Square Wave Generator for a Given Frequency and Amplitude

```
def squareWave(freq,amplitude,seconds):

  # Get a blank sound
  square = makeEmptySoundBySeconds(seconds)

  # Set music constants
  samplingRate = getSamplingRate(square)     # sampling rate
  # Build tools for this wave
  # seconds per cycle: make sure floating point
  interval = 1.0 * seconds / freq
  # creates floating point since interval is fl point
  samplesPerCycle = interval * samplingRate
  # we need to switch every half-cycle
  samplesPerHalfCycle = int(samplesPerCycle / 2)
  sampleVal = amplitude
  s = 1
  i = 1

  for s in range (0, getLength(square)):
    # if end of a half-cycle
```

```
      if (i > samplesPerHalfCycle):
        # reverse the amplitude every half-cycle
        sampleVal = sampleVal * -1
        # and reinitialize the half-cycle counter
        i = 0
      setSampleValueAt(square,s,sampleVal)
      i = i + 1

  return(square)
```

Use it like this:

```
>>> sq440=squareWave(440,4000,3)
>>> play(sq440)
>>> sq880=squareWave(880,8000,3)
>>> sq1320=squareWave(1320,10000,3)
  >>> writeSoundTo(sq440,getMediaPath("square440.wav"))
  Note: There is no file at C:/ip-book/mediasources/
  square440.wav
  >>> addSounds(sq880,sq440)
  >>> addSounds(sq1320,sq440)
  >>> play(sq440)
  >>> writeSoundTo(sq440,getMediaPath("squarecombined440.wav"))
  Note: there is no file at C:/ip-book/pmediasources/
  squarecombined440.wav
```

How It Works

This program creates sine waves that are square in shape and all the sample values are either the passed amplitude or −1 times the amplitude. Let's walk through what happens when sq440 = squareWave(440,4000) is executed.

- First, we create a silent sound that is long enough for seconds number of seconds, called square.
- Next, we calculate the number of samples per cycle based on the sampling rate, frequency, and length in seconds. This is $(1.0 * 1/440) * 22{,}050$, which is about 50.11363.
- We calculate the number of samples in half of a cycle as an integer (25) so that half of the values in a cycle will be positive and half negative. We use i to track how many values have been set in square in order to check if we have done half a cycle. We set the sampleVal to be the passed amplitude.
- If we reach the end of a half cycle (i == samplesPerHalfCycle), we multiply the sampleVal by −1 to negate it. If sampleVal was positive, it will become negative. And if it was negative, it will become positive. We also reset i to zero to start counting the next half cycle.
- We set the sample value in square to sampleVal. We increment i.
- After the loop finishes, we return the square sound.

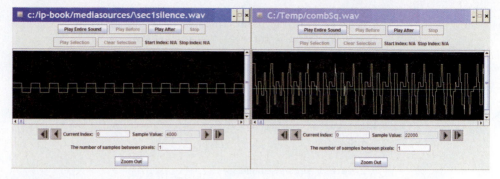

FIGURE 9.7
The 440 Hz square wave (*left*) and additive combination of square waves (*right*).

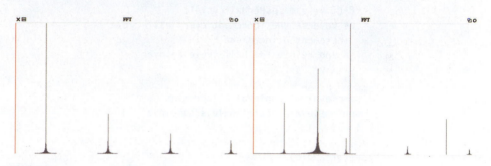

FIGURE 9.8
FFTs of the 440 Hz square wave (*left*) and additive combination of square waves (*right*).

You'll find that the waves really do look square (Figure 9.7) but the most amazing thing is all the additional spikes in FFT (Figure 9.8). Square waves really do result in a much more complex sound.

9.5.5   Triangular Waves

You can create triangular waves instead of square waves with this program (Figure 9.9).

Program 124: Generate Triangular Waves

```
def triangleWave(freq, theAmplitude, seconds):

  # Get a blank sound
  triangle = makeEmptySoundBySeconds(seconds)

  # Set music constants
  # use the passed amplitude
  amplitude = theAmplitude
  # sampling rate (samples per second)
  samplingRate = 22050

  # Build tools for this wave
  # seconds per cycle: make sure floating point
```

```
interval = 1.0 * seconds / freq
# creates floating point since interval is fl point
samplesPerCycle = interval * samplingRate
# we need to switch every half-cycle
samplesPerHalfCycle = int(samplesPerCycle / 2)
# value to add for each subsequent sample; must be integer
increment = int(amplitude / samplesPerHalfCycle)
# start at bottom and increment or decrement as needed
sampleVal = -amplitude
i = 0

# create 1 second sound
for s in range (0, samplingRate):

  # if end of a half-cycle
  if (i == samplesPerHalfCycle):
    # reverse the increment every half-cycle
    increment = increment * -1
    # and reinit the half-cycle counter
    i = 0

  sampleVal = sampleVal + increment
  setSampleValueAt(triangle,s,sampleVal)
  i = i + 1

play(triangle)
return triangle
```

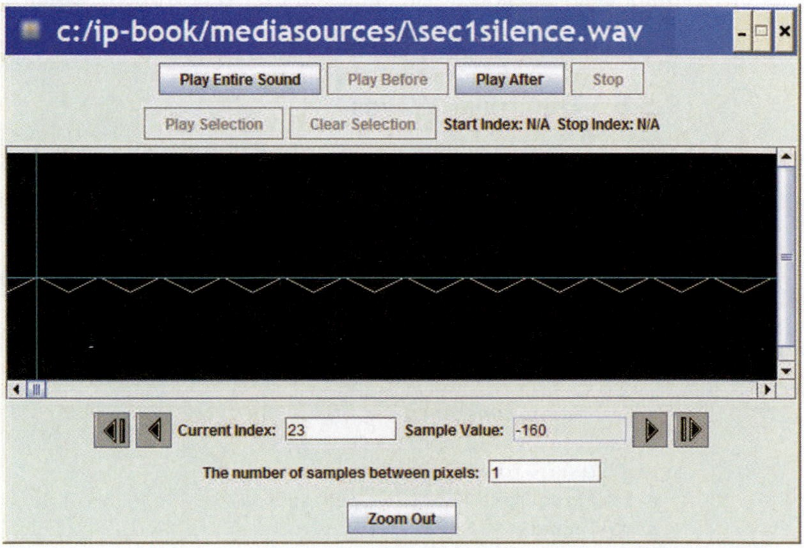

FIGURE 9.9
Exploring a triangular wave.

Use it like this (Figure 9.9):

```
>>> tri440=triangleWave(440,4000,3)
>>> explore(tri440)
```

How It Works

This recipe is similar to the one that creates square waves but these waves are triangular in shape. The `sampleValue` will be initialized to the negation of the passed amplitude. An increment is added to the `sampleValue` each time through the loop. The variable i tracks where we are in the cycle and when we reach halfway through a cycle it negates the `increment` and resets the value of i to zero.

9.6   MODERN MUSIC SYNTHESIS

Additive synthesis is how early music synthesizers worked. Nowadays, additive synthesis isn't too common because the sounds it generates don't sound natural. Synthesizing from recorded sounds is quite common.

The most common synthesis technique today is probably **frequency modulation synthesis** or **FM synthesis**. In FM synthesis, an oscillator (a programmed object that generates a regular series of outputs) controls (modulates) frequencies with other frequencies. The result is a richer sound, less tinny or computer-sounding.

Another common technique is **subtractive synthesis**. In subtractive synthesis, *noise* is used as the input, and then *filters* are applied to remove unwanted frequencies. The result is, again, a richer sound, though typically not as rich as FM synthesis.

Why would we want to create sounds or music with computers anyway? What's the point when there are lots of great sounds, music, and musicians in the world? The point is that if you want to tell someone else *how* you got that sound, so that they could replicate the process or even modify the sound in some way (perhaps making it better), a program is the way to do it. A program succinctly captures and communicates a process—how a sound or a piece of music is generated.

9.6.1   MP3

Nowadays, the audio files on your computer are most commonly MP3 files (or perhaps MP4 or one of its related or descendant file types). MP3 files are sound (and video, in some cases) encodings based on the MPEG-3 standard. They are audio files but compressed in special ways.

One way in which MP3 files are compressed is called **lossless compression**. As we know, there are techniques for storing data that use fewer bits. For example, we know that every sample is typically two bytes wide. What if we didn't store every sample but instead stored the *difference* from the last sample to this sample? The difference between samples is usually much smaller than 32,767 to −32,768—it might be +/− 1000. That takes fewer bits to store.

But MP3 also uses **lossy compression**. It actually throws away some of the sound information. For example, if there's a really soft sound immediately after or simultaneous with a really loud sound, you won't be able to hear the soft sound. An *analog* recording (the type used in records) keeps all those frequencies. MP3 throws away the ones you can't actually hear. Analog recordings are different than digital recordings in that they continuously record the sound, while digital recordings take samples at time intervals.

WAV files are compressed, but not as much as MP3, and they only use lossless techniques. MP3 files tend to be much smaller than the same sound in a WAV format. AIFF files are similar to WAV files.

9.6.2   MIDI

MIDI is the *Musical Instrument Digital Interface*. It's really a set of agreements between manufacturers of computer music devices (sequencers, synthesizers, drum machines, keyboards, etc.) for how their devices will work together. Using MIDI, you can control various synthesizers and drum machines from different keyboards.

MIDI is not used for encoding sound as much as encoding music. MIDI doesn't record what something sounds like, but how it is played. Literally, MIDI encodes information like, "Press the key down on synthesized instrument X at pitch Y," then later "Release the key Y on instrument X." The quality of MIDI sound depends entirely on the synthesizer, the device generating the synthesized instrument.

MIDI files tend to be very small. Instructions like "Play key #42 on track 7" are only some five bytes long. This makes MIDI attractive in comparison with large sound files. MIDI has been particularly popular for karaoke machines.

MIDI has an advantage over MP3 or WAV files in that it can specify a lot of music in very few bytes. But MIDI can't record sounds. For example, if you want to record a specific person's style of playing an instrument, or record *anyone* singing, you don't want to use MIDI. To capture actual sounds, you need to record the actual samples, so you'll need MP3 or WAV.

Most modern operating systems have pretty good synthesizers built into them. We can use them from Python. JES has built into it a function playNote that takes as input a MIDI note, a duration (how long to play the sound) in milliseconds, and an intensity (how hard to strike the key) from 0 to 127. playNote will always use a piano-sounding instrument. MIDI notes correspond to keys, not to frequencies. C in the first octave is 1, C# is 2. C in the fourth octave is 60, D is 62, and E is 64.

Here's a simple example of playing some MIDI notes from JES. We can use for loops to specify loops in the music.

Program 125: Playing MIDI Notes (Example)

```
def song():
    playNote(60,200,127)
    playNote(62,500,127)
    playNote(64,800,127)
    playNote(60,600,127)
```

PROGRAMMING SUMMARY

`if`	Allows Python to make decisions. `if` takes an expression to test for true or false (basically, anything that evaluates to 0 is false, and everything else is true). The block that follows the `if` is executed if the test is true.
`int`	Returns the integer part of the input value, throwing away anything after the decimal.
`setMediaPath()`	Lets you pick a folder where you get and store media.
`getMediaPath(baseFileName)`	Takes an input of a base filename, then returns the complete path to that file (assuming it's in the media folder that you set using `setMediaPath()`).
`playNote`	Takes as input the note, duration, and intensity. Each note is represented as an integer value from 0 to 127 and middle C is 60. The duration is specified in milliseconds. The intensity can also range from 0 to 127. If you leave this out JES will use 64 for the intensity.

PROBLEMS

9.1 What are each of the following:

1. MIDI
2. MP3
3. Analog
4. Amplitude
5. Sampling rate

9.2 What is the difference between lossless compression and lossy compression? Which type of sound files use what type of compression?

9.3 Rewrite the echo function (Program 111 (page 258)) to generate *two* echoes back, each `delay` samples previous. (*Hint:* Start your index loop at `2*delay + 1`, then access one echo sample at `index-delay` and another at `index-2*delay`.)

9.4 Write a general blend function that takes the two sounds to blend as input and returns a new sound.

9.5 Generalize your general blend function even more. Take in the number of samples to use from the first sound before the blend begins and the number of samples to blend.

9.6 How long is a sound compared to the original when it's been frequency doubled (Program 116 (page 261))? How long is a sound compared to the original when only every fourth sound value is copied into the target sound?

9.7   Write a function to input a sound, then create a canvas sound of the same length. Copy samples from the input into the canvas *every other* position, i.e., copy from index 0 in the input into the canvas at index 0, then copy from index 2 (skipping index 1) in the input into the canvas at index 1. What do you hear in the canvas sound? Same sound? Faster? Slower?

9.8   Write a function to input a sound, then create a canvas sound of the same length. Copy samples from the input into the canvas *every third* position, i.e., copy from index 0 in the input into the canvas at index 0, then copy from index 3 (skipping index 1 and 2) in the input into the canvas at index 3. What do you hear in the canvas sound? Same sound? Faster? Slower?

9.9   Write a function that will input two sounds. Create a new sound with one half of the first sound, then add the two sounds together for the length of the two sounds, and then add the second half of the second sound. This is easiest to do if the sounds have the same length.

9.10   Write a function that will blend three sounds together. Start with part of the first sound, then a blend of sound1 and sound2, and then a blend of sound2 and sound3, and end with the rest of sound3.

9.11   Blend in some words over some music. Start with the music at 75% and the words at 25% and gradually make the words 75% and the music 25%.

9.12   Write a function that inputs a frequency, a maximum amplitude, and length in seconds. Create two sounds, one a square and one a triangle, using the same inputs. Add the sounds together. What do you get?

9.13   Write a function that inputs a frequency, a maximum amplitude, a percentage of blend (e.g., 0.25 to represent 25%), and length in seconds. Create two sounds, one a square and one a triangle, using the same inputs. Add the sounds together, with the blend percentage of the square and 100—*blend* of the triangle. How does the sound change if you try 0.25, 0.5, and 0.75 as the blend percentages?

9.14   Write a function to change the frequency of a sound 10 times—five times *lower* than the original frequency, and five times *higher*.

9.15   Create a new version of the shift function that creates the target to be as big as the resulting sound should be. So if the factor is less than one it would create a larger sound and if greater than one a smaller sound.

9.16   Does the shift function work with a factor of 0.3? If it doesn't, can you fix it to copy each source value three times into the target?

9.17   Hip-hop DJs spin turntables back and forth so that sections of sound are played forwards and backwards quickly. Try combining backwards play (Program 108 (page 248)) and frequency shifting (Program 116 (page 261)) to get the same effect. Play a second of a sound quickly forward, then quickly backward, two or three times. (You might have to move faster than just double the speed.)

9.18   Consider changing the `if` block in the frequency shift recipe (Program 119 (page 264)) to `sourceIndex = sourceIndex - getLength(source)`.

What's the difference from just setting the `sourceIndex` to 0? Is this better or worse? Why?

9.19 If you use the shifting recipe (Program 119) with a factor of 2.0 or 3.0, you'll get the sound repeated or even triplicated. Why? Can you fix it? Write `shiftDur` that takes a number of samples (or even seconds) to play the sound.

9.20 Using the sound tools, figure out the characteristic pattern of different instruments. For example, pianos tend to have a pattern the opposite of what we created—the amplitudes *decrease* as we get to higher sine waves. Try creating a variety of patterns and see how they sound and how they look.

9.21 When musicians work with additive synthesis, they will often wrap *envelopes* around the sounds, and even around each added sine wave. An envelope *changes* the amplitude over time—it might start out small, then grow (rapidly or slowly), then hold at a certain value during the sound, and then drop before the sound ends. That kind of pattern is sometimes called the *attack-sustain-decay (ASD) envelope*. Pianos tend to attack quickly, then decay quickly. Flutes tend to attack slowly and sustain as long as you want. Try implementing that for the sine and square wave generators.

9.22 Create a function to play your school's fight song using MIDI.

9.23 The Web site `https://musopen.org/` has copyright-free sheet music. Take any one of those songs and translate it into MIDI notes, and write a function to play it.

9.24 **Challenging:** Take any song you want and play it by using the recorded *bassoon* notes in the media folder, shifting them up and down in frequency to create the right notes.

TO DIG DEEPER

Good books on computer music say a lot about creating sounds from scratch, as in this chapter. One of Mark's favorites for understandability is *Computer Music: Synthesis, Composition, and Performance* by Dodge and Jerse [10]. The "bible" of computer music is Curtis Roads' massive *The Computer Music Tutorial* [11].

One of the most powerful tools for playing with this level of computer music is *CSound*. It's a software music synthesis system, free, and totally cross-platform. The book by Richard Boulanger [39] has everything you need for playing with CSound.

10 Building Bigger Programs

Chapter Learning Objectives

- To demonstrate two different design strategies: top-down and bottom-up.
- To demonstrate different testing strategies, such as black box and glass box.
- To demonstrate several debugging strategies to use when figuring out programming problems.
- To identify challenges to engineering of large programs.

The computer science goals for this chapter are:

- To use methods for accepting user input and generating output for the user.
- To use an indefinite iteration structure, the `while` loop.
- To access global variables.

For many problems that you might solve with a program, the kinds of programs we have been writing so far in this book will work just fine. Relatively small programs with maybe a dozen lines of code can solve many interesting problems and make many interesting creations. There are many, many more problems and creations, though, that *could* be solved with larger and more complex programs. That's what this chapter is about. These are the issues that are addressed by the field of *software engineering*.

Writing larger programs involves solving problems that have to do with managing the activity of programming itself.

- What program lines are you going to write? How are you going to decide what functions you need? This is the process of *design*. There are many approaches to design, but the two most common are **top-down** and **bottom-up**. In top-down design, you figure out what has to be done, refine the *requirements* until you think you can identify the pieces, and then you write the pieces (typically from the highest level first). In bottom-up design, you start with what you know, and keep adding to it until you've got your program.

- Things won't work the first time. Programming has been defined as "the art of debugging a blank sheet of paper."[1] Debugging is figuring out what *doesn't* work, why, and how to fix it. The activity of programming and the activity of *debugging* are intricately connected. Learning to debug is an important skill that leads to figuring out how to make programs that actually *run*.

- Even if things work the first time, it's unlikely that you got it completely right. Big programs have lots of parts to them. You need to use *testing* techniques to make sure that you got all (or even most) of the mistakes (*bugs*) in the program.

- Even after testing and debugging, most large programs are not "done." Many large programs get used over a long period of time to solve problems that come up often (like bookkeeping or tracking inventory). These large programs are *never* finished. Instead, new features are added, or newly discovered bugs have to be squashed. The *maintenance* stage of program development goes on for as long as the program is in use. Overall, over the course of a lifetime of a program, maintenance is *by far* the most expensive part.

- Design done well is iterative. Use of the program inspires thinking about new things that the program might do. Maintenance leads to rethinking how the program was designed the first (or last) time. Design is an iterative process, and both top-down and bottom-up are only about one pass through the cycle.

10.1   DESIGNING PROGRAMS TOP-DOWN

Top-down design is how most engineering disciplines recommend designing. You start out by developing a list of *requirements*: what needs to be done, using English or math, that can be iteratively refined. Refining requirements means making them clearer and more specific. The goal of refining requirements in top-down design is to get to the point where the statements of the requirements can be directly implemented as program code.

The top-down process is often preferred because it's understandable and you can plan for it—it's really what makes the business of software possible. Imagine working with a customer who wants you to program something. You are given a problem statement and then work with the customer to refine it into a set of requirements. You go build the program. If the customer is not happy with it, you can test to see if the software meets the requirements. If it does, and the customer agreed to the requirements, then you've met your agreement. If it doesn't, then you need to make it meet the requirements—but not necessarily meet the customer's changed needs.

---

[1] Definition of "programming" from The Jargon File v. 4.4.8. The Jargon File © 2003 by Eric S. Raymond. Reprinted with permission.

In detail, the process looks something like this:

- Start out with the problem statement. If you don't have one, write one. What are you trying to do?

- Start refining the problem statement. Are there parts to the program? Perhaps you should use **hierarchical decomposition** to define subfunctions? Do you know that you have to open some pictures or set some constant values? And then are there some loops? How many do you need?

- Keep refining the problem statement until you get to statements or commands or functions that you know (or know how to write).

- When you are working on a large program, you are almost certainly going to use functions that call other functions (*subfunctions*). Start by writing the functions you might call from the Command Area, then the lower-level functions, until you get to the subfunctions.

10.1.1   A Top-Down Design Example

If we followed this process and defined functions (*procedures*) instead of lines of code, we would be using **procedural abstraction**. In procedural abstraction, you define high-level functions that call lower-level functions. The lower-level functions are easy to write and test, and the higher-level functions become easy to read, because they're simply calling lower-level functions.

We have seen some procedural abstraction earlier in the book. An example is when we redefined the collage in terms of lower-level functions that did copying of pixels for us. These lower-level functions are a form of abstraction. By naming those lines of code with a function name, we can stop thinking in terms of those individual lines, and instead use a meaningful name for those lines. By providing parameters to the function, we make the function reusable.

Let's build a simple *adventure game*. An adventure game is a kind of video game where the player explores a world, moving between rooms and spaces in the game using commands like "go north" and "take the key." Often there are puzzles to solve and battles to wage. The original adventure game was written in the 1970s by William Crowther and then extended by Don Woods. It was based on exploration of a set of caves. The genre was made popular in the 1980s with the Infocom games like *Zork* and *Hitchhiker's Guide to the Galaxy*. Modern adventure games tend to be graphical, like *Dreamfall* and *Portal*. The original text-based adventure games blended gaming with storytelling, which is what we'll aim for.

At this point, we need to define our problem. What kind of adventure game are we going to build? What size? What will the user be able to do? We want to define the problem within the limitations of what we can develop.

Let's build an adventure game where the user can walk between rooms and that's it. No puzzles and no real game play. We want just a simple example. Here's a sketch of how a simple set of rooms might be laid out. Just to make it interesting, let's pretend it's a setting for a horror or thriller story.

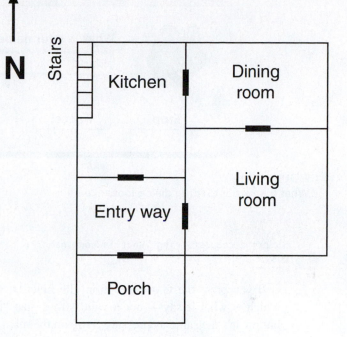

10.1.2 Designing the Top-Level Function

How will our program work? We can come up with an outline for how it might run:

1. We start out by telling the player the basics of how to play the game.
2. We describe the room to the player. Let's put the player in a particular room to start.
3. We get the player's command ("north" or "quit") typed in.
4. We figure out which room the user goes into next, because of her (or his) command choice (e.g., what direction the user wants to go in).
5. We repeat from step 2 on until the user says to quit.

We can actually write the function that will do these things right now. We need to know a couple of additional functions in Python that we haven't seen yet.

- printNow is a function[2] that takes a string as input then prints it to the Command Area *as soon as it executes*. printNow is useful for displaying things during the game.
- To get input from the user, we can use requestString. The function request String takes as input a prompt that will appear in the window requesting user input (Figure 10.1). (In Python, the ability to read a string input from the user is called raw_input.) The function returns the string that the user types in.

---

[2]In Python 3.0, even print is a function, so it's not as strange as it might seem.

FIGURE 10.1
What the requestString dialog looks like.

```
>>> print requestString("What is your name?")
Mark
```

If you press the CANCEL button, the function requestString returns None which is what it says—not a valid string, just "none." If you press the STOP button, it's the same as pressing STOP on the main JES window. That allows you to stop a program even while in an input dialog.

```
>>> print requestString("What is your name?") # Cancel
None
>>> print requestString("What is your name?") # Stop
[The program was stopped by the stop button.]
```

- Another challenge is how to just keep repeating some lines of code *indefinitely* until something specific happens. We can't do that with a for loop.

  We'll use a while loop which allows us to loop without specifying for how many steps, indices, or values in a loop (e.g., getPixels). A while loop takes a test (like an if). What's different, compared with if, is that the while loop repeats the body of the loop *indefinitely* until the test becomes false. The below executes when x is 0, 1, and 2, but when x is 3, it's not true that x < 3, so the loop doesn't execute.

```
>>> x = 0
>>> while (x < 3):
...          print "Counting..."
...          x = x + 1
...
Counting...
Counting...
Counting...
```

With these three pieces, we can write the function that corresponds to the outline that appeared earlier.

Program 126: Top-Level Function of Adventure Game

```
def playGame():
  location = "Porch"
  showIntroduction()
  while not (location == "Exit") :
    showRoom(location)
    direction = requestString("Which direction?")
    location = pickRoom(direction, location)
```

This function is pretty close to the outline we presented earlier, line-for-line. What may be strange here is that we have not seen or written some of these functions, like showIntroduction, showRoom, and pickRoom. That is one of the points of top-down design—we can make the *plan* for how the whole program should work, and what functions we will need in the full program, long before we write all the parts.

How It Works

- We will use the variable location to store the room where the player currently is. We'll start out on the "Porch."
- The function showIntroduction will display the instructions to the user.
- We will use the location "Exit" to represent the player's request to leave the game. While the location is *not* "Exit," we will keep playing the game.
- At the start of each turn, we show the description of the current room. The function showRoom will display the room's description, using the player's location as the input for which room to show.
- We get the user's request for a new direction via requestString.
- We pick a new room for the user via the pickRoom function, based on the inputs of the requested direction and the current room location.

Notice that we know *nothing* about how these subfunctions will work. We cannot possibly know how they will work right now, since we have not written them yet. What this means is that this top-level function, playGame, is *decoupled* from the lower-level subfunctions. We define them in terms of the inputs, outputs, and what they should do. Somebody else could write these functions for us now. That's another reason why top-level design is so commonly used for engineering.

- It makes it easier to maintain, since the different pieces can change without changing the whole thing.
- We plan functions before we write them.
- We can allow different programmers to work together on the same program, working from the plan.

10.1.3   Writing the Subfunctions

Now that we have the plan, we can just go ahead and write the rest of the subfunctions to make this work. For right now, we will put all these functions in the file together to make it work right. We could also put useful functions in a separate file and `import` the functions. For now, let's just complete our design and implementation of the adventure game.

Program 127: `showIntroduction` for the Adventure Game

```
def showIntroduction():
  printNow("Welcome to the Adventure House!")
  printNow("In each room, you will be told")
  printNow(" which directions you can go.")
  printNow("You can move north, south, east, or west")
  printNow(" by typing that direction.")
  printNow("Type help to replay this introduction.")
  printNow("Type quit or exit to end the program.")
```

How It Works

Showing the introduction simply displays information for the user/player, via the `printNow` function. We tell the player how to move (by typing a direction), and how to get help or quit. Notice that, in so doing, we are further defining the later functions. In our `pickRoom` function, we will have to manage inputs like "help," "quit," and "exit."

Program 128: `showRoom` for the Adventure Game

```
def showRoom(room):
  if room == "Porch":
    showPorch()
  if room == "Entryway":
    showEntryway()
  if room == "Kitchen":
    showKitchen()
  if room == "LivingRoom":
    showLR()
  if room == "DiningRoom":
    showDR()
```

How It Works

We could make `showRoom` into a long function with lots of `printNow` function calls. However, that would be tedious to write and challenging to maintain. What if you wanted to change the description of the living room? You could wade through a long function and find the right `printNow` to change. Or, you could simply change the `showLR` function. That's how we set it up here.

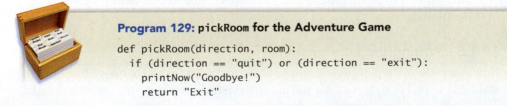

Program 129: `pickRoom` for the Adventure Game

```
def pickRoom(direction, room):
  if (direction == "quit") or (direction == "exit"):
    printNow("Goodbye!")
    return "Exit"
```

```
    if direction == "help":
      showIntroduction()
      return room
    if room == "Porch":
      if direction == "north":
        return "Entryway"
    if room == "Entryway":
      if direction == "north":
        return "Kitchen"
      if direction == "east":
        return "LivingRoom"
      if direction == "south":
        return "Porch"
    if room == "Kitchen":
      if direction == "east":
        return "DiningRoom"
      if direction == "south":
        return "Entryway"
    if room == "LivingRoom":
      if direction == "west":
        return "Entryway"
      if direction == "north":
        return "DiningRoom"
    if room == "DiningRoom":
      if direction == "west":
        return "Kitchen"
      if direction == "south":
        return "LivingRoom"
```

How It Works

This function is defined by the map. Given a current room and the desired direction, this function returns the name of the new room for the player to be located in.

Program 130: Showing Rooms in the Adventure Game

```
def showPorch():
 printNow("You are on the porch of a frightening looking house.")
 printNow("The windows are broken. It's a dark and stormy night.")
 printNow("You can go north into the house. If you dare.")

def showEntryway():
 printNow("You are in the entry way of the house.")
 printNow(" There are cobwebs in the corner.")
 printNow("You feel a sense of dread.")
 printNow("There is a passageway to the north and another to the east.")
 printNow("The porch is behind you to the south.")

def showKitchen():
 printNow("You are in the kitchen. ")
 printNow("All the surfaces are covered with pots,")
```

```
   printNow(" pans, food pieces, and pools of blood.")
   printNow("You think you hear something up the stairs")
   printNow(" that go up the west side of the room.")
   printNow("It's a scraping noise, like something being dragged")
   printNow(" along the floor.")
   printNow("You can go to the south or east.")

def showLR():
 printNow("You are in a living room.")
 printNow("There are couches, chairs, and small tables.")
 printNow("Everything is covered in dust and spider webs.")
 printNow("You hear a crashing noise in another room.")
 printNow("You can go north or west.")

def showDR():
 printNow("You are in the dining room.")
 printNow("There are remains of a meal on the table.")
 printNow("  You can't tell what it is,")
 printNow(" and maybe don't want to.")
 printNow("Was that a thump to the west?")
 printNow("You can go south or west")
```

⌐These lines of the program should continue with the next lines. A single command in Python may not break across multiple lines.   ■

How It Works

For each room, there are simply some printNow invocations to describe that room. From a programming sense, these are very simple functions. From the author's perspective, this is where the fun and creative stuff is.

We now have enough to play our game. We start it by invoking our top-level function, by typing playGame(). Descriptions show up in the Command Area and prompts appear in a dialog box above the game (Figure 10.2). A run of the program might look like this:

```
>>> playGame()
Welcome to the Adventure House!
In each room, you will be told
 which directions you can go.
You can move north, south, east, or west
 by typing that direction.
Type help to replay this introduction.
Type quit or exit to end the program.
You are on the porch of a frightening looking house.
The windows are broken. It's a dark and stormy night.
You can go north into the house. If you dare.
You are in the entry way of the house.
 There are cobwebs in the corner.
You feel a sense of dread.
There is a passageway to the north and another to the east.
The porch is behind you to the south.
You are in the kitchen.
All the surfaces are covered with pots,
```

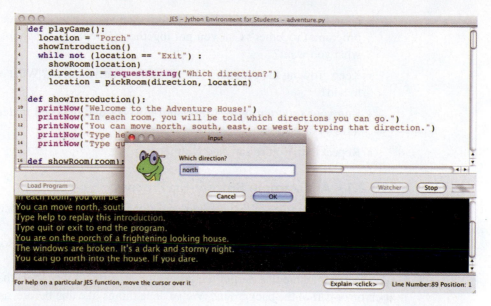

FIGURE 10.2
Screenshot of adventure game play.

```
pans, food pieces, and pools of blood.
You think you hear something up the stairs
 that go up the west side of the room.
It's a scraping noise, like something being dragged
 along the floor.
You can go to the south or east.
Goodbye!
```

10.2 DESIGNING PROGRAMS BOTTOM-UP

Bottom-up is a different process that can end up in essentially the same place. You start with some idea of what you want to do—you could call it a problem statement. But instead of refining the problem, you focus on building the solution program. You want to reuse code from other programs as much as possible.

The most important thing you do with bottom-up design is to *try* your program *very often*. Does it do what you want? Does it do what you *expect*? Does it make sense? If not, add `print` statements and explore the code until you understand what it's doing. If you don't know what it does, you can't change it into what you want.

Here's what the bottom-up process typically looks like, starting from a problem statement:

- How much of the problem do you already know how to do? How much of it can you get from other programs that you've written? For example, does the problem say that you have to manipulate sound? Try a couple of sound programs in the book to remember how to do that. Does it say that you have to change red levels? Can you find a function that does that and try it?

- Now, can you add some of these pieces (that you can write or can steal from other programs) together? Can you put together a couple of functions that do *part* of what you want?

- Keep growing the program. Is it closer to what you need? What else do you need to add?

- Run your program *often*. Make sure it works and that you understand what you have so far.

- Repeat until you're satisfied with the result.

10.2.1   An Example Bottom-Up Process

Most of the examples in this book are developed in a bottom-up process. The way we did background subtraction and chromakey is a good example. We started out with the idea of removing the background of someone and putting that someone in a new picture. Where do we start?

We can imagine that part of the problem is finding all the pixels that are part of the person or part of the background. We've done things like that before, as when we found all the brown in Katie's hair in order to turn it red (Program 48 (page 116)). That tells us that we're going to want to check if there's a large enough distance between a person's color and a background color, and if so, we want to bring in a new background's pixel's color—the pixel at the same point. We've done things like that, too, as when we copied pictures into the canvas.

At this point, we could probably write something like:

```
if distance(personColor,bgColor)<someThresholdValue:
    bgColor = getColor(getPixel(newBackground,x,y))
    setColor(getPixel(personPicture,x,y),bgColor)
```

That's the care of the background subtraction algorithm. The rest of it is simply setting up the variables (Program 56 (page 129)). But then, when we tried it, we found that it didn't work very well, for a variety of reasons. That's what led us to chromakey (Program 57 (page 132)). Chromakey is a better way of figuring out which pixels are part of the background and which are part of the foreground but the basic process is the same as swapping the background—so most of the program is reusable in the new context.

The key process here is to take ideas (or even lines of code) from other projects, and combine them, *testing* what you're doing all the time. Bottom-up programming is quite close to "debugging a blank sheet of paper." Debugging is a critical skill in bottom-up design or programming.

10.3   TESTING YOUR PROGRAM

It is really hard to test your programs well, especially for a new programmer. You wrote the code, so you assume that it does what you wrote! Becoming a good tester requires a large helping of humility. You have to accept the fact that you may have written something incorrectly or that you may not have completely understood *what* to write.

There are two main approaches to testing programs. One is called *glass-box testing*, which is where you test every possible path through your program. The approach is called "glass-box" because you actually look at your program and think through how to test each and every line of your program. You know what the structure of your program is, so you test according to that structure.

To use glass-box testing of our adventure game, we would traverse every door, in both directions. For example, go from the Porch north to the Entryway, then south back to the Porch. Did you go to the right place each time? Did the rooms display correctly? We would test what happens in response to the commands "help," "quit," and "exit." That would make sure that we test each and every line of our program.

The second approach is called *black-box testing*, where you do not consider how the program is written. Instead, you consider how the program is supposed to behave, and in particular, in response to both valid and *invalid* inputs. The player will not necessarily type the right commands. The player might make a mistake and mistype something or may try a command that she thinks is reasonable but you did not consider.

For example, let's use black-box testing with the pickRoom function. First we should test all the correct inputs to pickRoom, like this:

```
>>> pickRoom("north","Porch")
"Entryway"
>>> pickRoom("north","Entryway")
"Kitchen"
```

Now, let's try some invalid inputs—some misspellings and things that should not work.

```
>>> pickRoom("nrth","Porch")
>>> pickRoom("Entryway","Porch")
```

That's a real problem. In response to invalid input, pickRoom does not return anything. When we try to set the variable location from the response, we will not be able to get a valid room. The variable location will be empty. Further, the player won't get any response that something has gone wrong.

We need to change pickRoom so that, if no other response matches, some reasonable reply is made, and a reasonable value is returned. Probably the most reasonable return is simply to return the same room—leave the player where she is.

Program 131: Improved pickRoom for the Adventure Game

```
def pickRoom(direction, room):
  if (direction == "quit") or (direction == "exit"):
    printNow("Goodbye!")
    return "Exit"
  if direction == "help":
    showIntroduction()
    return room
  if room == "Porch":
    if direction == "north":
      return "Entryway"
  if room == "Entryway":
```

```
    if direction == "north":
      return "Kitchen"
    if direction == "east":
      return "LivingRoom"
    if direction == "south":
      return "Porch"
  if room == "Kitchen":
    if direction == "east":
      return "DiningRoom"
    if direction == "south":
      return "Entryway"
  if room == "LivingRoom":
    if direction == "west":
      return "Entryway"
    if direction == "north":
      return "DiningRoom"

  if room == "DiningRoom":
    if direction == "west":
      return "Kitchen"
    if direction == "south":
      return "LivingRoom"
printNow("You can't (or don't want to) go in that direction.")
return room
```

Now, our program will work a bit more reasonably in response to incorrect input.

```
>>> pickRoom("nrth","Porch")
You can't (or don't want to) go in that direction.
'Porch'
>>> pickRoom("Entryway","Porch")
You can't (or don't want to) go in that direction.
"Porch"
```

The first sentence here is just saying that the input direction is not allowed and that the second line ('Porch') is the room that the player is now in.

10.3.1 Testing the Edge Conditions

Professional programmers test every program extensively to make sure that it works the way they expect. One of the black-box items they focus on is testing the *edge conditions*. What's the smallest input that the program should work with? What's the largest input that the program should work with? Make sure that the program can work with both the smallest and largest possible inputs is what we mean by testing the edge conditions.

You can also use this strategy for testing your programs that manipulate media. Let's say that your picture-manipulation program fails (generates an error or doesn't seem to stop) with a particular picture and you've tried to trace the program but can't figure out why it's failing. Try it with a different picture. Does it work with a smaller picture? How about with an empty (all white or all black) picture? Maybe you'll find that your program works but is just so slow that you didn't think it was working with the larger picture.

Sometimes functions that manipulate indices (e.g., scaling programs) may fail on programs of one size but not another. For example, mirroring programs may work with odd-number indices but not even-number indices. Try inputs with different kinds of sizes to see which succeed or fail.

10.4   TIPS ON DEBUGGING

How do you figure out what your program is doing if it runs but isn't doing what you want? This is the process of *debugging*. Debugging is figuring out what your program is doing, how that differs from what you *want* it to be doing, and how to get the program from where it is to where you need it to be.

Starting from an error message is the *easiest* kind of debugging. You have some indication from Python about what the error is, and you have some idea (a line number) about where the error is. That tells you where to look to fix the problem and make the error go away.

The much harder kind of debugging is where the program works but doesn't do what you want. Now you have to figure out what the program is doing and what you want it to be doing.

The first step is *always* to **figure out what the program is doing**. Whether you have explicit error messages or not, this is always the first thing to do. If you get an error, the important question is why the program worked up to there, and what variable values were present at that point such that the error occurred.

> **Computer Science Idea: Learn to Trace Code!**
> The most important thing you can do when debugging your programs is to be able to trace your code. Think about your program the way the computer does. Walk through each line and figure out what it does.

Start out debugging by walking the code, at least the lines around where the error is occurring. What does the error say? What might be causing the error? What are the values of the variables before and after that point? The interesting question is why the error occurred *now*. Why didn't it happen earlier in the program?

If you can, run the program. It's always easier to have the computer *tell* you what's happening instead of having to figure it out yourself. That said, simply executing your functions won't give you the answer. Add `print` statements to your code to show you the values of the variables.

> **Debugging Tip: Print Statements Are Your Friends!**
> Print out what's going on in your programs. Do this when you can't figure out what's going on from tracing the program. Print out the values of equations that are too complex. Print out simple statements like "I'm in this function now!" to let you know that you are reaching the functions you think you're calling. Let the computer *tell* you what it's doing.

Sometimes, especially in a loop, you'll want to use printNow. Since printNow prints the input string to the Command Area *as soon as it occurs*, it is more useful than print for debugging. You want to be able to see what's happening *when* it's happening.

> **Debugging Tip: Don't Be Afraid to Change the Program**
>
> Save a new copy of your program, then edit out all the parts you're confused about. Can you get the rest to run? Now start adding pieces back in (copy–paste) from the original copy of your program. Changing the program so that you're only running part of it at a time is a great way to figure out what's going on.

10.4.1   Finding Which Statement to Worry About

The bugs that are often hardest to figure out are the ones that *look* just fine. Spacing errors and mismatched parentheses fall into this category. These are particularly hard to find in large programs, where the error just says that there's a problem "somewhere" around a given line, but Python isn't exactly sure where.

A time-honored strategy for figuring out what's wrong is to get rid of all the statements that you're sure about. Simply put a "#" in front of the statements that you think are okay. If you comment out an if or for, make sure that you also comment out the block after the statement. Now try again.

If the error goes away, then you were wrong—you actually commented out the statements where the problem is. Uncomment a few and try again. When the error message comes back, the error is in one of the lines that you just uncommented.

If the error is still there, you now have only a few statements to check—the ones that are still uncommented. Eventually, the error either goes away or you have a single line that's uncommented. Either way, you can now figure out where the error is.

10.4.2   Seeing the Variables

Besides printing, there are other tools built into JES to help you figure out what your programs are doing. The showVars function will show you all the variables and their values at the point when it's executed (Figure 10.3). It will show you both the variables in the *current* context and the variables in the *global* context (accessible even from the Command Area). You can use showVars() in the Command Area to see the variables you've created there—perhaps you'd forgotten their names or wanted to see what the values were in several variables at once.

The other powerful tool in JES is the *Watcher*. The Watcher allows you to see which lines are being executed *as* they are executed. Figure 10.4 shows the Watcher running the code given below—the makeSunset() function from Program 38 (page 96). We simply open the Watcher (from the DEBUG menu or from the WATCHER button), then use the Command Area as normal. Whenever we execute our own functions, the Watcher will run.

```
def makeSunset(picture):
  reduceBlue(picture)
  reduceGreen(picture)
```

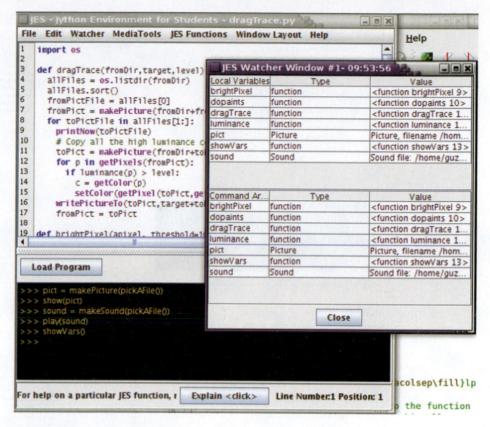

FIGURE 10.3
Showing variables in JES.

```
def reduceBlue(picture):
  for p in getPixels(picture):
    value=getBlue(p)
    setBlue(p,value*0.7)

def reduceGreen(picture):
  for p in getPixels(picture):
    value=getGreen(p)
    setGreen(p,value*0.7)
```

We can PAUSE execution, then STEP through it from there. We can also STOP execution, go FULL SPEED, or even set a speed from slow to fast. When you have the Watcher open, the program *will* run more slowly. The faster the program runs, the less information will be displayed (i.e., not every line executed will show up in the Watcher).

Besides stepping through execution and seeing which statements get executed when, you can also observe particular variables. After clicking ADD VARIABLE, you will be prompted for the name of the variable. Then, when the Watcher runs, the value of the variable will be displayed along with the line. When the variable doesn't have a value yet, you'll see that too (Figure 10.5).

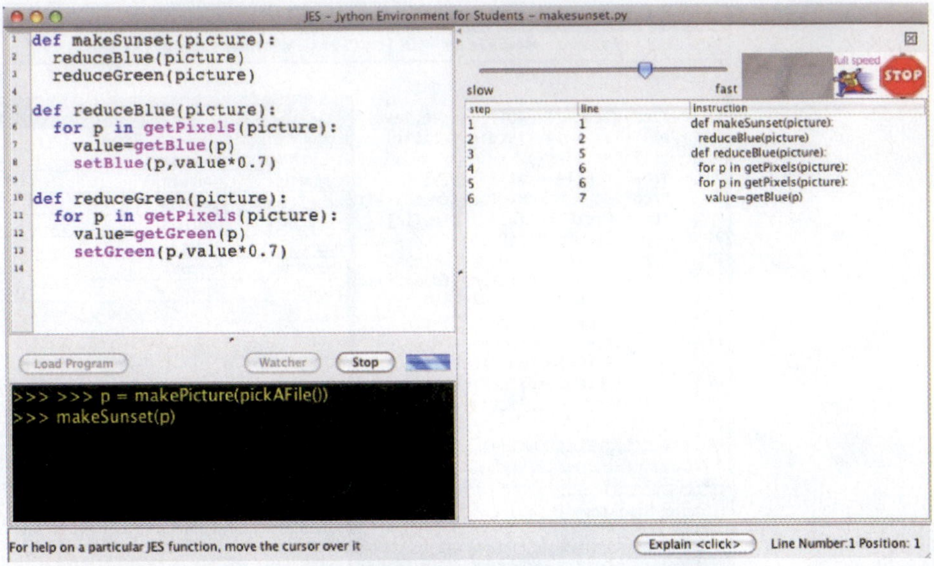

FIGURE 10.4
Stepping through the makeSunset() function with the Watcher.

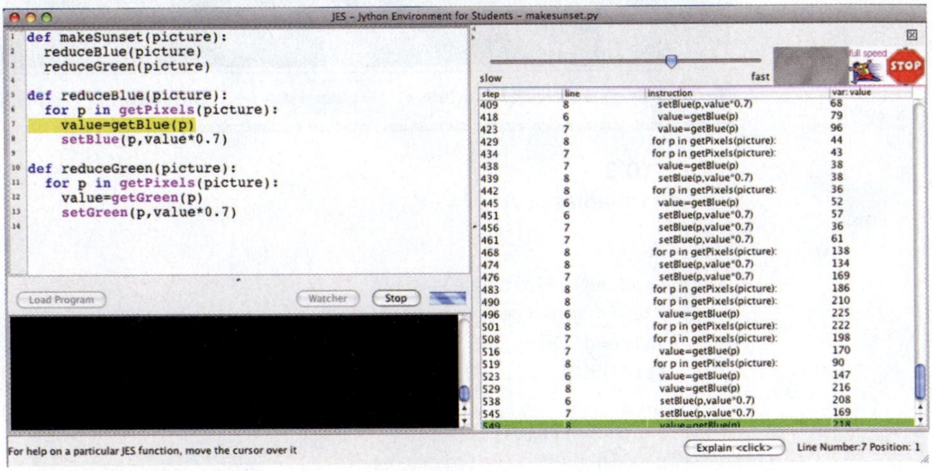

FIGURE 10.5
Watching the variable value in the makeSunset() function with the Watcher.

10.4.3   Debugging the Adventure Game

Let's use some of these techniques with the adventure game. The problem that we have with the adventure game is that it basically works! There are no obvious error messages generated. By going through our testing process, we were able to figure out that we were not handling invalid input correctly. What else could be a problem?

Let's look at what happens when we run the program:

```
>>> playGame()
Welcome to the Adventure House!
```

```
In each room, you will be told
 which directions you can go.
You can move north, south, east, or west
 by typing that direction.
Type help to replay this introduction.
Type quit or exit to end the program.
You are on the porch of a frightening looking house.
The windows are broken. It's a dark and stormy night.
You can go north into the house. If you dare.
You are in the entry way of the house.
 There are cobwebs in the corner.
You feel a sense of dread.
There is a passageway to the north and another to the east.
The porch is behind you to the south.
You are in a living room.
There are couches, chairs, and small tables.
Everything is covered in dust and spider webs.
You hear a crashing noise in another room.
You can go north or west.
You are in the dining room.
There are remains of a meal on the table.
  You can't tell what it is,
 and maybe don't want to.
Was that a thump to the west?
You can go south or west.
You are in the kitchen.
All the surfaces are covered with pots,
 pans, food pieces, and pools of blood.
You think you hear something up the stairs
 that go up the west side of the room.
It's a scraping noise, like something being dragged
 along the floor.
You can go to the south or east.
You are in the entry way of the house.
 There are cobwebs in the corner.
You feel a sense of dread.
There is a passageway to the north and another to the east.
The porch is behind you to the south.
Goodbye!
```

What's wrong with that? Here are two problems that we have with that printout:

1. It's really hard to look back and figure out which room was which. The room descriptions all blur together.

2. We can't go back and figure out what we typed where. If this was a big map with lots of rooms, we would want to be able to scroll back and figure out what we typed to get to different rooms.

Let's deal with the first one. We need some kind of space or separator to appear between room descriptions. Where would we put that statement? Certainly, it has to be *inside* the main top-level loop. It could go inside the showRoom function, maybe as the first line. Or it could go in the top-level function, just before or after we show the room.

On the grounds that it's better to make detail changes in the subfunctions, let's change showRoom.

Program 132: Improved showRoom for the Adventure Game

```
def showRoom(room):
  printNow("===========")
  if room == "Porch":
    showPorch()
  if room == "Entryway":
    showEntryway()
  if room == "Kitchen":
    showKitchen()
  if room == "LivingRoom":
    showLR()
  if room == "DiningRoom":
    showDR()
```

Now, let's deal with the second one. We should print out what the player typed. We have to do this *after* the call to requestString. This change could, again, be in the top-level loop, or could be at the start of pickRoom. Both could work. This time, let's take the opposite choice. The function pickRoom is pretty complicated already. Let's respond right after the player makes a choice.

Program 133: Improved playGame for the Adventure Game

```
def playGame():
  location = "Porch"
  showIntroduction()
  while not (location == "Exit") :
    showRoom(location)
    direction = requestString("Which direction?")
    printNow("You typed: "+direction)
    location = pickRoom(direction, location)
```

Now we can try our debugged program.

```
>>> playGame()
Welcome to the Adventure House!
In each room, you will be told
 which directions you can go.
You can move north, south, east, or west
 by typing that direction.
Type help to replay this introduction.
Type quit or exit to end the program.
===========
You are on the porch of a frightening looking house.
The windows are broken. It's a dark and stormy night.
You can go north into the house. If you dare.
You typed: north
```

```
============
You are in the entry way of the house.
 There are cobwebs in the corner.
You feel a sense of dread.
There is a passageway to the north and another to the east.
The porch is behind you to the south.
You typed: east
============
You are in a living room.
There are couches, chairs, and small tables.
Everything is covered in dust and spider webs.
You hear a crashing noise in another room.
You can go north or west.
You typed: north
============
You are in the dining room.
There are remains of a meal on the table.
  You can't tell what it is,
 and maybe don't want to.
Was that a thump to the west?
You can go south or west.
You typed: west
============
You are in the kitchen.
All the surfaces are covered with pots,
 pans, food pieces, and pools of blood.
You think you hear something up the stairs
 that go up the west side of the room.
It's a scraping noise, like something being dragged
 along the floor.
You can go to the south or east.
You typed: south
============
You are in the entry way of the house.
 There are cobwebs in the corner.
You feel a sense of dread.
There is a passageway to the north and another to the east.
The porch is behind you to the south.
You typed: exit
Goodbye!
```

10.5   ALGORITHMS AND DESIGN

Algorithms are general descriptions of processes that can be implemented in any specific programming language. Knowledge of algorithms is one of the tools in professional programmers' toolboxes. We've seen several algorithms so far:

- The *sampling algorithm* is a process that can be used to shift a sound's frequency up or down or to scale a picture smaller or larger. We don't have to talk about loops or incrementing source or target indices to describe the sampling algorithm. The sampling algorithm works by changing how we copy samples or pixels from a source to a target—instead of taking every sample or pixel, we can take every other sample/pixel, or every sample/pixel twice, or some other pattern of sampling.

- We've also seen how we copy pixels or samples from a source to a target. We simply keep track of where we are in both the source and target.
- We've seen that blending is essentially the same for both pixels and samples. We apply a weighting to each of the pixels or samples being summed, then add the weighted values to create a blended sound or a blended picture.

The role of algorithms in design is to allow us to *abstract* a description of the program to be designed, above the basic program code. Professional programmers know lots of algorithms and this allows them to think through program design problems at a higher level. We can talk about negating pictures and mirroring the negated pictures *without* talking about loops or source and target indices. We can focus on more abstract names like "mirroring" without focusing on code.

Programmers also know a lot *about* the algorithms they know. They know how to make the algorithms efficient, and when they're not useful, and what the hitches about them might be. For example, we know that when scaling sound, we have to be careful not to go beyond the bounds of the sound. There are better and worse algorithms, in terms of how quickly they execute and how much memory they require. We will say more about speed of algorithms in Chapter 13.

We made decisions in this program that we might have made differently. For example, we have described the rooms and how they connect to one another in the code of the program. We could imagine storing the descriptions as strings in variables. We could even use some other *data structures* like arrays or sequences to describe how the rooms connect to one another. The program would then look very different. It would process the *data* in the variables more than describe the rooms themselves. Making choices among alternative ways of writing a program is called *designing the program*. We can think about the design of the program, that is, the possible decisions and their strengths and weaknesses, entirely apart from the code of the program itself.

10.6   CONNECTING TO DATA OUTSIDE A FUNCTION

Games today often have nonplayer characters (NPCs) which are characters in a game that are not controlled by the user. Let's add a ghost to our game. The ghost will appear in one room and then disappear. Revisiting that room will not show the ghost anymore. But if you visit a second specific room, the ghost appears—then disappears. Now, it will show up again in the first room.

From a programming perspective, this is a challenging problem. Our ghost does not need to appear in *every* function. It would probably be overkill to pass the state of the ghost into each and every function as an input. But we will need to access the ghost data (i.e., what room it should appear in) from different functions—both of the room display functions, at the least.

This is a general problem in software engineering. How do we access data needed in different modules or parts of a program, but not in all, and do so without the data getting messed up in some way? We are going to solve it in this case with a *global*, which will work but is not the best way to solve the problem.

We will create a `ghost` variable at the top of the file, before the `playGame` function.

```
ghost = 0

def playGame():
  location = "Porch"
  showIntroduction()
  while not (location == "Exit") :
    showRoom(location)
    direction = requestString("Which direction?")
    printNow("You typed: "+direction)
    location = pickRoom(direction, location)
```

Executing `ghost = 0` before and outside all other functions creates a variable in the scope of the *file*. It is not local to any function. But that creates a problem. If we access the variable `ghost` inside another function, it will be scoped as local to that function. How do we tell Python to access the variable `ghost` which is at the file scope?

The statement `global` tells Python, "Look for this variable outside of this scope." We can rewrite two of the room descriptions to use the `ghost` variable.

Program 134: Adding Access to the Ghost Global Variable

```
def showEntryway():
 global ghost
 printNow("You are in the entry way of the house.")
 printNow(" There are cobwebs in the corner.")
 printNow("You feel a sense of dread.")
 if ghost == 0:
   printNow("You suddenly feel cold.")
   printNow("You look up and see a thick mist.")
   printNow("It seems to be moaning.")
   printNow("Then it disappears.")
   ghost = 1
 printNow("There is a passageway to the north and another to the east.")
 printNow("The porch is behind you to the south.")

def showKitchen():
 global ghost
 printNow("You are in the kitchen. ")
 printNow("All the surfaces are covered with pots,")
 printNow(" pans, food pieces, and pools of blood.")
 printNow("You think you hear something up the stairs")
 printNow(" that go up the west side of the room.")
 printNow("It's a scraping noise, like something being dragged")
 printNow(" along the floor.")
 if ghost == 1:
   printNow("You see the mist you saw earlier.")
   printNow("But now it's darker, and red.")
   printNow("The moan increases in pitch and volume")
   printNow("  so now it sounds more like a yell!")
```

```
    printNow("Then it's gone.")
    ghost = 0
printNow("You can go to the south or east.")
```

■

If the ghost variable is 0, then the ghost shows up (a ghost description appears) in the Entryway. But once it shows up in the Entryway, the value of the ghost variable changes to 1. Now, if the value is 1, the ghost shows up in the Kitchen—and then changes the value back to 0.

A run of the program shows the ghost appearing and disappearing.

```
>>> playGame()
Welcome to the Adventure House!
In each room, you will be told
 which directions you can go.
You can move north, south, east, or west
 by typing that direction.
Type help to replay this introduction.
Type quit or exit to end the program.
============
You are on the porch of a frightening looking house.
The windows are broken. It's a dark and stormy night.
You can go north into the house. If you dare.
You typed: north
============
You are in the entry way of the house.
 There are cobwebs in the corner.
You feel a sense of dread.
You suddenly feel cold.
You look up and see a thick mist.
It seems to be moaning.
Then it disappears.
There is a passageway to the north and another to the east.
The porch is behind you to the south.
You typed: east
============
You are in a living room.
There are couches, chairs, and small tables.
Everything is covered in dust and spider webs.
You hear a crashing noise in another room.
You can go north or west.
You typed: west
============
You are in the entry way of the house.
 There are cobwebs in the corner.
You feel a sense of dread.
There is a passageway to the north and another to the east.
The porch is behind you to the south.
You typed: north
============
You are in the kitchen.
All the surfaces are covered with pots,
```

```
pans, food pieces, and pools of blood.
You think you hear something up the stairs
 that go up the west side of the room.
It's a scraping noise, like something being dragged
 along the floor.
You see the mist you saw earlier.
But now it's darker, and red.
The moan increases in pitch and volume
  so now it sounds more like a yell!
Then it's gone.
You can go to the south or east.
You typed: east
============
You are in the dining room.
There are remains of a meal on the table.
  You can't tell what it is,
 and maybe don't want to.
Was that a thump to the west?
You can go south or west.
You typed: west
============
You are in the kitchen.
All the surfaces are covered with pots,
 pans, food pieces, and pools of blood.
You think you hear something up the stairs
 that go up the west side of the room.
It's a scraping noise, like something being dragged
 along the floor.
You can go to the south or east.
You typed: south
============
You are in the entry way of the house.
 There are cobwebs in the corner.
You feel a sense of dread.
You suddenly feel cold.
You look up and see a thick mist.
It seems to be moaning.
Then it disappears.
There is a passageway to the north and another to the east.
The porch is behind you to the south.
You typed: exit
Goodbye!
```

Using a global variable really does work. But it also creates a problem. Imagine that you leave the program and come back to make some changes a few months later. Now, you want the ghost to appear in three different rooms. You set the value of ghost to "DiningRoom"—forgetting that you originally used integer values. And which integer values represented what rooms? The values of ghost are now spread all over the program, with no one place that makes clear what the values mean (e.g., that 0 is the Entryway and 1 is the Kitchen).

Global variables are easy to use, and they solve the problem of connecting different modules with shared data. However, they are harder to maintain. This was a problem identified decades ago, and there are many different solutions for the problem. For now, we will use the easy but not robust solution of global variables.

10.7   RUNNING PROGRAMS OUTSIDE OF JES

Python programs can be run in many ways. If you build larger and more complex programs, you will want to run them outside of JES. What you are learning in this book is *directly* usable in Python (or Jython). Commands like `for` and `print` work in both Python and Jython. System libraries like `ftplib` and `urllib` are exactly the same in Python and Jython.

However, the media tools we're using are not built-in to Python or Jython. It's possible to use the media libraries in Python. There are Python implementations like Myro (`http://myro.roboteducation.org`) that include the same image functions as in JES. There is also the *Python Imaging Library (PIL)* which provides similar functionality, with differently named functions.

You can use the libraries that we provide in Jython. Jython is available at `http://www.jython.org` for most computer systems. Our media libraries work in Jython with only a few extra commands. Figure 10.6 shows the use of the media library in Jython in Linux.

Here's how we make the media functions work in traditional Jython.

- To find modules to `import`, Python uses a variable called `sys.path` (from the built-in system library `sys`) to list all the directories where it should look for modules. If you want to use the JES media library in Jython, you need to put the location of those module files in your `sys.path`. (This is what `setLibPath` does for you in JES.)

    You need to `import sys` to get access to the `sys.path` variable. To manipulate that variable, we use the method `append` to put the JES **Sources** directory at the end of your path of library directories (see Figure 10.6). On the Macintosh, you will need to reference the Java and Jython code inside the JES application, typing something like `sys.path.append ("/users/guzdial/JES.app/Contents/Resources/Java")`.

- You then use `from media import *` to make things like `pickAFile` and `makePicture` available in Jython.

    The statement `from media import *` is actually inserted (invisibly to you, the student programmer) into your Program Area each time you press the LOAD button. That's how the special media features of JES are made available to your programs.

Here's how it works to generate the image in Figure 10.6 from Linux:

```
guzdial@guzdial-laptop:~$ jython
Jython 2.2.1 on java1.6.0_07
Type "copyright", "credits" or "license" for more
  information.
>>> import sys
```

FIGURE 10.6
Using Jython to do media functions outside of JES in Linux.

```
>>> sys.path.append("/media/MyUSB/jes-4-0/Sources")
>>> from media import *
>>> p = makePicture(pickAFile())
>>> show(p)
```

Dr. Manuel A. Pérez-Quiñones at Virginia Tech and his students figured out how to use the media libraries in Mac OS X with Jython. They started up Jython using a *UNIX shell* file that looked like this:

```
# Running the jython inside of JES (assumes jes-4-3.app
#is in the /Applications folder and jython is inside the
#JES app, which is the default configuration)

# Set some variables
# (the next two are of my own creation, no special meaning
# beyond this use)
# This is the path on the Mac to where the java/jython
```

```
# files are stored JESHOME="/Applications/jes-4-3.app/
# Contents/Resources/Java"

# These are all the jar files that JES uses, they are all
# at the directory above JESJARS=$JESHOME/AVIDemo.jar:$
# JESHOME/customizer.jar:$JESHOME/jl1.0.jar:$JESHOME/
# jmf.jar:$JESHOME/junit.jar:$JESHOME/jython.jar:$JESHOME/
# mediaplayer.jar:$JESHOME/multiplayer.jar

# run jython
# some of the extra options are from jython documentation
# you need to setup several paths: CLASSPATH for java to
# find jars, and jython.home for jython to find some python
# files (for now, one more below)
java -Xmx512m -Xss1024k -Dfile.encoding=UTF-8 -classpath
$JESJARS:$CLASSPATH -Dpython.home=$JESHOME/jython-2.2.1
-Dpython.executable=./jython org.python.util.jython
```

Inside of Jython, then, you type:

```
>>> import sys
>>> sys.path.insert(0, "/Applications/jes-4-3.app/
    Contents/Resources/Java/")
>>> from media import *   # import them
>>> #Then everything should work
>>> show(makePicture(pickAFile()))
```

PROGRAMMING SUMMARY

printNow	Prints the input to the function *immediately* while the program is still running. Whereas print doesn't print the input until the program finishes executing.
requestString	Displays a dialog box with the input prompt, accepts a string from the user, and returns that string. The analogous functions requestNumber, requestInteger, and even requestIntegerInRange (which restricts the entered integer to being between two input values) also exist in JES.
showVars	Displays all the existing variables and their values.
while	Loops through the statements in the block of statements following the while statement as long the test specified in the while statement is true.
global	Declares to Python that a named variable should be found outside the local context of this function.

PROBLEMS

10.1   Typically, one does not *optimize* a program (make it run faster or with less use of memory) until after it is running, well-debugged, and well-tested. (Of course, you still have to test again after each optimizing modification.) Here is an optimization that we could make to the adventure game. Currently, showRoom compares the room variable to each possible room—even if it matched earlier. Python gives us a way of only testing once, by using an elif instead of later if statements. The statement `elif` means "else if." You only test the `elif` statement if the earlier `if` was false. You may have as many `elif` statements as you like after an `if`. You might use it like this:

```
if (room == "Porch"):
    showPorch()
elif (room == "Kitchen"):
    showKitchen()
```

Rewrite the `showRoom` method more optimally by using `elif`.

10.2   A function like `pickRoom` is hard to read with all the nested `if` statements. It can be made clearer with appropriate use of comments to explain what each section of the code is doing—checking the room, then checking the possible directions in the room. Add comments to `pickRoom` to make it easier to read.

10.3   Add comments to *all* the methods, to make it easier for someone else to read the function.

10.4   Add another global variable for the player, called a `hand`. Make the hand initially empty. Change the description so that there is a "key" in the Living Room. If the player types the command `key` while in the Living Room, the key gets put in the hand. Now, if the player has the key when entering the Kitchen, the stairs become accessible, allowing the player to go "west" and up the stairs. You will have to add some rooms to the game to make this work.

10.5   Create the ability to go down from the Porch, to explore a secret underground world.

10.6   Add additional secret items to have in the player's hand to allow different rooms to be accessed, such as a lantern to allow access to a tunnel under the Porch.

10.7   Add a "bomb" in the Dining Room. If the player types `bomb` in the Dining Room, the bomb goes in the hand. If the player types `bomb` in the upstairs where the Ogre is, the bomb is dropped and the Ogre is blasted to smithereens.

10.8   Add the ability for the player to *lose* the game (perhaps die). When the player loses, the game should print what happened, and then the game exits. Perhaps finding the Ogre *without* the bomb in the player's hand will make the player lose the game.

10.9   Add the ability for the player to *win* the game. When the player wins, the game should print what happened and exit the game. Perhaps finding the secret treasure room under the Porch would make the player win the game.

10.10 Room descriptions do not have to be wholly verbal. Play a relevant sound when the player enters a particular room. Use `play`, so that game play can continue while the sound is playing.

10.11 Room descriptions can be visual, as well as textual and auditory. Display a picture relevant to the room when the room is entered. For extra credit, only `show` a picture once, and if the room is reentered, `repaint` the picture to bring it back to the front again.

10.12   A source of possible error in this adventure game is that the names for the rooms appear in several places. If the Dining Room is spelled "DiningRoom" in one place and "DinngRoom" (missing the second "i") in another place, the game won't work correctly. The more rooms you add, and the more places where you have the room names typed, the odds increase that the error will be made.

There are a couple of ways of making this error less likely to occur:

- Do not name the rooms with strings of characters. Instead, use numbers. It's easier to type and check "4" than "DiningRoom."

- Use a *variable* for `DiningRoom` and use that one variable for checking the location. Then it doesn't matter if you're using numbers or strings (and strings are much easier to read and understand).

Use one of these techniques to rewrite the adventure game with fewer potential errors.

10.13   Currently, the user must get the case right when typing the directions. Use the `lower()` method on strings (introduced in Chapter 3) to make the input all in lowercase, so that both "North" and "north" will work as input.

10.14   Let's start over with a new map. Below is a map of a castle.

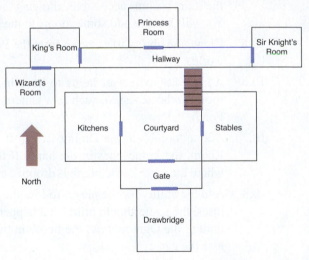

Create a new adventure game based on this map. Think *Lord of the Rings* or maybe *Game of Thrones*. The player should start on the drawbridge.

10.15   In the castle game, the player must answer a riddle correctly or provide a password in order to pass through to the Courtyard. Add that to your game.

10.16   Games often have *nonplayer characters* (NPC) which are characters that are not controlled by the player. Add an Evil Wizard to the castle game. When you first play the game, the Evil Wizard is in the Courtyard, and his description says that he is in the Courtyard, but then disappears. Every other time after the first time you enter the Courtyard, the Evil Wizard does not appear in the description. But if you visit the Wizard's Room, the Evil Wizard can be found there. You defeat him and win the game.

10.17   Use the `in` operator from Chapter 3 to provide some flexibility to the castle game. Allow the player in the Courtyard to go "north" or "up" to the upper Hallway, or "down" or "south" to return to the Courtyard from the Hallway.

10.18   The function `printNow` is not the only way to present information to the user during the running of a program. We might also use the function `showInformation` which takes a string as input, then displays it in a dialog box. Currently, our `showRoom` subfunctions presume that we will display the room information via `printNow`. If functions like `showPorch` *returned a string* with the description, then the function `showRoom` could either use `printNow` to display the room description or `showInformation`.

    Rewrite the room showing functions to return a string, then modify `showRoom` to easily change between printing the room information and showing it in a dialog box.

10.19   Consider this program:

```
def testMe(p,q,r):
  if q > 50:
    print r
  value = 10
  for i in range(1,p):
    print "Hello"
    value = value - 1
  print value
  print r
```

If we execute `testMe(5,51,"Hello back to you!")`, what will print?

10.20

```
def newFunction(a, b, c):
    print a
    list1 = range(1,5)
    value = 0
    for x in list1:
        print b
        value = value +1
    print c
    print value
```

If you call the preceding function by typing `newFunction("I", "you", "walrus")`, what will the computer print?

TO DIG DEEPER

Textual adventure games today are typically called *interactive fiction*. There are Web sites and archives where you can download and play interactive fiction. Even better, there are programming languages especially designed for building video games, like *Inform 7*.

Probably the best book ever written on software engineering is *The Mythical Man-Month: Essays on Software Engineering, Anniversary Edition (2nd Edition)*, by Frederick P. Brooks (Addison-Wesley, 1995). Brooks points out that many of the issues of developing software are organizational issues. We highly recommend this book.

TEXT, FILES, NETWORKS, DATABASES, AND UNIMEDIA

CHAPTER 11

Manipulating Text with Methods and Files

Chapter Learning Objectives

The media learning goals for this chapter are:

- To generate text in a form-letter style.
- To manipulate structured text, such as phone and address listings.
- To generate random structured text.

The computer science goals for this chapter are:

- To access object components using dot notation.
- To read and write files.
- To understand file structures like trees.
- To write programs that manipulate programs, which leads to powerful ideas like interpreters and compilers.
- To use the modules in the Python Standard Library, such as the random and os utilities.
- To get a sense of the functionality available in the Python Standard Library.
- To broaden the understanding of the import capability.

11.1 TEXT AS UNIMEDIA

Nicholas Negroponte, founder of the MIT Media Lab, said that what makes computer-based multimedia possible is the fact that the computer is actually **unimedia**. The computer really understands only one thing: zeros and ones. We can use the computer for multimedia because any medium can be encoded as zeros and ones.

He might as well have been talking about *text* as the unimedia. We can encode any medium to text. What's even better than using zeros and ones, we can *read* the text. Later in this book, we map sounds to text and then back to sounds, and we do the same with pictures. But once we have our media in text, we don't have to go back to the original medium: we can map sounds to text and then to pictures, and thus create *visualizations* of sounds.

The World Wide Web is primarily text. Visit any Web page, then go to the menu of your Web browser and choose to "VIEW THE SOURCE." What you will see is text. Every Web page is actually text. The text references the pictures, sounds, and animations that appear when you view the page, but the page itself is defined as text. The words in the text are in a notation called *HyperText Markup Language (HTML)*.

In this chapter, we continue the exploration of text. We manipulated text as a medium in Chapter 3, and we manipulated pictures and sounds after that. In this chapter, we deal with more structured text, which allows us to do more sophisticated manipulations.

11.2   MANIPULATING PARTS OF STRINGS

We use the square bracket notation ([]) to reference parts of strings.

- `string[n]` returns the *n*th character in the string, where the first character in the string is zero.
- `string[n:m]` returns a *slice* of the string starting at the *n*th character and up to *but not including* the *m*th (similar to how the `range()` function works). You can optionally leave out *n* or *m*. If *n* is missing, it's assumed to be zero (the start of the string). If *m* is missing, it's assumed to be the end of the string. We can also use negative numbers at either end to trim off that much from that side.

We can think about the characters of the string as being in boxes, each with its own index number.

H	e	l	l	o
0	1	2	3	4

```
>>> hello = "Hello"
>>> print hello[1]
e
>>> print hello[0]
H
>>> print hello[2:4]
ll
>>> print hello
Hello
>>> print hello[:3]
Hel
>>> print hello[3:]
lo
>>> print hello[:]
Hello
>>> print hello[-1:]
o
>>> print hello[:-1]
Hell
```

11.2.1   String Methods: Introducing Objects and Dot Notation

Everything in Python is actually more than just a value—it's an *object*. An object combines data (like a number or a string or a list) with the *methods* that can act upon that object. Methods are like functions except that they're not globally accessible. You can't execute a method the way you can execute `pickAFile()` or `makeSound()`. A method is a function that can only be accessed *through* an object.

Strings in Python are objects. They are not only sequences of characters—they also have methods that are not globally accessible but are known only to strings. To execute a method of a string, you use *dot notation*. You type `object.method()`.

An example method known only to strings is `capitalize()`. It capitalizes the string it's called upon. It will not work on a function or on a number.

```
>>> test="this is a test."
>>> print test.capitalize()
This is a test.
>>> print capitalize(test)
A local or global name could not be found. You need
to define the function or variable before you try to
use it in any way.
NameError: capitalize
>>> print 'this is another test'.capitalize()
This is another test
>>> print 12.capitalize()
Your code contains at least one syntax error, meaning
it is not legal jython.
```

There are *many* useful string methods.

- `startswith(prefix)` returns true if the string starts with the given prefix. Remember that `true` in Python is anything 1 or greater and `false` is zero.

```
>>> letter = "Mr. Mark Guzdial requests the pleasure of your company..."
>>> print letter.startswith("Mr.")
1
>>> print letter.startswith("Mrs.")
0
```

- `endswith(suffix)` returns true if the string ends with the given suffix. `endswith` is particularly useful for checking whether a filename is the right kind for a program.

```
>>> filename="barbara.jpg"
>>> if filename.endswith(".jpg"):
...         print "It's a picture"
...
It's a picture
```

- `find(str)` and `find(str,start)` and `find(str,start,end)` all find the `str` in the object string and return the index number where the string starts. In the optional forms, you can tell it what index number to start from, and even where to stop looking.

This is very important: the `find()` method returns −1 if it fails. Why −1? Because any value from 0 to 1 less than the length of the string *could* be a valid index where a search string might be found.

```
>>> print letter
Mr. Mark Guzdial requests the pleasure of your company...
>>> print letter.find("Mark")
4
>>> print letter.find("Guzdial")
9
>>> print len("Guzdial")
7
>>> print letter[4:9+7]
Mark Guzdial
>>> print letter.find("fred")
-1
```

There also exists `rfind(findstring)` (and the same variations with optional parameters) that searches from the end of the string toward the front.

- `upper()` translates the string to uppercase.
- `lower()` translates the string to lowercase.
- `swapcase()` makes all uppercase into lowercase and vice versa.
- `title()` makes just the first characters uppercase and the rest lower.

  These methods can be *cascaded*—one modifying the result of another.

  ```
  >>> string="This is a test of Something."
  >>> print string.swapcase()
  tHIS IS A TEST OF sOMETHING.
  >>> print string.title().swapcase()
  tHIS iS a tEST oF sOMETHING.
  ```

- `isalpha()` returns true if the string is not empty and is all letters—no numbers and no punctuation.
- `isdigit()` returns true if the string is not empty and is all numbers. You might use this if you were checking the results of some search you were doing. Say that you were writing a program to look for stock prices. You want to parse out a current *price*, not a stock name. If you get it wrong, maybe your program might make buys or sells that you don't want. You could use `isdigit()` to check your result automatically.
- `replace(search,replace)` searches for the `search` string and replaces it with the `replace` string. It returns the result but doesn't change the original string.

  ```
  >>> print letter
  Mr. Mark Guzdial requests the pleasure of your company...
  >>> letter.replace("a","!")
  'Mr. M!rk Guzdi!l requests the ple!sure of your comp!ny...'
  >>> print letter
  Mr. Mark Guzdial requests the pleasure of your company...
  ```

11.2.2   Lists: Powerful, Structured Text

Lists are very powerful structures that we can think about as a kind of *structured text*. Lists are defined with square brackets with commas between their elements but they can contain just about anything—including sublists. Like strings, you can reference parts with square bracket notations, and you can add them together with +. Lists are also sequences, so you can use a for loop on them to walk through their pieces.

```
>>> myList = ["This","is","a", 12]
>>> print myList
['This', 'is', 'a', 12]
>>> print myList[0]
This
>>> for i in myList:
...        print i
...
This
is
a
12
>>> print myList + ["Really!"]
['This', 'is', 'a', 12, 'Really!']
>>> anotherList=["this","has",["a",["sub","list"]]]
>>> print anotherList
['this', 'has', ['a', ['sub', 'list']]]
>>> print anotherList[0]
this
>>> print anotherList[2]
['a', ['sub', 'list']]
>>> print anotherList[2][1]
['sub', 'list']
>>> print anotherList[2][1][0]
sub
>>> print anotherList[2][1][0][2]
b
```

Lists have a set of methods that they understand that strings do not.

- append(something) puts something in the list at the end.
- remove(something) removes something from the list if it's there.
- sort() puts the list in alphabetical order.
- reverse() reverses the list.
- count(something) tells you the number of times that something is in the list.
- max() and min() are functions we've seen before that take a list as input and give you the maximum and minimum values in the list.

```
>>> list = ["bear","apple","cat","elephant","dog","apple"]
>>> list.sort()
>>> print list
['apple', 'apple', 'bear', 'cat', 'dog', 'elephant']
```

```
>>> list.reverse()
>>> print list
['elephant', 'dog', 'cat', 'bear', 'apple', 'apple']
>>> print list.count('apple')
2
```

One of the most important string methods, `split(delimiter)`, converts a string into a list of substrings, separating on a delimiter string that you provide. This allows us to convert strings into lists.

```
>>> print letter.split(" ")
['Mr.', 'Mark', 'Guzdial', 'requests', 'the',
'pleasure', 'of', 'your', 'company...']
```

Using `split()` we can process **formatted text**—text where the separation between parts is a well-defined character, like **tab-delimited text** or **comma-delimited text** from a spreadsheet. Here's an example using structured text to store a phone book. The phone book has lines separated by newline characters and parts separated by colons. We can split on the newline characters, then the colons, to get a list of sublists. Searches through this can be made with a simple for loop.

Program 135: A Simple Phone Book Application

```
def phonebook():
  return """
Mary:893-0234:Realtor:
Fred:897-2033:Boulder crusher:
Barney:234-2342:Professional bowler:"""

def phones():
  phones = phonebook()
  phonelist = phones.split('\n')
  newphonelist = []
  for list in phonelist:
    newphonelist = newphonelist + [list.split(":")]
  return newphonelist

def findPhone(person):
  for people in phones():
    if people[0] == person:
      print "Phone number for",person,"is",people[1]
```

How It Works

There are three functions here: one to provide the phone text, the other to create the phone list, and the third to look up a phone number.

- The first function, phonebook, creates the structured text and returns it, using triple quotes so that the lines can be formatted with newline characters. The format is name, colon, phone number, colon, and job, then colon and end of the line.

```
>>> print phonebook()
```

```
Mary:893-0234:Realtor:
Fred:897-2033:Boulder crusher:
Barney:234-2342:Professional bowler:
```

- The second function, phones, returns a list of all the phones. It accesses the phone list through phonebook, then splits it into lines. The result of split is a list comprising a string with colons in it. The loop in phones then chops up each list using split on the colons. What phones returns, then, is a list of lists.

  ```
  >>> print phones()
  [["], ['Mary', '893-0234', 'Realtor', "],
  ['Fred', '897-2033', 'Boulder crusher', "],
  ['Barney', '234-2342', 'Professional bowler', "]]
  ```

- Finally, the third function, findPhone, takes a name as input and finds the corresponding phone number. It loops over all the sublists that phones returns and finds the one where the first item in the sublist (index number 0) is the input name. It then prints the result

  ```
  >>> findPhone('Fred')
  Phone number for Fred is 897-2033
  ```

11.2.3   Strings Have No Font

Strings have no **font** (characteristic look of the letters) or **style** (typically the boldface, italics, underline, and other effects applied to the string) associated with them. Font and style information are added to strings using word-processors and other programs. Typically, these are encoded as **style runs**.

A style run is a separate representation of the font and style information with indices into the string to show where the changes should take place. For example, **The old** brown fox runs might be encoded as [[bold 0 6][italics 8 12]].

Think about strings with style runs. What do you call this combination of related information? It's clearly not a single value. Could we encode the string with the style runs in a complex list? Sure—we can do just about *anything* with lists!

Most software that manages formatted text will encode strings with style runs as an **object**. Objects have data associated with them, perhaps in several parts (like strings and style runs). Objects know how to act upon their data, using *methods* that may be known only to objects of that type. If the same method name is known to multiple objects, it probably does the same thing, but probably not in the same way.

This is foreshadowing. Objects will be discussed in more detail later.

11.3   FILES: PLACES TO PUT YOUR STRINGS AND OTHER STUFF

Files are large, named collections of bytes on your hard disk. Files typically have a **base name** and a **file suffix**. The file **barbara.jpg** has the base name of "barbara" and a file suffix of "jpg" that tells you that the file is a JPEG picture.

Files are clustered into **directories** (sometimes called **folders**). Directories can contain other directories as well as files. There is a base directory on your computer which is referred to as the **root directory**. On a computer using the Windows operating system, the base directory will be something like **C:**. A complete description of what directories to visit to get to a particular file from the base directory is called a **path**.

```
>>> file=pickAFile()
>>> print file
C:\ip-book\mediasources\640x480.jpg
```

The path that is printed tells us how to go from the root directory to the file **640x480.jpg**. We start at **C:**, choose the directory **ip-book**, then the directory **mediasources**.

We call this structure a **tree** (Figure 11.1). We call **C:** the **root** of the tree. The tree has **branches** where there are subdirectories. Any directory can contain more directories (branches) or files, which are referred to as **leaves**. Except for the root, each **node** of the tree (branch or leaf) has a single **parent** branch node, though a parent can have multiple **children** branches and leaves.

We need to know about directories and files if we're going to manipulate files, especially lots of files. If you're dealing with a big Web site, you are going to be working with a lot of files. If you are going to be dealing with video, you will have about 30 files (individual frames) for each second of video. You don't really want to write a line of code to open each frame. You want to write programs that will walk directory structures to process Web or video files.

We can also represent trees in lists. Because lists can contain sublists, just as directories can contain subdirectories, it's a pretty easy encoding. The important point is that lists allow us to represent complex, hierarchical relationships, like trees (Figure 11.2).

```
>>> tree = [["Leaf1","Leaf2"],[["Leaf3"],["Leaf4"],
"Leaf5"]]
>>> print tree
```

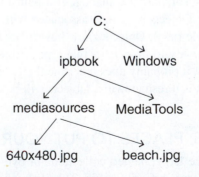

FIGURE 11.1
Diagram of a directory tree.

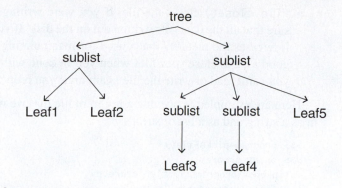

FIGURE 11.2
Diagram for a list.

```
[['Leaf1', 'Leaf2'], [['Leaf3'], ['Leaf4'], 'Leaf5']]
>>> print tree[0]
['Leaf1', 'Leaf2']
>>> print tree[1]
[['Leaf3'], ['Leaf4'], 'Leaf5']
>>> print tree[1][0]
['Leaf3']
>>> print tree[1][1]
['Leaf4']
>>> print tree[1][2]
Leaf5
```

11.3.1   Opening and Manipulating Files

We open files in order to read or write them. We use a function named (not surprisingly) open(filename, how). The filename can be a complete path or just a base filename and suffix. If you don't provide a path, the file will be opened in the current JES directory. The how input is a string describing what you want to do with the file.

- "rt" means "read the file as text—translate the bytes into characters for me."
- "wt" means "write the file as text."
- "rb" and "wb" mean "read and write bytes" (respectively). You use these if you are going to manipulate **binary files** (like JPEG, WAV, Word, or Excel files).

The function open() returns a file object that you then use to manipulate the file. The file object understands a set of methods.

- file.read() reads the whole file as a giant string. (If you opened the file for writing, don't try to read from it.)
- file.readlines() reads the whole file into a list where each element is a single line. You can only use read() or readlines() once per file opening.
- file.write(somestring) writes somestring to the file. (If you opened the file for reading, don't try to write to it.)

- `file.close()` closes the file. If you were writing to the file, closing it makes sure that all the data gets written out on the disk. If you were reading from the file, it releases the memory that's used for manipulating the file. In either case, it's a good idea to close your files when you're done with them. Once you close a file, you can't read or write the file again until you reopen it.

Here are examples of opening a program file that we wrote earlier and of reading it in as a string and as a list of strings.

```
>>> program=pickAFile()
>>> print program
C:\ip-book\programs\littlePicture.py
>>> file=open(program,"rt")
>>> contents=file.read()
>>> print contents
def littlePicture():
  canvas=makePicture(getMediaPath("640x480.jpg"))
  addText(canvas,10,50,"This is not a picture")
  addLine(canvas,10,20,300,50)
  addRectFilled(canvas,0,200,300,500,yellow)
  addRect(canvas,10,210,290,490)
  return canvas
>>> file.close()
>>> file=open(program,"rt")
>>> lines=file.readlines()
>>> print lines
['def littlePicture():\n', '
canvas=makePicture(getMediaPath("640x480.jpg"))\n', '
addText(canvas,10,50,"This is not a picture")\n', '
addLine(canvas,10,20,300,50)\n', '
addRectFilled(canvas,0,200,300,500,yellow)\n', '
addRect(canvas,10,210,290,490)\n', '   return canvas']
>>> file.close()
```

Here's an example of writing a silly file. The \n creates the new lines in the file.

```
>>> writeFile = open("myfile.txt","wt")
>>> writeFile.write("Here is some text.")
>>> writeFile.write("Here is some more.\n")
>>> writeFile.write("And now we're done.\n\nTHE END.")

>>> writeFile.close()
>>> writeFile=open("myfile.txt","rt")
>>> print writeFile.read()
Here is some text.Here is some more.
And now we're done.

THE END.
>>> writeFile.close()
```

11.3.2 Generating Form Letters

Not only can we write programs to take apart structured text, we can also write programs that *assemble* structured text. One of the classic structured texts that we're all too familiar with is spam or form letters. The really good spam writers (if that's not a contradiction in terms) fill in details that actually refer to *you* in the message. How do they do this? It's pretty easy—they have a function that takes in the relevant input and plugs it into the right places.

Program 136: A Form-Letter Generator

```
def formLetter(gender,lastName,city,eyeColor):
 file = open("formLetter.txt","wt")
 file.write("Dear ")
 if gender=="F":
  file.write("Ms. "+lastName+":\n")
 if gender=="M":
  file.write("Mr. "+lastName+":\n")
 file.write("I am writing to remind you of the offer ")
 file.write("that we sent to you last week. Everyone in ")
 file.write(city+" knows what an exceptional offer this is!")
 file.write("(Especially those with lovely eyes of"+eyeColor+"!)")
 file.write("We hope to hear from you soon.\n")
 file.write("Sincerely,\n")
 file.write("I.M. Acrook, Attorney at Law")
 file.close()
```

How It Works

This function takes a gender, a last name (family name), city, and eye color as input. It opens a **formLetter.txt** file, then writes out an opening, tuned to the gender of the recipient. It writes out a bunch of text, inserting the input into the right places. Then closes the file.

When this is executed with `formLetter("M","Guzdial","Decatur", "brown")`, it generates:

```
Dear Mr. Guzdial:
I am writing to remind you of the offer that we
sent to you last week. Everyone in Decatur knows what
an exceptional offer this is!(Especially those with
lovely eyes of brown!)We hope to hear from you soon.
Sincerely,
I.M. Acrook,
Attorney at Law
```

11.3.3   Reading and Manipulating Data from the Internet

Being able to manipulate text is quite important for gathering data on the Internet. Most of the Internet is just text. Go to your favorite Web page, then use the VIEW SOURCE (or something like this) option in the menu. That's the text that defines the page you're seeing in the browser. Later, we'll learn how to download pages directly from the Internet, but for now, let's assume that you've saved (*downloaded*) pages or files from the Internet onto your disk, and then we'll do searches from there.

For example, there are places on the Internet where you can grab sequences of nucleotides associated with things like parasites. I found a file of this type that looks like this:

```
>Schisto unique AA825099
gcttagatgtcagattgagcacgatgatcgattgaccgtgagatcgacga
gatgcgcagatcgagatctgcatacagatgatgaccatagtgtacg
>Schisto unique mancons0736
ttctcgctcacactagaagcaagacaatttacactattattattattatt
accattattattattattattactattattattattattactattattta
ctacgtcgctttttcactccctttattctcaaattgtgtatccttccttt
```

Let's say that we had a subsequence (like "ttgtgta") and wanted to know which parasite it was part of. If we read in this file into a string, we could search for the subsequence. If it's there (i.e., the find result is not equal <> to −1), we search *backwards* from there to find the ">" that starts each parasite name, then *forward* to the end of line (newline character) to get the name of the file. If we don't find the subsequence (find() returns a −1), the subsequence isn't there.

Program 137: Finding a Subsequence in Parasite Nucleotide Sequences

```
def findSequence(seq):
  sequencesFile = getMediaPath("parasites.txt")
  file = open(sequencesFile,"rt")
  sequences = file.read()
  file.close()
  # Find the sequence
  seqLoc = sequences.find(seq)
  #print "Found at:",seqLoc
  if seqLoc <> -1:
    # Now, find the ">" with the name of the sequence
    nameLoc = sequences.rfind(">",0,seqLoc)
    #print "Name at:",nameLoc
    endline = sequences.find("\n",nameLoc)
    print "Found in ",sequences[nameLoc:endline]
  if seqLoc == -1:
    print "Not found"
```

How It Works

The function findSequence takes a part of a sequence as an input. It opens the **parasites.txt** file (in the media folder specified with setMediaPath) and reads the whole thing into the string sequences. We look for the sequence in the string sequences using find. If it's found (i.e., the result isn't −1), then we look *backwards* from where we found the sequence (seqLoc) to the beginning of the string (0) to find the ">" which starts the sequence. We then search forward from the greater-than sign to the end of the line ("\n"). This gives us where in the original sequences string we can find the name of the parasite that our input subsequence is from.

We have been reading the entire contents of a file into one big string and then processing the string. We can also use the readlines method to read all the files into a list of strings. But, if you have very large files it might be better to process the contents one line at a time. You can do this using the `readline` method which returns a single line each time we call it. For example, if you want to change every occurrence of a string in a file you could use the following function.

Program 138: Replacing All Occurrences of a Word in a File

```
def replaceWord(fileName,origWord,repWord):
  file = open(getMediaPath(fileName),"rt")
  outFile = open(getMediaPath("out-" + fileName),"wt")
  line = file.readline()
  while line <> ":
    newLine = line.replace(origWord,repWord);
    outFile.write(newLine)
    line = file.readline()
  file.close()
  outFile.close()
```

How It Works

The function `replaceWord` accepts a filename as input that is presumed to be in the media folder. It also accepts a word to search for, and a word to replace it with. We open the file by using `getMediaPath` with the input `fileName`.

Common Bug: You Must Use getMediatPath to Get the Full Pathname

We did not have to provide the full pathname for makePicture and makeSound because those are JES functions. JES functions know to search in the media folder if they are not given a full path as input. The function open is a standard Python function which accepts a full file path as input. By using getMediaPath, we can create the full file path for a file in the media folder.

We open the input file which will be referenced with the variable `file`, and we open an output file with the variable `outFile`. We then read the first line in the file with `file.readline()` into the variable `line`. We use a `while` loop to say "Keep reading as long as there is a line to process," by testing on `line <> "` where " is an *empty string*. It is what `readline` will return if there is no other lines to read. We then use the `replace` method to swap out the `origWord` for `repWord`. We store the replaced line into `outFile`.

Very importantly, the *last* thing we do in the loop is to read a new line from the input file with `line = file.readline()`. This is important because the *top* of the loop is then a test to see if `line` is empty. When the loop ends (because `line` is in fact the empty string), we close the two files.

If the input file `test.txt` in the media folder contained this:

```
This is a test of how well we can swap
one word for another.  Our test will be
showing that we can remove the word test
```

```
and replace it with a test replacement
word.
```

We might run replaceWord("test.txt","test","demonstration"), which would generate the file out-test.txt in the media folder:

```
This is a demonstration of how well we can swap
one word for another.  Our demonstration will be
showing that we can remove the word demonstration
and replace it with a demonstration replacement
word.
```

11.3.4   Scraping Information from a Web Page

There are programs that wander the Internet, gathering information from Web pages. For example, Google's news page (http://news.google.com) isn't written by reporters. Google has programs that go out and snag headlines out of *other* news sites. How do these programs work? There are a variety of mechanisms for getting information from Web sites. One of these is called *RSS* for Rich Site Summary, and sometimes Real Simple Syndication. RSS provides articles (e.g., from news sites, from blogs) in chunks of strings that are easy to manipulate.

Another way of getting these data is by *scraping* a Web site. This means that you get the source code (HTML) of the page, then remove the data you want by searching for it within the HTML. It's not the easiest method for getting data, but it does allow you to read *any* HTML page.

For example, let's say that you wanted to write a function that would give you the current temperature by reading it off a local weather page. In Atlanta, a good weather page is http://www.ajc.com/weather—the weather page of the *Atlanta Journal-Constitution*. By viewing the source, we can find where the current temperature appears on the page, and what the key features of the text are around it to grab just the temperature. Here's the relevant part of the page that Mark found one day:

```
<td ><img src="/shared-local/weather/images/ps.gif"
width="48" height="48" border="0"><font size=-2><br>
    </font>
<font size="-1"
face="Arial, Helvetica, sans-serif"><b>Currently
    </b><br>
Partly sunny<br> <font size="+2">54<b>&deg;</b><
    /font>
<font face="Arial, Helvetica, sans-serif" size="+1">
F</font></font></td> </tr>
```

You can see the word Currently in there, then the temperature just before the characters <b>°. We can write a program to chop out those pieces and return the temperature, given that the weather page is saved in a file named **ajc-weather.html**. Now this program won't *always* work with the current AJC weather page. The page format may change, and the key text we're looking for might move or disappear. But as long as the format is the same, this recipe will work.

Program 139: Get the Temperature off a Weather Page

```
def findTemperature():
  weatherFile = getMediaPath("ajc-weather.html")
  file = open(weatherFile,"rt")
  weather = file.read()
  file.close()
  # Find the Temperature
  currLoc = weather.find("Currently")
  if currLoc <> -1:
    # Now, find the "<b>&deg;" following the temp
    temploc = weather.find("<b>&deg;",currLoc)
    tempstart = weather.rfind(">",0,temploc)
    print "Current temperature:",weather[tempstart+1:temploc]
  if currLoc == -1:
    print "They must have changed the page format--can't find¬
    the temp"
```

How It Works

This function assumes that the file **ajc-weather.html** is stored in the media folder specified with `setMediaPath`. The function `findTemperature` opens and reads the file as text, then closes it. We look for the word "Currently." If we find it (the result is not −1), we look for the degree marker after the "Currently" (stored in `currLoc`). We then search backwards for the end of the previous tag, ">." The temperature is between these points. If `currLoc` is −1, we give up because we couldn't find the word "Currently."

11.3.5   Reading CSV Data

There are Web sites on the Internet where data are shared. Probably the most common format in which those data are shared is CSV files, or *comma-separated values*. CSV files list data in columns, where columns are separated by commas. CSV files can be read by spreadsheets, but they can also be processed by programs in Python to do things that might be hard in a spreadsheet.

There are efforts on the Internet to share more data, to let everyone have access to important data. For example, the US Census Bureau makes all of their population and demographic information available on the Internet in CSV files (e.g., see `https://www.census.gov`). The British newspaper *The Guardian* is making an effort to make all of the data that they use in their stories available on the Web. They call it *data journalism*, and we found all of their data at `http://www.theguardian.com/news/datablog/interactive/2013/jan/14/all-our-datasets-index`.[1]

The US Census data is especially nice to use because the US Federal Government is not allowed to copyright census data. We can freely share it and work with it. We have downloaded some state population data in the file `state-populations.csv`. We can

[1] Accessed on 5 August 2014.

actually open the file in JES or any other text file to see what is in it. The first few lines look like this:

```
SUMLEV,REGION,DIVISION,STATE,NAME,POPESTIMATE2013,POPEST18PLUS2013,PCNT_POPEST18PLUS
10,0,0,0,United States,316128839,242542967,76.7
40,3,6,1,Alabama,4833722,3722241,77
40,4,9,2,Alaska,735132,547000,74.4
40,4,8,4,Arizona,6626624,5009810,75.6
```

We see that the first line gives us the headings for the data. The meaning of all these headings is available on the Census website. We are just going to look at *State* and *PopEstimate2013* (population estimate for 2013) for a simple example. Let's write a function to return the population of a given state.

Program 140: Find a Given State's Population in 2013

```
def findPopulation(state):
  file = open(getMediaPath("state-populations.csv"),"rt")
  lines = file.readlines()
  file.close()
  for line in lines:
    parts = line.split(",")
    if parts[4] == state:
      return int(parts[5])
  return -1
```

Here's what it looks like to use this function:

```
>>> findPopulation("Georgia")
9992167
>>> findPopulation("Michigan")
9895622
>>> findPopulation("Maine")
1328302
```

How It Works

The function findPopulation takes a state name as input in the variable state. We open the state-populations.csv file as readable text, via file = open(getMediaPath("state-populations.csv"),"rt"). The file is relatively small, so we read all of its lines at once, then close the file.

Now, we process each line in the lines of the file. We use the method split with a split character of "," in order to split up the line into its columns. So, if the line were "40,3,6,1,Alabama,4833722,3722241,77", then we could split it like this:

```
>>> "40,3,6,1,Alabama,4833722,3722241,77".split(",")
['40', '3', '6', '1', 'Alabama', '4833722', '3722241', '77']
```

The state name is at index 4 in this list.

```
>>> line = "40,3,6,1,Alabama,4833722,3722241,77"
>>> parts = line.split(",")
>>> parts[4]
'Alabama'
```

The function then searches through the lines to find a `line` where the state part is the input name. When we get to the state we want, the function returns the next part (index 5) because that is the population we want. The function `int` converts the string from the file into a number that we could process if we wanted.

Now, if the function returns, the function ends. The loop *only* ends if we go through all the lines in the file and we *don't* find the state we want. If that happens, we `return` a *sentinel value* – a value that can't naturally happen, so we use that to indicate that the state wasn't found. No US state has a population of −1, so that works as a sentinel value.

11.3.6 Writing Out Programs

Let's use our ability to write text files to write something somewhat unusual—let's write a program to *change* another program. We'll read the **littlePicture.py** file and change the text string that's inserted into the picture. We'll `find()` the `addText()` function, then search for each of the double quotes. Then we'll write out a new file with everything from **littlePicture.py** up to the first double quote, insert our new string, and put in the rest of the file from the second double quote to the end.

Program 141: A Program to Change the `littlePicture` Program

```
def changeLittle(filename,newString):
  # Get the original file contents
  programFile="littlePicture.py"
  file = open(programFile,"rt")
  contents = file.read()
  file.close()
  # Now, find the right place to put our new string
  addPos= contents.find("addText")
  #Double quote after addText
  firstQuote = contents.find('"',addPos)
  #Double quote after firstQuote
  endQuote = contents.find('"',firstQuote+1)
  # Make our new file
  newFile = open(filename,"wt")
  newFile.write(contents[:firstQuote+1]) # Include the quote
  newFile.write(newString)
  newFile.write(contents[endQuote:])
  newFile.close()
```

How It Works

This program opens up the file **littlePicture.py** (the name assumes that it's in the JES directory, since no path is provided). It reads the whole thing in as a big string, then closes the file. Using the `find` method, it finds where the `addText` is, where the first double quote is, and where the last double quote is. It then opens up a new file (for writable text: "wt") and writes out all of the little program up to the first double quote. Then it writes out the input string. Then it writes out the rest of the little program from the last double quote on. Thus, it replaces the string that's added. Finally, it closes the new file.

When we run this with `changeLittle("sample.py","Here is a sample of changing a program")`, we get in **sample.py**:

```
def littlePicture():
    canvas=makePicture(getMediaPath("640x480.jpg"))
    addText(canvas,10,50,"Here is a sample of changing a program")
    addLine(canvas,10,20,300,50)
    addRectFilled(canvas,0,200,300,500,yellow)
    addRect(canvas,10,210,290,490)
    return canvas
```

This is how vector-based drawing programs work. When you change a line in Auto-CAD or Flash or Illustrator, you're actually changing the underlying representation of the picture—in a real sense, a little program whose execution results in the picture you're working with. When you change the line, you're actually changing the program, which is then reexecuted to show you the updated picture. Is this process slow? Computers are fast enough that we just don't notice.

11.4 THE PYTHON STANDARD LIBRARY

In every programming language, there's a way of extending the basic functions of the language with new ones. In Python, this functionality is referred to as **importing a module**. As we saw earlier, a **module** is simply a Python file with new capabilities defined in it. When you `import` a module, it's as if you typed that Python file in at that point and all the objects, functions, and variables in it become defined at once.

Python comes with an extensive library of modules that you can use to do a wide range of things, such as accessing the Internet, generating random numbers, and accessing files in a directory—a useful thing to do when developing Web pages or working with videos.

Let's use that as our first example. The module we'll use is the `os` module. The function in the `os` module that knows how to list the files in a directory is `listdir()`. We access the piece of the module using dot notation.

```
>>> import os
>>> print os.listdir("C:\ip-book\mediasources\pics")
['students1.jpg', 'students2.jpg', 'students5.jpg',
 'students6.jpg', 'students7.jpg', 'students8.jpg']
```

We can use `os.listdir()` to title pictures in a directory or to insert a statement, such as a copyright claim. Now `listdir()` just returns the base filename and suffix. That's enough to make sure that we have pictures and not sounds or something else.

But it doesn't give us complete paths for makePicture. To get a complete path, we can combine the input directory with the base filename from listdir()—but we need a path delimiter between the two pieces. Python has a standard that if a filename has a "//" in it, then that will be replaced with whatever the right path delimiter is for the operating system you're using.

Program 142: Title a Set of Pictures in a Directory

```
import os

def titleDirectory(dir):
  for file in os.listdir(dir):
    print "Processing:",dir+"//"+file
    if file.endswith(".jpg"):
      picture = makePicture(dir+"//"+file)
      addText(picture,10,10,"Property of CS1315 at Georgia Tech")
      writePictureTo(picture,dir+"//"+"titled-"+file)
```

How It Works

The function titleDirectory takes a directory (path name, as a string) as input. It then walks through each filename file in the directory. If the filename ends with ".jpg," it's probably a picture. So we make the picture from the file in the given **dir** directory. We add text to the picture, then write the picture back out as "titled-" plus the filename, in the given **dir** directory.

11.4.1   More on Import and Your Own Modules

There are actually several forms of the import statement. The one we're using here, import module, makes all of the modules available through dot notation. These are several other options:

- We can import just a few things from a module, but then access them without using dot notation. This form is from module import name.

  ```
  >>> from os import listdir
  >>> print listdir(r"C:\Documents and Settings")
  ['Default User', 'All Users', 'NetworkService',
  'LocalService', 'Administrator', 'Driver',
  'Mark Guzdial']
  ```

  We can use the form from module import * to import *everything* from the module and access it without using dot notation at all.

- We can import module as newname if we'd like to import a module but then use newname to reference the module. You can use this to make it easier to access Java libraries from Jython. Java libraries sometimes have long names like java.awt.event. We can use this syntax to create a shorthand, for example,

  ```
  import java.awt.event as event
  ```

  Then you can reference elements in java.awt.event as event.

A module is just a Python file. As we saw earlier in this book, you can import your own code as a module. If you have the function findTemperature in the file **findTemperatureFile.py** in the JES directory, you can simply execute import findTemperature from findTemperatureFile and then use findTemperature as if it were typed into your Program Area.

11.4.2   Adding Unpredictably to Your Program with Random

Another fun and useful module is random. The base function random.random() generates random numbers (evenly distributed) between 0 and 1.

```
>>> import random
>>> for i in range(1,10):
...          print random.random()
...
0.8211369314193928
0.6354266779703246
0.9460060163520159
0.904615696559684
0.33500464463254187
0.08124982126940594
0.0711481376807015
0.7255217307346048
0.2920541211845866
```

Random numbers can be fun when they're applied to tasks like picking random words from a list. The function **random.choice()** does that.

```
>>> for i in range(1,5):
...          print random.choice(["Here", "is", "a",
"list", "of", "words", "in", "random", "order"])
...
list
a
Here
list
```

From there, we can generate random sentences by randomly picking nouns, verbs, and phrases from lists.

Program 143: Randomly Generate Language

```
import random

def sentence():
  nouns = ["Mark","Adam","Angela","Larry","Jose","Matt","Jim"]
  verbs = ["runs", "skips", "sings", "leaps", "jumps", "climbs",¬
  "argues", "giggles"]
  phrases = ["in a tree", "over a log", "very loudly", "around¬
  the bush", "while reading the newspaper"]
  phrases = phrases + ["very badly", "while skipping", "instead¬
  of grading", "while typing in Wikipedia."]
```

```
print random.choice(nouns), random.choice(verbs),¬
random.choice(phrases)
```

¬These lines of the program should continue with the next lines. A single command in Python may not break across multiple lines.   ■

How It Works

We simply create lists for nouns, verbs, and phrases—taking care that all the combinations make sense in terms of number. The `print` statement defines the desired structure: a random noun, then a random verb, then a random phrase.

```
>>> sentence()
Jose leaps while reading the newspaper
>>> sentence()
Jim skips while typing on the CoWeb.
>>> sentence()
Matt sings very loudly
>>> sentence()
Adam sings in a tree
>>> sentence()
Adam sings around the bush
>>> sentence()
Angela runs while typing on the CoWeb.
>>> sentence()
Angela sings around the bush
>>> sentence()
Jose runs very badly
```

The basic process here is common in simulation programs. What we have is a structure defined in the program: a definition of what counts as a noun, a verb, and a phrase, and a statement that what we want is a noun, then a verb, then a phrase. The structure gets filled in with random choices. The interesting question is how much can be simulated with a structure and randomness. Could we simulate intelligence this way? And what's the difference between a *simulation* of intelligence and a really thinking computer?

Imagine a program that reads input from the user and then generates a random sentence. Maybe there are a few *rules* in the program that search for keywords and respond to them, like:

```
if input.find("Mother") <> -1:
    print "Tell me more about your Mother"
```

Joseph Weizenbaum wrote a program like this many years ago, called *Doctor* (later known as *Eliza*). His program would act like a Rogerian psychotherapist, echoing back whatever you said, with some randomness, but searching for keywords so that it would seem to really be "listening." The program was meant as a joke, not as a real effort to create a simulation of intelligence. To Weizenbaum's dismay, people took it seriously. They started treating it like a therapist. Weizenbaum changed his research direction from *artificial intelligence* to concern over the ethical use of technology and how easily people can be fooled by technology.

11.4.3   Reading CSV Files with a Library

There is a standard module named csv that can make reading CSV files a little easier. You don't have to do split. Programs like Excel can sometimes generate CSV files that are hard to read, and this module takes care of that. The CSV module creates a reader function that returns a specially formatted list. The below function does the *same* thing as our earlier findPopulation, but uses the CSV module.

Program 144: Find the Population Using the CSV Module

```
from csv import *

def findPopulation2(state):
  file = open(getMediaPath("state-populations.csv"),"rb")
  csvfile = reader(file)
  for row in csvfile:
    if row[4] == state:
      return int(row[5])
```

11.4.4   A Sampling of Python Standard Libraries

We have seen some of the Python standard modules like os, sys, and random so far. There are *lots* of modules in the Python Standard Library. There are lots of reasons for using these modules.

- They are written very well—fast, well-documented, and well-tested. You can trust them and save yourself effort.

- It is always a good idea to reuse program code. It's a good practice to get into.

- In a bottom-up design process, starting from existing modules is a great way to start on a new project.

Some of the modules that you might want to explore include:

- time knows how to measure time (e.g., how long is this code running, which we use in Chapter 6) and how to pause execution with sleep, which we use with turtles in Chapter 17.

- datetime and calendar modules know how to manipulate dates, time, and calendars. For example, you can find out what day of the week it was when the U.S. Declaration of Independence was signed in 1776.

  ```
  >>> from datetime import *
  >>> independence = date(1776,7,4)
  >>> independence.weekday()
  3
  >>> #0 is Monday, so 3 is Thursday
  ```

- The math module knows lots of important mathematical functions, like sin (sine) and sqrt (square root).

- The module zipfile knows how to read and write compressed "zip" files.

- The module `email` provides facilities for writing your own program to manipulate email (e.g., like a spam filter).
- `SimpleHTTPServer` is actually a Web server all by itself—programmable in Python, to boot!

PROGRAMMING SUMMARY

GENERAL PROGRAM PIECES

csv	Module for processing CSV files.
random	Module for generating random numbers or making random choices.
os	Module for manipulating the operating system.

STRING FUNCTIONS, FUNCTIONS, METHODS, AND PIECES

string[n], string[n:m]	Returns the character in the string at position *n* ([n]) or the substring from *n* to *m* − 1. Remember that these start at index 0.
startswith	Returns true if the string starts with the input string.
endswith	Returns true if the string ends with the input string.
find	Returns the index if the input string is found in the string; −1 otherwise.
upper, lower	Returns a new string converted to the specified case.
isalpha, isdigit	Returns true if the whole string is alphabetic or numeric (digits), respectively.
replace	Takes two input substrings—replaces all instances of the first with the second in the given string.
split	Bursts a string into a list of substrings using the input string as the delimiter.

LIST FUNCTIONS AND PIECES

append	Appends the input to the end of the list.
remove	Removes the input from the list.
sort	Sorts the list.
reverse	Reverses the list.
count	Counts the number of times the input appears in the list.
max, min	Returns the maximum or minimum (respectively) value from a list of numbers as input in the list.

PROBLEMS

11.1   Create a string variable that contains the sentence "Don't do that!" in it. Create a string variable that contains double quotes in it. Create a string variable that has a tab in it. Create a string variable that has a filename in it with backslashes.

11.2   Write a function that prints every other letter in a string.

11.3   Write a function that takes a string and prints out the letters in the string in reverse order.

11.4   Write a function that finds and removes the second occurrence of a given string in a passed string.

11.5   Write a function to uppercase every other word in a passed sentence. So given "The dog ran a long way," it would output "The DOG ran A long WAY."

11.6   Write a function that takes a passed sentence and an index and returns the sentence with the word at the index uppercased. For example, if the function takes in a sentence "I love the color red" and the index 4 it returns "I love the color RED."

11.7   Change the function `findPopulation` to change the input and the comparison word both to lowercase. Now, it will match even if we executed `findPopulation("CALIFORNIA")`.

11.8   Write a function that takes a sentence as input and returns it scrambled (the order of the words mixed up in some way). For example, if it is passed "Does anything rhyme with orange?" it might return "Orange with does anything rhyme?".

11.9   Write a function that can find the zip code for a person from a delimited string for an address. For example, it might read a string that has in it "name:line1: line2: city:state:zipCode" and return the zip code.

11.10   Modify the `changeLittle` function to use `readLines` instead of `read`.

11.11   Modify the `changeLittle` function to use `readLine` instead of `read`.

11.12   Create a secret message by encoding each character of a string into a number using `ord`. For each character in the message, print the `rod` of that character.

11.13   Create a function that reverses the items in a list.

11.14   Create a function that replaces a passed string in a list of strings with a new string.

11.15   Are the numbers returned from the `random.random()` function really random? How are they generated? You will have to look up some information on random numbers on the Internet to answer this question.

11.16   Write short essay responses to these questions:

(a) Give me one example of a task for which you would not write a program and give me another example of a task for which you would write a program.

(b) What's the difference between an array, a matrix, and a tree? Give an example where we have used each to represent some data of interest to us.

(c) What is dot notation and when do you use it?

(d) Why is red a bad color to use for chromakey?

(e) What's the difference between a function and a method?

(f) Why is a tree a better representation than an array for files on a disk? Why do you have many directories on your disk, and not just one gigantic one?

(g) What are some advantages that vector-based graphics have over bitmap graphical representations (like JPEG, BMP, GIF)?

11.17 Extend the form-letter recipe to take an input of a pet's name and type, and reference the pet in the form letter. `"Your pet "+petType+","+petName+" will love our offer!"` might generate `"Your pet poodle, Fifi, will love our offer!"`.

11.18 Imagine that you have a list of the genders (as single characters) of all the students in your class, in order of their last name. The list will look something like "MFFMMMFFMFMMFFFM" where M is male and F is female. Write a function (below) `percentageGenders(string)` to accept a string that represents the genders. You are to count all of the M's and F's in the string and print out the ratio (as a decimal) of each gender. For example, if the input string were "MFFF," then the function should print something like, "There are 0.25 males, 0.75 females." (*Hint*: Better multiply something by 1.0 to make sure that you get floats not integers.)

11.19 You worked late into the night on an assignment and didn't realize that you wrote a huge section of your term paper with your fingers on the wrong keys.

Where you meant to type: "This is an unruly mob." You actually typed: "Ty8s 8s ah 7hr7o6 j9b."

Basically you swapped: 6 for Y, 7 for U, 8 for I, 9 for O, 0 for P, U for J, I for K, O for L, H for N, and J for M. (Those were the only keystrokes you got wrong—you caught yourself before you got much further.) You also never touched the shift key, so it's only lowercase letters that you care about.

Knowing Python as you do, you decide to write a quick program to fix your text. Write a function `fixItUp` that takes a string as input and returns a string with the characters put the way that they ought to have been.

*11.20 Write a function `doGraphics` that will take a list as input. The function `doGraphics` will start by creating a canvas from the **640x480.jpg** file in the **mediasources** folder. You will draw on the canvas according to the commands in the input list. Each element of the list will be a string. There will be two kinds of strings in the list:

- "b 200 120" means to draw a black dot at *x* position 200 and *y* position 120–(200, 120). The numbers, of course, will change, but the command will

*More challenging problem

always be a "b." You can assume that the input numbers will always have three digits.

- "1 000 010 100 200" means to draw a line from position (0, 10) to position (100, 200).

So an input list might look like: ["b 100 200","b 101 200","b 102 200","1 102 200 102 300"] (but have any number of elements).

11.21   Write a function findLargestState that figures out which state has the largest population and returns that.

11.22   Write a function findSmallestState that figures out which state has the smallest population and returns that.

11.23   In the media folder available at MediaComputation.org, there is another piece of census data that includes city information, state-city-populations.csv. The first few lines of this file look like this:

```
SUMLEV,STATE,COUNTY,PLACE,COUSUB,CONCIT,FUNCSTAT,NAME,STNAME,

CENSUS2010POP,ESTIMATESBASE2010,POPESTIMATE2010,POPESTIMATE2011,

POPESTIMATE2012,POPESTIMATE2013
040,01,000,00000,00000,00000,A,Alabama,Alabama,4779736,4779758,4785570,

4801627,4817528,4833722 162,01,000,00124,00000,00000,A,Abbeville
city,Alabama,2688,2688,2683,2690,2658,2651
162,01,000,00460,00000,00000,A,Adamsville
city,Alabama,4522,4522,4519,4496,4474,4448 1
```

Write the below functions in two ways: One with split and another with the csv module.

- Write the findCityPopulation function that returns the population in 2013 (last field) of an input city.

- Write a function findLargestCityInState and findSmallestCity InState to find the city with the largest and the smallest population (respectively) within a given state.

- Use both your state and city functions to answer some questions. Find the state with the largest population, and the state with the smallest population. Is the smallest city in the largest state larger or smaller than the smallest city in the smallest state? Is the largest city in the largest state larger or smaller than the largest city in the smallest state?

TO DIG DEEPER

The book that Mark uses for making his way through the Python modules is Frederik Lundh's *Python Standard Library* [16]. You can find the listing of library modules, with their documentation, at http://docs.python.org/library/.

12 Advanced Text Techniques: Web and Information

Chapter Learning Objectives

The media learning goals for this chapter are:

- To write programs to directly access and use text information from the Internet.
- To translate a sound or picture to text and translate text back to a sound or picture.
- To hide a message (text or audio) in a picture.

The computer science goals for this chapter are:

- To write a program to access the Internet and return processed information.
- To show that information can be encoded in many ways.

12.1 NETWORKS: GETTING OUR TEXT FROM THE WEB

A *network* is formed whenever computers communicate with one another. Rarely does the communication take place with voltages over wires, the way that a computer encodes 0's and 1's internally. It's too hard to maintain specific voltages over distances. Instead, 0's and 1's are encoded in some other way. For example, a **modem** (literally *modulator-demodulator*) is a gadget that maps 0's and 1's to different audio frequencies. To humans, it sounds like a bunch of buzzing bees, but to modems and computers, it's pure binary.

Like onions and ogres, networks have layers. At the bottom level is the physical substrate. How are the signals being passed? Higher levels define how data is encoded. What makes up a zero? A one? Do we send one bit at a time? A **packet** of bytes at a time? Even higher levels define the **protocol** for communication. How does one computer tell another computer that it wants to talk and what it wants to talk about? How do we address your computer at all? By thinking about these distinct layers, and keeping them distinct, we can easily swap out one part without changing the others.

For example, most people with a direct connection to a network use a wired connection to an **Ethernet** network, but Ethernet is actually a mid-level protocol that works over wireless networks, too.

Think about how you can access the same Web pages with a cell phone, a laptop via Wi-Fi, or a desktop computer with a direct, wired connection to the Internet. The top layers of the protocol are very different in each of these three examples. A cell phone accesses the Internet via the cellular network. The laptop using Wi-Fi is using a radio-frequency top layer that connects to the rest of the Internet through a *router*. At the intermediate and bottom layers of the network, though, all three devices are accessing the exact same information in the exact same way. The protocols for how a browser asks for information from a Web server are all the same, no matter what kind of device and what kind of layer is being used to access the network.

Humans also have protocols. If Mark walks up to you, holds out his hand, and says, "Hi, my name is Mark," you will most certainly hold out your hand and say something like "My name is Carolina" (assuming that your name is Carolina—if it wasn't, that would be pretty funny). In each culture, there's a protocol about how people greet one another. Computer protocols are about the same things but they're written down to communicate the process exactly. What's said isn't too different. One computer may send the message "HELO" to another to start a conversation (we don't know why the protocol writers couldn't spare the extra L to spell it right), and a computer may send BYE to end the conversation. (We even sometimes call the start of a computer protocol the *handshake*.) It's all about establishing a connection, and making sure that both sides understand what's going on.

The **Internet** is a network of networks. If you have a device in your home so that your computers can talk to one another (e.g., a **router**), then you have a network. With just that, you can probably copy files around between computers and print. When you connect your network to the wider Internet (through an **Internet Service Provider (ISP)**), your network becomes part of the Internet.

The Internet is based on a set of agreements about a whole bunch of things:

- *How computers are addressed*: Currently, each computer on the Internet has a 32-bit number associated with it—four byte values that are usually written like this separated by periods "101.132.64.15." These are called **IP addresses** (for Internet Protocol addresses).

  There is a system of **domain names** by which people can refer to specific computers without knowing their IP addresses. For example, when you access `http://www.cnn.com`, you are actually accessing `http://157.166.226.26/`. That worked for us last time we tried it but it could change. There is a network of *domain name servers* that keep track of names like "www.cnn.com" and map them to addresses like "157.166.226.26." The fact that the numbers can change is one of the advantages of the domain name server—the name stays the same and can point at any address. You can be connected to the Internet and still not be able to get to your favorite Web sites if your domain name server is broken. You might be able to get to it if you type in the IP address directly.

- *How computers communicate*: Data is placed in *packets* that have a well-defined structure, including the sender's IP address, the receiver's IP address, and a number of bytes per packet.

- *How packets are routed around the Internet*: The Internet was designed in the time of the *Cold War*. It was designed to withstand a nuclear attack. If a section of the Internet is destroyed (or damaged, or blocked as a form of censorship), the packet-routing mechanism of the Internet will simply find a route around the damage.

But the topmost layers of the network define what the data being passed around *means*. One of the first applications placed on top of the Internet was electronic mail. Over the years, the mail protocols have evolved to standards like **POP (post office protocol)** and **SMTP (simple mail transfer protocol)**. Another old and important protocol is **FTP (file transfer protocol)**, which allows us to transfer files between computers.

These protocols aren't super-complicated. When the communication ends, one computer will probably say BYE or QUIT to the other. When one computer tells another computer to accept a file via FTP, it literally says "STO filename" (again, early computer developers didn't want to spare the two more bytes to say "STORE").

The *World Wide Web* is yet another set of agreements, developed mostly by Tim Berners-Lee. The Web is based on top of the Internet, simply adding more protocols on top of the existing ones.

- *How to refer to things on the Web*: Resources on the Web are referenced using **URLs (uniform resource locators)**. A URL specifies the protocol to use to address the resource, the domain name of the **server** that can provide the resource, and the **path** to the resource on that server. For example, a URL like `http://www.cc.gatech.edu/index.html` says, "Use the HTTP protocol to talk to the computer at `www.cc.gatech.edu` and ask it for the resource index.html."

  Not every file on every computer attached to the Internet is accessible via a URL. There are some preconditions before a file is accessible via a URL. First, an Internet-accessible computer has to be running a piece of software that understands a protocol that Web browsers understand, typically **HTTP (hypertext transfer protocol)** or FTP. We call a computer that is running such a piece of software a *server*. A browser that accesses a server is called a **client**. Second, a server typically has a *server directory* accessible via that server. Only files in the directory, or subdirectories within the directory, are available.

- *How to serve documents*: The most common protocol on the Web is HTTP. It defines how resources are served on the Web. HTTP is really simple—your browser literally says to a server things like "GET index.html" (just those letters!).

- *How documents will be formatted*: Documents on the Web are formatted using **HTML (HyperText Markup Language)**.

You'll notice the term **HyperText** showing up frequently in reference to the Web. HyperText is literally nonlinear text. Ted Nelson invented the term *hypertext* to describe the kind of reading that we all do on the Web but that didn't exist before computers:

read a little on one page, then click a link and read a little over there, then click BACK and continue reading where you left off. The basic idea of HyperText dates back to Vannevar Bush, who was one of the President Franklin Roosevelt's science advisers, but it wasn't until the computer came along that we could envision implementing Bush's model of a *Memex*—a device for capturing flows of thought. Tim Berners-Lee invented the Web and its protocols as a way of supporting rapid publication of research findings with connections between documents. The Web is certainly not the ultimate HyperText system. Systems like the ones that Ted Nelson worked on wouldn't allow "dead links" (links that are no longer accessible). But for all its warts, the Web *works*.

A browser (e.g., Internet Explorer, Google Chrome, Opera) understands a lot about the Internet. It usually knows several protocols, such as HTTP, FTP, *gopher* (an early HyperText protocol), or *mailto* (SMTP). It knows HTML, how to format it, and how to grab resources referenced within the HTML, like JPEG pictures. It is also possible to access the Internet without nearly that much overhead. Mail clients (e.g., Outlook and Apple Mail) know some of these protocols without knowing all of them. Even JES understands a little bit about SMTP and HTTP to support turn-in of assignments.

Python, like other modern languages, provides modules to support access to the Internet without all the overhead of a browser. Basically, you can write small programs that are clients. Python's module `urllib` allows you to open URLs and read them as if they were files. Here we access the news Web site `http://www.cnn.com` and display the first 100 characters of the Web page that gets returned.

```
>>> import urllib
>>> connect = urllib.urlopen("http://www.cnn.com")
>>> news = connect.read()
>>> connect.close()
>>> news[0:100]
'\n<!DOCTYPE HTML>\n<html lang="en-US">\n<head>\n<title>CNN.com -
    Breaking News, U.S., World, Weather, En'
```

Earlier, we made a temperature-reading program to get information from a saved weather page directly from the Internet. We can still do that with sites like `http://www.weather.com`. But we can also get other information live from other Web sites. That's called *scraping*, where we download a Web page and then try to grab information directly out of the source of the page.

To scrape information typically requires a lot of trial-and-error explanation to make it work right. We use the module `urllib` to read the Web page as a string and then search the string in the same way that we did the file previously. Of course, all of this breaks just as soon as the Web site changes how they display whatever information you are interested in. It's an inelegant and inefficient way of gathering data. The data being gathered are publicly available—scraping is simply automating that process. There is nothing illegal in that. However, it could be counter to the use agreements for some Web sites.

Let's consider Web scraping from Facebook as an example. The Facebook member agreement (at least, at the time of this writing) says, "[Y]ou agree not to use automated scripts to collect information from the Service or the Site." If you wrote a program to scrape from Facebook, you would be using an automated script to collect information from the Facebook site. What if your program accessed the site anonymously, not as a member of Facebook and not logged in as anyone? That would likely be legal and not counter to the member agreement—but Facebook (and similar sites) typically limits access without being signed in. Instead, Facebook provides an interface for accessing information automatically. That would be a more elegant and less complicated way of gathering information.

12.1.1   Automating Access to CSV Data

In the previous chapter, we showed how to process CSV data downloaded from the Web. Using the `urllib`, we can process CSV data without downloading it first. CSV files are one way that a Web site can provide data (even data that is regularly updated) in a way that is easy for others to manipulate—and far more reliable than scraping.

If you recall, we processed USA census data via CSV files that we downloaded. We downloaded that data from `https://www.census.gov/popest/data/datasets.html`. We can actually process that data right where it's at, by getting the URL for a particular CSV file. By right clicking on a DATA link, we can choose to copy the link address, and then we can paste it into our code. The data set that we were using in the last chapter can be found at the URL: `https://www.census.gov/popest/data/state/asrh/2013/files/SCPRC-EST2013-18+POP-RES.csv`.[1] Now, we can look for a state's population without downloading the data.

Program 145: Find a Population from a CSV File at a Given URL

```
import urllib

def findPopulationURL(state):
  con = urllib.urlopen("https://www.census.gov/popest/data/state/
    asrh/2013/files/SCPRC-EST2013-18+POP-RES.csv")
  lines = con.readlines()
  con.close()
  for line in lines:
    parts = line.split(",")
    if parts[4] == state:
      return int(parts[5])
  return -1
```

How It Works

This version of the file works just like the one in the last chapter, except that we are reading from a URL rather than a file. In the first line, we open a connection `con` to a URL via the `urllib` using the `urlopen` function. We can use `readlines` just as we did with a file, then close the connection. The rest of the function is exactly the same— to check each line for the state (in `parts[4]`) we want, then return the population (`parts[5]`).

We can even use two modules at once, using both the `urllib` and the `csv` libraries.

---

[1]When you look, it may have a different URL. You may have to go fetch a new one.

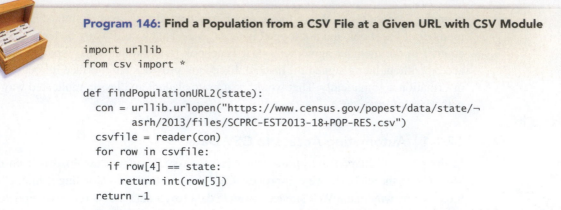

Program 146: Find a Population from a CSV File at a Given URL with CSV Module

```
import urllib
from csv import *

def findPopulationURL2(state):
  con = urllib.urlopen("https://www.census.gov/popest/data/state/¬
        asrh/2013/files/SCPRC-EST2013-18+POP-RES.csv")
  csvfile = reader(con)
  for row in csvfile:
    if row[4] == state:
      return int(row[5])
  return -1
```

¬These lines of the program should continue with the next lines. A single command in Python may not break across multiple lines.   ∎

Sometimes, a CSV file is freely accessible, but can't be opened via `urllib.urlopen`. In that case, you will have to download the file, store it somewhere on your disk, and then process it as a file. For example, *The Guardian* has a large collection of CSV files as part of its *Data Journalism* project. At `http://www.theguardian.com/news/datablog/interactive/2013/jan/14/all-our-datasets-index`, we found a CSV file about executions all over the world. When we tried to access CSV file via its URL (`https://spreadsheets.google.com/feeds/download/spreadsheets/Export?exportFormat=csv&key=0AonYZs4Mz1ZbdGJiUzRwTVh1M25DWD1PdjBmNURjOUE`), we found that `urllib.urlopen` wouldn't work. So we downloaded the file as `"Death penalty.csv"` into our media folder in order to process it.

The format of the code is described in Figure 12.1. The index 0 column contains the country name, the index 14 column has number of executions by that country, and the index 15 contains the number sentenced to death 2007–2012. So, what country has executed the most people in 2007–2012?

Turns out to be a little harder to process than you think. Not all the values in the 14th column are numbers. If we try to use `int` to get the value, we will get an error. There is a mechanism in Python by which we can say, "*Try* to do this, and if it doesn't work, just *pass* to the next value." The code is literally `try: except: pass`. Here is the program that does it.

0   **15**

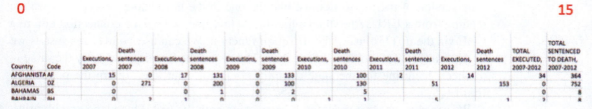

FIGURE 12.1
Format of Death penalty.csv.

Program 147: **Find the Country Who Executed the Most People 2007–2012**

```
from csv import *

def highestExecutions():
  file = open(getMediaPath("Death penalty.csv"),"rb")
  csvfile = reader(file)
  max = -1
  maxcountry = "None"
  for row in csvfile:
    try:
      country = row[0]
      executions = int(row[14])
      if executions > max:
       max = executions
       maxcountry = country
    except:
      pass
  print maxcountry,max
```

How It Works

This function is built assuming that the file `"Death penalty.csv"` has been down-loaded from *The Guardian* and stored in the media folder. The function opens the file, and starts up a `csvreader` on the data. We are going to find the maximum number of executions in `max` and the country in `maxcountry`. When we start, we'll give `max` a value of −1.

Now, we process each `row` in the `csvfile`. We `try` to get the country (from `row[0]`) and the number of executions (from `int(row[14])`). If the `executions` are greater than the current maximum value in `max`, we define a new maximum and save the `maxcountry` name. If anything goes wrong, that triggers the `except:` clause, and we just `pass` to the next row. At the very end of the program, we print out the maximum country name and the number of executions.

```
>>> highestExecutions()
SAUDI ARABIA 423
```

12.1.2 Accessing FTP

We can access FTP data sources via the `ftplib` in Python.

```
>>> import ftplib
>>> connect = ftplib.FTP("cleon.cc.gatech.edu")
>>> connect.login("guzdial","mypassword")
'230 User guzdial logged in.'
>>> connect.storbinary("STOR barbara.jpg",open(getMediaPath("barbara.jpg")))
'226 Transfer complete.'
>>> connect.storlines("STOR JESintro.txt",open("JESintro.txt"))
'226 Transfer complete.'
>>> connect.close()
```

To create interaction on the Web, we need programs that actually generate HTML. For example, when you type a phrase into a text area and then click the SEARCH button, you are actually causing a program to execute on the server that executes your search and then *generates* the HTML (Web page) that you see in response. Python is a common language for this kind of programming. Its modules, ease of quoting, and ease of writing make it excellent for writing interactive Web programs.

12.2   USING TEXT TO SHIFT BETWEEN MEDIA

As we said at the beginning of this chapter, we can think about text as *unimedia*. We can map from sound to text and back again and the same with pictures. And more interestingly, we can go from sound to text ... to pictures.

Why would we want to do any of this? Why should we care about transforming media in this way? For the same reasons that we care about digitizing media at all. Digital media transformed into text can be more easily transmitted from place to place, checked for errors, and even corrected for errors. The international standards for Internet email[2] require binary files (like pictures and sounds) sent via an email message to be converted to text first. That isn't very hard to do, and happens pretty much invisibly to you as an email user. *Information can be put in many different representations. We can choose new representations for information to allow us to do new things.*

Mapping sound to text is easy. Sound is just a series of samples (numbers). We can easily write these out to a file.

Program 148: Write a Sound to a File as Text Numbers

```
def soundToText(sound,filename):
    file = open(filename,"wt")
    for s in getSamples(sound):
        file.write(str(getSampleValue(s))+"\n")
    file.close()
```

How It Works

We're taking an input sound and a filename as input, then opening the filename for writable text. We then loop through each sample and write it to the file. We're using the function str() here to convert a number into its string representation so that we can add a newline to it and write it to a file.

What do we do with sound as text? Manipulate it as a series of numbers, as with Excel (Figure 12.2). We can quite easily do modifications, such as multiplying each sample by 2.0 here. We can even graph the numbers, and see the same kind of sound graph as we've seen in MediaTools (Figure 12.3). (You will get an error, though—Excel doesn't like to graph more than 32,000 points, and at 22,000 samples per second, 32,000 samples is not a long sound.)

[2]RFC 822, in case you were interested. Internet email is actually defined as being text-only.

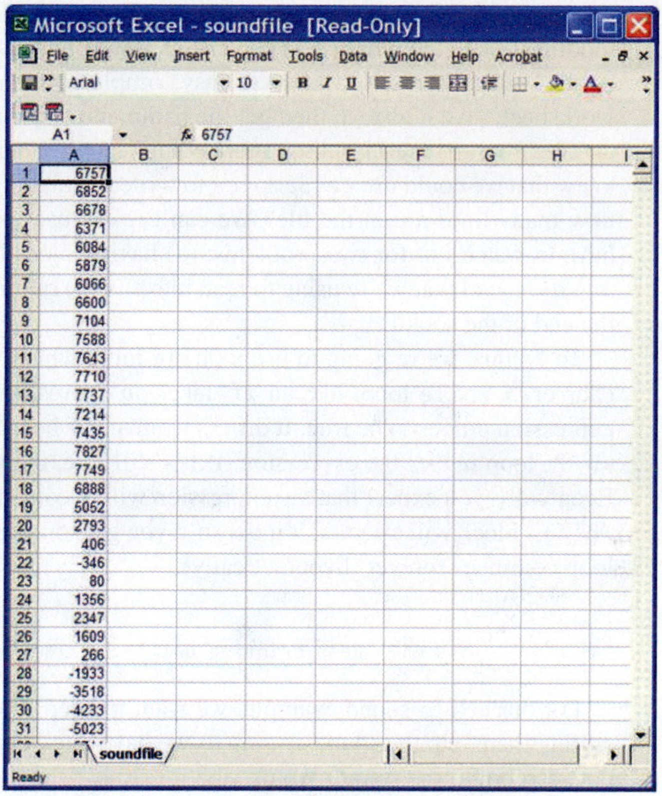

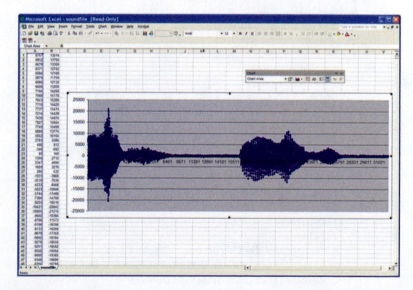

FIGURE 12.2
Sound-as-text file read into Excel. *Source*: Screenshots from Microsoft Excel 2003. Copyright © 2003 by Microsoft Corporation. Reprinted with permission.

FIGURE 12.3
Sound-as-text file graphed in Excel. *Source*: Screenshots from Microsoft Excel 2003. Copyright © 2003 by Microsoft Corporation. Reprinted with permission.

How do we convert a series of numbers back into a sound? Say that you do some modification to the numbers in Excel and now you want to hear the result. How do you do it? The mechanics of Excel are easy: simply copy the column you want into a new worksheet, save it as text, then get the pathname of the text file to use in Python.

The program itself is a little more complicated. When going from sound to text, we knew that we could use `getSamples` to write out all the samples. But how do we know how many lines are in the file? We can't really use `getLines`—it doesn't exist. We have to watch out for two problems: (a) having more lines in the file than we can fit into the sound that we're using to read into and (b) running out of lines before we reach the end of the sound.

To do this, we're going to use a `while` loop, which we did see briefly in an earlier chapter. A `while` loop, like an `if`, takes an expression and executes its block if the expression proves to be true. It differs from an `if` because *after* executing the block, a `while` loop *retests* the expression. If it's still true, the whole block is executed again. Eventually, you expect that the expression will become false, and then the line after the `while`'s block will execute. If it doesn't, you get something called an *infinite loop*—the loop continues forever (hypothetically).

```
while 1==1:
    print "This will keep printing until the computer is turned off."
```

For our text-to-sound example, we want to keep reading samples from the file and storing them into the sound *as long as* we have numbers in the file *and as long as* there is still room in the sound. We use the function `float()` to convert the string number into a real number. (`int` would work, too, but this gives us the chance to introduce `float`.)

```
>>> print 2*"123"
123123
>>> print 2 * float("123")
246.0
```

Program 149: Convert a File of Text Numbers into a Sound

```
def textToSound(filename):
    #Set up the sound
    sound = makeSound(getMediaPath("sec3silence.wav"))
    soundIndex = 0
    #Set up the file
    file = open(filename,"rt")
    contents=file.readlines()
    file.close()
    fileIndex = 0
    # Keep going until run out of sound space or run out of file contents
        while (soundIndex < getLength(sound)) and (fileIndex < len(contents)):
        sample=float(contents[fileIndex])
        #Get the file line
        setSampleValueAt(sound,soundIndex,sample)
```

```
        fileIndex = fileIndex + 1
        soundIndex = soundIndex + 1
    return sound
```

How It Works

The function `textToSound` takes a filename as input that contains the samples as numbers. We open up a silent three-second sound to hold the sound. `soundIndex` stands for the next sample to read, and `fileIndex` stands for the next number to read for the file list `contents`. The `while` loop says to keep going until *either* the `soundIndex` goes past the length of the sound *or* the `fileIndex` goes past the end of the file (in the list `contents`). In a loop we convert the next string in the list to a float, set the sample value to that, then increment both `fileIndex` and `soundIndex`. When we're done (by either condition in the `while`), we `return` the input sound.

12.3   MOVING INFORMATION BETWEEN MEDIA

We don't *have* to map from sounds to text and back to sounds. We could decide to go to a picture instead. The program below takes a sound and maps each sample to a pixel. All we have to do is define our mapping which is how we want to represent the samples. We chose a very simple one: if the sample is greater than 1000, the pixel is red; if less than −1000 it is blue, and everything else is green (Figure 12.4).

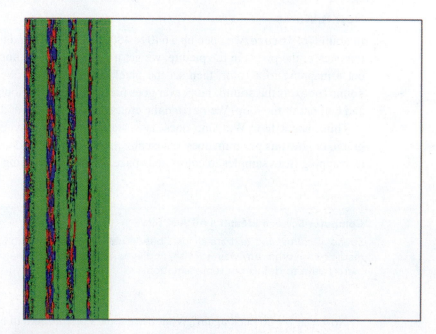

FIGURE 12.4
A visualization of the sound "This is a test."

We now have to deal with the case where we run out of samples before we run out of pixels. To do this, we use yet another new programming construct: a `break`. A `break` statement stops our current loop and goes to the line below it. In this example, if we run out of samples, we stop the `for` loop that is processing the pixels.

Program 150: Visualizing Sound

```
def soundToPicture(sound):
  picture = makePicture(getMediaPath("640x480.jpg"))
  soundIndex = 0
  for p in getPixels(picture):
    if soundIndex > getLength(sound):
      break
    sample = getSampleValueAt(sound,soundIndex)
    if sample > 1000:
      setColor(p,red)
    if sample < -1000:
      setColor(p,blue)
    if sample <= 1000 and sample >= -1000:
      setColor(p,green)
    soundIndex = soundIndex + 1
  return picture
```

How It Works

In `soundToPicture`, we open up a 640×480 blank picture and take a sound as input. For each of the pixels in the picture, we get a sample value at `soundIndex` and figure out a mapping to a color, then set the pixel `p` to that color. We then increment the `soundIndex`. If the `soundIndex` ever goes past the end of the sound, we simply `break` and bail out of the loop. We `return` the created picture at the end.

Think about how WinAmp does its visualizations, or how Excel or MediaTools graph, or how this program does its visualization. Each is just deciding a different way of mapping from samples to colors and space. It's just a mapping. It's all just bits.

Computer Science Idea: It's All Just Bits
Sound, pictures, and text are all just "bits." They're just information. We can map from media to the other any way we wish, and even convert back to the original media. We merely have to define our representation.

Now, can we go back again? What if we took a picture like in Figure 12.4 and fed it into a function that knew about the mapping? Could we get a sound back again? If the sound was speech, could we hear the speech again?

Program 151: Hearing a Picture

```
def pictureToSound(picture):
  sound = makeEmptySoundBySeconds(10)
  sndIndex = 0
  for p in getPixels(picture):
    if sndIndex == getLength(sound):
      break
    if getRed(p) > 200:
      setSampleValueAt(sound,sndIndex,1000)
    elif getBlue(p) > 200 :
      setSampleValueAt(sound,sndIndex,-1000)
    elif getGreen(p) > 200:
      setSampleValueAt(sound,sndIndex,0)
    sndIndex = sndIndex + 1
  return(sound)
```

How It Works

In `pictureToSound`, we input a picture and return a sound from it. We start out by creating an empty sound of 10 seconds in length (`makeEmptySoundBySeconds(10)`). The idea is to have a big sound to fill, but it's also a limitation—we can't process more than 10 seconds of sound.

We use a variable `sndIndex` to represent the next sample that we'll fill in our target `sound`. We use `p` to represent each pixel. If we get to the end of the sound before we get to the end of the pixels (`sndIndex == getLength(sound)`), we `break` and stop.

We could check that the pixel `p` is exactly red (e.g., red component is 255 and green and blue components are both 0), green, or blue, but given that we are using JPEG (a lossy format), that's unlikely. However, we did put in just red, green, and blue colors, so we can assume that a pixel with *lots* of red is probably red. So we'll check if the red component is greater than 200, and if so, make the corresponding sample (at `sndIndex`) 1000. If it's a lot of blue, we make the sample −1000, and if there is a lot of green, we make the sample 0. We are using `elif` here as an abbreviation for `else if`. No matter what sample value we assign, we will then move to the next sample (`sndIndex = sndIndex + 1`) before moving on to the next pixel. At the end, we `return(sound)`.

If we encoded somebody speaking words, from a sound to a picture, then converted it back with `pictureToSound`, do you think we could make out the words? Back in Chapter 6, we maximized sound and was able to make out words—and we really only had one bit per sample. In this case, we have three values or two bits per sample. Plenty of information! Yes, we can make out the words pretty clearly.

We have now seen that we can put speech information inside a picture. How many pictures on the Internet actually have speech hidden inside them, perhaps using a more sophisticated mapping between samples and pixels? The key idea here is that the speech information is just *information* that can be represented in multiple media.

12.4   USING LISTS AS STRUCTURED TEXT FOR MEDIA REPRESENTATIONS

Lists, as we have already said, are very powerful. It's pretty easy to go from sound to lists.

Program 152: Map Sounds to Lists

```
def soundToList(sound):
  list = []
  for s in getSamples(sound):
    list = list + [getSampleValue(s)]
  return list

>>> list = soundToList(sound)
>>> print list[0]
6757
>>> print list[1]
6852
>>> print list[0:100]
```

```
[6757, 6852, 6678, 6371, 6084, 5879, 6066, 6600,
7104, 7588, 7643, 7710, 7737, 7214, 7435, 7827,
7749, 6888, 5052, 2793, 406, -346, 80, 1356, 2347,
1609, 266, -1933, -3518, -4233, -5023, -5744,
-7394, -9255, -10421, -10605, -9692, -8786, -8198,
-8133, -8679, -9092, -9278, -9291, -9502, -9680,
-9348, -8394, -6552, -4137, -1878, -101, 866, 1540,
2459, 3340, 4343, 4821, 4676, 4211, 3731, 4359, 5653,
7176, 8411, 8569, 8131, 7167, 6150, 5204, 3951, 2482,
818, -394, -901, -784, -541, -764, -1342, -2491,
-3569, -4255, -4971, -5892, -7306, -8691, -9534,
-9429, -8289, -6811, -5386, -4454, -4079, -3841,
-3603, -3353, -3296, -3323, -3099, -2360]
```

Going from pictures to lists is similarly easy—we simply have to define our representation. How about mapping each pixel as its *X* and *Y* positions, then its red, green, and blue channels? We have to use double square brackets because we want these five values as sublists inside the big list.

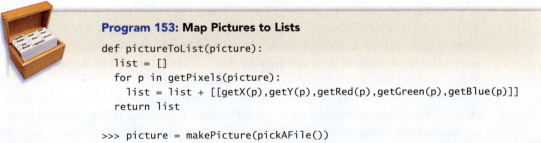

Program 153: Map Pictures to Lists

```
def pictureToList(picture):
  list = []
  for p in getPixels(picture):
    list = list + [[getX(p),getY(p),getRed(p),getGreen(p),getBlue(p)]]
  return list

>>> picture = makePicture(pickAFile())
>>> piclist = pictureToList(picture)
```

```
>>> print piclist[0:5]
[[1, 1, 168, 131, 105], [1, 2, 168, 131, 105], [1, 3, 169,
132, 106], [1, 4, 169, 132, 106], [1, 5, 170, 133, 107]]
```

Going back again is also easy. We simply have to make sure that our *X* and *Y* positions are within the bounds of our canvas.

Program 154: Map Lists to Pictures

```
def listToPicture(list):
  picture = makePicture(getMediaPath("640x480.jpg"))
  for p in list:
    if p[0] <= getWidth(picture) and p[1]<= getHeight(picture):
      setColor(getPixel(picture,p[0],p[1]),makeColor(p[2],p[3],p[4]))
  return picture
```

We can figure out that this will work because we can see how the mapping works both ways and then consider just the mapping from lists to pictures. The numbers don't *have* to have come from a picture. We could just as easily have mapped from weather data or stock ticker data or just about anything into a list of numbers that we then visualize. It's all bits . . .

All we're really doing here is changing the encoding. We're not changing the base information at all. Different encodings offer us different capabilities.

A really smart mathematician, Kurt Gödel, used the notion of encodings to come up with one of the most brilliant proofs of the 20th century. He proved the **Incompleteness theorem**, thereby demonstrating that any powerful mathematical system cannot prove all mathematical truths. He figured out a mapping from mathematical statements of truth to numbers. This was long before we had ASCII, where such mappings are commonplace. Once these statements were numbers, he was able to show that there are numbers representing true statements that could not be derived from the mathematical system. In this way, he showed that no system of logic can prove all true statements. By changing his encoding, he gained new capabilities, and thus was able to prove something that no one knew before.

Claude Shannon was an American engineer and mathematician who developed *information theory*. Information theory describes how information can be represented in different media. When we map a picture into text or sounds, we are applying information theory.

12.5 HIDING INFORMATION IN A PICTURE

Steganography is about hiding information in ways that can't be easily detected. If we have a text message displayed in black on a white picture, we can hide it inside another picture. We will do this by first changing all the red values in the original picture to even. Then we will loop through the pixels of the text we want to hide and if the pixel color is close to black, then we will make the red value odd in the modified picture.

Program 155: Encoding the Message

```
def encode(msgPic,original):
  # Assume msgPic and original have same dimensions
  # First, make all red pixels even
  for pxl in getPixels(original):
    # Using modulo operator to test oddness
    if (getRed(pxl) % 2) == 1:
      setRed(pxl, getRed(pxl) - 1)
  # Second, wherever there's black in msgPic
  # make odd the red in the corresponding original pixel
  for x in range(0,getWidth(original)):
    for y in range(0,getHeight(original)):
      msgPxl = getPixel(msgPic,x,y)
      origPxl = getPixel(original,x,y)
      if (distance(getColor(msgPxl),black) < 100.0):
        # It's a message pixel! Make the red value odd.
        setRed(origPxl, getRed(origPxl)+1)
```

Now we can hide a message in the picture of the beach by doing the following.

```
>>> beach = makePicture(getMediaPath("beach.jpg"))
>>> explore(beach)
>>> msg = makePicture(getMediaPath("msg.jpg"))
>>> encode(msg,beach)
>>> explore(beach)
>>> writePictureTo(beach,getMediaPath("beachHidden.png"))
```

You should save the picture using either the png or bmp format. Don't save the picture using the JPEG (jpg) format. The JPEG standard is lossy, which means that it doesn't save the picture exactly as originally specified. It throws away detail (like specific red values) that you normally wouldn't notice but in this case we want to save the picture exactly as it is so that we can decode it later.

Can you detect any difference between the original picture of the beach and the one with the message hidden in it (Figure 12.5)? We doubt it.

Now let's get back out the hidden message. Here is the function to do that.

Program 156: Decoding the Message

```
def decode(encodedImg):
  # Takes in an encoded image. Return the original message
  message = makeEmptyPicture(getWidth(encodedImg),getHeight(encodedImg))
  for x in range(0,getWidth(encodedImg)):
    for y in range(0,getHeight(encodedImg)):
      encPxl = getPixel(encodedImg,x,y)
      msgPxl = getPixel(message,x,y)
```

FIGURE 12.5
The original picture (*left*) and the picture with the hidden message (*right*).

```
    if (getRed(encPxl) % 2) == 1:
        setColor(msgPxl,black)
return message
```

■

We can decode the message using the following code. You should be able to read the resulting message (Figure 12.6).

```
>>> origMsg = decode(beach)
>>> explore(origMsg)
```

12.5.1   Hiding a Sound Inside a Picture

We figured out a while ago that we can use just one bit per sample to record completely understandable speech. We just figured out that we can change the red part of a pixel between even and odd (0 and 1) without seeing a change in the picture. We can combine these two facts to hide sound inside a picture.

Program 157: Encode a Sound in a Picture

```
def encodeSound(sound,picture):
  soundIndex = 0
  for p in getPixels(picture):
    # Clear out the red LSB
    r = getRed(p)
    if ((r % 2) == 1):
      setRed(p,r-1)
  for p in getPixels(picture):
    # Did we run out of sound?
    if soundIndex == getLength(sound):
      break
    # Get the sample value
```

FIGURE 12.6
The decoded message.

```
value = getSampleValueAt(sound,soundIndex)
if value > 0:
  setRed(p,getRed(p)+1)
soundIndex = soundIndex + 1
```

How It Works

We input a sound (like `"thisisatest.wav"`) and a picture. To encode the whole sound, we need to have more pixels in the picture than there are samples in the sound. We first walk through all the pixels and clear out the least significant bit (the even/odd bit) from the red part of each pixel. We then have a second loop. If we reach the end of the sound, we `break`. Otherwise, we get the sample value, and test to see if it's positive. If it is, we add one to the red component of the corresponding pixel. We go on to the next `soundIndex` and the next pixel p in the `for` loop.

Here's how it looks to encode:

```
>>> t = makeSound("thisisatest.wav")
>>> p = makePicture("llama.jpg")
>>> explore(p)
>>> encodeSound(t,p)
```

FIGURE 12.7
The original llama (*left*), and the llama (*right*) with the sound encoded in it.

The llama picture before and after encoding appears in Figure 12.7. We really can't tell that the sound is in there.

Decoding a sound is the reverse process. We check each pixel, and if the red is odd, put a large positive value in the corresponding sample. If the red is even, put a large negative value in the corresponding sound sample.

```
>>> newt = decodeSound(p)
>>> explore(newt)
```

As you might imagine, we can hear the words again after decoding.

Program 158: Decode a Sound from a Picture

```
def decodeSound(picture):
  sound = makeEmptySoundBySeconds(5)
  sndIndex = 0
  for p in getPixels(picture):
    # Did we run out of sound?
    if sndIndex == getLength(sound):
      break
    # Is it mostly red, mostly blue, or mostly green?
    if ((getRed(p) % 2) == 1):
      setSampleValueAt(sound,sndIndex,32000)
    else:
      setSampleValueAt(sound,sndIndex,-32000)
    sndIndex = sndIndex + 1
  return(sound)
```

PROGRAMMING SUMMARY
GENERAL PROGRAM PIECES

`while`	Creates a loop. Executes the body iteratively as long as the provided logical expression is true (i.e., not zero).
`try:except:pass`	Attempt to execute the statements in the block after `try:`. If any errors occur, pass on to the next value in the loop.
`break`	Breaks a loop immediately—jumps to the end of the `for` or `while`.
`urllib, ftplib`	Module for using URLs or FTP access.
`csv`	Module for manipulating CSV (comma-separated value) files.
`str`	Converts numbers (or other objects) to their string representations.
`float`	Converts a number or string to its floating-point equivalent representation.

PROBLEMS

12.1   Go to a page with a lot of text in it, like `http://www.cnn.com` and use your browser's menus to SAVE the file as something like **myPage.html**. Edit the file using JES or even an editor like Windows Notepad. Find some text in the page that you can see when you view the page, like a headline or article text. *Change it!* Instead of "protesters" rioting, make it "College students" or even "kindergarteners." Now OPEN that file in your browser. You've just rewritten the news!

12.2   Create a function that visits a news page (maybe for your college) and pulls out all the headers by Web scraping. Put them all in a text file.

12.3   Create a function that pulls a sound from a URL using `urllib` and creates a sound clip saved on your local machine.

12.4   Create a function that pulls a picture from a URL and creates a thumbnail saved on your local machine.

12.5   Match the letter of the definition next to the appropriate phrase below. *(Yes, you will have one unused definition.)*

____ **Domain Name Server** ____ **Web Server** ____ **HTTP** ____ **HTML**
____ **Client** ____ **IP Address** ____ **FTP** ____ **URL**

(a) A computer that matches names like *www.cnn.com* to their addresses on the Internet.

(b) A protocol used to move files between computers (e.g., from your personal computer to a larger computer that acts as a Web server).

(c) A string that explains how (what protocol) and on what machine (domain name) and where on the machine (path) a particular file can be found on the Internet.

(d) A computer that offers files through HTTP.

(e) The protocol on which most of the Web is built, a very simple form aimed at rapid transmission of small bits of information.

(f) What a browser (like Internet Explorer) is when contacting a server like *google.com*.

(g) The tags that go into Web pages to identify parts of the page and how they should be formatted.

(h) A protocol used for transmitting electronic mail between computers.

(i) The numeric identifier of a computer on the Internet—four numbers between 0 and 255, like *120.32.189.12*.

12.6 For each of the following, see if you can figure out the representation in terms of bits and bytes.

(a) Internet addresses are four numbers, each between 0 and 255. How many bits are in an Internet address?

(b) In the ancient programming language Basic, lines can be numbered, each one between 0 and 65,535. How many bits are needed to represent a line number?

(c) Each pixel's color has three components, red, green, and blue, each of which can be between 0 and 255. How many bits are needed to represent a pixel's color?

(d) A string in some systems can only be up to 1,024 characters. How many bits are needed to represent the length of a string?

12.7 What is a domain name server? What does it do?

12.8 Investigate how you would buy a domain name (like "mycooldomainname.org") and register it so that other users could find it. How long does it take your new domain name to be recognized across the Internet?

12.9 Why does it take any time at all for domain names to be accessible across the Internet?

12.10 What are FTP, SMTP, and HTTP? What are they each used for?

12.11 What is HyperText? Who invented it?

12.12 What is the difference between a client and a server?

12.13 How does knowing how to manipulate text help you in gathering and creating information on the Internet?

12.14 What is a Denial of Service Attack? Could you write a program to generate one?

12.15 What is an ISP? Can you give an example of one?

12.16 *The Guardian*'s Web site includes CSV data on how often the groundhog correctly predicts Spring on *Groundhog Day*. Write a program to grab that CSV file and add up the number of corrects and the number of incorrect predictions. Is the groundhog more accurate than chance (50%)?

12.17   Is it possible to hide a color picture in another color picture? Why or why not?

12.18   If you erase lower *two* bits in the red value, you can clear space for hiding values 0–4.

```
for p in getPixels(picture):
    # Clear out the red 2xLSB
    r = getRed(p)
    setRed(p,r-(r%4))
```

If you erase the lower two bits from red, green, and blue, you can save six bits. Six bits can encode 64 values. That's enough to encode all 27 letters, both upper and lowercase.

(a) Write a function to input a picture and a string. Save each character in the string in a pixel of the picture, by saving it across the least significant two bits in each of red, green, and blue. Can you tell the difference between the original picture and the picture with the encoded text message?

(b) Now write a function to decode the original text.

12.19   We can be trickier about how we encode text. Imagine that you (the sender) of the message and the receiver have a hidden sentence containing all the characters you might need in a coded message, like "The quick brown fox jumps over the lazy cat." You can now just encode the position of the character you want in the picture (e.g., a "t" could be 0 and an "h" could be 1). You don't even need six bits for this encoding. Rewrite the encoding and decoding function from the last exercise to use a hidden sentence for encoding.

TO DIG DEEPER

The book that Mark uses for making his way through the Python modules is Frederik Lundh's *Python Standard Library* [16]. You can find the listing of library modules, with their documentation, at `http://docs.python.org/library/`.

Making Text for the Web

Chapter Learning Objectives

The media learning goals for this chapter are:

- To gain some basic skill with HTML.
- To automatically generate HTML for input data, like an index page for a directory of images.
- To use databases to generate Web content.

The computer science goals for this chapter are:

- To use another number base, hexadecimal, for specifying RGB colors.
- To distinguish between XML and HTML.
- To explain what SQL is, and what it has to do with relational databases.
- To create and use subfunctions (utility functions).
- To demonstrate one use for hash tables (dictionaries).

13.1 HTML: THE NOTATION OF THE WEB

The World Wide Web is mostly text and most of the text is in the specification language **HTML (hypertext markup language)**. HTML is based on **SGML (standard generalized markup language)**, which is a way of adding additional text to one's text to identify logical parts of the document: "This here is the title," "This here is a heading," and "This is just a plain ol' paragraph." Originally, HTML (like SGML) was supposed to just identify logical parts of a document—how it *looked* was up to the browser. Documents were *expected* to look different from one browser to another. But as the Web evolved, two separate goals developed: being able to specify *lots* of logical parts (e.g., prices, part numbers, stocker ticker codes, temperatures), and being able to control formatting very carefully.

For the first goal, **XML (extensible markup language)** evolved. This allows you to define new tags like `<partnumber>7834JK</partnumber>`. For the second goal, things like **cascading style sheets** were developed. Yet another markup language, **XHTML**, was developed, which is HTML defined in terms of XML. XHTML is nearly identical to HTML 4.01. Today, we have HTML 5, which is supported on nearly every browser. For the most part, HTML 5 will accept XHTML as well. We'll focus on HTML 5, ignore the subtle distinctions, and talk about it as "HTML."

We're not going to have a complete tutorial for HTML here. There are many of these available, both in print and on the Web, and many are high quality. Enter "HTML tutorial" into your favorite search engine and take your pick. Instead, we'll talk here about some general notions of HTML, and mention the tags that you should really know.

A markup language means that text is inserted into the original text to identify the parts. In HTML, the inserted text (called **tags**) is delimited with angle brackets: less-than and greater-than signs. For example, <p> starts a paragraph, and </p> ends a paragraph.

Web pages have several parts, and the parts nest within each other. The first is a **doctype** right at the top of the page that announces the *kind* of page this is (i.e., whether the browser should try to interpret it as HTML5, XHTML, or something else). Following the doctype comes a head (<head>...</head>) and a body (<body>...</body>). The heading can contain information like the title *nested* within it—the ending of the title comes before the ending of the head. The body has many pieces nested within it, such as headings (**h1** starts and ends before the body ends) and paragraphs. All of the body and head nests within an <html>...</html> set of tags. Figure 13.1 shows a simple Web page's source and Figure 13.2 shows how the page appears in the open source browser, WebKit.[1]

Try this yourself. You can type in the text in Figure 13.1 into any text editor. Notepad on Windows works fine. On Mac OS X, you will probably want to get an application like TextWrangler or Sublime Text. But if you can't get any of those, JES will actually work as a plain text editor, too. Simply type in the HTML, save it with an .html file suffix, and then open it in a Web browser. The only difference between this file and any Web page is that this file lives on your disk. If it were on a Web server, it would be a Web page.

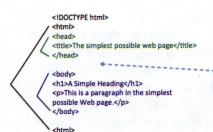

FIGURE 13.1
Simple HTML page source.

[1] https://www.webkit.org

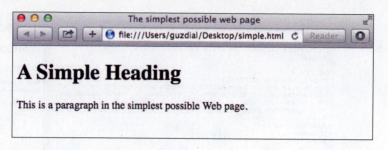

FIGURE 13.2
Simple HTML page open in open source Web browser WebKit.

Common Bug: Browsers Are Forgiving but Usually Wrong
Browsers are very forgiving. If you forget the DOCTYPE or make mistakes in the HTML, a browser will literally guess at what you meant and then try to show it. Murphy's Law, though, says that it will guess *wrong*. If you want your Web page to look just the way you want, get the HTML right.

Here are some of the tags that you should know well:

- The `<body>` tag can take parameters to set the background, text, and link colors. These colors can be simple color names like "red" or "green" or they can be specific RGB colors.

  You specify colors in **hexadecimal**. Hexadecimal is a number system with base 16, whereas the decimal number system is base 10. The decimal numbers 1 to 20 translate to hexadecimal 1, 2, 3, 4, 5, 6, 7, 8, 9, A, B, C, D, E, F, 10, 11, 12, 13, and 14. Think of hexadecimal "14" as one and 16 plus 4 ones gives a result of 20.

  The advantage of hexadecimal is that each digit corresponds to four bits. Two hexadecimal digits correspond to a byte. Thus, the three bytes of RGB colors are six hexadecimal digits, in RGB order. Hexadecimal FF0000 is red—255 (FF) for red, 0 for green, and 0 for blue. 0000FF is blue, 000000 is black, and FFFFFF is white.

- Headings are specified using tags `<h1>...</h1>` through `<h6>...</h6>`. Smaller numbers are more prominent.

- There are lots of tags for different kinds of styles: emphasis `<em>...</em>`, italics `<i>...</i>`, boldface `<b>...</b>`, bigger `<big>...</big>` and smaller `<small>...</small>` fonts, typewriter font `<tt>...</tt>`, preformatted text `<pre>...</pre>`, block quotes `<blockquote>...</blockquote>`, subscripts `<sub>...</sub>`, and superscripts `<sup>...</sup>`. See Figure 13.3 for demonstration of some of these. You can also control things like font and color using the `<font>...</font>` tags.

  Many of these are contrary to the original plan of HTML, to be a notation for the *structure* of a document but not the *appearance*. But people want to be able to control these aspects of their document, so these style tags were added in.

- You can insert breaks without new paragraphs using `<br />`.

FIGURE 13.3
HTML styles, editing the source in JES, viewing in WebKit.

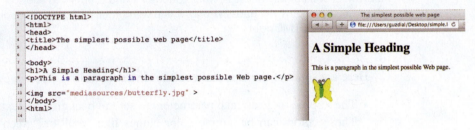

FIGURE 13.4
Inserting an image into an HTML page.

- You use the `<image src="image.jpg">` tag to insert images (Figure 13.4). The `image` tag takes an image as an `src=` parameter. What comes after that is an image specification, in one of several forms.

    - If it's just a filename (like **flower1.jpg** or **butterfly.jpg**), then it's assumed to be an image in the same directory as the HTML file referencing it.

    - If it's a path, it's assumed to be a path *from the same directory as the HTML page* to that image. So if there was an HTML page in MY DOCUMENTS that referenced an image in the **mediasources** directory, we might have a reference to **mediasources/flower1.jpg**. You can use UNIX conventions here (e.g., "`..`" references the parent directory, so **../images/flower1.jpg** would say to go to the parent directory, then down to **images** to grab image **flower1.jpg**).

    - It can also be a complete URL—you can reference images entirely on other servers.

    You can also manipulate the width and height of images with options to the image tag (e.g., `<image height="100" src="flower.jpg">` to limit the height to 100 pixels) and adjust the width so that the picture keeps its height:width ratio. Using the option `alt` you can specify text to be displayed if the image can't be displayed (e.g., for audio or Braille browsers).

- You use the *anchor tag* `<a href="someplace.html">anchor text</a>` to create links from anchor text somewhere else. In this example, `someplace.html` is the *target* for the anchor—it's where you go when you click on the *anchor*. The *anchor* is what you click on. It can be text, like `anchor text`, or it can be an image. As seen in Figure 13.5, the target can also be a complete URL.

  Note, too, in Figure 13.5, that line breaks in the source file don't show up in the browser. We can even have line breaks in the middle of an anchor tag and they don't affect the view. The breaks that *matter* (i.e., that show up in the browser view) are generated by tags like `<br />` and `<p>`.

- You create bullet lists (*unordered lists*) and numbered lists (*ordered lists*) using the `<ul>...</ul>` and `<ol>...</ol>` tags, respectively. Individual items are specified using tags `<li>...</li>`.

- Tables are created using `<table>...</table>` tags. Tables are constructed out of table rows using `<tr>...</tr>` tags, and each row consists of several table data items identified with `<td>...</td>` tags (Figure 13.6). Tables contain rows and rows contain table data items.

There is *lots* more to HTML, such as frames (having subwindows within one's HTML page window), divisions (`<div />`), horizontal rules (`<hr />`), applets and JavaScript. The items listed above are the most critical for understanding the rest of this chapter.

```
1  <!DOCTYPE html>
2  <html>
3  <head>
4  <title>The simplest possible web page</title>
5  </head>
6
7  <body>
8  <h1>A Simple Heading</h1>
9  <p>This is a paragraph in the simplest possible Web page.</p>
10
11 <img src="mediasources/butterfly.jpg" alt="Drawn butterfly">
12
13 <p>Here is a link to <a href="http://www.mediacomputation.org">
14 The Media Computation Page</a>.
15 </p>
16 </body>
17 <html>
18
```

FIGURE 13.5
An HTML page with a link in it.

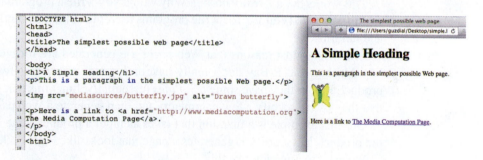

```
<table border="5">

<tr><td>Column
   1</td><td>Column
   2</td></tr>

<tr><td>Element in column
   1</td><td>Element in
   column 2</td></tr>

</table>
```

FIGURE 13.6
Inserting a table into an HTML page.

13.2   WRITING PROGRAMS TO GENERATE HTML

HTML itself is not a programming language. HTML can't specify loops, conditionals, variables, data types, or anything else we've learned about specifying process. HTML is used to describe structure, not process.

That said, we can easily write programs to generate HTML. Python's multiple ways of quoting strings come in *really* handy here!

Program 159: Generating a Simple HTML Page

```
def makePage():
  file=open("generated.html","wt")
  file.write("""<!DOCTYPE html>

<html>
<head> <title>The Simplest Possible Web Page</title>
</head>
<body>
<h1>A Simple Heading</h1>
<p>Some simple text.</p>
</body>
</html>""")
  file.close()
```

This works but it's really boring. Why would you write a program to write what you can do with a text editor? You write programs for replicability, communicating process, and tailoring.

One of the most reasons that Web pages are generated are for *catalogs*. Web sites like Amazon and E-Bay don't really have individual Web pages for each and every product. Rather they have some *templates* (essentially, functions that generate HTML) that they use to specify a few parameters and then generate a Web page.

Our first example is a function that takes as input a product name, an image file for the product, and a price. It generates a page that looks like Figure 13.7.

We call this function like this:

```
>>> makeCatalog("Seahorses","seahorses.jpg",32.75)
```

Program 160: A Catalog Page Generator

```
def makeCatalog(product, image, price):
  file=open(getMediaPath("catalog.html"),"wt")
  body = """<!DOCTYPE html>
<html>
<head>
<title>Catalog Page for:"""+ product+'''</title>
</head>
<body>
<h1>'''+product+""" is the greatest!</h1>
<p>You are so lucky to have found this page!
You have the opportunity to buy """+product+"""
```

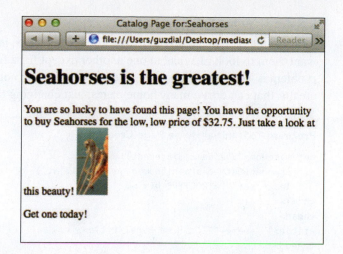

FIGURE 13.7
A sample catalog product page.

```
for the low, low price of $"""+str(price)+'''.
Just take a look at this beauty!
<img src="'''+image+'''" height = 100></p>
<p>Get one today!</p>
</body>
</html>'''
  file.write(body)
  file.close()
```

How It Works

Our function `makeCatalog` takes in a `product`, `image`, and `price`. We open a writable text file in the media folder named "*catalog.html*." We then make up a really big string named body.

- We use triple quotes so that we can put in returns within the string. We sometimes use triple double-quotes and sometimes triple single-quotes in order to make it easier to understand the quote marks inside the HTML.

- We escape the string to insert the `product` name into the title *Catalog Page for:* (in our case) *Seahorses*. Clearly, the program expects a singular product, not a plural. The sentences are grammatically incorrect with a plural word as input. Computers will do just what we tell them to do, even if it's wrong.

- We then expound upon the glories of this product, including the low, low price—which is a floating-point number, so we have to convert it into a string with `str(price)`.

- We again escape the string to insert the actual filename for the image.

After formatting the whole body string, we write it to a file and close the file.

13.2.1   Making Home Pages

Imagine that you and a group of your friends decide to make home pages, and you all want them to look identical to one another except for a few small details. The general problem is like the catalog page generator that we just solved. Let's make a home page creator that can create many home pages, just changing the name and interests.

Program 161: Initial Home Page Creator

```
def makeHomePage(name, interest):
  file=open(getMediaPath("homepage.html"),"wt")
  file.write("""<!DOCTYPE html>
<html>
<head>
<title>"""+name+"""'s Home Page</title>
</head>
<body>
<h1>Welcome to """+name+"""'s Home Page</h1>
<p>Hi!  I am """+name+""".  This is my home page!
I am interested in """+interest+"""</p>
</body>
</html>""")
  file.close()
```

Thus, executing `makeHomePage("Barb","horses")` will create:

```
<!DOCTYPE html>
<html>
<head>
<title>Barb's Home Page</title>
</head>
<body>
<h1>Welcome to Barb's Home Page</h1>
<p>Hi!  I am Barb.  This is my home page!
I am interested in horses</p>
</body>
</html>
```

Debugging Tip: Write the HTML First

Programs to generate HTML can be confusing. Before you start trying to write one, write the HTML. Make up a sample of what you want the HTML to look like. Make sure that it works in your browser. *Then* write the Python function that generates that kind of HTML.

Modifying this program is painful, though. There is so much detail in the HTML and all that quoting is hard to get around. We're better off using *subfunctions* to break up the program into pieces that are easier to manipulate. This is, again, an example of using **procedural abstraction**. Here's a version of the program where we confine the parts that we'll change most often to the top.

Program 162: Improved Home Page Creator

```
def makeHomePage(name, interest):
  file=open(getMediaPath("homepage.html"),"wt")
  file.write(doctype())
  file.write(title(name+"'s Home Page"))
  file.write(body("""
<h1>Welcome to """+name+"""'s Home Page</h1> <p>Hi!  I am
"""+name+""".  This is my home page! I am interested in
"""+interest+"""</p>"""))
  file.close()

def doctype():
  return '<!DOCTYPE html>'

def title(titlestring):
  return "<html><head><title>"+titlestring+"</title></head>"

def body(bodystring):
  return "<body>"+bodystring+"</body></html>"
```

We can grab content for our Web pages from anywhere we want. Here is a program that can pull information out of a directory provided as input and generates an index page of those images (Figure 13.8). We're not going to list the doctype() and other *utility functions* here—we'll just focus on the part we care about. And that is how we should think about it—just the part we care about; we write doctype() once, then forget about it!

Figure 13.8 takes a little explaining. We ran the code that appears below by executing makeSamplePage(getMediaPath("")). Then, we opened the generated file "samples.html." The generated page is all one line—which browsers have no trouble interpreting, but is hard for humans. We inserted some return characters to make it easier to read. The browser page to the right is what is seen when the HTML to the left is opened.

FIGURE 13.8
Creating a thumbnail page.

Program 163: Generate a Thumbnail Page

```
import os

def makeSamplePage(directory):
 samplesFile=open(directory+"/samples.html","wt")
 samplesFile.write(doctype())
 samplesFile.write(title("Samples from "+directory))
 # Now, let's make up the string that will be the body.
 samples="<h1>Samples from "+directory+" </h1>"
 for file in os.listdir(directory):
  if file.endswith(".jpg"):
    samples=samples+"<p>Filename: "+file
    samples=samples+'<image src="'+file+'"height="100"></p>'
 samplesFile.write(body(samples))
 samplesFile.close()
```

We can get content to add to our home pages from a wide range of sources. We could scrape information to add to our pages. In the previous chapters, we have built koan generators and random sentence generator. We can add something like that to our homepage generator. The function `tagline` randomly returns a tag line (a signature line) to the bottom of the home page.

Program 164: Home Page Generator with Random Tag Lines

```
import urllib
import random
```

```
import urllib
import random

def makeHomePage(name,interests):
   file=open(getMediaPath("homepage.html"),"wt")
   file.write(doctype())
   file.write(title(name+"'s Home Page"))
   text = "<h1>Welcome to "+name+"'s Home Page</h1> "
   text += "<p>Hi!  I am "+name+".  This is my home page!"
   text += " I am interested in "+interests+"</p>"
   text += "<p>Random thought for the day: "+tagline()+"</p>"
   file.write(body(text))
   file.close()

def tagline():
   tags = []
   tags += ["After all is said and done, more is said than done."]
   tags += ["Save time... see it my way."]
   tags += ["This message transmitted on 100% recycled electrons."]
   tags += ["Nostalgia isn't what it used to be."]
   tags += ["When you're in up over your head, the first thing to do is close your mouth."]
   tags += ["I hit the CTRL key but I'm still not in control!"]
```

```
tags += ["Willyoupleasehelpmefixmykeyboard?Thespacebarisbroken!"]
return random.choice(tags)
```

How It Works

Let's walk through the whole large example.

- We are going to need both `urllib` and `random` in this function, so we `import` both of them at the top of our Program Area.

- Our main function is `makeHomePage`. We call it with a name and a string of interests, like this:

  ```
  >>> makeHomePage("Dracula","bats and blood")
  ```

- At the top of `makeHomePage`, we open the HTML file we're writing, then write out the `doctype` using the utility function. (It's not listed here, but would have to be in the Program Area). We write out the title (using the `title` function) with the input `name` inserted.

- We build up the body of the page in the string variable `text`. We break it up across several lines to make it more readable. To do that, we use a shorthand in Python. The syntax `+=` means "Append the string on the right to the string variable on the left."

  Read the line:

  ```
  text += "<p>Hi!  I am "+name+".  This is my home page!"
  ```

  as:

  ```
  text = text + "<p>Hi!  I am "+name+".  This is my home page!"
  ```

  Thus, we build up the body in the string `text` with a heading, a paragraph with the owner's name, a statement about interests, and the random tag line. We write out the `name` and the return values from the functions by concatenating them into the middle of the HTML string. We then write that to the Web page body (using the `body` function).

- The function `tagline` creates a list of strings (using the same `+=` shorthand, but with a list of strings), then randomly chooses one (using the library function `random.choice`). Each time `tagline` is called, it returns a string with a random tagline.

  ```
  >>> tagline()
  "I hit the CTRL key but I'm still not in control!"
  >>> tagline()
  'Save time... see it my way.'
  ```

- Finally, back at `makeHomePage`, we close the HTML file, and we're done.

13.3 DATABASES: A PLACE TO STORE OUR TEXT

Large Web sites don't use big functions with all the values defined in them (like how we did our `tagline` function). Where do you think large Web sites get all their information? There are *so* many pages in those Web sites. Where do they get it all? Where do they store it all?

Large Web sites use **databases** to store their text and other information. Sites like eBay.com, Amazon.com, and CNN.com have large databases with lots of information in them. The pages at these sites aren't generated by somebody typing in information. Instead, programs walk over the database gathering all the information and generating HTML pages. They may do this on a timed basis, to keep updating the page.

Why databases rather than simple text files? There are four reasons:

- Databases are fast. Databases store *indices* that keep track of where key information (like last name or ID number) is in a file, so that you can find "Guzdial" right away. Files are indexed on filename but not on the content *in* the file.

- Databases are standardized. You can access the Microsoft Access, Informix, Oracle, Sybase, and MySQL databases from any number of tools or languages.

- Databases can be **distributed**. A great many users, on different computers across a network, can put information into a database and pull information out of it.

- Databases store **relations**. When we used lists to represent pixels, we had to keep in our heads which number meant what. Databases store names for *fields* of data. When a database knows which fields are important (e.g., which ones you're going to search on most often), it can be indexed on those fields.

Python has built-in support for several different databases and provides a general support for any kind of database called anydbm.

```
>>> # Get the database library
>>> import anydbm
>>> # Make a database
>>> db = anydbm.open(getMediaPath("mydbm"),"c")
>>> # Stores the string about Wilma under the key "fred"
>>> db["fred"] = "My wife is Wilma."
>>> db["barney"] = "My wife is Betty."
>>> db.close()
```

Keys go in square brackets and those are the fields that you get the fastest access through. Both keys and values can only be strings using anydbm. Here's an example of retrieving information from anydbm.

```
>>> db = anydbm.open(getMediaPath("mydbm"),"r")
>>> print db.keys()
['barney', 'fred']
>>> print db['barney']
My wife is Betty.
>>> for k in db.keys():
...          print db[k]
...
My wife is Betty.
My wife is Wilma.
>>> db.close()
```

Another standard Python database, shelve, allows you to put strings, lists, numbers, or just about anything in the value. The database shelve is useful because it's standard Python—it's always available. However, it is *not* a relational database.

```
>>> import shelve
>>> db=shelve.open(getMediaPath("myshelf"),"c")
```

```
>>> db["one"]=["This is",["a","list"]]
>>> db["two"]=12
>>> db.close()
>>> db=shelve.open(getMediaPath("myshelf"),"r")
>>> print db.keys()
['two', 'one']
>>> print db['one']
['This is', ['a', 'list']]
>>> print db['two']
12
```

13.3.1   Relational Databases

Most modern databases are **relational databases**. In relational databases, information is stored in tables (Figure 13.9). Columns in a relational table are named and rows of data are assumed to be related.

Complex relationships are stored across multiple tables. Let's say that you have a bunch of pictures of students and you want to keep track of which students are in which pictures—where there is more than one student in a given picture. You might record a structure like that in a collection of tables for recording students and student IDs, pictures and picture IDs, then the mapping between student IDs and picture IDs, as in Figure 13.10.

Fields

Name	Age
Mark	40
Matthew	11
Brian	38

The implied relation of this row is that Mark is 40 years old.

FIGURE 13.9
An example relational table.

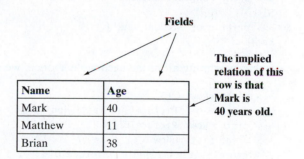

Picture	PictureID
Class1.jpg	P1
Class2.jpg	P2

StudentName	StudentID
Katie	S1
Brittany	S2
Carrie	S3

PictureID	StudentID
P1	S1
P1	S2
P2	S3

FIGURE 13.10
Representing more complex relationships across multiple tables.

How would you use tables like the one in Figure 13.10 to figure out which picture Brittany is in? You start up by looking up Brittany's ID in the student table, then look up the picture ID in the picture-student table, then look up the picture name in the picture table, to result in **Class1.jpg**. How about figuring out who's in that picture? You look up the ID in the picture table, then look up which student IDs are related to that picture ID, and then look up the student names.

This use of multiple tables to answer a **query** (a request for information from a database) is called a **join**. Database joins work best if the tables are kept simple, with only a single relation per row.

13.3.2   An Example Relational Database Using Hash Tables

To explain relational database ideas, this section builds a relational database using a simpler structure in Python. In this way, we can describe how some database ideas, like joins, work. This section is optional.

We can use a structure called a **hash table** or **dictionary** (other languages sometimes call them *associative arrays*) to create rows for database relational tables using shelve. Hash tables allow us to relate keys and values, like databases, but only in memory.

```
>>> row={'StudentName':'Katie','StudentID':'S1'}
>>> print row
{'StudentID': 'S1', 'StudentName': 'Katie'}
>>> print row['StudentID']
S1
>>> print row['StudentName']
Katie
```

Besides defining all of the hash table at once, we can fill in the hash table in pieces.

```
>>> pictureRow = {}
>>> pictureRow['Picture']='Class1.jpg'
>>> pictureRow['PictureID']='P1'
>>> print pictureRow
{'Picture': 'Class1.jpg', 'PictureID': 'P1'}
>>> print pictureRow['Picture']
Class1.jpg
```

Now we can create a relational database by storing each table in a separate shelve database and representing each row as a hash table.

Program 165: Creating a Relational Database Using shelve

```
import shelve
def createDatabases():
  #Create Student Database
  students=shelve.open(getMediaPath("students.db"),"c")
  row = {'StudentName':'Katie','StudentID':'S1'}
  students['S1']=row
  row = {'StudentName':'Brittany','StudentID':'S2'}
  students['S2']=row
```

```
row = {'StudentName':'Carrie','StudentID':'S3'}
students['S3']=row
students.close()
#Create Picture Database
pictures=shelve.open(getMediaPath("pictures.db"),"c")
row = {'Picture':'Class1.jpg','PictureID':'P1'}
pictures['P1']=row
row = {'Picture':'Class2.jpg','PictureID':'P2'}
pictures['P2']=row
pictures.close()
#Create Picture-Student Database
pictures=shelve.open(getMediaPath("pict-students.db"),"c")
row = {'PictureID':'P1','StudentID':'S1'}
pictures['P1S1']=row
row = {'PictureID':'P1','StudentID':'S2'}
pictures['P1S2']=row
row = {'PictureID':'P2','StudentID':'S3'}
pictures['P2S3']=row
pictures.close()
```

How It Works

The function `createDatabases` actually creates three different database tables.

- The first one is **students.db**. We create dictionaries (hash tables) representing Katie, who is "S1," then store that in the database `students` using the student ID "S1" as the index. We do the same for Brittany and Carrie—it's okay to use the same `row` variable for each of them, because we simply create the hash table and then store it to the database.

- Next we create the **pictures.db** database. We set up the relationship between the "Picture" **Class1.jpg** and its ID "P1." Then we store that in the `pictures` database. We repeat the process for the picture **Class2.jpg**. Could we have used a variable `database` for each database? Since we only open one at a time, then close it before the next one, we certainly could have. But it would have been less readable.

- Finally, we open and fill the **pict-students.db** database. We create rows relating the picture IDs to the student IDs, store them in the database, then close the database.

Using the databases we just created, we can do a *join*. Obviously, the idea is that we would be doing this lookup sometime after creating the database, and may be after adding lots more entries to it. (If we only had two pictures and three students in the database, this would be a pretty silly exercise in programming.) We have to loop through the data to find the values we need to match across databases.

Program 166: Doing a Join with Our `shelve` Database

```
def whoInClass1():
  # Get the pictureID
```

```
pictures=shelve.open(getMediaPath("pictures.db"),"r")
for key in pictures.keys():
  row = pictures[key]
  if row['Picture'] == 'Class1.jpg':
    id = row['PictureID']
pictures.close()
# Get the students' IDs
studentslist=[]
pictures=shelve.open(getMediaPath("pict-students.db"),"c")
for key in pictures.keys():
  row = pictures[key]
  if row['PictureID']==id:
    studentslist.append(row['StudentID'])
pictures.close()
print "We're looking for:",studentslist
# Get the students' names
students = shelve.open(getMediaPath("students.db"),"r")
for key in students.keys():
  row = students[key]
  if row['StudentID'] in studentslist:
    print row['StudentName'],"is in the picture"
students.close()
```

How It Works

Each of the parts of the join requires a different loop through our database.

- First, we open **pictures.db** and name it `pictures`. We loop through all the `keys`, getting each `row` (hash table), and checking if the `'Picture'` entry is **Class1.jpg**. When we find it, we store the picture ID in `id`. We close the database because we're done with it.

- Next, we open **pict-students.db** in `pictures` (it's okay to reuse the name). We know that there may be more than one student in a picture, so we create a list to store all the student IDs that we find, `studentslist`. For each key in `pictures`, we look for `"PictureID"` entries in the hash table that match our `id`. When we find one, we `append` the `"StudentID"` part of the hash table onto our `studentslist`.

- Finally, we open the **students.db** database in `students`. We loop through all the `keys` and get the hash table `row`. We use a neat feature of lists that we haven't seen previously: we can ask whether a string is `in` the list `studentslist`. If the given `'StudentID'` is one of those that we're looking for (in `studentslist`), then we print the corresponding `'StudentName'` from the `row` hash table. Finally, we close the `students` database to clean up.

Running this looks like this:

```
>>> whoInClass1()
We're looking for: ['S2', 'S1']
Brittany is in the picture
Katie is in the picture
```

13.3.3   Working with SQL

Real databases don't make you do loops to do joins. Instead, you typically use **SQL** (**Structured Query Language**) to manipulate and query databases. There are actually several languages in the SQL database language family but we're not going to make distinctions here. SQL is a large and complex programming language and we're not going to even attempt to go over all of it. But we are going to touch on enough of it to give you a sense of what SQL is like and how it's used.

SQL can be used with many different databases, including Microsoft Access. Python can talk to virtually all of them in the way that we'll be using it here. There are also freely available databases like **MySQL** that use SQL and can be controlled from Python. If you want to play with the examples we'll be doing here, you can install *MySQL* from `http://www.mysql.com` into JES. You need to set up MySQL, and you need to download the *JAR file* that allows Java to access MySQL and put that in your **JythonLib** folder.

To manipulate a MySQL database from JES, you need to create a *connection* that will provide you with a *cursor* to manipulate via SQL. Just as a cursor on the screen records where you're typing or copying (on what line, at what characters), the database cursor keeps track of where we are in the database. We use MySQL from JES with a function like the one below, so that we can execute `con = getConnection()`.

Program 167: Getting a MySQL Connection from Jython

We find all these details hard to remember, so we hide them in a function and just say `con = getConnection()` with the below in the Program Area.

```
from com.ziclix.python.sql import zxJDBC

def getConnection():
  db =zxJDBC.connect("jdbc:mysql://localhost/test", "root",
  None, "com.mysql.jdbc.Driver")
  con = db.cursor()
  return con
```

To execute SQL commands from here, we use an `execute` method on the connection. The method `execute` takes a string as input which are SQL commands. Here is an example:

```
con.execute("create table Person (name VARCHAR(50), age INT)")
```

Here's a very brief taste of SQL:

- To create a table in SQL, we use `create table tablename (columnname datatype,...)`. So in the example above, we're creating a *Person* table with two columns: a name with a variable number of characters up to 50 and an integer age. Other datatypes include numeric, float, date, time, year, and text.

- We insert data into SQL using `insert into tablename values (column-value1, columnvalue2,...)`. Here's where our multiple kinds of quotes come in handy.

```
con.execute('insert into Person values
   ("Mark",40)')
```

- Think about selecting data in a database as literally selecting, as you would in a word-processor or a spreadsheet, the rows that you want in the table. Some examples of selection commands in SQL are:

```
Select * from Person
Select name,age from Person
Select * from Person where age>40
Select name,age from Person where age>40
```

We can do all of this from Python. Our connection has an **instance variable** (like a method, but known only to objects of that type), rowcount, that tells you the number of rows selected. The method fetchone() gives you the next selected row, as a **tuple** (think of this as a special kind of list—we can use it just like a list for most purposes).

```
>>> con.execute("select name,age from Person")
>>> print con.rowcount
3
>>> print con.fetchone()
('Mark', 40)
>>> print con.fetchone()
('Barb', 41)
>>> print con.fetchone()
('Brian', 36)
```

We can also select using a condition.

Program 168: Selecting and Showing Data with a Conditional Select

```
def showSomePersons(con, condition):
  con.execute("select name, age from Person "+condition)
  for i in range(0,con.rowcount):
    results=con.fetchone()
    print results[0]+" is "+str(results[1])+" years old"
```

How It Works

The function showSomePersons takes the input of a database connection con and a condition, which is meant to be a string containing an SQL where clause. We then ask the connection to execute a select SQL command. We concatenate the condition onto the end of our select command. We then have a loop for each of the rows returned from the selection (using con.rowcount to get that number of rows). We use fetchone to get each response and print it. Note the use of normal list indexing on the returned tuple.

Here's an example of using showSomePersons:

```
>>> showSomePersons(con,"where age >= 40")
Mark is 40 years old
Barb is 41 years old
```

We can now think about doing one of our joins using a conditional select. The next code snippet says, "Return a picture and student name, from these three tables, where the student name is 'Brittany', where the students' ID is the same as the student ID in the student-picture IDs table, and the picture ID from the IDs table is the same as the ID in the picture table."

```
Select
    p.picture,
    s.studentName
From
    Students as s,
    IDs as i,
    Pictures as p
Where
    (s.studentName="Brittany") and
    (s.studentID=i.studentID) and
    (i.pictureID=p.pictureID)
```

13.3.4   Using a Database to Build Web Pages

Most of the Web pages on the Internet come from databases. Web sites like CNN, Amazon, and eBay have a handful of *templates* that describe the HTML to generate around database queries. That's not a special ability. We also can store information in our database, retrieve it, then put it in our Web page—just like Amazon, CNN, and eBay.

```
>>> import anydbm
>>> db=anydbm.open(getMediaPath("news"),"c")
>>> db["headline"]="Katie turns 8!"
>>> db["story"]="""Our daughter, Katie, turned 8 years old
    yesterday. She had a great birthday. Grandma and
    Grandpa came over. The previous weekend, she had three
    of her friends over for a sleepover."""
>>> db.close()
```

When we run the below program with `makeHomePage("Mark","beer and ukulele")`, we get a Web page that looks like Figure 13.11.

Program 169: Building a Web Page with Database Content

```
import urllib
import random
import anydbm

def makeHomePage(name,interests):
  file=open(getMediaPath("homepage.html"),"wt")
  file.write(doctype())
  file.write(title(name+"'s Home Page"))
  text = "<h1>Welcome to "+name+"'s Home Page</h1> "
  text += "<p>Hi!  I am "+name+".  This is my home page!"
  text += " I am interested in "+interests+"</p>"
  text += "<p>Random thought for the day: "+tagline()+"</p>"
```

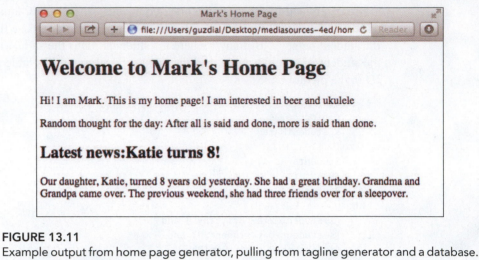

FIGURE 13.11
Example output from home page generator, pulling from tagline generator and a database. Created with `makeHomePage("Mark","beer and ukulele")`.

```
# Import the database content
db=anydbm.open(getMediaPath("news"),"r")
text += "<h2>Latest news:"+db["headline"]+"</h2>"
text += "<p>"+db["story"]+"</p>"
file.write(body(text))
file.close()

#Rest, like tagline(), from previous examples
```

Now we can think about how a large Web site like CNN.com works. Reporters enter stories into a database that are distributed all over the world. Editors (also distributed or all in one place) retrieve stories from the database, update them, then store them back. On a regular basis (perhaps more often when a hot story emerges), the Web page generation program runs, gathers up the stories, and generates the HTML. "POOF! You have a large Web site!" Databases are really critical to how large Web sites run.

PROBLEMS

13.1   Your father calls you. "My tech support people are saying that the company Web site is down because the database program is broken. What does the database have to do with our company Web site?" You explain to him how databases can be integral to running large Web sites. Explain both (a) how the Web site comes to be authored through the database and (b) how the HTML is actually created.

13.2   You have a new computer that seems to connect to the Internet but when you try to go to `http://www.cnn.com` you get a "Server Not Found" error. You call tech support and they tell you to try to go to `http://64.236.24.20`. That works. Now both you and the tech know what's wrong with your computer's settings. What isn't working properly, since you can get to a site via the Internet but can't get the domain name www.cnn.com to be recognized?

13.3   Given a folder with images in it, create an index HTML page with links to each image. Write a function that takes a string which is the path to a directory. You will create a page in the folder named **index.html** that should be an HTML page containing a link to every JPEG file in the directory.

You will also generate a thumbnail (half the size) copy of each image. Use makeEmptyPicture to create a blank picture of the right size, then scale down the original picture into the blank picture. Name the new image "half-" + the original filename (e.g., if the original filename was **fred.jpg**, save the half-size image as **half-fred.jpg**). The anchor in the link to each full-size picture should be the half-size image.

13.4   Use your favorite search engine to figure out what are the differences between SGML, HTML 5, XML, HTML 4.01, and XHTML.

13.5   Convert the following hexadecimal numbers to decimal: 2A3, 321, 16, 24, F3.

13.6   Convert the following decimal numbers to hexadecimal: 113, 64, 129, 72, 3.

13.7   Convert the following colors to hexadecimal: gray, yellow, pink, orange, and magenta. You can get the red, green, and blue values for each color using print color.

13.8   The makeCatalog function that we create in this chapter has a couple of significant errors.

- There should be a space in the title after the colon and before the product name. Fix that.

- The grammar of the example is awful, because the product we provided is plural ("Seahorses") but the text assumes a singular product. Fix it so that the text is right for the number of the input. There are several ways to fix this problem. One way is to take in a boolean input for singular or plural, then change the text accordingly. Another way is to create two catalog page generators, one for singular and one for plural, then let the user decide which to use. Implement one of these.

13.9   The makeSamplePage function generates all of the HTML on one line. Inserting the character \n will generate new lines. Put in some newline characters into a new version of that function to create readable HTML. Call it makeReadableSamplePage.

13.10   Write a function image that takes an image filename or URL, and a width, then returns the correct img tag for displaying that filename with a given width. Rewrite makeSamplePage to use your new image function for generating the ing tag for the samples.

13.11   Write a function to create a simple home page with your name, your picture, and a table with the titles of your courses and teacher names.

13.12   Write a function called `riddle` that returns a two line string, with a riddle and its answer. Modify `makeHomePage` to insert the riddle at the end of the page rather than the tagline.

13.13   Write a function to create a simple home page with your name, your picture, and your hometown. Provide a link to your home town in a search engine (like Google or Bing) and to a map of your home town (e.g., via Google Maps or Mapquest).

13.14   Go to `www.half.com` and look up a popular movie that they sell as a DVD. What database tables and fields do you think are needed to represent the data for a DVD?

13.15   Why should you use a relational database? Are there other kinds of databases? Who invented relational databases?

13.16   Do some Web searches to come up with answers to these questions about relational databases:

- What is a database table?
- What is a join?
- What is a query?
- What is a connection?

13.17   Do some Web searches to come up with answers to these questions about SQL:

- What is SQL?
- How do you create a table in SQL?
- How do you insert a row in a table in SQL?
- How do you get data from a table in SQL?

13.18   Write a function that reads delimited strings from a file with names and phone numbers and uses a database to store the names as the keys and the phone numbers as the values. Take as input the filename and the name of the person who's phone number you are looking for. How would you look up the phone number to find the name it belongs to?

13.19   Create a relational database that has a person table, a picture table, and a person–picture table. In the person table, store an ID, the person name, and the person's age. In the picture table, store a picture ID and filename. In the person–picture table, keep track of the people in each picture. Write a function that let you find all the pictures for people over a certain age.

13.20   Create a relational database that has a product table, a customer table, an order table, and an order item table. In the product table, store an ID, name, picture, description, and price. In the customer table, store the ID, name, and address. In the order table, store the order ID and customer ID. In the order item table, store the order ID, product ID, and quantity. Write a function to let you find all orders for a given customer. Write a function to let you find all orders with a total cost greater than some specified value.

13.21   Given a relational database with a person table that contains an ID, name, and age. What do each of the following return?

- Select * from person.
- Select age from person.
- Select ID from person.
- Select name, age from person.
- Select * from person where age > 20.
- Select name from person where age < 20.

13.22   Use a hash table to store texting shortcuts and their definitions. For example, "lol" means "laugh out loud." Use this hash table to decode a text message. Iterate through all the words in the text message input, and if any are found, replace them with their definitions. Return the decoded string.

TO DIG DEEPER

There are several good books on using Python and Jython for Web development and programming. We particularly recommend the books by Gupta [38] and Hightower [40] for their discussions of the use of Java in database contexts. You can find great resources on the Web about using databases from Jython.

PART **4** MOVIES

14 Creating and Modifying Movies

Chapter Learning Objectives

The media learning goals for this chapter are:

- To understand how a series of still images can be perceived as motion.
- To create animations with different motions and effects.
- To use video sources for animations and processing.
- To work out how a digital effect is implemented.

The computer science goals for this chapter are:

- To understand another example of using multiple functions to make coding easier.
- To understand a detailed example of bottom-up design and implementation.
- To use optional and named arguments to Python functions.

Movies (video) are actually very simple to manipulate. They are arrays of pictures (**frames**). You need to be concerned with the **frame rate** (the number of frames per second) but it's mostly just things you've seen before. We're going to use the term *movies* to refer generically to **animations** (motion generated entirely by graphical drawings) and **video** (motion generated by some kind of photographic process).

What makes movies work is a feature of our visual system called **persistence of vision**. We do not see every change that happens in the world. For example, you don't typically see your eyes blink, even though they do it quite often (typically 20 times a minute). But each time we blink, we don't panic and think, "Where'd the world go?" Instead, our eyes retain an image for a short time and keep telling the brain that the same image is there.

If we see one *related* picture after another fast enough, our eye retains the image and our brain sees continuous motion. "Fast enough" is about 16 frames per second—we see the 16 related pictures within a second, we think continuous motion. If the pictures aren't related, our brain reports a *montage*, a collection of disparate (though perhaps thematically connected) images. We refer to this 16 *frames per second* (*fps*) as the lower bound for the sensation of motion.

Early silent pictures were 16 fps. Motion pictures standardized on 24 fps to make sound smoother—16 fps didn't provide enough physical space on the film to encode enough sound data. (Ever wonder why silent pictures often look fast and jerky? Think about what happens when you scale up a picture or sound—that's exactly what happens if you play a 16 fps movie at 24 fps.) Digital video (e.g., video cameras) captures at 30 fps. How high is useful? There are some U.S. Air Force experiments suggesting that pilots can recognize a blurb of light in the shape of an aircraft (and figure out what kind it is) in 1/200 of a second. Video game players say that they can discern a difference between 30 fps video and 60 fps video.

Movies are challenging to work with because of the amount and speed of the data involved. **Real-time processing** of video (e.g., doing some modification to each frame as it comes in or goes out) is hard because whatever processing you do has to fit into 1/30 of a second. Let's do the math for how many bytes are needed to record video:

- One second of 640 × 480 frame size images at 30 fps means 30(*frames*) ∗ 640 ∗ 480(*pixels*) = 9,216,000 pixels.
- At 24-bit color (one byte for each of R, G, and B), that's 27,648,000 bytes, or 27 megabytes *per second*.
- For a 90-minute feature film, that's 90 ∗ 60 ∗ 27,648,000 = 149,299,200,000 bytes—149 gigabytes.

Digital movies are almost always stored in a compressed format. A DVD only stores 6.47 gigabytes, so even on a DVD the movie is compressed. Movie format standards like *MPEG*, *QuickTime*, and *AVI* are all compressed movie formats. They don't record every frame—they record *key frames* and then record the differences between one frame and the next. The *JMV* format is slightly different—it's a file of JPEG images, so every frame is there, but every frame is compressed.

Movies can use some different compression techniques than pictures or sounds. Think about watching someone walk across a frame of a camera. Between two successive frames, only a little bit changes—where the person just was and where they now are. If we recorded only those differences, and not all the pixels for the whole frame, then we save a lot of space.

An MPEG movie is really just an MPEG image sequence merged with an MPEG (like MP3) audio file. We're going to follow that lead and *not* deal with sound here. The tools described in the next section *can* create movies with sound, but the real trick of processing movies is handling all the images. That's what we're going to focus on here.

14.1   GENERATING ANIMATIONS

To make movies, we're going to create a series of JPEG frames and then reassemble them. We'll place all of our frames in a single directory and number them so that the tools know how to reassemble them into a movie in the right order. We'll literally name

frame00.jpg   frame02.jpg   frame50.jpg

FIGURE 14.1
A few frames from the first movie: moving a rectangle down and right.

our files **frame01.jpg**, **frame02.jpg**, and so on. It's important to include the leading zeroes, so that the files are listed in numeric order when placed in alphabetical order.

Here's our first movie-generating program, which simply moves a red rectangle from top left to bottom right (Figure 14.1).

Program 170: Create a Movie with a Moving Rectangle

```
def makeRectMovie(directory):
  for num in range(1,30): #29 frames (1 to 29)
    canvas = makeEmptyPicture(300,200)
    addRectFilled(canvas,num * 10, num * 5, 50,50, red)
    # convert the number to a string
    numStr=str(num)
    if num < 10:
      writePictureTo(canvas,directory+"\\frame0"+numStr+".jpg")
    if num >= 10:
      writePictureTo(canvas,directory+"\\frame"+numStr+".jpg")
  movie = makeMovieFromInitialFile(directory+"\\frame00.jpg");
  return movie
```

You can try this out by creating a directory called **rect** in the **Temp** directory and then executing the following.

```
>>>   rectM = makeRectMovie("c:\\Temp\\rect")
>>>   playMovie(rectM)
```

Making It Work Tip: Changing Path Names for Different Platforms
The function makeRectMovie uses "\\" as a file delimiter for Windows. Windows uses "\" as a file delimiter, and doubling it makes sure that it gets interpreted by Python as a backslash. We could also use "/" which will be interpreted correctly for Mac OS X, Windows, and Linux. If you are only writing for Windows and you want to make sure that your paths look the way they look elsewhere (e.g., when printing out what pickAFile() returns), then go ahead and use the backslash delimiter. By this point, you should be able to figure out path names so that they make sense for your operating system.

When you execute playMovie(movie), it will display all the frames of the movie in a movie player. Once the movie has finished displaying, you can use the PREV button to see the previous frame and the NEXT button to see the next frame in the movie.

The Play Movie button will play the entire movie again. The Delete All Previous button will delete all frames before the displayed frame in the directory. The Delete All After button will delete all the frames after the displayed frame in the directory. The Write Quicktime button will write out a QuickTime movie from all the frames in the directory. The Write AVI button will write out an AVI movie from all the frames in the directory. The movies will be in the directory with the frames and will have the same name as the directory.

How It Works

The key part of this recipe are the lines right after `makeEmptyPicture`. We have to compute a different position for the rectangle depending on the current frame number. The equations in the `addRectFilled()` functions compute different positions for different frames of the movie (Figure 14.2).

While `setPixel()` gets upset if you try to set a pixel outside the bounds of the picture, the graphics functions like `addText()` and `addRect()` don't generate errors for going beyond the borders. They'll simply *clip* the image for the picture (show only what they can), so you can create simple code to make animations and not worry about going out of bounds. This makes creating a tickertape movie really pretty easy (Figure 14.3).

Program 171: Generate a Tickertape Movie

```
def tickertape(directory,string):
  for num in range(1,100): #99 frames
    canvas = makeEmptyPicture(300,100)
    #Start at right, and move left
    addText(canvas,300-(num*10),50,string)
    # Now, write out the frame
```

FIGURE 14.2
The movie player showing the rectangle movie.

FIGURE 14.3
A tickertape movie.

```
# Have to deal with single digit vs. double digit frame numbers¬
differently
numStr=str(num)
if num < 10:
  writePictureTo(canvas,directory+"//frame0"+numStr+".jpg")
```

¬These lines of the program should continue with the next lines. A single command in Python may not break across multiple lines.

```
if num >= 10:
  writePictureTo(canvas,directory+"//frame"+numStr+".jpg")
```

■

How It Works

The function `tickertape` takes a directory in which the frames of the movie will be stored and a string to write out. For each of 99 frames (from 1 to 100, but not including 100), we make an empty picture of size (300, 100) and put the string into it as text. The *y* position is always at 50 (same position vertically), and the *x* position (horizontally) is at `300-(num*10)`. As the frame number, num, increases, this equation gets smaller. So each frame has the string drawn closer to the left side (smaller *x* values) of the frame. We convert the frame number num to a string numStr and use that to make a filename with the right number of leading zeroes.

Can we move more than one thing at once? Sure! Our drawing code just gets a little more complicated. We could just move things with linear motion like all the examples up until now, but let's try something different. Here's a recipe that uses *sine* and *cosine* to create circular motion to match our linear motion of Program 170 (page 387) (Figure 14.4).

Program 172: Move Two Objects at Once

```
def movingRectangle2(directory):
  for num in range(1,30): #29 frames
    canvas = makeEmptyPicture(300,250)
    #add a filled rect moving linearly
    addRectFilled(canvas,num*10,num*5, 50,50,red)

    # Let's have one just moving around
```

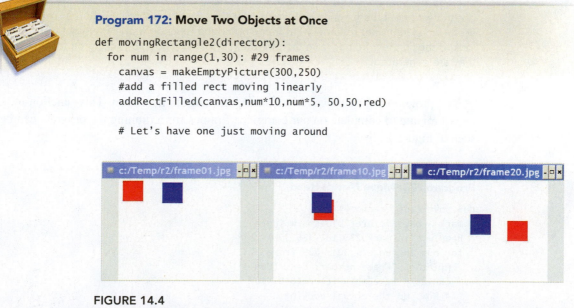

FIGURE 14.4
Moving two rectangles at once.

```
blueX = 100+ int(10 * sin(num))
blueY = 4*num+int(10* cos(num))
addRectFilled(canvas,blueX,blueY,50,50,blue)

# Now, write out the frame
# Have to deal with single digit vs. double digit
numStr=str(num)

if num < 10:
  writePictureTo(canvas,directory+"//frame0"+numStr+".jpg")
if num >= 10:
  writePictureTo(canvas,directory+"//frame"+numStr+".jpg")
```

How It Works

We know that $\sin$ and $\cos$ generate values between -1 and 1. (You remember that, right?) The x position of the blue box is set by $100 + \texttt{int}(10 * \sin(num))$. This means that the x position of the blue box will be around 100, plus or minus 10 pixels. It'll shift left to right and right to left as the values of $\sin$ change. The y position is determined by $4 * num + \texttt{int}(10 * \cos(num))$. The y position, then, is always increasing (the box is falling), but plus or minus 10, so there's a slight up-and-down motion while it's falling.

We don't have to create our animations only out of things that we can do with graphics primitives. We can use the same kinds of images we've used previously through `setColor()`. This kind of code runs pretty slowly.

Debugging Tip: `PrintNow()` to Print `NOW`

There is a JES function called `printNow()` that takes a string and prints it *immediately*—it doesn't wait until the function is done to print the line to the Command Area. That's useful when you want to know what frame number a function is on. You might want to go look at the first few frames from the operating system by double-clicking on them once they are generated.

The program below moves Mark's head around on the screen. This function took over a minute to complete on our computer. Frames from running the program can be seen in Figure 14.5.

Program 173: Move Mark's Head

```
def moveHead(directory):
  mark = makePicture("blue-mark.jpg")
  head = clip(mark,275,160,385,306)
  for num in range(1,30): #29 frames
    printNow("Frame number: "+str(num))
    canvas = makeEmptyPicture(640,480)
    # Now, do the actual copying
    copy(head,canvas,num*10,num*5)
```

FIGURE 14.5
A couple of frames from moving the head movie.

```
    # Now, write out the frame
    # Have to deal with single digit vs. double digit frame
    # numbers differently
    numStr=str(num)
    if num < 10:
      writePictureTo(canvas,directory+"//frame0"+numStr+".jpg")
    if num >= 10:
      writePictureTo(canvas,directory+"//frame"+numStr+".jpg")

def clip(picture,startX,startY,endX,endY):
  width = endX - startX + 1
  height = endY - startY + 1
  resPict = makeEmptyPicture(width,height)
  resX = 0
  for x in range(startX,endX):
    resY=0 # reset result y index
    for y in range(startY,endY):
      origPixel = getPixel(picture,x,y)
      resPixel = getPixel(resPict,resX,resY)
      setColor(resPixel,(getColor(origPixel)))
      resY=resY + 1
    resX=resX + 1
  return resPict

def copy(source, target, targX, targY):
  targetX = targX
  for sourceX in range(0,getWidth(source)):
    targetY = targY
    for sourceY in range(0,getHeight(source)):
      px=getPixel(source,sourceX,sourceY)
      tx=getPixel(target,targetX,targetY)
      setColor(tx,getColor(px))
      targetY=targetY + 1
    targetX=targetX + 1
```

How It Works

We've created a new method `clip` that creates and returns a new picture with just the pixels in the rectangle defined by the passed `startX`, `startY`, `endX`, and `endY`. We use this `clip` function to create a picture with just Mark's head in it. Then we use the general `copy` function (Program 78 (page 172)) to copy Mark's head to different locations in the `canvas` based on the frame number `num`.

Our movie programs are getting more complicated now. We might want to be able to write them in parts, with the frame-writing part kept separate. This means that we can focus in the main body of the function on what we want in the frame, not on writing the frame. This is an example of **procedural abstraction**.

Program 174: Move Mark's Head, Simplified

```
def moveHead2(directory):
  mark = makePicture("blue-mark.jpg")
  face = clip(mark,275,160,385,306)
  for num in range(1,30): #29 frames
    printNow("Frame number: "+str(num))
    canvas = makeEmptyPicture(640,480)
    # Now, do the actual copying
    copy(face,canvas,num*10,num*5)
    # Now, write out the frame
    writeFrame(num,directory,canvas)
def writeFrame(num,dir,pict):
  # Have to deal with single digit vs. double digit
  numStr=str(num)
  if num < 10:
    writePictureTo(pict,dir+"//frame0"+numStr+".jpg")
  if num >= 10:
    writePictureTo(pict,dir+"//frame"+numStr+".jpg")
```

But this `writeFrame()` function assumes two-digit maximum frame numbers. We could want more frames. Here's a version that allows for three-digit frame numbers.

Program 175: Writeframe() for Over 100 Frames

```
def writeFrame(num,dir,pict):
  # Have to deal with single digit vs. double digit
  numStr=str(num)
  if num < 10:
    writePictureTo(pict,dir+"//frame00"+numStr+".jpg")
  if num >= 10 and num<100:
    writePictureTo(pict,dir+"//frame0"+numStr+".jpg")
  if num >= 100:
    writePictureTo(pict,dir+"//frame"+numStr+".jpg")
```

We can use the image manipulations that we created in Chapter 3 over multiple frames to create quite interesting movies. Remember the sunset-generating program (Program 37 (page 95))? Let's modify it to *slowly* generate a sunset across many frames.

We modify it so that the difference between each frame is only 1%. This version actually goes too far, and generates a supernova, but the effect is still pretty interesting (Figure 14.6).

Program 176: Make a Slow-Sunset Movie

```
def slowSunset(directory):
  #outside the loop!
  canvas = makePicture("rotoroa.jpg")
  for num in range(1,100): #99 frames
    printNow("Frame number: "+str(num))
    makeSunset(canvas)
    # Now, write out the frame
    writeFrame(num,directory,canvas)

def makeSunset(picture):
  for p in getPixels(picture):
    value=getBlue(p)
    setBlue(p,int(value*0.99)) #Just 1% decrease!
    value=getGreen(p)
    setGreen(p,int(value*0.99))
```

■

How It Works

The key to this movie is that we create the `canvas` *before* the loop that creates each frame. Within the loop, we simply keep using the same base `canvas`. This means that each call to `makeSunset` increases the "sunsetness" (no, it's not a word) by 1%. (We're not going to show `writeFrame()` anymore, since we assume that you'll include it in your Program Area.) We use the `int` function since multiplying a value by 0.99 will not result in an integer, but a pixel value is always an integer.

The `swapBack()` program that we made a while ago can also be used for good effect for generating movies. We modify the function in Program 56 (page 129) to take a threshold as input, then we pass in the frame number as the threshold. The effect is a slow fade into the background image (Figure 14.7).

Program 177: Fade Out Slowly

```
def swapBack(pic1, back, newBg, threshold):
  for x in range(0,getWidth(pic1)):
    for y in range(0,getHeight(pic1)):
      p1Pixel = getPixel(pic1,x,y)
      backPixel = getPixel(back,x,y)
      if (distance(getColor(p1Pixel),getColor(backPixel))
        < threshold):
        setColor(p1Pixel,getColor(getPixel(newBg,x,y)))
  return pic1
def slowFadeout(directory):
  origBack = makePicture(getMediaPath("bgframe.jpg"))
  newBack = makePicture(getMediaPath("beach.jpg"))
  for num in range(1,60): #59 frames
```

FIGURE 14.6
Frames from the slow-sunset movie.

FIGURE 14.7
Frames from the slow-fade-out movie.

```
# do this in the loop
kid = makePicture(getMediaPath("kid-in-frame.jpg"))
swapBack(kid,origBack,newBack,num)
# Now, write out the frame
writeFrame(num,directory,kid)
```

How It Works

The frame number here is the threshold value for which we decide to swap in the new background instead of keeping the original pixels in swapBack. As the threshold increases, we replace more and more of the pixels of the original picture with new background pixels. As the frame number increases, then, we end up having more new background and less of both the old background and the old foreground. Note that here we create the kid picture *inside* the frame loop. We want the effect to be new for each frame, with the frame differences computed in swapBack with the changing threshold.

14.2   WORKING WITH VIDEO SOURCE

As we said earlier, dealing with real video, in real time, is very hard. We're going to cheat by saving the video as a sequence of JPEG images, manipulate the JPEG images, then convert back into a movie. This lets us use video as a source (e.g., for background images).

To manipulate movies that already exist, we have to break them into frames. There are various tools that can do this. The MediaTools application can do this for you for MPEG movies. Tools like Apple's QuickTime Pro can do the same for QuickTime and AVI movies.

14.2.1   Video Manipulating Examples

If you get the **mediasources** folder that we provide for this book, you will find a brief movie of our daughter dancing around when she was little. Let's create a movie of Mommy (Barb) watching her daughter—we'll simply composite Barb's head onto the frames of Katie dancing (Figure 14.8).

FIGURE 14.8
Frames from the Mommy watching Katie movie.

Program 178: Make Movie of Mommy Watching Katie

```
import os

def mommyWatching(directory):
  kidDir="/Users/guzdial/Desktop/mediasources-4ed/kid-in-bg-seq"
  barb = makePicture("barbaraS.jpg")
  face = clip(barb,22,9,93,97)
  num = 0
  for file in os.listdir(kidDir):
    if file.endswith(".jpg"):
      num = num + 1
      printNow("Frame number: "+str(num))
      framePic = makePicture(kidDir+"//"+file)
      # Now, do the actual copying
      copy(face,framePic,num*3,num*3)
      # Now, write out the frame
      writeFrame(num,directory,framePic)
```

How It Works

The directory where the video source images are stored is **/Users/guzdial/Desktop/mediasources-4ed/kid-in-bg-seq**. We put that in a variable and get Barb's picture. We then make a picture of just Barb's face using the `clip` function. The frame number, num, is incremented in the loop, because we're actually going to read each frame individually as a video source via `os.listdir` on the `kidDir` (directory where the kid video frames are). We're lucky that `os.listdir` returns the frames in alphabetical order, which (with leading zeroes) is also numeric order. We read the file, make sure it's one of our JPEG frames, then open it and copy Barb's head onto it. We then write out the frame using `writeFrame`.

We can certainly do more sophisticated image processing than simple composing or sunsets. For example, we can do *chromakey* on movie frames. That's how many computer-generated effects in real movies are made. To try this out, we took a simple video of our three children (Matthew, Katie, and Jenny) crawling in front of a blue screen (Figure 14.9). We didn't do the lighting right, so the background turned out to

FIGURE 14.9
Frames from the original kids crawling in front of a blue screen.

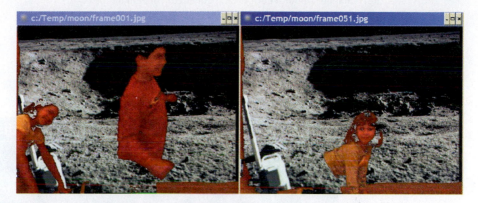

FIGURE 14.10
Frames from the kids on the moon movie.

be black instead of blue. That turned out to be a critical error. As a result, the chromakey also modified Matthew's pants, Katie's hair, and Jenny's eyes, so that you can see the moon right through them (Figure 14.10). Like red, black is a color that one should *not* use for the background when doing chromakey.

Program 179: Using Chromakey to Put Kids on the Moon

```
import os

def kidsOnMoon(directory):
  kids="C://ip-book//mediasources//kids-blue"
  back=makePicture("moon-surface.jpg")
  num = 0
  for frameFile in os.listdir(kids):
    num = num + 1
    printNow("Frame: "+str(num))
    if frameFile.endswith(".jpg"):
      frame=makePicture(kids+"//"+frameFile)
```

```
      for p in getPixels(frame):
        if distance(getColor(p),black) <= 100:
          setColor(p,getColor(getPixel(back,getX(p),getY(p))))
      writeFrame(num,directory,frame)
```

Mark took video of fish underwater. Water filters out red and yellow light, so the video looks too blue (Figure 14.11). Let's increase the red and green in the video (yellow is a mixture of red and green light). Let's also create a new function that multiplies the red and green values in a picture by some input factor. The result can be seen in Figure 14.12.

Program 180: Fix the Underwater Movie

```
import os

def changeRedAndGreen(pict,redFactor,greenFactor):
    for p in getPixels(pict):
        setRed(p,int(getRed(p) * redFactor))
        setGreen(p,int(getGreen(p) * greenFactor))

def fixUnderwater(directory):
  num = 0
```

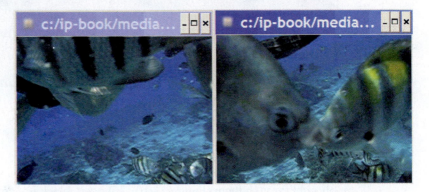

FIGURE 14.11
Frames from the too blue underwater movie.

FIGURE 14.12
Frames from the less blue movie.

```
dir="C://ip-book//mediasources//fish"
for frameFile in os.listdir(dir):
    num = num + 1
    printNow("Frame: "+str(num))
    if frameFile.endswith(".jpg"):
        frame=makePicture(dir+"//"+frameFile)
        changeRedAndGreen(frame,2.0,1.5)
        writeFrame(num,directory,frame)
```

14.3   BUILDING A VIDEO EFFECT BOTTOM-UP

You may have seen the television commercials where actors "draw" in the air with a glow stick or flashlight, and the lines hang in the air as if drawn on a whiteboard. How do they do that? Given what we know about video and image processing, we can probably figure this out. Let's write a program to replicate the process, and we will do it in bottom-up, to exemplify that way of building programs.

Figure 14.13 shows four frames of a movie of someone drawing with a glows tick in the air. We made this movie when it was dark out so that the glow stick would be a sharp contrast with the rest. How would we get the bright pixels from the glows tick to appear in all successive frames? We want the last frame of the created movie to look

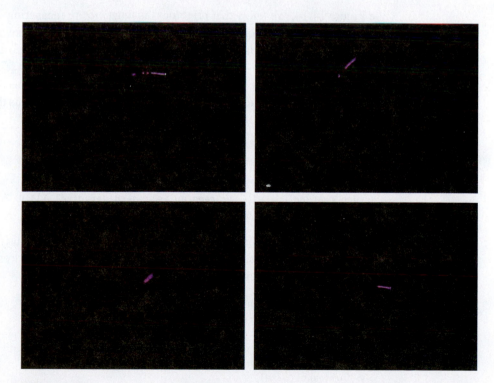

FIGURE 14.13
Frames of the source movie, with the glow stick being drawn in the air.

FIGURE 14.14
Final frame of target movie, with the trace of the glow stick visible.

like Figure 14.14. We know that brightness is what we are measuring with luminance. What we could do is to copy from one frame to the next all those pixels above a certain luminance level. If we just repeat this for all frames, all those pixels that are brighter will get collected.

In bottom-up process, we start gathering the pieces that we need from standard libraries, or writing the pieces that we think we will need. It's obvious that we will have to implement luminance at some point.

Program 181: Luminance for Combining Bright Pixels

```
def luminance(apixel):
  return (getRed(apixel)+getGreen(apixel)+getBlue(apixel))/3.0
```

We should also test our pieces, as we develop them. Does our luminance function do what we expect? Let's make a pixel, and set its color to some extreme values to see if it is responding as we might expect.

```
>>> pict = makeEmptyPicture(1,1)
>>> pixel=getPixelAt(pict,0,0)
>>> white
Color(255, 255, 255)
>>> setColor(pixel,white)
>>> luminance(pixel)
255.0
>>> black
```

```
Color(0, 0, 0)
>>> setColor(pixel,black)
>>> luminance(pixel)
0.0
```

Next, we'll need something that will tell us whether a pixel is bright *enough*. We need a *threshold* value as a comparison point. One might want the method `brightPixel` in a couple of different ways: where you provide a threshold value or where a default threshold value is used. Python gives us a way of doing both, by providing *keyword arguments* or sometimes called *optional arguments*. We specify an argument for a function with a default value.

Program 182: `brightPixel` for Combining Bright Pixels

```
def brightPixel(apixel, threshold=100):
  if luminance(apixel) > threshold:
    return true
return false
```

How It Works

`brightPixel` takes a pixel as input, and optionally, a threshold value whose default value is 100. If the luminance of the pixel is greater than the threshold value, it returns true. If not, execution reaches the last line and it returns false. We can build `brightPixel` to take advantage of the fact that we've already written `luminance`.

We can use `brightPixel` by specifying the threshold value, or by leaving it out, or even by specifying it with an assignment.

```
>>> red
Color(255, 0, 0)
>>> setColor(pixel,red)
>>> luminance(pixel)
85.0
>>> brightPixel(pixel)
0
>>> brightPixel(pixel,80)
1
>>> brightPixel(pixel,threshold=80)
1
>>> setColor(pixel,white)
>>> brightPixel(pixel,threshold=80)
1
>>> brightPixel(pixel)
1
>>> setColor(pixel,black)
>>> brightPixel(pixel,threshold=80)
0
>>> brightPixel(pixel)
0
```

What other functions do we need? We can look over our description of the statement. We need to be able to get a list of all files from a directory, to get all the frames. Given a list of files, we will need to be able to get the `firstFile` as distinct from the rest of the files, `restFiles`, so that we take the first file, copy the pixels to the first of the rest of the files, and then continue the process. Let's write those pieces.

Program 183: **Functions to Manipulate File Lists for Combining Bright Pixels**

```
import os

def allFiles(fromDir):
  listFiles = os.listdir(fromDir)
  listFiles.sort()
  return listFiles

def firstFile(filelist):
  return filelist[0]

def restFiles(filelist):
  return filelist[1:]
```

How It Works

We have seen all three of these kinds of code before, so we are building on other elements. Here, we are just giving them good names and turning them into parameterized functions. `allFiles` just gets our list of files, then sorts it (to make sure it's in increasing order), and returns it. The `[0]`th item of a list is the first one, and `[1:]` is from the second item to the end of the list. Thus `firstFile` and `restFiles` give us the elements of the file we want. We should test these, to make sure that they work as we want.

```
>>> files = allFiles("/")
>>> files
['Recycled', '_314109_', 'bin', 'boot', 'cdrom',
'dev', 'etc', 'home', 'initrd', 'initrd.img',
'initrd.img.old', 'lib', 'lost+found', 'media',
'mnt', 'opt', 'proc', 'root', 'sbin', 'srv', 'sys',
'tmp', 'usr', 'var', 'vmlinuz', 'vmlinuz.old']
>>> firstFile(files)
'Recycled'
>>> restFiles(files)
['_314109_', 'bin', 'boot', 'cdrom', 'dev', 'etc',
'home', 'initrd', 'initrd.img', 'initrd.img.old',
'lib', 'lost+found', 'media', 'mnt', 'opt', 'proc',
'root', 'sbin', 'srv', 'sys', 'tmp', 'usr', 'var',
'vmlinuz', 'vmlinuz.old']
```

Now that we have built and tested all the individual pieces, we can write the top-level function, in terms of these smaller functions.

Program 184: **Combining Bright Pixels into a New Movie**

```
def brightCombine(fromDir,target):
  fileList = allFiles(fromDir)
```

```
fromPictFile = firstFile(fileList)
fromPict = makePicture(fromDir+fromPictFile)
for toPictFile in restFiles(fileList):
  printNow(toPictFile)
  # Copy all the high luminance colors from fromPict to toPict
  toPict = makePicture(fromDir+toPictFile)
  for p in getPixels(fromPict):
    if brightPixel(p):
      c = getColor(p)
      setColor(getPixel(toPict,getX(p),getY(p)),c)
  writePictureTo(toPict,target+toPictFile)
  fromPict = toPict
```

How It Works

brightCombine takes two directories as input: where to get the frames of moving bright pixels and where to write the frames where the bright pixels are copied over. We get the list of frames, and make a picture (fromPict) from the first frame in the list. Now, toPictFile will be each of the other frame filenames, one at a time, and we will make a picture from it in variable toPict. We check all the pixels in the fromPict and those that are bright enough get written to the toPict. We then make the *to* picture be the *from* picture, fromPict = toPict, and move on to the next frame. In this way, we copy all the bright pixels forward.

Of course, we should test brightCombine but we leave it to the reader to try it out. What you see in this process is building up individual elements, testing them, and building on top of those elements. The end result, the top-level function, might end up pretty much the same as in the top-down process. In the bottom-up process, we might not have a clear idea of where we're going (in this case, we did have a pretty good idea), and we focus on building from smaller to larger elements.

PROBLEMS

14.1   How many frames would you need for a two-hour movie with a picture size of 1024 width by 728 height and 60 frames per second? How much disk space would this movie need if you stored every pixel's color? Remember that each pixel would require 24 bits to store the color.

14.2   Look on the Internet for answers to these questions:
  - How do the AVI and QuickTime movie formats differ?
  - How do they compare to MPEG4?
  - When would you want to use each movie format?

14.3   Look up "persistence of vision" on the Internet and how it relates to making animations.

14.4   Only the first example in this chapter uses the movie object. Rewrite any of the other example programs to create a movie object and return the movie object.

14.5   Write a function to create a movie where one item is moving from the top to the bottom and another item is moving from the bottom to the top.

14.6   Write a function to create a movie where one item is moving from the left to the right and another item is moving from the right to the left.

14.7   Write a function to create a movie where one item is moving in a diagonal line from top left to bottom right and another item is moving from the right to the left.

14.8   Create a new movie that has two rectangles moving a random amount (from −5 to 5) in each direction in each frame.

14.9   Create a movie that has the frames slowly becoming sepia-toned from left-to-right. Maybe you make sepia-toned the leftmost 10 columns of pixels in the first frame, then the leftmost 20 columns are made sepia-tones in the second frame, and so on.

14.10   Create a movie where an input picture becomes wider and wider with successive frames. For example, the first frame of the movie might just have the middle 5 columns of pixels, then the second frame might have the middle 10 columns of pixels, then 15 columns, and so on.

14.11   Create a movie where an input picture becomes smaller with successive frames. Paste the whole picture into the first frame, then reduce the size by 5% in successive frames.

14.12   Create a movie where an input picture becomes more cropped with successive frames. Paste the whole picture into the first frame. In the second frame, copy the whole picture, but make the 5 columns of pixels on the left and 5 columns on the right all white. In the second frame, make it 10 frames.

14.13   Create a function that takes a picture and creates a movie with the picture slowing turning into the negative from left-to-right. Maybe you do the leftmost 10 columns of pixels in the first frame, then the leftmost 20 columns are made negative in the second frame, and so on.

14.14   One of the most common transitions in movies is *fade to black*. Let's implement that. Take a picture as input and copy that into the first frame of the movie. For the next 5 frames, copy the picture but make every 10th pixel black. Then for the next 5 frames, make every 9th and 10th pixel black. Continue the process until all the pixels are black.

14.15   Find another slide transition in PowerPoint or Keynote or some other presentation software, and implement it as a movie.

14.16   Create a new version of the `lineDetect` function (Program 55 (page 128)) that takes in a threshold and create a movie using `lineDetect` where the threshold changes depending on the frame number.

14.17   Write a function that draws a sun on the picture of a beach at different places on the picture in successive frames. The goal is to make it look like the sun is moving across the sky through the day.

14.18   Write a function to make a movie with text that starts out large near the bottom of the movie and then moves up toward the top and gets smaller each time it moves up. You can create a font style using `makeStyle(family,type,size)`.

14.19   Take a movie of some of your friends dancing in front of a green screen and use chromakey to make it look like they are dancing on the beach.

14.20   Take a movie of a location and a movie shot in front of a green screen and use chromakey to blend the two movies together.

14.21   Build an animation of at least three seconds in duration (30 frames at 10 fps, or 75 frames at 25 fps). You must have at least three things in motion during this sequence. You must use at least one composited image (a JPEG image that you scale (if necessary) and copy into the image) and one drawn image (a rectangle or line or text or oval or arc—anything that you draw). For at least one of the things in motion, change its *velocity* part way through the animation—change the direction or the speed.

14.22   `http://abcnews.go.com` is a popular news site. Let's make a movie of it. Write a function that will input a directory as a string. Then:

   • Visit `http://abcnews.go.com` and pick out the top three news story head-lines. (*Hint:* the anchors for the news story headlines all have `<a href="/wire/` before them. Find that tag, then search for the beginning of the anchor `<a href="/wire/`, then you can find the anchor text, which is the headline.)

   • Create a tickertape movie on the 640 × 480 canvas of all three news stories. Have one come across at $y = 100$, another at $y = 200$, and the third at $y = 300$. Generate 100 frames, and don't have the words move more than 5 pixels per frame. (In 100 frames, you won't make it all the way across the screen—that's fine.) Store the frames to files in the input directory.

14.23   Create a movie where a person seems to be fading out of the scene. You can base this on the `slowFadeout` function (Program 177 (page 393)).

14.24   Remember the blending of pictures in Chapter 6? Try blending one picture into another as a movie, slowly increasing the percentage of the second (incoming) image while decreasing the percentage of the original (outgoing) image.

14.25   The example of tracing bright pixels in this chapter used the **paint1** folder in the **mediasources**. There is another example in **paint2**. Try running that one.

14.26   The end-result pixels are pretty dull in the bright pixel tracing example. Use the `makeLighter` function to brighten up the pixels that you copy across.

14.27   Will the bright pixel tracing function *only* work in darkness? Make your own movie with someone writing with a glow stick or flashlight, in normal bright-ness. Does the function still work? Do you need to use a different threshold value? Do you have to try a different approach to identify "bright" pixels (e.g., perhaps by comparing luminance a particular pixel to the pixels around it)?

CHAPTER 15 Speed

Chapter Learning Objectives

- To choose between compiled and interpreted programming languages, based on an understanding of machine language and how computers work.
- To know the categories of algorithms based on their complexity and to avoid intractable algorithms.
- To consider processor choice based on an understanding of clock rates.
- To make decisions about computer storage options when aiming for optimizing speed.

15.1 FOCUSING ON COMPUTER SCIENCE

At this point, you probably have a lot of questions about what you've been doing in this book. You may be asking, for instance:

- Why is Photoshop so much faster than anything we do in JES?
- How fast can we get our programs to go?
- Does it always take this long to write programs? Can you write smaller programs to do the same things? Can you write programs more easily than this?
- What does programming look like in other programming languages?

The answers to most of these questions are known or are studied in *computer science*. This part of the book is an introduction to some of those topics, as a signpost to get you started in exploring computer science further.

15.2 WHAT MAKES PROGRAMS FAST?

Where does the speed go? You buy a really fast computer and Photoshop seems really fast on it. Colors change as quickly as you change the slider. But then you run programs in JES and they just take *forever* (or 30 seconds, whichever comes first). Why?

15.2.1   What Computers Really Understand

In reality, computers do not understand Python, or Java, or any other language. The basic computer understands only one kind of language—**machine language**. Machine-language instructions are just values in the bytes in memory and they tell the computer to do very low-level activities. In a real sense, the computer doesn't even "understand" machine language. The computer is just a machine with lots of switches that make data flow this way or that. Machine language is just a bunch of switch settings that make other switches in the computer change. We *interpret* these data switchings as addition, subtraction, loading data, and storing data.

Each kind of computer can have its own machine language. Windows computers can't run programs for older Apple computers, not because of any philosophical or marketing differences but because each kind of computer has its own **processor** (the core of the computer that actually executes the machine language). They *literally* don't understand one another. That's why an .exe program from Windows won't run on an older Macintosh and a Macintosh application won't run on a Windows computer. Executable files are (almost always) machine-language programs.

Machine language looks like a bunch of numbers—it's not particularly user-friendly. **Assembly language** is a set of human-understandable words (or near-words) that corresponds one-to-one with machine language. Machine-language instructions tell the computer to do things like store numbers into particular memory locations or into special locations (variables or registers) in the computer, test numbers for equality or comparison, or add numbers together or subtract them.

An assembly program to add two numbers together and store them somewhere (and the corresponding machine language generated by an **assembler**) might look like this:

```
LOAD #10,R0      ; Load special variable R0 with 10
LOAD #12,R1      ; Load special variable R1 with 12
SUM R0,R1        ; Add special variables R0 and R1
STOR R1,#45      ; Store the result into memory
                   location #45


01 00 10
01 01 12
02 00 01
03 01 45
```

An assembly program that can make a decision could look like this:

```
LOAD R1,#65536   ; Get a character from keyboard
TEST R1,#13      ; Is it an ASCII 13 (Enter)?
JUMPTRUE #32768  ; If true, go to another part of
                   the program
CALL #16384      ; If false, call func. to process
                   the new line

Machine Language:

05 01 255 255
10 01 13
```

```
20 127 255
122 63 255
```

Input and output devices are often just memory locations to the computer. Maybe, when you store a 255 to location 65,542, the red component of the pixel at (101, 345) is suddenly set to maximum intensity. Maybe each time the computer reads from memory location 897,784, it's a new sample just read from the microphone. In this way, these simple loads and stores can also handle multimedia.

Machine language is executed very quickly. Mark typed the first version of this chapter on a computer with a 900-megahertz (MHz) processor. What that means *exactly* is hard to define but roughly it means that this computer processes 900 *million* machine-language instructions *per second*. A 2-gigahertz (GHz) processor handles 2 *billion* instructions per second. A 12-byte machine-language program that corresponds to something like a = b + c executes on Mark's old computer in something like 12/900,000,000 of a second.

15.2.2 Compilers and Interpreters

Applications like Adobe Photoshop and Microsoft Word are typically **compiled**. This means that they were written in a computer language like C or C++ and then *translated* into machine language using a program called a **compiler**. The programs then execute at the speed of the base processor.

However, programming languages like Python, Java, Scheme, Squeak, Director, and Flash are actually (in most cases) *interpreted*. They execute at a slower speed. It's the difference between *translating* and then doing instructions versus simply doing the instructions.

A detailed example might help. Consider this exercise:

Write a function doGraphics that will take a list as input. The function doGraphics will start by creating a 640 × 480 empty canvas. You will draw on the canvas according to the commands in the input list.

Each element of the list will be a string. There will be two kinds of strings in the list:

- "b 200 120" means to draw a black dot at *x* position 200 and *y* position 120. The numbers, of course, will change, but the command will always be a "b." You can assume that the input numbers will always have three digits.
- "l 000 010 100 200" means to draw a line from position (0, 10) to position (100, 200).

So an input list might look like ["b 100 200","b 101 200","b 102 200", "l 102 200 102 300"] (but have any number of elements).

Here's a solution to the exercise. We look at each string in the list, compare the first character as a "black pixel" command or a "list" command, then chop out the

```
>>> canvas=doGraphics(["b 100
    200","b 101 200","b 102
    200","l 102 200 102 300","l
    102 300 200 300"])
Drawing pixel at 100 : 200
Drawing pixel at 101 : 200
Drawing pixel at 102 : 200
Drawing line at 102 200 102 300
Drawing line at 102 300 200 300
>>> show(canvas)
```

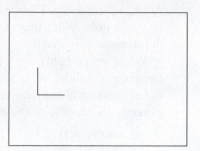

FIGURE 15.1
Running the doGraphics interpreter.

right coordinates (converting them to numbers with int()), and doing the appropriate graphics command. This solution works—see Figure 15.1.

Program 185: Interpret Graphics Commands in a List

```
def doGraphics(mylist):
  canvas = makeEmptyPicture(640,480)
  for command in mylist:
    if command[0] == "b":
      x = int(command[2:5])
      y = int(command[6:9])
      print "Drawing pixel at ",x,":",y
      setColor(getPixel(canvas, x,y),black)
    if command[0] =="l":
      x1 = int(command[2:5])
      y1 = int(command[6:9])
      x2 = int(command[10:13])
      y2 = int(command[14:17])
      print "Drawing line at",x1,y1,x2,y2
      addLine(canvas, x1, y1, x2, y2)
  return canvas
  return canvas
```

How It Works

We accept the list of graphics commands as input in mylist. We make a blank canvas for drawing on. For each string command in the input list, we check the first character (command[0]) to figure out what type of command it is. If it's a "b" (black pixel), we chop out the x- and y coordinates from the string (since they're always the numbers of the same length, we know exactly where they'll be), then draw the pixel on the canvas. If it's an "l" (line), we get the four coordinates and draw the line. At the end, we return the canvas.

What we've just done is implement a new language for graphics. We have even created an *interpreter* that reads the instructions for our new language and creates the picture that goes along with it. In principle, this is just what PostScript, PDF, Flash, and

AutoCAD are doing. Their file formats specify pictures in just the way that our graphics language does. When they draw (*render*) the image to the screen, they are *interpreting* the commands in that file.

While we probably can't tell from such a small example, this is a relatively slow language. Consider the program shown below—would it run faster than reading the list of commands and interpreting them? Both this program and the list in Figure 15.1 generate the exact same picture.

```
def doGraphics():
    canvas = makeEmptyPicture(640,480)
    setColor(getPixel(canvas, 100,200),black)
    setColor(getPixel(canvas, 101,200),black)
    setColor(getPixel(canvas, 102,200),black)
    addLine(canvas, 102,200,102,300)
    addLine(canvas, 102,300,200,300)
    show(canvas)
    return canvas
```

In general, we'd probably guess (correctly) that the direct instructions given above will run faster than reading the list and interpreting it. Here's an analogy that might help. Mark took French in college but he says he is really bad at it. Let's say that someone gave him a list of instructions in French. He could meticulously look up each word, figure out the instructions, and do them. What if he was asked to do the instructions again? Go look up each word again. Ten times? Ten lookups. Now let's imagine that he wrote down the English (his native language) translation of the French instructions. He can very quickly repeat doing the list of instructions as often as you like. It takes him hardly any time to look up any word. In general, figuring out the language takes up some time that is just overhead—simply *doing* the instructions (or drawing the graphics) will always be faster.

Here's an idea: Could we *generate* the above program? Could we write a program that takes as input the list graphics language we invented, then write a Python program that draws the same pictures? Turns out not to be that hard. This is a **compiler** for the graphics language.

Program 186: Compiler for New Graphics Language

```
def makeGraphics(mylist):
    file = open("graphics.py","wt")
    file.write('def doGraphics():\n')
    file.write('  canvas = makePicture(getMediaPath ("640 x 480.jpg"))\n');
    for i in mylist:
        if i[0] == "b":
            x = int(i[2:5])
            y = int(i[6:9])
            print "Drawing pixel at ",x,":",y
            file.write('  setColor(getPixel(canvas, '+str(x)+', '+str(y)+'),¬
            black)\n')
        if i[0] =="l":
```

¬These lines of the program should continue with the next lines. A single command in Python may not break across multiple lines.

```
       x1 = int(i[2:5])
       y1 = int(i[6:9])
       x2 = int(i[10:13])
       y2 = int(i[14:17])
       print "Drawing line at",x1,y1,x2,y2
       file.write('  addLine(canvas, '+str(x1)+','+str(y1)+','+str(x2)+',¬
       +str(y2)+')\n')
   file.write('  show(canvas)\n')
   file.write('  return canvas\n')
   file.close()
```

¬These lines of the program should continue with the next lines. A single command in Python may not break across multiple lines.

Common Bug: Change Filenames for Your Platform

In this program, we write to "graphics.py". On a Mac, where the default JES folder is inside the application itself, this probably won't work. It will work on Linux and Windows. By this point, you should be able to figure out how to change programs to make them work for your operating system.

How It Works

The compiler accepts the *same* input as the interpreter, but instead of opening a canvas to write to, we open a file. We write to the file the start of a doGraphics function—the def and the code to create a canvas (indented two spaces so that it's inside the block of the doGraphics function). Note that we're not really *making* the canvas here—we're simply writing out the command to make the canvas, which will be executed *later* when doGraphics is executed. Then, just like the interpreter, we figure out which graphics command it is ("b" or "l") and determine the coordinates from the input string. Then we write out to the file the commands to do the drawing. At the end, we write out commands to show and return the canvas, and finally we close the file.

Now the compiler has a lot of overhead. We still have to look up what the commands mean. If we only have a small graphics program to run, and we only need it once, we might as well just run the interpreter. But what if we needed to run the picture 10 times, or 100 times? Then we pay the overhead of compiling the program *once*, and the next 9 or 99 times, we run it as fast as we possibly can. That will almost certainly be faster than doing the interpretation overhead 100 times.

This is what compilers are all about. Applications like Photoshop and Word are written in languages like C or C++ and are then *compiled* to *equivalent* machine-language programs. The machine-language program does the same thing that the C language says to do, just as the graphics programs created from our compiler do the same things as our graphics language says to do. But the machine-language program runs *much* faster than we could interpret the C or C++.

Jython programs are actually *interpreted* and not once but *twice*. Jython is written in Java and Java programs don't typically compile to machine language. (Java *can* be compiled to machine language—it's just not the normal thing that people do with Java.) Java programs compile to a machine language for a *make-believe processor*—a **virtual**

machine. The *Java Virtual Machine* doesn't really exist as a physical processor. It's a definition of a processor. What good is that? It turns out that since machine language is *very* simple, building a machine-language *interpreter* is pretty easy to write.

The result is that a Java Virtual Machine interpreter can be very easily made to run on just about any processor. This means that a program in Java is compiled *once* and then runs *everywhere*. Devices as small as wristwatches can run the same Java programs that run on large computers.

When you run a program in JES, it's actually compiled to Java—an equivalent Java program is written for you. Then the Java is compiled for the Java Virtual Machine. Finally, the Java Virtual Machine interpreter runs the Java machine language of your program. All of which will always be slower than running a compiled form of the same thing.

That's the first part of the answer to the question, "Why is Photoshop always faster than JES?" JES is interpreted *twice*, which will always be slower than Photoshop running in machine language.

Then why have an interpreter at all? There are many good reasons. Here are three:

- Do you like the Command Area? Did you even once ever type in some example code just to *try* it? That kind of interactive, exploratory, trying-things-out programming is only available with interpreters. Compilers don't let you try things out line by line and print the results. Interpreters are good for learners.

- Once a program is compiled to Java machine language, it can be used *anywhere*, as-is, from huge computers to programmable toaster ovens. That's a big savings for software developers. They only ship one program and it runs on anything.

- Virtual machines are safer than machine language. A program running in machine language might do all kinds of nonsecure things. A virtual machine can carefully keep track of the programs it is interpreting to make sure that they only do safe things.

15.2.3   What Limits Computer Speed?

The raw power of compiled as compared to interpreted programs is only part of the answer of why Photoshop is faster. The deeper part, and one that can actually lead to interpreted programs being *faster* than compiled programs, is in the design of the *algorithms*. There's a temptation to think, "Oh, it's okay if it's slow now. Wait 18 months, we'll get double the processor speed, and then it will be fine." There are some algorithms that are *so* slow they will never end in your lifetime and others that can't be written at all. Rewriting the algorithm to be *smarter* about what we ask the computer to do can have a dramatic impact on performance.

An **algorithm** is a description of the way a computer must behave to solve a problem. A program (functions in Python) consists of executable interpretations of algorithms. The same algorithm can be implemented in many different languages. There is always more than one algorithm to solve the same problem—some computer scientists study algorithms and come up with ways to compare them and state which are better than others.

We've seen several algorithms that appear in different ways but are really doing the same things:

- Sampling to scale a picture up or down or to lower or raise the frequency of a sound.
- Blending to merge two pictures or two sounds.
- Mirroring of sounds and pictures.

We can compare algorithms based on several criteria. One is how much *space* the algorithm needs to run. How much memory does the algorithm require? This can become a significant issue for media computation because so much memory is required to hold all that data. Think about how bad an algorithm would be that needed to hold *all* the frames of a movie in a list in memory at the same time.

The most common criterion used to compare algorithms is *time*. How much time does the algorithm take? We don't mean clock time, but how many steps the algorithm requires. Computer scientists use **Big-Oh notation**, or $O()$ to refer to the magnitude of the running time of an algorithm. The idea of Big-Oh is to express how much slower the program gets as the input data get larger. It tries to ignore differences between languages, even between compiled versus interpreted, and focuses on the number of *steps* to be executed.

Think about our basic picture- and sound-processing functions like `increaseRed()` or `increaseVolume()`. Some of the complexity of these functions is hidden in functions like `getPixels()` and `getSamples()`. In general, though, we refer to these as being $O(n)$. The amount of time the program takes to run is proportional linearly to the input data. If the picture or sound doubled in size, we'd expect the program to take twice as long to run.

When we figure out Big-Oh, we typically clump the body of the loop into one step. We think about these functions as processing each sample or pixel once, so the real-time sink in these functions is the loop, and it doesn't really matter how many statements are in the loop.

But, if there is another loop in the loop body, it does matter. Loops are multiplicative in terms of time. Nested loops multiply the amount of time needed to run the body. Think about this toy program:

```
def loops():
  count = 0
  for x in range(1,5):
    for y in range(1,3):
      count = count + 1
      print x,y,"--Ran it ",count,"times"
```

When we run it, we see that it actually executes eight times—four for the x's, two for the y's, and $4 * 2 = 8$.

```
>>> loops()
1 1 --Ran it  1 times
1 2 --Ran it  2 times
2 1 --Ran it  3 times
2 2 --Ran it  4 times
```

```
3 1 --Ran it  5 times
3 2 --Ran it  6 times
4 1 --Ran it  7 times
4 2 --Ran it  8 times
```

How about movie code? Since it takes so long to process, is it actually a more complex algorithm? No, not really. Movie code is just processing each pixel once, so it's still $O(n)$. It's just that the n is really, *really* big!

Not all algorithms are $O(n)$. There is a group of algorithms called **sorting algorithms** that are used to sort data into alphabetical or numerical order. One simple algorithm called the **bubble sort** has a complexity of $O(n^2)$. In a bubble sort, you loop through elements in a list comparing two adjacent elements and swapping their values if they are out of order. You keep doing this until one pass through the list doesn't result in any swaps, which means the data is sorted.

For example, if we started with a list of (3, 2, 1) the following shows the changes in the list.

```
(3,2,1) # compare the 3 and 2 and swap order
(2,3,1) # compare the 3 and 1 and swap order
(2,1,3) # compare the 2 and 1 and swap order
(1,2,3) # no swaps, so the list is sorted
```

If a list has 100 elements, it'll take on the order of 10,000 steps to sort the 100 elements with this kind of sort. However, there are smarter algorithms (like the **quicksort**) that have complexity $O(n * log(n))$. In quicksort, one of the values in the list to be sorted is picked as a pivot. Then the values in the original list are broken into two lists with all the values that are less than the pivot moved into one list and all the values greater or equal to the pivot moved to the other list. Then the two new lists are also sorted using quicksort. A list of one element is sorted, so if any of the lists ever reach that size quicksort just returns that list.

```
(5 1 3 2 7) # pick 3 as pivot
(1 2) 3 (5 7) # pick 2 and 7 as pivots
(1) 2 3 (5) 7 # all lists are of size 1 so
  just return them
(1 2 3 5 7) # combine all returned lists
```

The same list of 100 elements would only take 460 steps to process using quicksort. These kinds of differences start to have huge real world, "measure it on a clock" differences when you're talking about processing 10,000 customers.

15.2.4   Does It Really Make a Difference?

You might be thinking that this sounds like a lot of mathematical gobbledygook. $O(n)$? $O(n^2)$? $O(n!)$? If you do small programs, does it matter if your program is slow?

Here's a thought experiment: imagine that you want to write a program that will generate hit songs for you. Your program will recombine bits of sounds that are some of the best riffs you've ever heard on various instruments—some 60 of them. You want to generate every combination of these 60 bits (some in, some out; some earlier in the song, some later). You want to find the combination that is less than 2 minutes

30 seconds (for optimal radio play time) and has the right amount of high and low volume combinations (and you've got a checkSound() function to do that).

How many combinations are there? Let's ignore order for right now. Let's say that you've got three sounds: *a, b,* and *c*. Your possible songs are *a, b, c, bc, ac, ab,* and *abc*. Try it with two sounds or four sounds and you'll see that the pattern is the same as what we saw earlier with bits: for *n* things, every combination of include-or-exclude is 2^n. (If we ignore the fact that there is an empty song, it's $2^n - 1$.)

Therefore, our 60 sounds will result in 2^{60} combinations to run through our length and sound checks. That's $1,152,921,504,606,846,976$ combinations. Let's imagine that we can do the checks in only a single instruction (unbelievable, of course, but we're pretending). On a 1.5-GHz computer, we can handle that many combinations in 768,614,336 seconds. Spell that out: that's 12,810,238 minutes, which is 213,504 hours, which is 8,896 days. That's 24 *years* to run the program. Now, since Moore's Law doubles process rates every 18 months, we will soon be able to run the program in much less time. Only *12 years!* If we cared about order, too (e.g., *abc* vs. *cba* vs. *bac*), the number of combinations has 63 zeroes in it.

Finding the absolutely optimal combination of just about anything is always time expensive. $O(2^n)$ like this is not an uncommon running time for these kinds of algorithms. But there are other problems that seem as if they should be do-able in a reasonable time but aren't.

One of these is the famous *Traveling Salesman Problem*. Imagine that you're a salesperson and you're responsible for many different clients—let's say 30, half the size of the optimization problem. To be efficient, you want to find the shortest path on the map that will let you visit each client exactly once, and not more than once.

The best-*known* algorithm that gives an optimal solution for the Traveling Salesman Problem is $O(n!)$. That's *n* factorial. There are algorithms that take less time to run that give close but not guaranteed shortest paths. For 30 cities, the number of steps to execute with one of these $O(n!)$ algorithms is 30!, or 265,252,859,812,191,058,636,308, 480,000,000. Go ahead and run that on a 1.5-GHz processor—it won't get done in your lifetime.

The really aggravating part is that the Traveling Salesman Problem isn't a made-up, toy problem. There really are people who have to plan the shortest routes in the world. There are similar problems that are basically the same algorithmically, like planning the route of a robot on a factory floor. This is a big, hard problem.

How big of a difference is $O(n)$ from $O(n!)$. Let's graph it. Our input *n* will vary from 1 to 10. The curves in Figure 15.2 represent various curves on a log scale (look how fast the numbers increase on the vertical axis). If to process *n* pieces of data takes about *n* steps (or even 5*n* or 1,000*n*), then our curve is *linear* and program isn't too slow. But if you get to *n*!, even at just 10 pieces of data, you are at nearly 10 million steps. If each step costs you one billionth of a second, you can process 10 pieces of data. But 20? 100? $O(n!)$ is too slow for most real problems.

But now does $O(n * log(n))$ versus $O(n^2)$ really make a difference? From looking at Figure 15.2, it doesn't look like there's much of a difference. As *n* gets bigger, though, the difference grows. Look at Figure 15.3. The curve for $O(n^2)$ grows much faster than

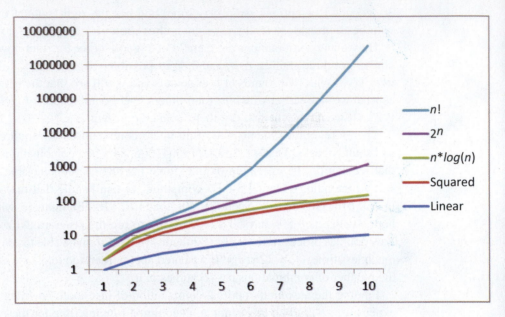

FIGURE 15.2
Various O curves, on a log scale.

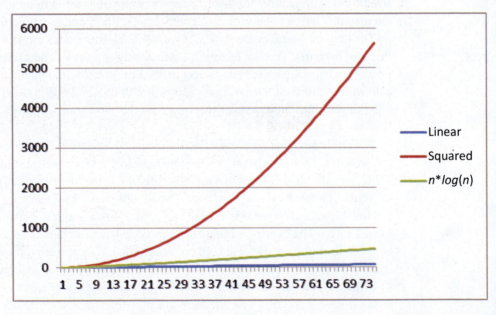

FIGURE 15.3
A few O curves, on a linear scale.

for $O(n * log(n))$. As your program processes more data, it will take *increasingly* longer for an $O(n^2)$ algorithm to run, compared to an $O(n * log(n))$ algorithm.

15.2.5   Making Searching Faster

Consider how you might look up a word in the dictionary. One way is to check the first page, then the next page, then the next page, and so on. That's called a *linear search* and it's $O(n)$. It's not very efficient. The *best case* (the fastest the algorithm could possibly be) is that the problem is solved in one step—the word is on the first page. The *worst case* is n steps where n is the number of pages—the word could be missing. The *average case* is $n/2$ steps—the word is halfway through.

We can implement this as searching in a list.

Program 187: Linear Search of a List

```
def findInSortedList(something, alist):
  for item in alist:
    if item == something:
      return "Found it!"
  return "Not found"
```

```
>>> findInSortedList ("bear",["apple","bear","cat","dog",
"elephant"])
'Found it!'
>>> findInSortedList ("giraffe",["apple","bear","cat",
"dog", "elephant"])
'Not found'
```

But let's use the fact that dictionaries are already in sorted order. We can be smarter about how we search for a word and do it in $O(log(n))$ time ($log(n) = x$, where $2^x = n$). Split the dictionary in the middle. Is the word before or after the page you're looking at? If after, look from the middle to the end (e.g., again split the book, but from the middle to end). If before, look from the start to the middle (split halfway between start and middle). Keep repeating until you find the word or it couldn't possibly be there. This is a more efficient algorithm. In the best case, the word is in the first place you look. In the average and worst case, it's $log(n)$ steps—keep dividing the n pages in half, and you'll have at most $log(n)$ splits.

Here's a simple (i.e., not the best possible, but illustrative) implementation of this kind of a search, called **binary search**.

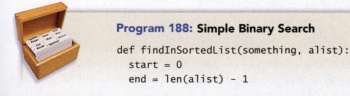

Program 188: Simple Binary Search

```
def findInSortedList(something, alist):
  start = 0
  end = len(alist) - 1
```

```
   while start <= end: #While there are more to search
      checkpoint = int((start+end)/2.0)
      if alist[checkpoint]==something:
        return "Found it!"
      if alist[checkpoint]<something:
        start=checkpoint+1
      if alist[checkpoint]>something:
        end=checkpoint-1
   return "Not found"
```

How It Works

We start with the low-end marker `start` at the beginning of the list (0) and `end` at the end of the list (length of the list minus 1). As long as `start` is less than or equal to `end`, we continue to search. We compute the `checkpoint` as halfway between the `start` and `end`. We then check to see if we found it. If so, we're done and we `return`. If not, we figure out whether we have to move `start` up to one past the `checkpoint` or `end` down to one less than the `checkpoint`. And we continue searching. If we ever get through the whole loop, we didn't take the "Found it!" `return`, so we `return` that we didn't find what we were searching for.

To see what this is doing, stick in a line after the calculation of the `checkpoint` that prints the values of `checkpoint`, `start`, and `end`:

```
printNow("Checking at: "+str(checkpoint)+"
  Start:"+str(start)+" End:"+str(end))
>>> findInSortedList("giraffe",["apple","bear","cat",
  "dog"])
Checking at: 1 Start:0 End:3
Checking at: 2 Start:2 End:3
Checking at: 3 Start:3 End:3
'Not found'
>>> findInSortedList("apple",["apple","bear","cat",
  "dog"])
Checking at: 1 Start:0 End:3
Checking at: 0 Start:0 End:0
'Found it!'
>>> findInSortedList("dog",["apple","bear","cat",
  "dog"])
Checking at: 1 Start:0 End:3
Checking at: 2 Start:2 End:3
Checking at: 3 Start:3 End:3
'Found it!'
>>> findInSortedList("bear",["apple","bear","cat",
  "dog"])
Checking at: 1 Start:0 End:3
'Found it!'
```

Notice that we said `checkpoint = int((start+end)/2.0)`, and not simply `checkpoint = (start+end)/2`. Is there any difference? The latter seems simpler.

15.2.6   Algorithms That Never Finish or Can't Be Written

Computer scientists classify problems into three piles:

- Many problems, like sorting, can be solved with an algorithm whose running time has a complexity that's a polynomial, like $O(n^2)$. We call these *class P* (P for polynomial) problems.

  Think of all the programs that we have written in this book. These are all in class P. Want to remove red eye? We can do that. Want to find the edges of a picture? We can do that. Want to create an echo effect in a sound? We can do that, too, all in polynomial time.

  Lots of other things that we may want to do are also solvable in polynomial time. Looking up the price of a book given an ISBN code can be done just like the searching we just did (or even faster, using other algorithms). Figuring out the best path from your house to your Grandmother's is also easily computed by your GPS device.

- Other problems, like optimization, have known algorithms that really work, but they are too slow even for small amounts of data. We call these problems *intractable*. That does not mean that we *cannot* solve these problems. The programs just run slowly.

  We *can* make some of them run faster—basically by cheating. We compute a solution that isn't *quite* optimal.

- Still other problems, like the Traveling Salesman, *seem* intractable, but maybe there's a solution in class P that we just haven't found yet. We call these *class NP*.

One of the biggest unsolved problems in theoretical computer science is proving either that class NP and class P are completely distinct (i.e., we'll never solve the Traveling Salesman optimally in polynomial time) or that class NP is within class P. Can we actually solve class NP problems in polynomial time (class P)? Or is it impossible?

You may be wondering whether *anything* can be proved about algorithms. There are so many different languages and different ways of writing the same algorithm. How can we positively *prove* that something is doable or not doable? We can, it turns out. In fact, Alan Turing proved that there are even algorithms that *can't be written*.

The most famous algorithm that can't be written is the solution to the *Halting Problem*. We've already written programs that can read other programs and write out other programs. Imagine a program that can read one program and tell us things about it (e.g., how many `print` statements are in it). Can we write a program that will input another program (e.g., from a file), then tell us whether the input program will ever *stop*? Think about the input program having some complex `while` loops where it's hard to tell whether the expression in the `while` loop is ever `false`. Now imagine a bunch of these, all nested within one another.

Alan Turing proved that such an analysis program could never be written. You can't write a program that can analyze an input program and tell you conclusively if it would ever stop. He used proof by absurdity. He showed that if such a program (call it H) could be written, you could try feeding that program to itself as input. Now H takes input, a program, right? What if you modified H (call it H2) so that if H said, "This one halts!" H2 would loop forever (e.g., while 1:). Turing showed that such a setup would announce that the program would halt only if it loops forever, and would halt only if it announces that it would loop forever.

The really amazing thing is that Turing came up with this proof in 1936—almost 10 years before the first computers were built. He defined a mathematical concept of a computer called a *Turing machine* and was able to make such proofs before physical computers even came into existence.

Here's another thought experiment: Is human intelligence computable? Our brains are executing a process that enables us to think, right? Can we write down that process as an algorithm? And if a computer executes that algorithm, is it thinking? Is a human reducible to a computer? This is one of the big questions in the field of **artificial intelligence**.

Artificial intelligence gives us a whole set of practical techniques for dealing with really hard problems. These techniques are sometimes called *heuristics*, rules of thumb that let you get a good-enough answer. Think about the problem of translating one human language to another. To do this completely *right*, to understand every word and its meaning, and to understand human language syntax is all a really hard problem. How is that Web services can do it today? They often use a *machine learning* approach. They compare lots of documents in both languages, and figure out statistical probabilities that (for example) this word in French matches this word in English. Using these probabilities, they can create a document that is *likely* to be an understandable translation, but isn't actually *exactly* right. Often, that's all you need.

15.2.7   Why Is Photoshop Faster than JES?

We can now answer the question of why Photoshop is faster than JES. First, Photoshop is compiled, so it runs at raw machine-language speeds.

But, secondly, Photoshop has algorithms that are smarter than what we're doing. For example, think about the programs where we searched for colors, like in chromakey or in making Katie's hair red. We know that the background color and the hair color were clumped next to one another. What if, instead of linearly searching all the pixels, you just searched from where the color was what you were looking for until you didn't find that color anymore? Finding the boundary this way would be a smarter search. That's the kind of thing that Photoshop does.

15.3   WHAT MAKES A COMPUTER FAST?

Computers are getting faster all the time—Moore's Law promises us that. But knowing this doesn't help us to compare computers that all belong to the same Moore's Law generation. How do you compare ads in the paper and figure out which of the listed computers is *really* the fastest?

Simply being fast is only one criterion for picking a computer, of course. There are issues of cost, how much disk space you need, what kind of expansion features you need, and so on. But in this section we'll explicitly deal with what the various factors in computer ads mean in terms of computer speed (see Figure 15.4 for some examples).

> **Processor:** Intel® Atom™ Processor Dual-Core N570, (1.66GHz, 1MB L2 cache, 667MHz FSB)
> **Graphics:** Intel® Graphics Media Accelerator 3150
> **Display:** 10.1" WSVGA (1024x600)
> **Memory:** 1024MB DDR3 SDRAM Memory
> **Storage Drive:** 250GB 5400RPM SATA Hard Drive

> Key features: Intel® Core™ i3-2120 processor; 4GB DDR3 memory; 1TB hard drive;
> Windows 7 Home Premium; built-in wireless networking;
> HDMI output; 21.5" widescreen LED monitor included

FIGURE 15.4
A couple of sample computer advertisements.

15.3.1   Clock Rates and Actual Computation

When computer ads state that they have a "Some-brand Processor 2.8 GHz" or "Other-brand Processor 3.0 GHz," what they're talking about is the *clock rate*. The processor is the smarts of your computer—it's the part that makes decisions and does computation. It does all this computing work at a certain *pace*. Imagine a drill sergeant shouting, "Go! Go! Go! Go!" That's what the clock rate is—it tells you how fast the drill sergeant shouts "Go!" A clock rate of 1.66 GHz means that the clock *pulses* (the drill sergeant shouts "Go!") 1.66 *billion* times per second.

This doesn't mean that the processor actually does something useful with every "Go!" Some computations have several steps, so it may take several pulses of the clock to complete a single useful computation. But *in general* a faster clock rate implies faster computation. Certainly, for the same *kind* of processor, a faster clock rate implies faster computation.

Is there really any difference between 1.66 GHz and 2.0 GHz? Or is 1.0 GHz with processor X about the same as 2.0 GHz with processor Y? These are much tougher questions. It's not really that much different from arguing over Dodge versus Ford trucks. Most processors have their advocates and their critics. Some will argue that processor X can do a certain search in very few clock pulses because of how well it's designed, so it's clearly faster even at a slower clock rate. Others will say that processor Y is still faster overall because its average number of clock pulses per computation is so low—and how common is the type of search that X does so fast, anyway? It's almost like arguing about whose religion is better.

Many computers that you will purchase today have multiple *cores*. Each core is literally a whole other processor. A *dual core* computer then actually has *two* processors on its main chip. *Quad core* computers have *four* processors. Does this mean that these computers are two or four times faster? Unfortunately, it doesn't work that cleanly. Not all programs are written to take advantage of the multiple cores. It's hard to write a program that essentially says, "Okay, now the next piece of the computation can be done in *parallel*, so here's this piece and there's that piece, and here's how we'll put it together in the end." If none of your software is written to take advantage of multiple cores, then having them will not make things much faster at all. One of computer science's great challenges today is how to take advantage of all these multiple cores to make computers work faster for people.

The real answer is to try some realistic work on the computer that you're considering. Does it feel fast enough? Check reviews in computer magazines—they often use realistic tasks (like sorting in Excel and scrolling in Word) to test the speed of computers.

Most of the computers that you use these days are hidden from you or are difficult to compare in terms of processor speed. Is a Blackberry faster or slower than an iPhone or a Droid? Smartphones are not typically sold in terms of processor speed. Smartphones are comparable on many other factors of more importance, like network speed and display quality. Power is actually a big deal with respect to speed—faster processors typically do take more power, so sometimes a manufacturer will use a slower processor to save battery life. Most of the computers that you interact with every day are hidden from you (sometimes called *embedded computing*), from your watch to your microwave, and even the motion detection switch that might turn off the lights when no one is moving (or turn on the video camera at night when no one is *expected* to be moving). In those cases, you don't really care about clock speed. You simply care whether the computer can do its job.

15.3.2   Storage: What Makes a Computer Slow?

The speed of your processor is only one factor in what makes a computer fast or slow. Probably a bigger factor is where the processor goes to get the data it works with. Where are your pictures when your computer goes to work on them? That's a much more complex question.

You can think about your storage as being in a hierarchy, from the fastest to the slowest.

- Your fastest storage is your **cache memory**. Cache is memory that is physically located on the same silicon chip as your processor (or very, very close to it). Your processor takes care of putting as much as possible in the cache and leaving it there as long as it's needed. Cache is accessed far faster than anything else on your computer. The more cache memory you have, the more things the computer can access very quickly. But cache (of course) is also your most expensive storage.

- Your *RAM* storage (whether it's called **SDRAM** or any other kind of **RAM**) is your computer's main *memory*. **RAM** (an acronym for **random access memory**) of 256 MB (megabytes) means 256 *million* bytes of information. Memory of 1 GB (gigabyte) means 1 billion bytes of information. RAM storage is where your programs reside when they're executing and it's where the data that your computer is directly acting upon is located. Things are in your RAM storage before they're loaded into the cache. RAM is less expensive than cache memory and is probably your best investment in terms of making your computer faster.

- Your **hard disk** is where you store all your **files**. Your program that you're executing now in RAM started out as an .exe (executable) file on your hard disk. All your digital pictures, digital music, word-processing files, spreadsheet files, and so on, are stored on your hard disk. Your hard disk is your *slowest* storage but it's also your largest. A hard disk of 256 GB (*gigabyte*) means that you can store 256 *billion* bytes on it. That's a *lot* of space—and it's pretty small these days. A hard disk of 1 TB (*terabyte*) can store 1,000 gigabytes, or one *trillion* bytes.

Movement between levels in the hierarchy means a huge speed difference. It has been said that if the speed of access of cache memory is like reaching for a paper clip on your desk, then getting something off the hard disk means traveling to Alpha Centauri—four light-years away from Earth. Obviously, we *do* get things off our disk at reasonable speeds (which really implies that cache memory is phenomenally fast!) but the analogy does emphasize how very different the levels of the hierarchy are in respect to speed. The bottom line is that the more you have of the faster memory, the faster your processor can get the information you want and the faster your overall processing will be.

You'll see advertisements occasionally mentioning the **system bus**. The system bus is how signals are sent around your computer—from video or network to hard disk, from RAM to the printer. A faster system bus clearly implies a faster overall system but may not influence (for example) the speed of your experience with JES or Photoshop. First, even the fastest bus is much slower than the processor—400 million pulses per second versus 4 billion pulses per second. Second, the system bus doesn't usually influence the access to cache or memory, and that's where most of the speed is won or lost anyway.

There are things that you can do to make your hard disk as fast as possible for your computation. The speed of the disk isn't that significant for processing time—even the fastest disks are still far slower than the slowest RAM. Leaving enough free space on your disk for **swapping** is important. When your computer doesn't have enough RAM for what you're asking it to do, it stores some of the data that it isn't currently using from RAM on your hard disk. Moving data to and from your hard disk is a slow process (relatively speaking, compared to access to RAM). Having a fast disk with enough free space that the computer doesn't have to search around for **swap space** helps with processing speed.

How about the network? In terms of speed, the network doesn't really help you. The network is magnitudes slower than your hard disk. There are differences in network speeds that do influence your overall experience but not necessarily the speed of processing of your computer. Wired Ethernet connections tend to be faster than wireless Ethernet connections. Modem connections are slower.

15.3.3   Display

How about the display? Does the speed of your display really affect the speed of your computer? No, not really. Computers are really, *really* fast. The computer can repaint everything even on really large displays faster than you can perceive.

The only application where the display speed may matter is really high-end computer gaming. Some computer gamers claim that they can perceive a difference between 50 frames per second and 60 frames per second updates of the screen. If your display was really large and everything had to be repainted with every update, then *maybe* a faster processor would make a difference you could perceive. But most modern computers update so quickly that you just wouldn't notice a difference.

PROBLEMS

15.1   Explain what the difference is between an interpreter and a compiler.

15.2   What is machine language? How is it similar or different than *bytecodes* for the Java Virtual Machine? You will probably have to investigate on the Internet to answer these questions.

15.3   Explain the difference between RAM and cache memory.

15.4   There are lots of different kinds of sorting algorithms. Investigate some on the Internet. Which ones are considered fast, and under what conditions?

15.5   Find animations of different sorting algorithms on the Internet. How would you describe difference between a bubble sort and a quicksort in terms of what you see in the animations?

15.6   Write a function to do an insertion sort on a list.

15.7   Write a function to do a selection sort on a list.

15.8   Write a function to do a bubble sort on a list.

15.9   Write a function to do a quicksort on a list.

15.10   How many times will the following code print out the message?
```
for x in range(0,5):
   for y in range(0,10):
      print "I will be good"
```

15.11   How many times will the following code print out the message?
```
for x in range(1,5):
   for y in range(0,10,2):
      print "I will be good"
```

15.12   How many times will the following code print out the message?
```
for x in range(0,3):
   for y in range(1,5):
      print "I will be good"
```

15.13   What is the Big-Oh of the method `clearBlue`?

15.14   What is the Big-Oh of the method `lineDetect`?

15.15   Trace through the binary search algorithm in `findInSortedList` given the following input.
```
findInSortedList("8",["3","5","7","9","10"])
```

15.16   Trace through the binary search algorithm in `findInSortedList` given the following input.
```
findInSortedList("3",["3","5","7","9","10"])
```

15.17   Trace through the binary search algorithm in `findInSortedList` given the following input.
```
findInSortedList("1",["3","5","7","9","10"])
```

15.18   Trace through the binary search algorithm in `findInSortedList` given the following input.
```
findInSortedList("7",["3","5","7","9","10"])
```

15.19   You've now seen some examples of class P problems (e.g., sorting and searching), intractable problems (optimization of the song elements), and class NP problems (e.g., the Traveling Salesman Problem). Search the Web and find at least one more example of each class of problem.

15.20   Try something that takes a while in JES (e.g., chromakey on a large image). Use the `time` module to time how long it takes. Now time the same JES task on several different computers with different amounts of memory and different clock rates (and different amounts of cache, if you can). See what difference the different factors make in terms of the time it takes to complete the task in JES.

15.21   Alan Turing is known for another important finding in computer science, besides the proof that the Halting Problem is unsolvable. He gave us our test for whether a computer has actually achieved intelligence. What is the name of this test and how does it work? Do you agree that it is a test of intelligence?

15.22   How do people get answers to problems that have algorithms that would take way too long to find the optimal result? Sometimes they use *heuristics*: rules that don't lead to a perfect solution, but find a solution. Look up some heuristics used to compute the next move in a chess playing program.

15.23   Find an algorithm that solves the Traveling Salesman Problem in reasonable run time but isn't optimal.

15.24   The program *Watson* successfully beat humans at the game *Jeopardy*. Find articles on the Internet that explain how Watson did it. Does it guarantee that it always finds the best solution?

TO DIG DEEPER

To learn more about what makes a program work *well*, we recommend reading *Structure and Interpretation of Computer Programs* [17]. It's not about gigahertz and cache memories but it tells a lot about how you should think about your programs to make them work well.

Functional Programming

Chapter Learning Objectives

- To write programs more easily with more functions.
- To use functional programming to make powerful programs quickly.
- To understand what makes functional programming different from procedural or imperative programming.
- To be able to use `else` in Python.
- To be able to use `global` in Python.

16.1   USING FUNCTIONS TO MAKE PROGRAMMING EASIER

Why do we use functions? How can we use them to make programming easier? We have been talking about multiple functions at various points in this book. Let's summarize some of the benefits here, before we start talking about programming with functions in a more powerful way.

Functions are for managing complexity. Can we write all our programs as one large function? Sure, but it gets *hard*. As programs grow in size, they grow in complexity. We use functions:

- To hide away details so that we only focus on what we care about.
- To find the right place to make changes as you need to in a program—finding the right function is easier than finding a single line in few thousand lines of code.
- To make it easier to test and debug our programs.

If we break a program into smaller pieces, we can test each piece separately. Think about our HTML programs. We can test functions like `doctype()`, `title()`, and `body()` separately from the Command Area, rather than always having to test the whole thing. This way, you can deal with the smaller functions and smaller problems until they are solved—then you can ignore them and focus on the bigger problems.

```
>>> print doctype()
<!DOCTYPE html>
>>> print title("My title string")
<html><head><title>My title string</title></head>
>>> print body("<h1>My heading</h1>")
<body><h1>My heading</h1></body></html>
```

Being able to test small functions as shown above is useful when you are looking for problems (bugs). It also enables you to *trust* your functions. Try them in different ways. Convince yourself that the function always performs the task you're asking it to do. Once you have this trust, you can ask the function to do its task without thinking about it—then you can do some amazingly powerful things (see the next section).

Adding additional functions makes the whole program easier, if the functions are chosen well. If we have subfunctions that do smaller pieces of the overall task, we talk about changing the **granularity** of the functions. If the granularity gets too small, it swaps one kind of complexity for another. But at the right level, it makes the overall program easier to understand and to change.

Think about a home page program like this, with much smaller granularity than what we were doing before:

Program 189: Smaller Granularity Home Page Generator

```
def makeHomePage2(name,interests):
  file=open(getMediaPath("homepage.html"),"wt")
  file.write(doctype())
  file.write(startHTML())
  file.write(startHead())
  file.write(title2(name+"'s Home Page"))
  file.write(endHead())
  file.write(startBody())
  file.write(heading(1,"Welcome to "+name+"'s Home Page"))
  text = "Hi!  I am "+name+".  This is my home page!"
  text += " I am interested in "+interests
  file.write(paragraph(text))
  file.write(paragraph("Random thought for the day: "+tagline()))
  file.write(endBody())
  file.write(endHTML())
  file.close()

def doctype():
  return '<!DOCTYPE html>'

def startHTML():
  return '<html>'

def startHead():
  return '<head>'

def endHead():
  return '</head>'
```

```
def heading(level,string):
  return "<h"+str(level)+">"+string+"</h"+str(level)+">"

def startBody():
  return "<body>"

def paragraph(string):
  return "<p>"+string+"</p>"

def title2(titlestring):
  return "<title>"+titlestring+"</title>"

def endBody():
  return "</body>"

def endHTML():
  return "</html>"
```

■

This version is even easier to test. It has a big advantage over our earlier versions in that the home page generation function doesn't have any HTML in it at all. All of the HTML has been hidden inside of subfunctions. That's useful.

But now there's a new complexity. There are all those function names to remember. We have to remember the required ordering of all those functions (e.g., that you have to endHead() before you startBody()). This level of granularity may be too much.

Making It Work Tip: Use Subfunctions for the Hard Parts

Whenever you have a hard part in a program, break it into subfunctions so that you can debug and fix each of them separately.

■

Think about the HTML program to generate a samples page. The loop was the hard part of the program, so let's break it into a separate subfunction. This makes it easier to change how links are formatted—it's all down in the subfunction.

Program 190: Samples Page Creator with a Subfunction

```
def makeSamplePage2(directory):
  samplesFile=open(directory+"/samples.html","wt")
  samplesFile.write(doctype())
  samplesFile.write(title("Samples from "+directory))
  # Now, let's make up the string that will be the body.
  samples=heading(1,"Samples from "+directory)
  for file in os.listdir(directory):
   if file.endswith(".jpg"):
     samples += fileEntry(file)
  samplesFile.write(body(samples))
  samplesFile.close()
```

```
def fileEntry(file):
    text  ="<p>Filename: "+file
    text += '<image src="'+file+'"height="100"></p>'
    return(text)
```

Breaking out the pieces like this is part of **procedural abstraction**. The steps in procedural abstraction are:

- State the problem. Figure out what you want to do.
- Break the problem into subproblems.
- Keep breaking the subproblems into smaller problems until you know how to write the program that solves the smaller problem.
- Your goal is for the main function to basically tell all the subfunctions what to do. Each subfunction should do *one and only one* logical task.

We can think about procedural abstraction as filling in a *tree* of functions (see Figure 16.1). Making modifications is a matter of changing *one* node (function) on this tree and making additions is a matter of adding a node. For example, adding in the functionality to handle WAV files in our samples page only requires changing the function `fileEntry`, when it's broken down like this (Figure 16.2).

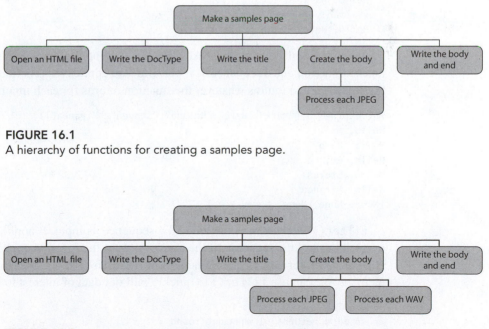

FIGURE 16.1
A hierarchy of functions for creating a samples page.

FIGURE 16.2
Changing the program is only a slight change to the hierarchy.

16.2   FUNCTIONAL PROGRAMMING WITH MAP AND REDUCE

If you're willing to trust your functions, you can write fewer lines of code and get the same programs written. When you really understand functions, and trust that your functions do what you meant them to do, you can do amazing things in a very few lines of code. We can write functions that apply functions to data and even have functions call themselves in a process called **recursion**.

Functions are just names that are associated with values that are pieces of code, rather than lists or sequences or numbers or strings. We invoke or call a function by stating its name followed by inputs in parentheses. Without parentheses, the name of the function still has a value—it's the function's code. Functions can also be *data*—they can be passed as inputs to *other* functions!

```
>>> print makeSamplePage2
<function makeSamplePage2 at 0x21>
>>> print fileEntry
<function fileEntry at 0x22>
```

The function `apply()` calls another function specified as input to `apply()`. The inputs for the called function are also inputs to `apply()`, as a sequence or list. Literally, `apply()` applies the function to the input.

```
def hello(someone):
  print "Hello,",someone
>>> hello("Mark")
Hello, Mark
>>> apply(hello,["Mark"])
Hello, Mark
>>> apply(hello,["Betty"])
Hello, Betty
```

A more useful function that takes functions as input is `map()`. It's a function that takes a function and a sequence as input. But map applies the function to *each* input in the sequence and returns whatever the function returns for each input.

```
>>> map(hello,["Mark","Barb","Briana","Steven","Miranda"])
Hello, Mark
Hello, Barb
Hello, Briana
Hello, Steven
Hello, Miranda
[None, None, None, None, None]
```

`filter()` also takes a function and a sequence as input. It applies the function to each element of the sequence. If the *return value* of the function on that element is true (1), then the filter returns that element. If the return is false (0), then the filter skips that element. We can use `filter()` to quickly pull out data of interest to us.

```
def rInName(someName):
  # find returns -1 when not found
  if someName.find("r") == -1:
    return 0
```

```
    # if not -1 then found
    if someName.find("r") != -1:
      return 1

>>> rInName("January")
1
>>> rInName("July")
0
>>> filter(rInName, ["Mark","Betty","Matthew","Jenny"])
['Mark']
```

We can rewrite rInName() above (a function that returns true if the input word contains an "r") in a much shorter form. Expressions actually do evaluate to 1 or 0 (true or false). We can perform operations on these *logical values*. One of these **logical operators** is not—it returns the opposite of its input value. So here's rInName() written using logical operators.

```
def rInName2(someName):
  return not(someName.find("r") == -1)


>>> filter(rInName2, ["Mark","Betty","Matthew","Jenny"])
['Mark']
```

reduce() also takes a function and a sequence but reduce *combines* the results. Below is an example where we total all the numbers: $1 + 2$, then $(1 + 2) + 3$, then $(1 + 2 + 3) + 4$, and finally $(1 + 2 + 3 + 4) + 5$. The total so far is passed in as the a input.

```
def add(a,b):
  return a+b


>>> reduce(add,[1,2,3,4,5])
15
```

Let's look at the example again: Doesn't it seem like a waste to have to create that add function when it's so small and does so little? It turns out that we don't have to give a function a name in order to be able to use it. A nameless function is called a lambda. This is a very old term in computer science, one that dates back to one of the original programming languages, Lisp. Wherever you would otherwise use a function name, you can just stick in a lambda. The syntax of a lambda is the word lambda followed by input variables separated by commas, then a colon, then the body of the function. Here are some examples, including the above reduce example recreated with lambda. As you can see, we can define functions that are virtually identical to the ones typed in the Program Area by assigning a name to a lambda.

```
>>> reduce(lambda a,b:a+b, [1,2,3,4,5])
15
>>> (lambda a:"Hello,"+a)("Mark")
'Hello,Mark'
>>> f=lambda a:"Hello, "+a
>>> f
<function <lambda> 6>
>>> f("Mark")
'Hello, Mark'
```

How it Works

The first line creates an unnamed function (a "lambda") that takes in two numbers, then returns the sum of those two numbers. When we use `reduce` with that `lambda` on `[1,2,3,4,5]`, we get 1+2 (3), then 3+3 (6), then 6+4 (10), then 10+5, to return 15. In the second line, we apply a lambda that adds `"Hello, "` before the input, `"Mark"`, which gives us `"Hello, Mark"`. We take that new "Hello" function and actually name it with `f`. The variable `f` has a value of a function, and we can apply it to `"Mark"` just like the unnamed version.

Using `reduce` and `lambda`, we can do real computation. Here's a function that computes the **factorial** of the passed number. The factorial of some number n is the product of all the positive integers less or equal to n. For example, the factorial of 4 is $(4*3*2*1)$.

Program 191: Calculating Factorial Using `lambda` and `reduce`

```
def factorial(a):
  return reduce(lambda a,b:a*b, range(1,a+1))
```

How It Works

It's easier to read this program right to left. The first thing we do is to create a list of all the numbers from 1 to a with `range(1,a+1)`. We then use `reduce` to apply a function (the `lambda`) that multiplies all the numbers in the input list one by the next, by the next, and on until finished.

```
>>> factorial(2)
2
>>> factorial(3)
6
>>> factorial(4)
24
>>> factorial(10)
3628800
```

You might be thinking at this point, "Okay, map, `filter`, and `reduce` look like they might be useful. *Might*. Sometimes. But why in the world would anyone want to use `apply`? That's the same as just typing the function call ourselves, isn't it?" That's true but we can actually *make* map, `filter`, and `reduce` using `apply`. We can literally make any version of these that we might want ourselves using `apply`.

```
def myMap(function,list):
  for i in list:
    apply(function,[i])

>>> myMap(hello, ["Fred","Barney","Wilma","Betty"])
Hello, Fred
Hello, Barney
Hello, Wilma
Hello, Betty
```

This style of programming is called **functional programming**. What we've been doing in Python up to now might be called *procedural programming*, because our focus is on defining procedures, or *imperative programming*, because we are mostly telling the computer to do things and change variable values (also called *state*). Focusing on functions as data and on functions that use functions as input are key ideas in functional programming.

Functional programming is amazingly powerful. You apply layers upon layers of functions to other functions and you end up doing a lot in a few lines of program code. Functional programming is used in building artificial intelligence systems and in building prototypes. These are areas where the problems are hard and ill-defined, so you want to be able to do a lot with only a few lines of program code—even if those few lines are pretty hard to read for most people.

16.3   FUNCTIONAL PROGRAMMING FOR MEDIA

Remember the function to turn Katie's hair red—Program 48 (page 116)? Here it is again:

```
def turnRed():
  brown = makeColor(42,25,15)
  picture=makePicture("katieFancy.jpg")
  for px in getPixels(picture):
    color = getColor(px)
    if distance(color,brown)<50.0:
      redness=int(getRed(px)*2)
      blueness=getBlue(px)
      greenness=getGreen(px)
      setColor(px,makeColor(redness,blueness,greenness))
  show(picture)
  return(picture)
```

We can write it as only a *single line* of program code. We need two utility functions—one that will check a single pixel for whether we want to turn the pixel red and another that will actually do it. Our single line of program code filters out the pixels that match our criteria for changing, then maps the change function to those pixels. In functional programming, you don't write functions with big loops. Instead, you write small functions and apply them to the data. It's like we're bringing the function to the data, rather than making the function go get all the data.

Program 192: Turn Hair Red, Functionally
```
def turnHairRed(pic):
  map(turnRed,filter(checkPixel,getPixels(pic)))

def checkPixel(aPixel):
  brown = makeColor(42,25,15)
  return distance (getColor(aPixel),brown)<50.0

def turnRed(aPixel):
  setRed(aPixel,getRed(aPixel)*2)
```

How It Works

The function `turnRed` takes a single pixel and doubles its redness percentage. The function `checkPixel` returns true or false if an input pixel is close enough to brown. The function `turnHairRed` takes a picture as input, then applies `checkPixel` using `filter` to all the pixels in the input picture (using `getPixels`). If the pixel is brown enough, `filter` returns it. We then use `map` to apply `turnRed` to all the pixels that `filter` returns.

Here's how we use it:

```
>>> pic=makePicture("KatieFancy.jpg")
>>> map(turnRed, filter(checkPixel, getPixels(pic)))
```

16.3.1   Media Manipulation without Changing State

Another important aspect of functional programming is programming *without state*. Our color manipulation functions (for example) change the object that is provided to the function as an input. Good functional programs do not do that. If an object is to be changed, a good functional program makes a copy of the object then modifies and returns the copied object. The advantage is that one can nest functions, passing the output of one to the input of the other, just as one can nest mathematical functions. No one expects that $sine(cosine(x))$ should change x any more than just $sine(x)$ changes x. Functions in the functional programming style should work the same. We say that these functions have no *side effects*. The functions only do what they are supposed to do and *return* a result. They don't change the inputs in any way.

Let's see what it would look like to create media manipulation functions that do not change state.

Program 193: Changing Colors without Changing the Picture

```
def decreaseRed(aPicture):
  returnPic = makeEmptyPicture(getWidth(aPicture),getHeight(aPicture))
  for x in range(getWidth(aPicture)):
    for y in range(getHeight(aPicture)):
      srcPixel = getPixelAt(aPicture,x,y)
      returnPixel = getPixelAt(returnPic,x,y)
      setColor(returnPixel,getColor(srcPixel))
      setRed(returnPixel, 0.8*getRed(srcPixel))
  return returnPic


def increaseBlue(aPicture):
  returnPic = makeEmptyPicture(getWidth(aPicture),getHeight(aPicture))
  for x in range(getWidth(aPicture)):
    for y in range(getHeight(aPicture)):
      srcPixel = getPixelAt(aPicture,x,y)
      returnPixel = getPixelAt(returnPic,x,y)
      setColor(returnPixel,getColor(srcPixel))
      setBlue(returnPixel, 1.2*getBlue(srcPixel))
  return returnPic
```

How It Works

Both of these functions have the same basic structure. An object to be returned, `returnPic`, is created of the same size as the input picture. For each pixel in the input picture, we copy the color to the corresponding pixel in the `returnPic` picture. We then decrease red or increase blue. Finally, we return the `returnPic`.

With these functions, we can apply these to a picture without changing the original picture. We can nest the functions in any way we want. Now the functions are much more like mathematical functions.

```
>>> newp = increaseBlue(decreaseRed(p))
>>> show(newp)
>>> show(decreaseRed(p))
>>> show(decreaseRed(increaseBlue(p)))
>>> show(increaseBlue(p))
```

16.4 RECURSION: A POWERFUL IDEA

Recursion is writing functions that call *themselves*. Instead of writing loops, you write a function that loops by calling itself again and again and again. When you write a recursive function, you always have at least two pieces:

- What to do when you're done (e.g., when you're processing the very last item in the data); and
- What to do when the data are larger, which usually involves processing one element of the data, then recalling the function to deal with the rest.

Let's explore recursion with some simple textual functions, before we tackle media with recursion. Let's think about how we could write a function to do the following:

```
>>> downUp("Hello")
Hello
ello
llo
lo
o
lo
llo
ello
Hello
```

Recursion can be hard to get your head around. It really relies on you *trusting* your functions. Does the function do what it's supposed to do? Then just call it, and it'll do the right thing.

We're going to talk about recursion in three ways to help you understand it. The first way is procedural abstraction—breaking the problem down into the smallest pieces that we can write down easily as functions and reusing as much as possible.

Let's think about downUp for one-character words. That's easy:

```
def downUp1(word):
  print word
```

```
>>> downUp1("I")
I
```

Now let's do `downUp` for two-character words. We'll reuse `downUp1` because we have it already.

```
def downUp2(word):
  print word
  downUp1(word[1:])
  print word
>>> downUp2("it")
it
t
it
>>> downUp2("me")
me
e
me
```

Now for three-character words:

```
def downUp3 (word):
  print word
  downUp2 (word[1:])
  print word

>>> downUp3("pop")
pop
op
p
op
pop
>>> downUp3("top")
top
op
p
op
top
```

Are we seeing a pattern yet? Let's try it:

```
def downUpTest(word):
  print word
  downUpTest(word[1:])
  print word

>>> downUpTest("hello")
hello
ello
llo
lo
o
```

```
The error was:java.lang.StackOverflowError
I wasn't able to do what you wanted.
The error java.lang.StackOverflowError has occured
Please check line 101 of C:\ip-book\programs\
    functional
```

The error is slightly different in regular Python, but means essentially the same thing.

```
>>> downUpTest("hello")
...
    File "<stdin>", line 3, in downUpTest
    File "<stdin>", line 3, in downUpTest
RuntimeError: maximum recursion depth exceeded
```

What happened? When we got down to one character, we just kept recalling downUpTest until we ran out of memory in an area called the *Stack*. We need to be able to tell our function "If we're down to only a single character, just print it and do *not* call yourself again!" The function shown below works.

Program 194: downUp Recursively

```
def downUp(word):
  print word
  if len(word)==1:
    return
  downUp(word[1:])
  print word
```

Here's our second way of thinking about recursion: good old tracing! We'll insert comments indented.

```
>>> downUp("Hello")
```

	The len(word) is not 1, so we print the word
Hello	
	Now we call downUp("ello") Still not one character, so print it
ello	
	Now we call downUp("llo") Still not one character, so print it
llo	
	Now we call downUp("lo") Still not one character, so print it
lo	
	Now call downUp("o") *Thats one character!* Print it, and return

o	
	downUp("lo") now continues from its call to downUp("o") It prints again and ends.
lo	
	downUp("llo") now continues (back from downUp("lo")) It prints and ends.
llo	
	downUp("ello") now continues. It prints and ends.
ello	
	Finally, the last line of the original downUp("Hello") can run.
Hello	

A third way of thinking about this is to imagine a *function invocation* as an *elf*—a little person inside the computer who's going to do what you say.

Here are the downUp instructions to the elves:

1. Accept a word as input.

2. If your word has only one character, write it on the screen and you're done. Stop and sit down.

3. Write your word down on the screen.

4. Hire another elf to do the same instructions and give the new elf your word minus the first character.

5. Wait until the elf you hired is done.

6. Write your word down on the screen again. You're done.

I suggest trying this in your own class—it's fun and helps recursion make sense. It works something like this:

- We start out hiring our first elf with the input "Hello."

Hello

(Think of this as an abstraction of an elf.)

- The elf carrying "Hello" follows the instructions. He accepts the word as input, sees that it has more than one character, and writes it on the screen: Hello. It then hires a new elf and gives it the input "ello."

- The "ello"-carrying elf accepts the input, sees that it has more than one character, and writes it on the screen (ello, right under Hello). She then hires a new elf and hands it the input "llo."

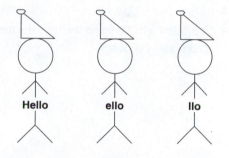

- At this point, we can make a few observations. Each elf is only aware of the elf to his left—the one he hired. He has to wait for that elf to finish before he can finish. When the elves start finishing, the first ones to finish will be the ones to the right, who were the last ones to be hired. We call this a **stack**—the elves "stack up" left to right, and the *last* one up is the *first* one out.

  If the original input was a really big word (e.g., "antidisestablishmentarianism"), you could imagine not having enough room for all the elves to stack up. We'd call that **stack overflow**—that's literally the error that Python gives you if the recursion gets too deep (i.e., too many elves).

- Imagine that we continue the simulation. We hire elves for "lo" and "o." The "o" elf writes down her o, then sits down.

- The "lo" elf now finishes up. She writes lo on the screen—which is below the o below the lo. And the "lo" elf sits down. That leaves us with three more elves awaiting their turns.

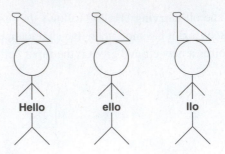

- The "llo" elf writes `llo` and sits down.

- The "ello" elf has been waiting for the "llo" elf to finish. He writes `ello` on the screen and sits down.

- Finally, the "Hello" elf writes down `Hello` for the second time and sits down. The stack is now empty.

Why do we use functional programming and recursion? Because it lets you do a lot in very few lines of code. It's a very useful technique for dealing with hard problems. Any kind of loop can be implemented with recursion. So many people feel that it's the most flexible, elegant, and powerful form of looping.

16.4.1 Recursive Directory Traversals

The earliest recursive structure that we discussed in this book was a directory tree. A folder can contain other folders, and so on, to any depth of folders. The easiest way to *traverse* (touch every file) in a directory structure is with a recursive method.

We know how to get all the files in a directory, using `os.listdir`. The challenge is to identify which of these files are directories. Fortunately, Java knows how to do this with its `File` object, which we can easily use from Jython. When we do find a directory, we can process just as we did the very first directory requested.

Program 195: Print All Filenames in a Directory Tree

```
import os
import java.io.File as File

def printAllFiles(directory):
  files = os.listdir(directory)
  for file in files:
    fullname = directory+"/"+file
    if isDirectory(fullname):
      printAllFiles(fullname)
    else:
      print fullname

def isDirectory(filename):
  filestatus = File(filename)
  return filestatus.isDirectory()
```

How It Works

We will need both Python's `os` module and Java's `java.io.File` class. To `print AllFiles` in a given `directory`, we get a list of all the files in the directory using `os.listdir`. For each of those files, we add the directory and the filename to get a full path. We then ask if that's a directory using `isDirectory`. Using the Java `File` object, we can ask it if it is a directory, then return that response.

Normally in this book, when we have two things to test, we use two `if` statements. Thus, we would write the first function above as:

```
def printAllFiles(directory):
  files = os.listdir(directory)
  for file in files:
    fullname = directory+"/"+file
    if isDirectory(fullname):
      printAllFiles(fullname)
    if not isDirectory(fullname):
      print fullname
```

However, every test of `isDirectory` requires a fairly complex file operation. That's expensive in terms of processing time. Rather than doing it repeatedly, we say, "If it's *not* a directory, that is, `else`, do this." Thus, we use the `else` construct. An `else` is not as readable as the double `if` statements, but it does prevent us from repeating a test, and is thus, more efficient.

We will test this function on the folder shown in Figure 16.3.

```
>>> printAllFiles("/home/guzdial/Documents/sampleFolder")
/home/guzdial/Documents/sampleFolder/
```

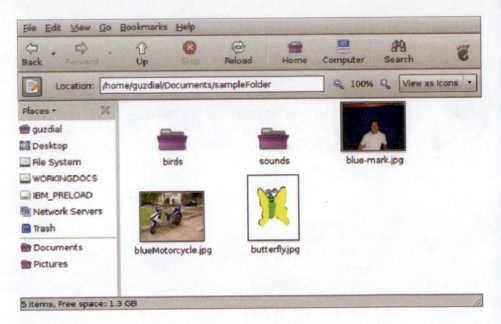

FIGURE 16.3
What's in the sampleFolder.

```
   blueMotorcycle.jpg
/home/guzdial/Documents/sampleFolder/sounds/
   bassoon-c4.wav
/home/guzdial/Documents/sampleFolder/sounds/
   bassoon-g4.wav
/home/guzdial/Documents/sampleFolder/sounds/
   bassoon-e4.wav
/home/guzdial/Documents/sampleFolder/birds/bird3.jpg
/home/guzdial/Documents/sampleFolder/birds/bird2.jpg
/home/guzdial/Documents/sampleFolder/birds/bird1.jpg
/home/guzdial/Documents/sampleFolder/birds/bird5.jpg
/home/guzdial/Documents/sampleFolder/birds/bird4.jpg
/home/guzdial/Documents/sampleFolder/birds/bird6.jpg
/home/guzdial/Documents/sampleFolder/blue-mark.jpg
/home/guzdial/Documents/sampleFolder/butterfly.jpg
```

16.4.2   Recursive Media Functions

We can think about writing media functions like decreaseRed() recursively, like this.

Program 196: Decrease Red, Recursively

```
def decreaseRedR(aList):
  if aList == []: # empty
    return
  setRed(aList[0],getRed(aList[0])*0.8)
  decreaseRedR(aList[1:])
```

How It Works

If the input list of pixels is empty, then we stop (`return`). Otherwise, we take the first pixel in the list (`alist[0]`) and decrease its red by 20% (multiply by 0.8). Then we call `decreaseRedR` on the *rest* of the list (`alist[1:]`).

We'd call this version like this: `decreaseRedR(getPixels(pic))`. *Warning*: It actually won't work even for reasonable-size pictures. Python (and the Java underlying Jython) don't expect recursion of this level of depth, so they run out of memory. It does work with *really* small pictures. This version of `decreaseRed` actually has two problems:

- First, it recurses once for every pixel. That's hundreds of thousands of times.

- Second, it passes the whole list of pixels for each call. That means, for every pixel processed, a copy of all the pixels is also stored in memory. That's a huge amount of memory.

We can write this function differently, so that we correct that second problem. We can avoid passing the whole list of pixels by declaring the variable containing the list of pixels as `global`. Then the variable is shared among the functions.

Program 197: Recursive decreaseRed with a Global Variable

```
aPicturePixels=[]

def decreaseRedR(aPicture):
  global aPicturePixels
  aPicturePixels=getPixels(aPicture)
  decreaseRedByIndex(len(aPicturePixels)-1)

def decreaseRedByIndex(index):
  global aPicturePixels
  pixel = aPicturePixels[index]
  setRed(pixel, 0.8 * getRed(pixel))
  if index == 0: # empty
    return
  decreaseRedByIndex(index - 1)
```

How It Works

We first create the variable `aPicturePixels` outside of any function. The `global` statements tell Python that `aPicturePixels` should be one defined at the level of the file (module), not just local to this function. `decreaseRedR` puts all the pixels into `aPicturePixels`, then calls the helper function `decreaseRedByIndex` with the last index in the list of picture pixels, the length (`len`) of the list minus one. The function `decreaseRedByIndex` gets the pixel at the specified index and decreases the red in it by 80%. If the index is zero, the very first pixel, we simply `return` and stop. If it is not zero, we continue decreasing red by one less than the current index.

The problem is that this version still recurses once for every pixel. For even relatively small pictures (640 × 480), the stack overflows before we complete the picture processing. In general, processing pixel-by-pixel recursively is hard, maybe impossible, to do in Jython.

PROGRAMMING SUMMARY

Following are some of the functions and programming pieces that we met in this chapter.

FUNCTIONAL PROGRAMMING

`apply`	Inputs a function and a list as input to the function, where the list has as many elements as the function takes as input. Calls the function on the input.
`map`	Inputs a function and a list of several inputs to the function. Calls the function on each of the inputs and returns a list of the outputs (`return` values).
`filter`	Inputs a function and a list of several inputs to the function. Calls the function on each of the list elements and returns the *input element* if the function returns true (nonzero) for that element.
`reduce`	Inputs a function that takes two inputs and a list of several inputs to the function. The function is applied to the first two list elements, then the result of that is used as input with the next list element, then the result of that is used as input with the *next* list element, and so on. The overall result is returned at the end.
`else:`	After an `if`, executes the following block of code only if the test in the `if` statement is *false*.
`global`	Variables listed after the statement `global` are meant to reference a variable created *before* this function, at the level of the file (or module). This allows us to share a reference to an object, rather than duplicate it.

PROBLEMS

16.1   Here's a puzzle. You have six blocks. One of them weighs more than the other. You have a scale but you can only use it twice. Find the heaviest one. (a) Write down your process as an algorithm. (b) What search is this like?

16.2   Mathematicians talk about the *Fibonacci Sequence*, which is a series of numbers *defined* recursively. The first Fibonacci number is 0, and the second is 1. From there on out, the nth Fibonacci number is $Fib(n) = Fib(n-2) + Fib(n-1)$. Write a function to input an integer index and then calculate that index value in the Fibonacci sequence.

16.3   Compound interest means that you add the interest (say, 2%) to a starting balance (say, $100) for a period of time (say it's a year) to get a new balance ($102.00 in this example). During the next period of time, we apply the same interest rate to the *new* balance. In our example, during the second year, our 2% interest on $102 would give us $104.04 as our new balance. Write a function `compoundInterest` that takes in an interest rate, a starting balance, and a number of years, then returns what the new balance would be. (*Hint*: Recursion can be useful here.)

16.4   Write a function to convert Celsius to Fahrenheit.

16.5   Write a function to convert Farenheit to Celsius.

16.6   If you have both of the last two functions (Celsius to Farenheit, and Farenheit to Celsius), are the exact inverses of one another? If you convert 32 degree Farenheit to Celsius, and then back to Farenheit, do you get 32 again? Try out different values. When does it work, and when doesn't it—and why?

16.7   Write a function to calculate a person's body mass index given his/her weight and height.

16.8   Write a function to calculate a tip of 20%.

16.9   Change the functional `turnHairRed()` in Program 192 (page 433) into *only* a single line by recoding the utility functions as `lambda` functions.

16.10   Describe what this function does. Try different numbers as input.

```
def test(num):
  if num > 0:
    return test(num-1)
  else:
    return 0
```

16.11   Describe what this function does. Try different numbers as input.

```
def test(num):
  if num > 0:
    return test(num-1) + num
  else:
    return 0
```

16.12   Describe what this function does. Try different numbers as input.

```
def test(num):
  if num > 0:
    return test(num-1) * num
  else:
    return 0
```

16.13   Describe what this function does. Try different numbers as input.

```
def test(num):
  if num > 0:
    return num - test(num-1)
  else:
    return 0
```

16.14   Describe what this function does. Try different numbers as input.

```
def test(num):
  if num > 0:
    return test(num-2) * test(num-1)
  else:
    return 0
```

16.15   Write a recursive method to list all the files in a directory and in all subdirectories.

16.16   Try writing upDown():

```
>>> upDown("Hello")
Hello
Hell
Hel
He
H
He
Hel
Hell
Hello
```

Try to write upDown() *both* recursively and without recursion. Which is easier? Why?

16.17   Using map, increase the value of a sound by applying a function to each sample of the sound.

16.18   Using map and filter, maximize a sound—if a sample's value is greater than or equal to 0, make the sample value 32, 767, and if not, make it −32, 768.

16.19   Try writing any other of our sound and picture examples from the earlier chapters *functionally*, using structures like filter and map.

17 Object-Oriented Programming

Chapter Learning Objectives

The media learning goals for this chapter are:

- To use turtles for graphics—in particular, to create complex recursive patterns.
- To use object-oriented programming to make programming easier to do in teams
- To use object-oriented programming to make programs easier to debug and even more robust.
- To understand such features of object-oriented programs as polymorphism, encapsulation, inheritance, and aggregation.
- To be able to choose between different styles of programming for different purposes.

17.1 HISTORY OF OBJECTS

The most common style of programming today is **object-oriented programming**. We're going to define it in contrast with the procedural programming that we've been doing up until now.

Back in the 1960s and 1970s, procedural programming was the dominant form of programming. People used *procedural abstraction* and defined lots of functions at high and low levels, and reused their functions wherever possible. This worked reasonably well—up to a point. As programs got really large and complex, with many programmers working on them at the same time, procedural programming started to break down.

Programmers ran into problems with procedure conflicts. People would write programs that modified data in ways that other people didn't expect. They would use the same names for functions and find that their code couldn't be integrated into one large program.

There were also problems in *thinking* about programs and the tasks the programs were supposed to perform. Procedures are about *verbs*—tell the computer to do this, tell the computer to do that. But it's not clear whether that's the way people think best about problems.

Object-oriented programming is *noun-oriented programming*. Someone building an object-oriented program starts by thinking about what the nouns are in the *domain* of the problem—what are the people and things that are part of this problem and its solution? The process of identifying the objects, what each of them knows about (with respect to the problem), and what each of them has to do is called **object-oriented analysis**.

Programming in an object-oriented way means that you define variables (called **instance variables**) and functions (called **methods**) *for the objects*. In the most object-oriented languages, programs have very few or even *no* global functions or variables—things that are accessible everywhere. In the original object-oriented programming language, Smalltalk, objects could *only* get things done by asking each other to do things via their methods. Adele Goldberg, one of the pioneers of object-oriented programming, calls this "Ask, don't touch." You can't just "touch" data and do whatever you want with it—instead, you "ask" objects to manipulate their data through their methods. That is a good goal even in languages like Python or Java where objects *can* manipulate each others' data directly.

The term *object-oriented programming* was invented by Alan Kay. Kay is a brilliant multidisciplinary scholar—he holds undergraduate degrees in mathematics and biology, a Ph.D. in computer science, and has been a professional jazz guitarist. In 2004, he was awarded the ACM Turing Award, which is sort of the Nobel Prize of computing. Kay saw object-oriented programming as a way of developing software that could truly scale to large systems. He described objects as being like biological *cells* that work together in well-defined ways to make the whole organism work. Like cells, objects would:

- Help manage *complexity* by distributing responsibility for tasks across many objects rather than one big program.
- Support *robustness* by making the objects work relatively independently.
- Support *reuse* because each object would provide *services* to other objects (tasks that the object would do for other objects, accessible through its methods), just as real-world objects do.

The notion of starting from nouns is part of Kay's vision. **Software**, he said, is actually a *simulation* of the world. By making software *model* the world, it becomes clearer how to make software. You look at the world and how it works, then copy that into software. Things in the world *know* things—these become **instance variables**. Things in the world can *do* things—these become **methods**.

Of course, we've been using objects already. Pictures, sounds, samples, and colors are all objects. Our lists of pixels and samples are examples of *aggregation*, which is creating collections of objects. The functions we've been using are actually just covering up the underlying methods. We can just call the objects' methods directly, which we will do later in this chapter.

17.2 WORKING WITH TURTLES

Seymour Papert, at MIT, used robot turtles to help children think about how to specify procedures in the late 1960s. The turtle had a pen in the middle of it that could be raised and lowered to leave a trail of its movements. As graphical displays became available, he used a virtual turtle on a computer screen instead of a robotic turtle.

Part of the media support in JES provides graphical turtle objects. Turtles make a great introduction to the ideas of objects. We manipulate turtle objects that move around a world. The turtles know how to move and turn. The turtles have a pen in the middle of them that leaves a trail to show their movements. The world keeps track of the turtles that are in it.

17.2.1 Classes and Objects

How does the computer know what we mean by a turtle and a world? We have to define what a turtle is, what it knows about, and what it can do. We have to define what a world is, what it knows about, and what it can do. In Python we do this by defining classes. A class defines what things or objects (instances) of that class know and can do. The media package for JES defines classes that define what we mean by a turtle and a world.

Object-oriented programs consist of objects. We create objects from classes. The class knows what each object of that class needs to keep track of and what it should be able to do. You can think of a class as an object factory. The factory can create many objects. A class is also like a cookie cutter. You can make many cookies from one cookie cutter and they will all have the same shape. Or you can think of the class as a blueprint and the objects as the houses that you can create from the blueprint.

To create and initialize a world you use `makeWorld()`. To create a turtle object, you can use `makeTurtle(world)`. That looks pretty similar to `makePicture` and `makeSound`—there is a pattern here, but we will introduce a new one, a more standard Python syntax in just a bit. Let's create a new world object.

```
>>> makeWorld()
```

This will create a world object and display a window that shows the world. It will just start as an all-white picture in a frame titled, "World." But we can't refer to it since we didn't name it.

Here we name the world object that gets created `earth`, and then create a turtle object in the world named `earth`. We will name the turtle object `tina`.

```
>>> earth = makeWorld()
>>> tina = makeTurtle(earth)
>>> print tina
No name turtle at 320, 240 heading 0.0.
```

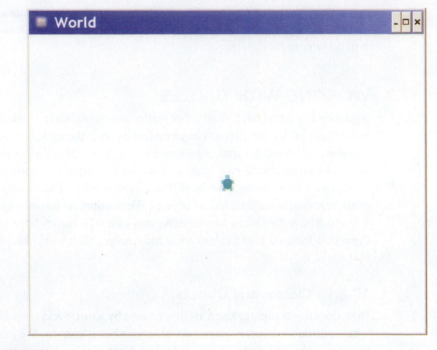

FIGURE 17.1
Creating a turtle in the world.

The turtle object appears in the center of the world (320, 240) and facing north (*a heading of* 0) (Figure 17.1). The turtle hasn't been assigned a name yet.

The turtle support in JES allows us to create many turtles. Each new turtle will appear in the center of the world.

```
>>> sue = makeTurtle(earth)
```

17.2.2   Sending Messages to Objects

We can ask the turtle to do things by sending a message to the turtle object, which we also think of as calling a method on an object. We do this using *dot notation*. In dot notation we ask an object to do something by specifying the name of the object and then a "." and then the function to execute (`name.function(parameterList)`). We saw dot notation with strings in Section 10.3.1.

```
>>> tina.forward()
>>> tina.turnRight()
>>> tina.forward()
```

Notice that only the turtle that we asked to do the actions moves (Figure 17.2). We can make the other one move by asking it to do things as well.

```
>>> sue.turnLeft()
>>> sue.forward(50)
```

Notice that different turtles have different colors (Figure 17.3). As you can see turtles know how to turn left and right, using `turnLeft()` and `turnRight()`. They also can

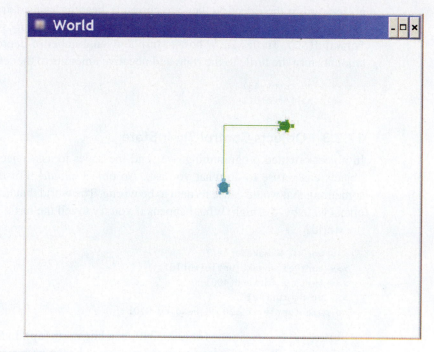

FIGURE 17.2
Asking one turtle to move and turn, while the other one remains.

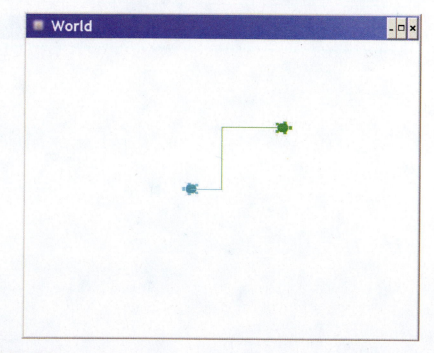

FIGURE 17.3
After the second turtle moves.

go forward in the direction they are currently heading using forward(). By default they go forward 100 pixels, but you can also specify how many pixels to go forward, forward(50). Turtles know how to turn a given number of degrees as well. Positive amounts turn the turtle to the right and negative amounts to the left (Figure 17.4).

```
>>> tina.turn(-45)
>>> tina.forward()
```

17.2.3   Objects Control Their State

In object-oriented programming, we send messages to ask objects to do things. The objects can refuse to do what you ask. An object *should* refuse if you ask it to do something that would cause its data to be wrong. The world that the turtles are in is 640 pixels wide by 480 high. What happens if you try to tell the turtle to go past the end of the world?

```
>>> world1 = makeWorld()
>>> turtle1 = makeTurtle(world1)
>>> turtle1.forward(400)
>>> print turtle1
No name turtle at 320, 0 heading 0.0.
```

Turtles are first positioned at (320, 240) heading north (up). In the world, the top left position is (0, 0) and x increases to the right and y increases going down. By asking the turtle to go forward 400, we are asking it to go to (320, 240 − 400) which would

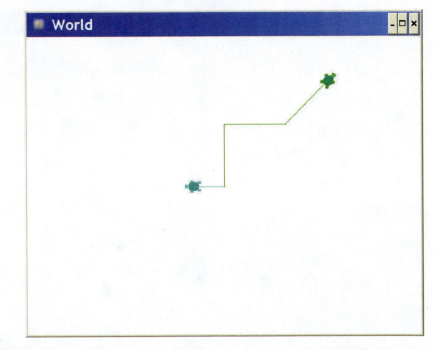

FIGURE 17.4
Turning a specified amount (−45).

result in a position of (320, −160). But, the turtle refuses to leave the world and instead stops when the center of the turtle is at (320, 0) (Figure 17.5). This means we won't lose sight of any of our turtles.

The point of this exercise is to show how methods control access to the object's data. If you do not want variables to have certain values in its data, you control that through the methods. The methods serve as the gateway to and gatekeeper for the object's data.

Turtles can do lots of other things as well as go forward and turn. As you have probably noticed, when the turtles move they draw a line that is the same color as the turtle. You can ask the turtle to pick up the pen using penUp(). You can ask the turtle to put down the pen using penDown(). You can ask the turtle to move to a particular position using moveTo(x,y). If the pen is down when you ask the turtle to move to a new position, the turtle will draw a line from the old position to the new position (Figure 17.6).

```
>>> worldX = makeWorld()
>>> turtleX = makeTurtle(worldX)
>>> turtleX.penUp()
>>> turtleX.moveTo(0,0)
>>> turtleX.penDown()
>>> turtleX.moveTo(639,479)
```

You can change the color of a turtle using setColor(color). You can stop drawing the turtle using setVisible(false). You can change the width of the pen using setPenWidth(width).

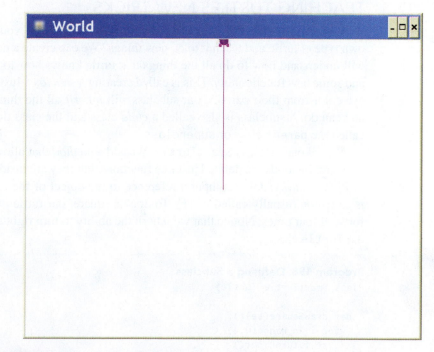

FIGURE 17.5
A turtle stuck at the edge of the world.

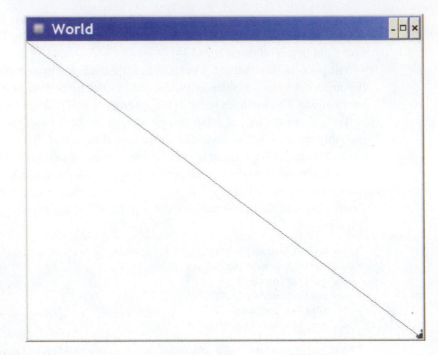

FIGURE 17.6
Using the turtle to draw a diagonal line.

17.3   TEACHING TURTLES NEW TRICKS

We have already defined a `Turtle` class for you. But, what if you want to create your own type of turtle and teach it to do new things? We can create a new type of turtle that will understand how to do all the things that turtle knows how to do, and we can also add some new functionality. This is called creating a *subclass*. Just like children inherit eye color from their parents, our subclass will *inherit* all the things that turtles know and can do. A subclass is also called a *child* class and the class that it inherits from is called the `parent` class or `superclass`.

We call our subclass `SmartTurtle`. We add a *method* that allows our turtle to draw a square. Methods are defined just like functions, but they are inside the class. Methods in Python *always* take as input a reference to the object of the class that the method is called on (usually called `self`). To draw a square, our turtle will turn right and go forward four times. Notice that we inherit the ability to turn right and go forward from the `Turtle` class.

Program 198: Defining a Subclass

```python
class SmartTurtle(Turtle):

    def drawSquare(self):
        for i in range(0,4):
            self.turnRight()
            self.forward()
```

Since the `SmartTurtle` is a kind of `Turtle`, we can use it in much the same way. But, we will need to create the `SmartTurtle` in a new way. We have been using `makePicture`, `makeSound`, `makeWorld`, and `makeTurtle` to make our objects. These are functions we have created to make it easier to make these objects. But, the actual way in Python to create a new object is to use `ClassName(parameterList)`. To create a world you can use `worldObj = World()` and to create a `SmartTurtle` you can use `turtleObj = SmartTurtle(worldObj)`.

```
>>> earth = World()
>>> smarty = SmartTurtle(earth)
>>> smarty.drawSquare()
```

Our `SmartTurtle` now knows how to draw a square (Figure 17.7). But, it can only draw squares of size 100. It would be nice to be able to draw different size squares. Python can have *optional inputs* to a function. In the method below, `drawSquare` *can* take a `width` input, but if one isn't given, `width` will have a *default* value of 100.

Program 199: Defining a Subclass
```
class SmartTurtle(Turtle):

  def drawSquare(self,width=100):
    for i in range(0,4):
      self.turnRight()
      self.forward(width)
```

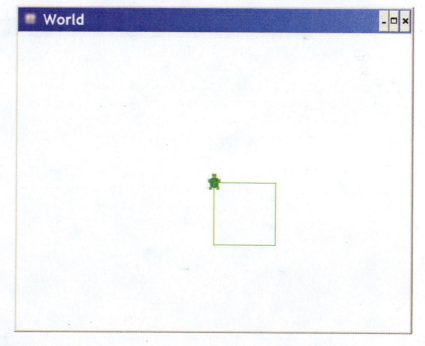

FIGURE 17.7
Drawing a square with our SmartTurtle.

How It Works

You can use this to draw different size squares (Figure 17.8).

```
>>> mars = World()
>>> tina = SmartTurtle(mars)
>>> tina.drawSquare(30)
>>> tina.drawSquare(150)
>>> tina.drawSquare(100)
>>> # Does the same thing
>>> tina.drawSquare()
```

17.3.1 Overriding an Existing Turtle Method

A subclass can redefine a method that already exists in the superclass. You might do this to create a specialized form of the existing method.

Here's the class ConfusedTurtle, which redefines forward and turn so that it does the Turtle class's forward and turn, but by a random amount. You use it just like a normal turtle—but it won't go forward or turn as much as you request. The below example will have goofy go forward not-quite-100 and turn nowhere-near-90.

```
>>> pluto = World()
>>> goofy = ConfusedTurtle(pluto)
>>> goofy.forward(100)
>>> goofy.turn(90)
```

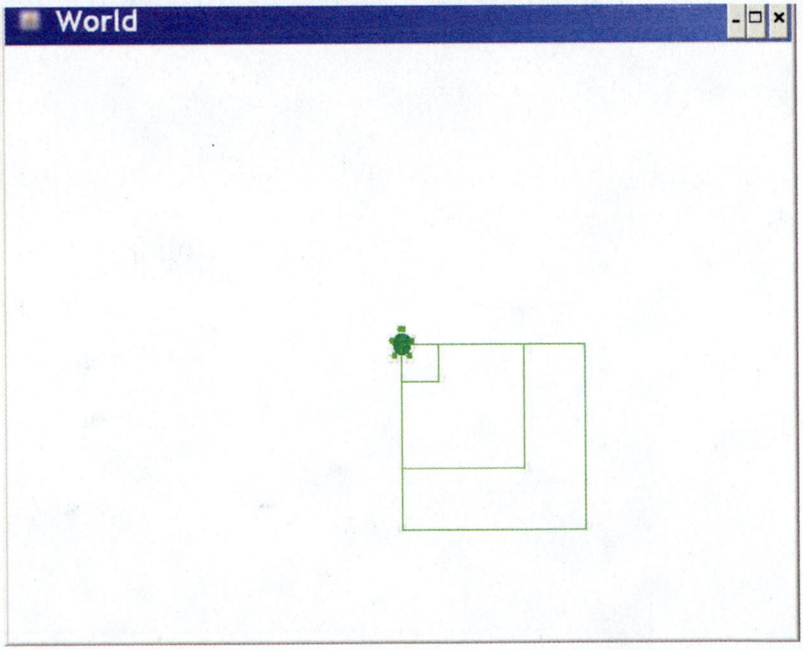

FIGURE 17.8
Drawing different size squares.

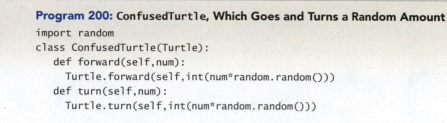

Program 200: ConfusedTurtle, Which Goes and Turns a Random Amount

```
import random
class ConfusedTurtle(Turtle):
    def forward(self,num):
      Turtle.forward(self,int(num*random.random()))
    def turn(self,num):
      Turtle.turn(self,int(num*random.random()))
```

How It Works

We declare the class ConfusedTurtle to be a subclass of Turtle. We define two methods in ConfusedTurtle: forward and turn. Like any other method, they take self and whatever the method input is. In these cases, the input to both is a number, num.

What we want to do is to call the *superclass* (i.e., Turtle) and have it do the normal forward and turn, but with the input multiplied by a random number. Each method's body is only a single line, but it's a fairly complicated line.

- We have to tell Python explicitly to call Turtle's forward.
- We have to pass in self, so that the right object's data gets used and updated.
- We multiply the input num by random.random(), but we need to convert it to an integer (using int). The random number returned will be between 0 and 1 (a floating-point number), but we need an integer for forward and turn.

17.3.2 Working with Multiple Turtles at Once

Turtles have a bunch of methods that allow for interesting graphical effects. For example, turtles are aware of each other. They can turnToFace(anotherTurtle) to change the heading so that the turtle is "facing" another turtle (so that if keeps going forward, it will reach the other turtle). In the below example, we set up four turtles (al, bo, cy, and di) in four corners of a square, then repeatedly have them move toward the one on the left. The result is Figure 17.9.

Program 201: Chase Turtles

```
def chase():
  # Set up the four turtles
  earth = World()
  al = Turtle(earth)
  bo = Turtle(earth)
  cy = Turtle(earth)
  di = Turtle(earth)
  al.penUp()
  al.moveTo(10,10)
  al.penDown()
  bo.penUp()
  bo.moveTo(10,400)
```

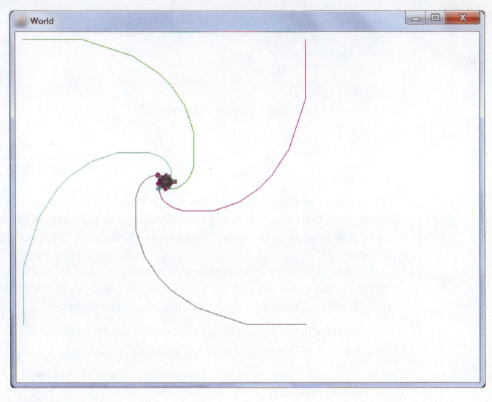

FIGURE 17.9
Four turtles chasing each other.

```
    bo.penDown()
    cy.penUp()
    cy.moveTo(400,10)
    cy.penDown()
    di.penUp()
    di.moveTo(400,400)
    di.penDown()
    # Now, chase for 300 steps
    for i in range(0,300):
      chaseTurtle(al,cy)
      chaseTurtle(cy,di)
      chaseTurtle(di,bo)
      chaseTurtle(bo,al)

def chaseTurtle(t1,t2):
  t1.turnToFace(t2)
  t1.forward(4)
```

How It Works

The main function here is `chase()`. The first few lines create a world and the four turtles, and place each of them in the corners $(10, 10)$, $(10, 400)$, $(400, 400)$, and

(400, 10). For 300 steps (a relatively arbitrary number), each turtle is told to "chase" (chaseTurtle) the one next to it, clockwise. So, the turtle that starts at (10, 10) (a1) is told to chase the turtle that starts at (10, 400) (cy). To chase means that the first turtle turns to face the second turtle, then moves forward four steps. (Try different values—we liked the visual effect of four the most.) Eventually, the turtles spiral into the center.

These functions are valuable for creating *simulations*. Imagine that we had brown turtles to act as deer, and gray turtles to act as wolves. Wolves would turnToFace deer when they saw them, and chase them. To run away, deer might turnToFace an oncoming wolf, then turn 180 and run away. Simulations are among the most powerful and insight-providing uses of computers.

> **Computer Science Idea: Parameters Work a Bit Differently with Objects**
>
> When you call a function and pass in a number as an input, the parameter variable (the local variable that accepts the input) essentially gets a *copy* of the number. Changing the local variable does not change the input variable.
>
> In the chasing turtles example, we used methods like turnToFace that are only available as methods. There are not any global functions in JES for turnToFace. There are actually quite a few World and Turtle methods available. These are listed at the end of the chapter.
>
> Look at the function chaseTurtle. When we call the function with chaseTurtle-(a1,cy), we *do* change the position and heading of the turtle whose name is a1. Why is it so different? It isn't really. The variable a1 doesn't actually hold a turtle—it holds a *reference* to a turtle. Think of it as an address (in memory) of where the turtle object can be found. If you make a copy of an address, the address still references the same place. The same turtle is being manipulated inside and outside the function. We still can't make a1 reference a new object from within a function like chaseTurtle. We can only change the object that a1 references.

17.3.3   Turtles with Pictures

Turtles also know how to drop pictures. When a turtle drops a picture, the turtle stays at the upper-left-hand corner of the picture—at whatever heading the turtle is facing (see Figure 17.10).

```
>>> # I chose Barbara.jpg for this
>>> p=makePicture(pickAFile())
>>> # Notice that we make the World and Turtle here
>>> earth=World()
>>> turtle=Turtle(earth)
>>> turtle.drop(p)
```

Turtles can also be placed on pictures, as well as World instances. When you put a turtle on a picture, its body doesn't show up by default (though you can make it visible) so that it doesn't mess up the picture. The pen is down, and you can still draw. Putting a turtle on a picture means that we can create interesting graphics on top of existing pictures or use existing pictures in your turtle manipulations.

One of our favorite techniques is spinning a picture: have the turtle move a little, turn a little, drop a copy of the picture, then keep going. Here's an example in Figure 17.11.

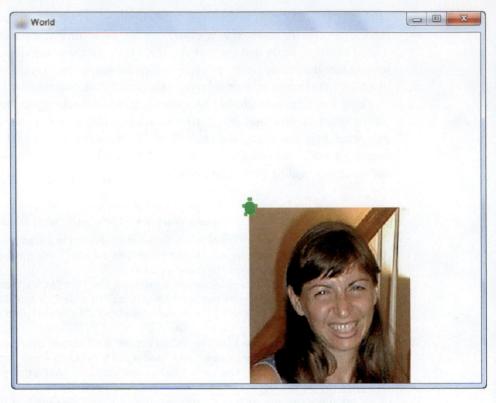

FIGURE 17.10
Dropping a picture on a world.

Below is the code that made the picture. We called it with the same picture of Barb from the previous example, show(spinAPicture(p)).

Program 202: Spinning a Picture by Dropping It from a Turning Turtle

```
def spinAPicture(apic):
  canvas = makeEmptyPicture(640,480)
  ted = Turtle(canvas)
  for i in range(0,360):
    ted.drop(apic)
    ted.forward(10)
    ted.turn(20)
  return canvas
```

17.3.4   Dancing Turtles

Working with multiple turtles is fun to create complex figures through their interaction, but it is difficult to actually *see* the turtles. They move too quickly. If we make them pause occasionally, we can see the turtles move. Then, they start to look like they're *dancing* (Figure 17.12).

FIGURE 17.11
Dropping a picture on a picture, while moving and turning.

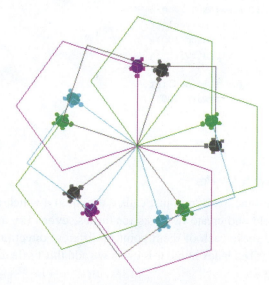

FIGURE 17.12
Multiple turtles "dancing" as they make a figure.

The `time` module has a function called `sleep` which pauses the current execution for an input period of time. If we pause for a short while (like 0.2 seconds), the execution slows down enough to see the turtles. In the below example, ten turtles are created – in an `evenlist` and a `oddlist` (based on the number of the turtles). We then have them move differently, based on which list they're in. We pause occasionally, so that we can see the motion.

Program 203: Dancing Turtles with Sleep

```
from time import sleep

def dance():
  makesquare()

def makesquare():
  w = makeWorld()
  evenlist = []
  oddlist = []
  for turtles in range(10):
    t = makeTurtle(w)
    t.turn(turtles*36)
    if turtles % 2 == 0:
      evenlist = evenlist + [t]
    else:
      oddlist = oddlist + [t]
  for times in range(20):
   for sides in range(5):
    if times % 2 == 0:
      for t in evenlist:
        t.forward(100)
        t.turn(90)
    else:
        for t in oddlist:
        t.forward(100)
        t.turn(72)
    sleep(0.2)
```

How It Works

The function `dance` just calls `makesquare` which does all the real work. We make a world and create two lists for turtles, `evenlist` and `oddlist`. We make 10 turtles, and make each of them point in different directions (`t.turn(turtles*36)`). If the `turtles` index number is even, we add this turtle to the even list, and otherwise to the odd list.

Then comes the dancing. For 20 steps, we make five sides each. If an even step, all the even turtles are told to go forward 100 and turn 90. If an odd step, all the odd turtles are told to go forward 100 and turn 72. After each round, we sleep for 0.2 seconds.

17.3.5   Recursion and Turtles

We can combine the turtles of this chapter with the recursive functions of the last chapter to create remarkably complex designs. The basic idea is to call a drawing function with a particular `size`. If the size is too small, stop—that's our stopping rule. Otherwise, draw with the given size, then recursively call the function with a small size.

Here's a simple example. We will start with the code for drawing a triangle. We use the code below like this, `triangle(myturtle,100)`.

Program 204: Draw a Triangle
```
def triangle(turtle,size):
  for sides in range(3):
    forward(turtle,size)
    turn(turtle,120)
```

■

Now let's make some recursive variations.[1] First, let's nest a call to make another triangle inside the loop where we make sides. We'll make another, smaller triangle just before we draw each side and angle. We call this one just like the `triangle` function, `nestedTri(myturtle,100)`, and the effect is remarkable (Figure 17.13).

Program 205: Nest Triangles
```
def nestedTri(t,size):
  if size < 10:
    return
  for sides in range(3):
    nestedTri(t,size/2)
    forward(t,size)
    turn(t,120)
```

■

FIGURE 17.13
Nesting triangles inside one another.

[1]You should use JES 5.0 or later for recursive drawings. JES 4.3 and earlier had an error in the turtle calculations which sometimes created incorrect recursive turtle drawing.

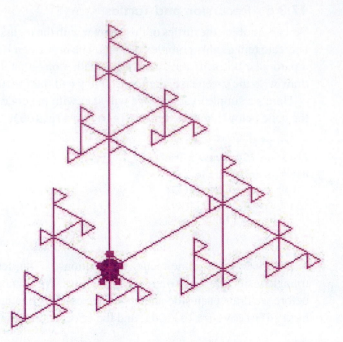

FIGURE 17.14
Putting triangles in the corners.

Here's another option: Let's create triangles *after* we draw the line and *before* we turn the corner. The result (Figure 17.14) is triangles sticking out away from other triangles.

Program 206: Corner Triangles

```
def cornerTri(t,size):
  if size < 10:
    return
  for sides in range(3):
    forward(t,size)
    cornerTri(t,size/2)
    turn(t,120)
```

17.4   AN OBJECT-ORIENTED SLIDE SHOW

Let's use object-oriented techniques to build a slide show. Let's say that we want to show a picture, then play a corresponding sound and wait until the sound is done before going on to the next picture. We'll use the function (first seen in Chapter 7) *blockingPlay( )*, which plays a sound and waits for it to finish before executing the next statement.

Program 207: Slide Show as One Big Function

```
def playSlideShow():
    pic = makePicture(getMediaPath("barbara.jpg"))
    sound = makeSound(getMediaPath("bassoon-c4.wav"))
    show(pic)
    blockingPlay(sound)
    pic = makePicture(getMediaPath("beach.jpg"))
    sound = makeSound(getMediaPath("bassoon-e4.wav"))
    show(pic)
    blockingPlay(sound)
    pic = makePicture(getMediaPath("church.jpg"))
    sound = makeSound(getMediaPath("bassoon-g4.wav"))
    show(pic)
    blockingPlay(sound)
    pic = makePicture(getMediaPath("jungle2.jpg"))
    sound = makeSound(getMediaPath("bassoon-c4.wav"))
    show(pic)
    blockingPlay(sound)
```

This isn't a very good program from any perspective. From a procedural programming perspective, there's an awful lot of duplicated code here. It would be nice to get rid of it. From an object-oriented programming perspective, we should have slide objects.

As we mentioned, objects have two parts. Objects *know* things—these become *instance variables*. Objects can *do* things—these become *methods*. We're going to access both of these using dot notation.

So what does a slide know? It knows its *picture* and its *sound*. What can a slide do? It can *show* itself, by showing its picture and playing its sound.

To define a slide object in Python (and many other object-oriented programming languages, including Java and C++), we must define a `Slide` **class**. We have already seen a couple of class definitions. Let's go through it again, slowly, building a class from scratch.

As we have already seen, a class defines the instance variables and methods for a set of objects—that is, what each object of that class knows and can do. Each object of the class is an *instance* of the class. We'll make multiple slides by making multiple instances of the `Slide` class. This is aggregation: collections of objects, just as our bodies might make multiple kidney cells or multiple heart cells, each of which knows how to do certain kinds of tasks.

To create a class in Python, we start with:

```
class Slide:
```

What comes after this, indented, are the methods for creating new slides and playing slides. Let's add a *show()* method to our `Slide` class.

```
class Slide:
    def show(self):
```

```
      show(self.picture)
      blockingPlay(self.sound)
```

To create new instances, we call the class name like a function. We can define new instance variables by simply assigning them. So here is how to create a slide and give it a picture and sound.

```
>>> slide1=Slide()
>>> slide1.picture = makePicture(getMediaPath("barbara.jpg"))
>>> slide1.sound = makeSound(getMediaPath("bassoon-c4.wav"))
>>> slide1.show()
```

The `slide1.show()` function shows the picture and plays the sound. What is this `self` stuff? When we execute `object.method()`, Python finds the method in the object's class, then calls it, using the instance object as an *input*. It's Python style to name this input variable `self` (because it is the object itself). Since we have the object in the variable `self`, we can then access its picture and sound by saying `self.picture` and `self.sound`.

But this is still pretty hard to use if we have to set up all the variables from the Command Area. How could we make it easier? What if we could pass in the sound and picture for the slides as *inputs* to the `Slide` class, as if the class were a real function? We can do this by defining something called a **constructor**.

To create new instances with some inputs, we must define a function named `__init__`. That's "underscore-underscore-i-n-i-t-underscore-underscore." It's the predefined name in Python for a method that *initializes* new objects. Our `__init__` method needs three inputs: the instance itself (because all methods get that), a picture, and a sound.

Program 208: A `Slide` Class

```
class Slide:
   def __init__(self, pictureFile,soundFile):
      self.picture = makePicture(pictureFile)
      self.sound = makeSound(soundFile)

   def show(self):
      show(self.picture)
      blockingPlay(self.sound)
```

We can use our `Slide` class to define a slide show like this.

Program 209: Playing a Slide Show, Using Our `Slide` Class

```
def playSlideShow2():
   pictF = getMediaPath("barbara.jpg")
   soundF = getMediaPath("bassoon-c4.wav")
   slide1 = Slide(pictF,soundF)
   pictF = getMediaPath("beach.jpg")
```

```
soundF = getMediaPath("bassoon-e4.wav")
slide2 = Slide(pictF,soundF)
pictF = getMediaPath("church.jpg")
soundF = getMediaPath("bassoon-g4.wav")
slide3 = Slide(pictF,soundF)
pictF = getMediaPath("jungle2.jpg")
soundF = getMediaPath("bassoon-c4.wav")
slide4 = Slide(pictF,soundF)
slide1.show()
slide2.show()
slide3.show()
slide4.show()
```

One of the features of Python that make it so powerful is that we can mix object-oriented and functional programming styles. Slides are now objects that can easily be stored in lists, like any other kind of Python object. Here's an example of the same slide show where we use map to show the slide show.

Program 210: Slide Show, In Objects and Functions

```
def showSlide(aSlide):
  aSlide.show()

def playSlideShow3():
    pictF = getMediaPath("barbara.jpg")
    soundF = getMediaPath("bassoon-c4.wav")
    slide1 = Slide(pictF,soundF )
    pictF = getMediaPath("beach.jpg")
    soundF = getMediaPath("bassoon-e4.wav")
    slide2 = Slide(pictF,soundF)
    pictF = getMediaPath("church.jpg")
    soundF = getMediaPath("bassoon-g4.wav")
    slide3 = Slide(pictF,soundF)
    pictF = getMediaPath("jungle2.jpg")
    soundF = getMediaPath("bassoon-c4.wav")
    slide4 = Slide(pictF,soundF)

    map(showSlide,[slide1,slide2,slide3,slide4])
```

Is the object-oriented version of the slide show easier to write? It certainly has less replication of code. It features **encapsulation** in that the data and behavior of the object are defined in one and only one place, so that any change to one is easily changed in the other. Being able to use lots of objects (like lists of objects) is called **aggregation**. This is a powerful idea. We don't always have to define new classes—we can often use the powerful structures we know, like lists with existing objects, to great impact.

17.4.1 Making the Slide Class More Object-Oriented

What happens if we need to change the picture or sound of some class? We can. We can simply change the picture or sound instance variables. But if you think about it, you realize that that's not very safe. What if someone else used the slide show and decided to store movies in the `picture` variable? It could easily be made to work, but now we have two different uses for the same variable.

What you really want is to have a method that handles getting or setting a variable. And if it becomes an issue that the wrong data is being stored in the variable, the set-the-variable method can be changed to check the value, to make sure it's the right type and valid, before setting the variable. In order for this to work, *everyone* that uses the class has to agree to use the methods for getting and setting the instance variables, and *not* directly mess with the instance variables. In languages such as Java, one can ask the compiler to keep instance variables `private` and do not allow any uses that directly touch the instance variables. In Python, the best we can do is to create the setting-and-getting methods and encourage their use only.

We call those methods (simply enough) *setters and getters*. Here is a version of the class where we define setters and getters for the two instance variables—as you can see, they are quite simple. Notice how we change the `show` and even the `__init__` methods so that, as much as possible, we use the setters and getters instead of direct access of the instance variables. This is the style of programming that Adele Goldberg meant when she talked about, "Ask, don't touch."

Program 211: Class `Slide` with Getters and Setters

```
class Slide:
  def __init__(self, pictureFile,soundFile):
      self.setPicture(makePicture(pictureFile))
      self.setSound(makeSound(soundFile))

  def getPicture(self):
    return self.picture
  def getSound(self):
    return self.sound

  def setPicture(self,newPicture):
    self.picture = newPicture
  def setSound(self,newSound):
    self.sound = newSound

  def show(self):
      show(self.getPicture())
      blockingPlay(self.getSound())
```

Here is something cool about our revised class. We don't have to change *anything* in our `playSlideShow3` function. It just works, still, even though we made several changes to how the class `Slide` works. We say that the function `playSlideShow3` and the class `Slide` are *loosely coupled*. They work together, in well-defined ways, but the inner workings of either can change without impacting the other.

17.5   OBJECT-ORIENTED MEDIA

As we said, we have been using objects throughout this book. We have been creating `Picture` objects with the function `makePicture`. We can also create a picture using the normal Python constructor.

```
>>> pic=Picture(getMediaPath("barbara.jpg"))
>>> pic.show()
```

Here's how the *function* `show()` is defined. You can ignore `raise` and `__class__`. Those lines are checking that the input to show is in fact a Picture, and if it isn't, an error should be identified ("raised"). The key point is that the function is simply executing the existing picture method `show`.

```
def show(picture):
    if not picture.__class__ == Picture:
        print "show(picture): Input is not a picture"
        raise ValueError
    picture.show()
```

We could have other classes that also know how to `show`. Objects can have their own methods with names that other objects also use. Much more powerful is that each of these methods with the same name can achieve the same *goal*, but in different ways. We defined a class for slides, and it knew how to `show`. For both slides and pictures, the method `show()` says, "Show the object." But what's really happening is different in each case: pictures just show themselves, but slides show their pictures and play their sounds.

> **Computer Science Idea: Polymorphism**
>
> When the same name can be used to invoke different methods that achieve the same goal, we call that **polymorphism**. It's very powerful for the programmer. You simply tell an object show()—you don't have to care exactly what method is being executed and you don't even have to know exactly what object it is that you're telling the object to show. You the programmer simply specify your *goal* to show the object. The object-oriented program handles the rest.

There are several examples of polymorphism built into the methods that we're using in JES.[2] For example, both pixels and colors understand the methods `setRed`, `getRed`, `setBlue`, `getBlue`, `setGreen`, and `getGreen`. This allows us to manipulate the colors of the pixels without pulling out the color objects separately. We could have defined the functions to take both kinds of inputs or to provide different functions for each kind of input, but both of those options get confusing. It's easy to do with methods.

```
>>> pic=Picture(getMediaPath("barbara.jpg"))
>>> pic.show()
>>> pixel = pic.getPixel(100,200)
>>> print pixel.getRed()
```

---

[2]Recall that JES is an environment for programming in Jython, which is a specific kind of Python. The media supports are part of what JES provides—they're not part of the core of Python.

```
73
>>> color = pixel.getColor()
>>> print color.getRed()
73
```

Another example is the method `writeTo()`. The method `writeTo(filename)` is defined for both pictures and sounds. Did you ever confuse `writePictureTo()` and `writeSoundTo()`? Isn't it easier to just always write `writeTo(filename)`? That's why that method is named the same in both classes, and why polymorphism is so powerful. (You may be wondering why we didn't introduce this in the first place. Were you ready in Chapter 2 to talk about dot notation and polymorphic methods?)

Overall, there are actually many more methods defined in JES than functions. More specifically, there are a bunch of methods for drawing on pictures that aren't available as functions.

- As you would expect, pictures understand `pic.addRect(color,x,y,width, height)`, `pic.addRectFilled(color,x,y,width,height)`, `pic.addOval (color,x,y,width,height)`, and `pic.addOvalFilled(color,x,y,width, height)`.

  See Figure 17.15 for examples of rectangle methods drawn from the following example.

```
>>> pic=Picture (getMediaPath("640x480.jpg"))
>>> pic.addRectFilled (orange,10,10,100,100)
>>> pic.addRect (blue,200,200,50,50)
>>> pic.show()
>>> pic.writeTo("newrects.jpg")
```

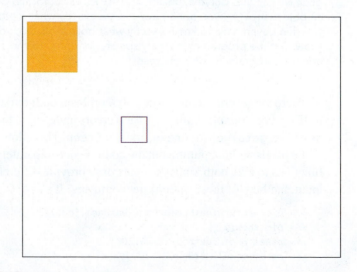

FIGURE 17.15
Examples of rectangle methods.

FIGURE 17.16
Examples of oval methods.

See Figure 17.16 for examples of ovals drawn from the following example.

```
>>> pic=Picture (getMediaPath("640x480.jpg"))
>>> pic.addOval (green,200,200,50,50)
>>> pic.addOvalFilled (magenta,10,10,100,100)
>>> pic.show()
>>> pic.writeTo("ovals.jpg")
```

- Pictures also understand *arcs*. Arcs are literally parts of a circle. The two methods are `pic.addArc(color,x,y,width,height,startAngle,arcAngle)` and `pic.addArcFilled(color,x, y, width, height, startAngle, arcAngle)`. They draw arcs for `arcAngle` degrees, where `startAngle` is the starting point. 0 degrees is at 3 o'clock on the clock face. A positive arc is counter clockwise and negative is clockwise. The center of the circle is the middle of the rectangle defined by (*x*, *y*) with the given `width` and `height`.

- We can also now draw colored lines, using `pic.addLine(color,x1,y1, x2,y2)`.

  See Figure 17.17 for examples of arcs and lines drawn from the following example.

```
>>> pic=Picture (getMediaPath("640x480.jpg"))
>>> pic.addArc(red,10,10,100,100,5,45)
>>> pic.show()
>>> pic.addArcFilled (green,200,100,200,100,1,90)
>>> pic.repaint()
>>> pic.addLine(blue,400,400,600,400)
>>> pic.repaint()
>>> pic.writeTo("arcs-lines.jpg")
```

- Text in Java can have styles, but these are limited to make sure that all platforms can replicate them. `pic.addText(color,x,y,string)` is the one we would expect

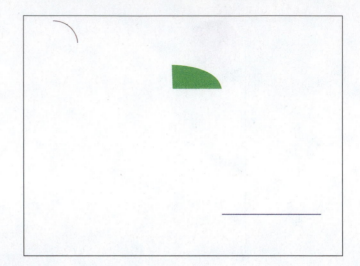

FIGURE 17.17
Examples of arc methods.

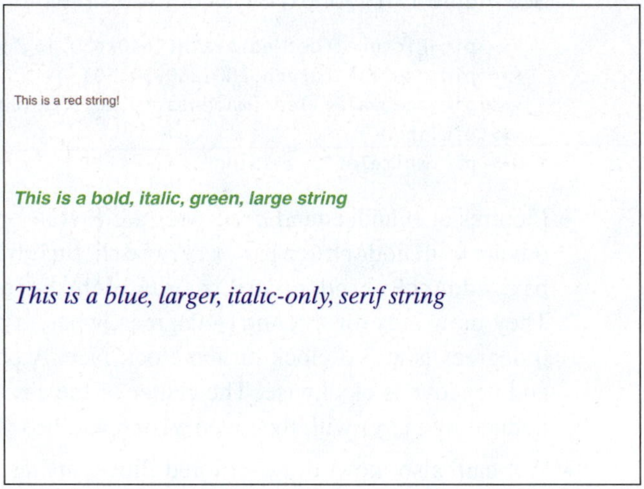

FIGURE 17.18
Examples of text methods.

to see. There is also `pic.addTextWithStyle(color,x,y,string,style)`, which takes a style created from `makeStyle(font,emphasis,size)`. The `font` is `sansSerif`, `serif`, or `mono`. The `emphasis` is `italic`, `bold`, or `plain`, or sum them to get combinations (e.g., `italic+bold.size` is a point size).

See Figure 17.18 for examples of text drawn from the following example.

```
>>> pic=Picture (getMediaPath("640x480.jpg"))
>>> pic.addText(red,10,100,"This is a red string!")
>>> pic.addTextWithStyle (green,10,200,"This is a¬
    bold, italic, green, large string",¬
```

```
        makeStyle(sansSerif, bold+italic,18))
>>> pic.addTextWithStyle (blue,10,300,"This is a¬
    blue, larger, italic-only, serif string",¬
    makeStyle(serif, italic,24))
>>> pic.writeTo("text.jpg")
```

¬These lines of the program should continue with the next lines. A single command in Python may not break across multiple lines.

The older media functions that we wrote can be rewritten in method form. We will need to create a subclass of the `Picture` class and add the method to that class.

Program 212: Making a Sunset Using a Method

```
class MyPicture(Picture):
  def makeSunset(self):
    for p in getPixels(self):
      p.setBlue(int(p.getBlue()*0.7))
      p.setGreen(int (p.getGreen()*0.7))
```

This can be used like this.

```
>>> pict = MyPicture(getMediaPath("beach.jpg"))
>>> pict.explore()
>>> pict.makeSunset()
>>> pict.explore()
```

We can also create new subclasses of the Sound class and new methods to work on sound objects. The methods for accessing sound sample values are `getSampleValue()` and `getSampleValueAt(index)`.

Program 213: Reverse a Sound with a Method

```
class MySound(Sound):
  def reverse(self):
    target = Sound(self.getLength())
    sourceIndex = self.getLength() - 1
    for targetIndex in range(0,target.getLength()):
      sourceValue = self.getSampleValueAt(sourceIndex)
      target.setSampleValueAt(targetIndex,sourceValue)
      sourceIndex = sourceIndex - 1
    return target
```

This can be used like this.

```
>>> sound = MySound(getMediaPath("always.wav"))
>>> sound.explore()
>>> target = sound.reverse()
>>> target.explore()
```

17.6   JOE THE BOX

The earliest example used to teach object-oriented programming was developed by Adele Goldberg and Alan Kay. It's called *Joe the Box*. There is nothing new in this example, but it does provide a *different* example from another perspective, so it's worth reviewing.

Imagine that you have a class Box like the one below:

```
class Box:
  def __init__(self):
    self.setDefaultColor()
    self.size=10
    self.position=(10,10)
  def setDefaultColor(self):
    self.color = red
  def draw(self,canvas):
    addRectFilled(canvas, self.position[0],self.
    position[1], self.size, self.size, self.color)
```

What will you see if you execute the following code?

```
>>> canvas = makeEmptyPicture(400,200)
>>> joe = Box()
>>> joe.draw(canvas)
>>> show(canvas)
```

Let's trace it out:

- Obviously, the first line just creates a white canvas that is 400 pixels wide and 200 pixels high.
- When we create joe, the __init__ method is called. The method setDefault Color is called on joe, so he gets a default color of red. When self.color=red is executed, the *instance variable* color is created for joe and gets a value of red. We return to __init__, where joe is given a size of 10 and a position of (10,10) (size and position both become new instance variables).
- When joe is asked to draw himself on the canvas, he's drawn as a red, filled rectangle (addRectFilled), at *x* position 10 and *y* position 10, with a size of 10 pixels on each side.

We could add a method to Box that allows us to make joe change his size.

```
class Box:
  def __init__(self):
    self.setDefaultColor()
    self.size=10
    self.position=(10,10)
  def setDefaultColor(self):
    self.color = red
  def draw(self,canvas):
    addRectFilled(canvas, self.position[0],self.
    position[1], self.size, self.size, self.color)
  def grow(self,size):
    self.size=self.size+size
```

Now we can tell `joe` to `grow`. A negative number like -2 will cause `joe` to shrink. A positive number will cause `joe` to grow—though we'd have to add a `move` method if we wanted him to grow much and still fit on the canvas.

Now consider the following code added to the same Program Area.

```
class SadBox(Box):
  def setDefaultColor(self):
    self.color=blue
```

Note that `SadBox` lists `Box` as a superclass (parent class). This means that `SadBox` *inherits* all the methods of `Box`. What will you see if you execute the code below?

```
>>> jane = SadBox()
>>> jane.draw(canvas)
>>> repaint(canvas)
```

Let's trace it out:

- When `jane` is created as a `SadBox`, the method `__init__` is executed in class `Box`.
- The first thing that happens in `__init__` is that we call `setDefaultColor` *on the input object* `self`. That object is now `jane`. So we call `jane`'s `setDefaultColor`. We say that `SadBox`'s `setDefaultColor` *overrides* `Box`'s.
- The `setDefaultColor` for `jane` sets the color to blue.
- We then return to executing the rest of `Box`'s `__init__`. We set `jane`'s size to 10 and position to (10,10).
- When we tell `jane` to draw, she appears as a 10×10 blue square at position (10,10). If we haven't moved or grown `joe`, he will disappear as `jane` is drawn on top of him.

Note that `joe` and `jane` are each a different *kind* of `Box`. They have the same instance variables (but different *values* for the same variables) and mostly know the same things. Because both understand `draw`, for example, we say that `draw` is *polymorphic*. The word *polymorphic* just means many forms.

A `SadBox` (`jane`) is slightly different in how it behaves when it created, so it knows some things differently. Joe and Jane highlight some of the basic ideas of object-oriented programming: inheritance, specialization in subclasses, and shared instance variables while having different instance variable values.

17.7   WHY OBJECTS?

One role for objects is to reduce the number of names that you have to remember. Through polymorphism, you only have to remember the name and the goal, not all the various global functions.

More importantly, though, objects encapsulate data and behavior. Imagine that you wanted to change the name of an instance variable and then all the methods that use the variable. That's a lot to change. What if you miss one? Changing them all in one place, together, is useful.

Objects reduce the *coupling* between program components, that is, how dependent they are on each other. Imagine that you have several functions that all use the same global variable. If you change one function so that it stores something slightly different in that variable, all the other functions must also be updated or they won't work. That's called *tight* coupling. Objects that only use methods on each other (no direct access to instance variables) are more *loosely* coupled. The access is well defined and easily changed in only one place. Changes in one object do not demand changes in other objects.

An advantage of loose coupling is ease in developing in team contexts. You can have different people working on different classes. As long as everyone agrees on how access will work through methods, nobody has to know how anybody else's methods work. Object-oriented programming can be particularly useful when working on teams.

Aggregation is also a significant benefit of object systems. You can have lots of objects doing useful things. Want more? Just create them!

Python's objects are similar to the objects of many languages. One significant difference is in access to instance variables, though. In Python, any object can access and manipulate any other object's instance variables. That's not true in languages like Java, C++, or Smalltalk. In these other languages, access to instance variables from other objects is limited and can even be eliminated entirely—then you can only access objects' instance variables through getter and setter methods.

Another big part of object systems is **inheritance**. As we saw with our turtle and box examples, we can declare one class (*parent class*) to be *inherited* by another class (*child class*) (also called superclass and subclass). Inheritance provides for instant polymorphism—the instances of the child automatically have all the data and behavior of the parent class. The child can then add more behavior and data to what the parent class had. This is called making the child a *specialization* of the parent class. For example, a 3D rectangle instance might know and do everything that a rectangle instance does by saying `class Rectangle3D(Rectangle)`.

Inheritance gets a lot of press in the object-oriented world but it's a trade-off. It reduces even further the duplication of code, which is a good thing. In actual practice, inheritance isn't used as much as other advantages of object-oriented programming (like aggregation and encapsulation), and it can be confusing. Whose method is being executed when you type the below? It's invisible from here, and if it's *wrong*, it can be hard to figure out where it's wrong.

```
myBox = Rectangle3D()
myBox.draw()
```

So when should you use objects? You should define your own object classes when you have data and behavior that you want to define for all instances of the group (e.g., pictures and sounds). You should use existing objects *all the time*. They're very powerful. If you're not comfortable with dot notation and the ideas of objects, you can stick with functions—they work just fine. Objects just give you a leg up on more complex systems.

PROGRAMMING SUMMARY

Following are some of the programming pieces that we met in this chapter.

OBJECT-ORIENTED PROGRAMMING

class	Lets you define a class. The keyword class takes a class name and an optional superclass in parentheses, ending with a colon. Methods for the class follow, indented within the class block.
__init__	The name of the method called on an object when it's first created. It's not required to have one.

GRAPHICS METHODS

addRect, addRectFilled	The methods in the Picture class for drawing rectangles and filled rectangles.
addOval, addOvalFilled	The methods in the Picture class for drawing ovals and filled ovals.
addArc, addArcFilled	The methods in the Picture class for drawing arcs and filled arcs.
addText, addTextWithStyle	The methods in the Picture class for drawing text and text with style elements (like boldface or sans serif).

addLine	The method in the Picture class for drawing a line.
getRed, getGreen, getBlue	The methods for both Pixel and Color objects for getting the red, green, and blue color components.
setRed, setGreen, setBlue	The methods for both Pixel and Color objects for setting the red, green, and blue color components.

TURTLE AND WORLD METHODS

Methods That Worlds Understand

getTurtleList()	Returns a list of all the turtles in the world.
getWidth()	Returns the width of the world in pixels.
getHeight()	Returns the height of the world in pixels.
repaint()	Forces the world to update and redraw all the turtles.

Methods That Turtles Understand

Some of the methods that turtles know (like `forward`, `turnRight`, `turnLeft`, and `turn`) do the same things as the global functions with the same name.

`penUp()`	Picks up the turtle's pen, so nothing gets drawn as the turtle moves.
`penDown()`	Puts down the turtle's pen, so lines get drawn as the turtle moves.
`isPenDown()`	Returns true if the pen is down.
`getPenColor()` and `setPenColor(color)`	Gets the current pen color, and sets the current pen color.
`getBodyColor()` and `setBodyColor(color)`	Gets the current color of the turtle's body, and sets the current body color.
`getShellColor()` and `setShellColor(color)`	Gets the current color of the turtle's shell, and sets the current shell color.
`getWidth()` and `setWidth(number)`	Gets the current width of the turtle itself, and sets the width of the turtle.
`getHeight()` and `setHeight(number)`	Gets the current height of the turtle itself, and sets the height of the turtle.
`getPenWidth()` and `setPenWidth(number)`	Gets the current width of the line that the pen draws, and sets the current pen width (in pixels).
`getHeading()` and `setHeading(number)`	Gets the current heading of the turtle, and sets the heading.
`hide()` and `show()`	Hides and shows the turtle, i.e., makes it invisible or visible while drawing.
`isVisible()`	Returns true if the turtle is visible.
`moveTo(x,y)`	Moves the turtle to the given x, y position, drawing a line if the pen is down.
`getDistance(x,y)`	Returns the distance from this turtle to the position x, y.
`backward(distance)`	Moves the turtle backwards the given distance.
`turnToFace(x,y)` and `turnToFace(turtle)`	Turns the turtle to face a given point x, y or a given turtle.

getXPos() and getYPos()	Returns the *x* or *y* position of the turtle.
drop(picture)	Drops the input picture into the world's (or picture) background, so that the turtle is at the top left of the picture; however, the turtle is turned.
clearPath()	Erases all the lines made by this turtle.

PROBLEMS

17.1 Look up Sierpinski's triangle. Write a recursive function with turtles to create Sierpinski's triangle.

17.2 Look up Koch's snowflake. Write a recursive function with turtles to create Koch's snowflake.

17.3 We can make all motions of a turtle slower by using a form of `forward` that includes `sleep`

```
def pausedForward(turtle,amount):
  sleep(0.2)
  turtle.forward(amount)
```

Rewrite the chase and dance functions to use `pausedForward`.

17.4 We can get the same effect as `sleep` by playing a sound with `blockingPlay`. Change the dance code to use a brief sound to pause the dance, rather than `sleep`.

17.5 Now, use `blockingPlay` on *different* sounds to get music to go with the dance.

17.6 The techniques we used to create recursive triangles can be used with other figures as well. Create nested and corner versions of squares and of pentagons.

17.7 Answer the following questions about object-oriented programming, using this chapter and explorations on the Web.

- What is the difference between an instance and a class?
- How are functions and methods different?
- How is object-oriented programming different from procedural programming?
- What is polymorphism?
- What is encapsulation?
- What is aggregation?
- What is a constructor?
- How did biological cells influence the development of the idea of objects?

17.8   Answer the following questions about how objects work, using this chapter and explorations on the Web.

- What is inheritance?
- What is a superclass?
- What is a subclass?
- What methods does a child class inherit?
- What instance variables (fields) does a child class inherit?

17.9   Add a method to the `Turtle` class to draw an equilateral triangle.

17.10 Add a method to the `Turtle` class to draw a rectangle given a width and height.

17.11 Add a method to the `Turtle` class to draw a simple house. It can have a rectangle for the house and an equilateral triangle as the roof.

17.12 Add a method to the `Turtle` class to draw a street of houses.

17.13 Add a method to the `Turtle` class to draw a letter.

17.14 Add a method to the `Turtle` class to draw your initials.

17.15 Create a movie with several turtles moving in each frame, like our dance function. Move each turtle, pause, and save it to a frame.

17.16 Add another constructor to the `Slide` class that takes *just* a picture filename and plays no sound when it plays.

17.17 Create a `SlideShow` class that holds a list of slides and shows each slide one at a time.

17.18 Create a `CartoonPanel` class that takes an array of `Pictures` and displays the pictures from left to right. It should also have a title and author, and display the title at the top left edge and the author at the top right edge.

17.19 Create a `Student` class. Each student should have a name and a picture. Add a method, `show`, that shows the picture for the student.

17.20 Add a field to the `SlideShow` class to hold the title and modify the `show` method to first show a blank picture with the title on it.

17.21 Create a `PlayList` class that takes a list of sounds and play them one at a time.

17.22 Use the methods in the `Picture` class to draw a smiling face.

17.23 Use the methods in the `Picture` class to draw a rainbow.

17.24 Rewrite the mirror functions as methods in the `MyPicture` class.

17.25 Make some modifications to Joe the Box.

- Add a method to `Box` named `setColor` that takes a color as input, then makes the input color the new color for the box. (Maybe `setDefaultColor` should call `setColor`?)
- Add a method to `Box` named `setSize` that takes a number as input, then makes the input number the new size for the box.
- Add a method to `Box` named `setPosition` that takes a list or tuple as a parameter, then makes that input the new position for the box.

- Change `__init__` so that it uses `setSize` and `setPosition` rather than simply setting the instance variables.

*17.26 Finish the Joe the Box example.

(a) Implement `grow` and `move`. The method `move` takes as input a relative distance like $(-10,15)$ to move 10 pixels left (x position) and 15 pixels down (y position).

(b) Draw patterns by creating `joe` and `jane`, then move a little and draw, grow a little and draw, then repaint the new canvas.

17.27 Create a movie with boxes growing and shrinking in it.

TO DIG DEEPER

There are lots more to do with Python in exploring procedural, functional, and object-oriented programming styles. Mark recommends the books by Mark Lutz (especially [34]) and Richard Hightower [40] as nice introductions to the deeper realms of Python. You might also explore some of the tutorials at the Python Web site (`http://www.python.org`).

We highly recommend the book *Turtle Geometry* [44]. The book is older, but there's none better for using turtles from biological modeling to exploring the theory of relativity.

*More challenging problem

A Quick Reference to Python

A.1 VARIABLES

Variables start with a letter and can be any word *except* one of the *reserved words*. These are: and, assert, break, class, continue, def, del, elif, else, except, exec, finally, for, from, global, if, import, in, is, lambda, not, or, pass, print, raise, return, try, while, yield.

We can use print to display the value of an expression (e.g., a variable). If we simply type the variable without print, we get the internal representation—functions and objects tell us about where they are in memory, and strings appear with their quotes.

```
>>> x = 10
>>> print x
10
```

```
>>> x
10
>>> y='string'
>>> print y
string
>>> y
'string'
>>> p=makePicture(pickAFile())
>>> print p
Picture, filename C:\ip-book\mediasources\
    7inX95in.jpg height 684 width 504
>>> p
<media.Picture instance at 6436242>
>>> print sin(12)
-0.5365729180004349
>>> sin
<java function sin at 26510058>
```

A.2   FUNCTION CREATION

We define functions with def. def x(a,b): defines a function named "x" that takes two input values which will be bound to variables "a" and "b." The body of the function comes after the def and is indented.

The function can return values using the return statement.

A.3   LOOPS AND CONDITIONALS

We create most of our loops using for, which takes an index variable and a list. The body of the loop is executed once for each element of the list.

```
>>> for p in [1,2,3]:
...        print p
...
1
2
3
```

The list in a for is often generated using a range function. range can take one, two, or three inputs. With one input, the range is from zero to the input. With two, the range starts at the first input and stops *before* the second. With three, the range starts at the first, takes steps of the third, and ends *before* the second.

```
>>> range(4)
[0, 1, 2, 3]
>>> range(1,4)
[1, 2, 3]
```

```
>>> range(1,4,2)
[1, 3]
```

The while loop takes a logical expression and executes its block as long as the logical expression is true.

```
>>> x = 1
>>> while x < 5:
...         print x
...         x = x + 1
...
1
2
3
4
```

A break immediately ends the current loop.

An if statement takes a logical expression and evaluates it. If it is true, the if's block is executed. If it is false, the else: clause is executed, if one exists.

```
>>> if a < b:
...         print "a is smaller"
... else:
...         print "b is smaller"
```

A.4 OPERATORS AND REPRESENTATION FUNCTIONS

+, -, *, /, **	Addition, subtraction, multiplication, division, and exponentiation. Order of precedence is algebraic.
<,>, ==, <=, >=	Logical operators less-than, greater-than, equal-to, less-than-or-equal, greater-than-or-equal.
<>, !=	Logical operators not-equal (both of them are equivalent).
and, or, not	Logical conjunctives and, or, and not.
int()	Returns the integer part of the input (floating-point number or string).
float()	Returns a floating-point version of the input.
str()	Returns a string representation of the input.
ord()	Given an input character, returns the ASCII numeric representation.

A.5   NUMERIC FUNCTIONS

abs()	Absolute value.
sin()	Sine.
cos()	Cosine.
max()	Maximum value of the inputs (including a list).
min()	Minimum value of the inputs (including a list).
len()	Returns the length of the input sequence.

A.6   SEQUENCE OPERATIONS

Sequences (strings, lists, tuples) can be added together, or concatenated (e.g., s1 + s2).

Elements of a sequence can be accessed using slices:

- seq[n] accesses the *n*-th element of the list (the first element is zero).
- seq[n:m] accesses the elements starting at the *n*-th up to *but not including* the *m*-th.
- seq[:m] accesses elements from the start up to but not including the *m*-th.
- seq[n:] accesses elements from the *n*-th to the end of the sequence.

A.7   STRING ESCAPES

\t	Tab character
\b	Backspace
\n	Newline
\r	Return
\uXXXX	Unicode character, hexadecimal XXXX

Precede a string with "r" as in r"C:\mediasources" to treat a string in raw mode, ignoring escapes.

A.8   USEFUL STRING METHODS

- count(sub): returns the number of times sub appears in the string.
- find(sub): returns the index where sub appears in the string, or returns −1 if not found. find can take an optional starting point and an optional ending point. rfind takes the same inputs but works right to left.
- upper(), lower(): convert the string to all upper or all lowercase.

- `isalpha()`, `isdigit()`: return true if all the characters in the string are alphabetic or all numeric, respectively.
- `replace(s,r)`: replaces all instances of "s" with "r" in the string.
- `split(d)`: returns a list of sublists where the character d is the split point.

A.9 FILES

Files are opened with `open` with two inputs: the filename and a file mode. The file mode is "r" for reading, "w" for writing, and "a" for appending, concatenated with a "t" for text or a "b" for binary. File methods include:

- `read()`: returns the whole file as a string.
- `readlines()`: returns the whole file as a list of strings delimited by lines.
- `write(s)`: writes the string s to the file.

A.10 LISTS

Lists are indexed like sequences using "[]". They are concatenated using +. List methods include:

- `append(a)`: appends the item a to the list.
- `remove(b)`: removes the item b from the list.
- `sort()`: sorts the list.
- `reverse()`: reverses the list.
- `count(s)`: returns the number of times that the element s appears in the list.

A.11 DICTIONARIES, HASH TABLES, OR ASSOCIATIVE ARRAYS

Dictionaries are created with {}. They can be accessed by a key.

```
>>> d = {'cat':'Diana', 'dog':'Fido'}
>>> print d
{'cat': 'Diana', 'dog': 'Fido'}
>>> print d.keys()
['cat', 'dog']
>>> print d['cat']
Diana
```

A.12 EXTERNAL MODULES

Modules are accessed using `import`. They can also be input as an alias, for example, `import javax.swing as swing`. Specific pieces can be imported, without any need for dot notation to access them, using `from module import n1, n2`. All pieces of a module can be imported and accessed without dot notation using `from module import *`.

A.13   CLASSES

Classes are created using the `class` keyword followed by the name of the class and, in parentheses, an optional superclass (one or more). Methods follow and are indented. *Constructors* (which are called when a new instance of the class is created) must be named `__init__`. You can have more than one constructor in a Python class as long as they take different parameters.

A.14   FUNCTIONAL METHODS

`apply`	Takes a function and a list as input to the function, where the list has as many elements as the function takes as input. Calls the function on the input.
`map`	Takes a function and a list of several inputs to the function. Calls the function on each of the inputs and returns a list of the outputs (`return` values).
`filter`	Takes a function and a list of several inputs to the function. Calls the function on each of the list elements and returns *the input element* if the function returns true (non zero) for that element.
`reduce`	Takes a function that has two inputs and a list of several inputs to the function. The function is applied to the first two list elements, the result of this is used as input with the next list element, then the result of this is used as input with the *next* list element, and so on. The overall result is returned at the end.

Bibliography

1. AAUW, *Tech-Savvy: Educating Girls in the New Computer Age*, American Association of University Women Education Foundation, New York, 2000.

2. ACM/IEEE, *Computing Curriculum 2001*, `http://www.acm.org/sigcse/cc2001` (2001).

3. ALAN J. DIX, JANET E. FINLAY, GREGORY D. ABOWD, AND RUSSELL BEALE, *Human–Computer Interaction*, 2d ed., Prentice Hall, Upper Saddle River, NJ, 1998.

4. ALLISON ELLIOT TEW, CHARLES FOWLER, AND MARK GUZDIAL, "Tracking an Innovation in Introductory CS Education from a Research University to a Two-Year College," *Proceedings of the 36th SIGCSE Technical Symposium on Computer Science Education*, ACM Press, New York, 2005, pp. 416–420.

5. AMY BRUCKMAN, "Situated Support for Learning: Storm's Weekend with Rachael," *Journal of the Learning Sciences* **9** (2000), no. 3, 329–372.

6. ANDREA FORTE AND MARK GUZDIAL, *Computers for Communication, Not Calculation: Media as a Motivation and Context for Learning*, HICSS 2004, Big Island, HI, IEEE Computer Society 2004.

7. ANN E. FLEURY, "Encapsulation and Reuse as Viewed by Java Students," *Proceedings of the 32nd SIGCSE Technical Symposium on Computer Science Education* (2001), pp. 189–193.

8. BETH ADELSON AND ELLIOT SOLOWAY, "The Role of Domain Experience in Software Design," *IEEE Transactions on Software Engineering* **SE-11** (1985), no. 11, 1351–1360.

9. BRIAN HARVEY, *Computer Science Logo Style*, 2d ed., Vol. 1: *Symbolic Computing*, MIT Press, Cambridge, MA, 1997.

10. CHARLES DODGE AND THOMAS A. JERSE, *Computer Music: Synthesis, Composition, and Performance*, Schirmer-Thomson Learning, New York, 1997.

11. CURTIS ROADS, *The Computer Music Tutorial*, MIT Press, Cambridge, MA, 1996.

12. CYNTHIA BAILEY LEE. Experience report: CS1 in matlab for non-majors, with media computation and peer instruction. In *Proceeding of the 44th ACM Technical Symposium on Computer Science Education*, SIGCSE '13, pages 35–40, New York, NY, USA, 2013. ACM.

13. DAN INGALLS, TED KAEHLER, JOHN MALONEY, SCOTT WALLACE, AND ALAN KAY, "Back to the Future: The Story of Squeak, a Practical Smalltalk Written in Itself," *OOPSLA'97 Conference Proceedings*, ACM, Atlanta, GA, 1997, pp. 318–326.

14. DAN OLSEN, *Developing User Interfaces*, Morgan Kaufmann Publishers, San Mateo, CA, 1998.

15. DANNY GOODMAN, *JavaScript & DHTML Cookbook*, O'Reilly & Associates, Sebastapol, CA, 2003.

16. FREDERIK LUNDH, *Python Standard Library*, O'Reilly and Associates, Sebastapol, CA, 2001.

17. HAROLD ABELSON, GERALD JAY SUSSMAN, AND JULIE SUSSMAN, *Structure and Interpretation of Computer Programs*, 2d ed., MIT Press, Cambridge, MA, 1996.

18. HEATHER PERRY, LAUREN RICH, AND MARK GUZDIAL, "A CS1 Course Designed to Address Interests of Women" *ACM SIGCSE Conference 2004*, Norfolk, VA, ACM, New York, 2004, pp. 190–194.

19. IDIT HAREL AND SEYMOUR PAPERT, "Software Design as a Learning Environment," *Interactive Learning Environments* **1** (1990), no. 1, 1–32.

20. JAMES D. FOLEY, ANDRIES VAN DAM, AND STEVEN K. FEINER, *Introduction to Computer Graphics*, Addison Wesley, Reading, MA, 1993.

21. JANE MARGOLIS AND ALLAN FISHER, *Unlocking the Clubhouse: Women in Computing*, MIT Press, Cambridge, MA, 2002.

22. JANET KOLODNER, *Case-Based Reasoning*, Morgan Kaufmann, San Mateo, CA, 1993.

23. JEANNETTE WING, "Computational Thinking," *Communications of the ACM* **49** (2006), no. 3, 33–35.

24. JENS BENNEDSEN AND MICHAEL E. CASPERSEN, "Failure Rates in Introductory Programming," *SIGCSE Bulletin* **39** (2007), no. 2, 32–36.

25. JOHN T. BRUER, *Schools for Thought: A Science of Learning in the Classroom*, MIT Press, Cambridge, MA, 1993.

26. KEN ABERNETHY AND TOM ALLEN, *Exploring the Digital Domain: An Introduction to Computing with Multimedia and Networking*, PWS Publishing, Boston, 1998.

27. LEO PORTER AND BETH SIMON. Retaining nearly one-third more majors with a trio of instructional best practices in CS1. In *Proceeding of the 44th ACM Technical Symposium on Computer Science Education*, SIGCSE '13, pages 165–170, New York, NY, USA, 2013. ACM.

28. MARGARET LIVINGSTONE, *Vision and Art: The Biology of Seeing*, Harry N. Abrams, New York, 2002.

29. MARK GUZDIAL AND ALLISON ELLIOT TEW, "Imagineering Inauthentic Legitimate Peripheral Participation: An Instructional Design Approach for Motivating Computing Education," paper presented at the International Computing Education Research Workshop, Canterbury, UK, ACM, New York, 2006.

30. MARK GUZDIAL AND KIM ROSE (eds.), *Squeak, Open Personal Computing for Multimedia*, Prentice Hall, Englewood, NJ, 2001.

31. MARK GUZDIAL, BARBARA ERICSON, TOM MCKLIN, AND SHELLY ENGELMAN. "Georgia Computes!" an intervention in a US state, with formal and informal education in a policy context. *Transactions on Computing Education*, 14(2):13:1–13:29, June 2014.

32. MARK GUZDIAL, *Squeak: Object-Oriented Design with Multimedia Applications*, Prentice Hall, Englewood, NJ, 2001.

33. MARK GUZDIAL. Exploring hypotheses about media computation. In *Proceedings of the Ninth Annual International ACM Conference on International Computing Education Research*, ICER '13, pages 19–26, New York, NY, USA, 2013. ACM.

34. MARK LUTZ AND DAVID ASCHER, *Learning Python*, O'Reilly & Associates, Sebastopol, CA, 2003.

35. MARTIN GREENBERGER, "Computers and the World of the Future," transcribed recordings of lectures at the Sloan School of Business Administration, April 1961, MIT Press, Cambridge, MA, 1962.

36. MATTHIAS FELLEISEN, ROBERT BRUCE FINDLER, MATTHEW FLATT, AND SHRIRAM KRISHNAMURTHI, *How to Design Programs: An Introduction to Programming and Computing*, MIT Press, Cambridge, MA, 2001.

37. MITCHEL RESNICK, *Turtles, Termites, and Traffic Jams: Explorations in Massively Parallel Microworlds*, MIT Press, Cambridge, MA, 1997.

38. RASHI GUPTA, *Making Use of Python*, Wiley, New York, 2002.

39. RICHARD BOULANGER (ed.), *The Csound Book: Perspectives in Synthesis, Sound Design, Signal Processing, and Programming*, MIT Press, Cambridge, MA, 2000.

40. RICHARD HIGHTOWER, *Python Programming with the Java Class Libraries*, Addison-Wesley, Reading, MA, 2003.

41. ROBERT H. SLOAN AND PATRICK TROY. CS 0.5: A better approach to introductory computer science for majors. In *Proceedings of the 39th SIGCSE Technical Symposium on Computer Science Education*, SIGCSE '08, pages 271–275, New York, NY, USA, 2008. ACM.

42. ROBERT SLOAN AND PATRICK TROY, "CS 0.5: A Better Approach to Introductory Computer Science for Majors," *Proceedings of the 39th SIGCSE Technical Symposium on Computer Science Education*, ACM Press, New York, 2008, pp. 271–275.

43. STEPHEN H. EDWARDS, DANIEL S. TILDEN, AND ANTHONY ALLEVATO. Pythy: Improving the introductory python programming experience. In *Proceedings of the 45th ACM Technical Symposium on Computer Science Education*, SIGCSE '14, pages 641–646, New York, NY, USA, 2014. ACM.

44. TURTLE GEOMETRY: *The Computer as a Medium for Exploring Mathematics* by Harold Abelson and Andrea diSessa (MIT Press: 1986).

Index